OECD/G20 Base Erosion and Profit Shifting Project

Harmful Tax Practices – 2020 Peer Review Reports on the Exchange of Information on Tax Rulings

INCLUSIVE FRAMEWORK ON BEPS: ACTION 5

OECD

BETTER POLICIES FOR BETTER LIVES

This document, as well as any data and map included herein, are without prejudice to the status of or sovereignty over any territory, to the delimitation of international frontiers and boundaries and to the name of any territory, city or area.

The statistical data for Israel are supplied by and under the responsibility of the relevant Israeli authorities. The use of such data by the OECD is without prejudice to the status of the Golan Heights, East Jerusalem and Israeli settlements in the West Bank under the terms of international law.

Note by Turkey
The information in this document with reference to "Cyprus" relates to the southern part of the Island. There is no single authority representing both Turkish and Greek Cypriot people on the Island. Turkey recognises the Turkish Republic of Northern Cyprus (TRNC). Until a lasting and equitable solution is found within the context of the United Nations, Turkey shall preserve its position concerning the "Cyprus issue".

Note by all the European Union Member States of the OECD and the European Union
The Republic of Cyprus is recognised by all members of the United Nations with the exception of Turkey. The information in this document relates to the area under the effective control of the Government of the Republic of Cyprus.

Please cite this publication as:
OECD (2021), *Harmful Tax Practices – 2020 Peer Review Reports on the Exchange of Information on Tax Rulings: Inclusive Framework on BEPS: Action 5*, OECD/G20 Base Erosion and Profit Shifting Project, OECD Publishing, Paris, *https://doi.org/10.1787/f376127b-en*.

ISBN 978-92-64-52253-4 (print)
ISBN 978-92-64-34440-2 (pdf)

OECD/G20 Base Erosion and Profit Shifting Project
ISSN 2313-2604 (print)
ISSN 2313-2612 (online)

Photo credits: Cover © ninog-Fotolia.com.

Corrigenda to publications may be found on line at: *www.oecd.org/about/publishing/corrigenda.htm*.

Foreword

The integration of national economies and markets has increased substantially in recent years, putting a strain on the international tax rules, which were designed more than a century ago. Weaknesses in the current rules create opportunities for base erosion and profit shifting (BEPS), requiring bold moves by policy makers to restore confidence in the system and ensure that profits are taxed where economic activities take place and value is created.

Following the release of the report Addressing Base Erosion and Profit Shifting in February 2013, OECD and G20 countries adopted a 15-point Action Plan to address BEPS in September 2013. The Action Plan identified 15 actions along three key pillars: introducing coherence in the domestic rules that affect cross-border activities, reinforcing substance requirements in the existing international standards, and improving transparency as well as certainty.

After two years of work, measures in response to the 15 actions were delivered to G20 Leaders in Antalya in November 2015. All the different outputs, including those delivered in an interim form in 2014, were consolidated into a comprehensive package. The BEPS package of measures represents the first substantial renovation of the international tax rules in almost a century. Once the new measures become applicable, it is expected that profits will be reported where the economic activities that generate them are carried out and where value is created. BEPS planning strategies that rely on outdated rules or on poorly co-ordinated domestic measures will be rendered ineffective.

Implementation is now the focus of this work. The BEPS package is designed to be implemented via changes in domestic law and practices, and in tax treaties. With the negotiation of a multilateral instrument (MLI) having been finalised in 2016 to facilitate the implementation of the treaty related BEPS measures, over 85 jurisdictions are covered by the MLI. The entry into force of the MLI on 1 July 2018 paves the way for swift implementation of the treaty related measures. OECD and G20 countries also agreed to continue to work together to ensure a consistent and co-ordinated implementation of the BEPS recommendations and to make the project more inclusive. Globalisation requires that global solutions and a global dialogue be established which go beyond OECD and G20 countries.

A better understanding of how the BEPS recommendations are implemented in practice could reduce misunderstandings and disputes between governments. Greater focus on implementation and tax administration should therefore be mutually beneficial to governments and business. Proposed improvements to data and analysis will help support ongoing evaluation of the quantitative impact of BEPS, as well as evaluating the impact of the countermeasures developed under the BEPS Project.

As a result, the OECD established the OECD/G20 Inclusive Framework on BEPS (Inclusive Framework), bringing all interested and committed countries and jurisdictions on an equal footing in the Committee on Fiscal Affairs and all its subsidiary bodies. The Inclusive Framework, which already has more than 140 members, is monitoring and peer reviewing the implementation of the minimum standards as well as completing the work on standard setting to address BEPS issues. In addition to BEPS members, other international organisations and regional tax bodies are involved in the work of the Inclusive Framework, which also consults business and the civil society on its different work streams.

This report was approved by the Inclusive Framework on 3 December 2021 and prepared for publication by the OECD Secretariat.

Abbreviations and acronyms

AGT	Angolan Tax Administration
AMPD	Administration Methodology and Procedures Department (Armenia)
APA	Advance pricing arrangement
ATR	Advance tax ruling
BEPS	Base Erosion and Profit Shifting
EOI	Exchange of Information
EU	European Union
FHTP	Forum on Harmful Tax Practice
GDT	General Directorate of Taxation (Albania)
ICD	International Cooperation Department (Armenia)
IP	Intellectual Property
ISTD	Income and Sales Tax Department (Jordan)
IRD	Saint Lucia's Inland Revenue Department
MAP	Mutual Agreement Procedure
MNE	Multinational Enterprise
OECD	Organization for Economic Co-operation and Development
PE	Permanent Establishment
R&D	Research and Development
RMO	Revenue Memorandum Order (Philippines)
SAARC	South Asian Association for Regional Cooperation
SRC	Seychelles Revenue Commission
SRC	State Revenue Committee (Armenia)
STA	Swedish Tax Agency
TAPA	Tax Administration and Procedures Act (Antigua and Barbuda)
ToR	Terms of reference
XML	Extensible Mark-Up Language

Table of contents

Executive summary

Context for the exchange of information on tax rulings (the "transparency framework")

The BEPS Action 5 minimum standard on the compulsory spontaneous exchange of information on tax rulings (the "transparency framework") provides tax administrations with timely information on rulings that have been granted to a foreign related party of their resident taxpayer or a permanent establishment, which can be used in conducting risk assessments and which, in the absence of exchange, could give rise to BEPS concerns.

The transparency framework requires spontaneous exchange of information on five categories of taxpayer-specific rulings: (i) rulings related to certain preferential regimes, (ii) unilateral advance pricing arrangements (APAs) or other cross-border unilateral rulings in respect of transfer pricing, (iii) rulings providing for a downward adjustment of taxable profits, (iv) permanent establishment (PE) rulings; and (v) related party conduit rulings.[1] The requirement to exchange information on the rulings in the above categories includes certain past rulings as well as future rulings, pursuant to pre-defined periods which are outlined in each jurisdiction's report and that varies according to the time when a certain jurisdiction has joined the Inclusive Framework or has been identified as a Jurisdiction of Relevance. The exchanges occur pursuant to international exchange of information agreements, which provide the legal conditions under which exchanges take place, including the need to ensure taxpayer confidentiality.

The inclusion of the above categories of rulings in the scope of the transparency framework is not intended to suggest that the issuance of such rulings constitutes a preferential regime or a harmful tax practice. In practice, tax rulings can be an effective way to provide certainty to taxpayers and reduce the risk of disputes. Rather, the need for transparency on rulings is that a tax administration's lack of knowledge or information on the tax treatment of a taxpayer in another jurisdiction can impact the treatment of transactions or arrangements undertaken with a related taxpayer resident in their own jurisdiction and thus lead to BEPS concerns. The availability of timely and targeted information about such rulings, as agreed in the template in Annex C of the Action 5 Report, Countering Harmful Tax Practices More Effectively, Taking Into Account Transparency and Substance (OECD, 2015[1]), is intended to better equip tax authorities to quickly identify risk areas.

This framework was designed with a view to finding a balance between ensuring that the information exchanged is relevant to other tax administrations and that it does not impose an unnecessary administrative burden on either the country exchanging the information or the country receiving it.

Scope of this review

This is the fifth annual peer review of the transparency framework, and covers 131 Inclusive Framework member jurisdictions. This comprises all Inclusive Framework members that joined prior to 30 June 2020 and Jurisdictions of Relevance identified by the Inclusive Framework prior to 30 June 2020. Of these 131 jurisdictions, there were 31 jurisdictions which are not able to legally, or in practice, issue rulings in scope of the transparency framework, and therefore no separate peer review report is included for these jurisdictions.[2]

Eight other members of the Inclusive Framework have not been assessed under the transparency framework, namely Anguilla, the Bahamas, Bahrain, Bermuda, the British Virgin Islands, the Cayman Islands, the Turks and Caicos Islands and the United Arab Emirates. These jurisdictions do not impose any corporate income tax, and therefore cannot legally issue rulings within scope of the transparency framework and nor do Inclusive Framework members exchange information on rulings with them. Therefore, these jurisdictions are considered to be outside the scope of the transparency framework.

The reviews contained in this annual report cover the steps jurisdictions have taken to implement the transparency framework during the calendar year 2020. The reviews have been prepared using information from each reviewed jurisdiction, input from peers who received exchanges of information under the transparency framework, and input from the delegates of the Forum on Harmful Tax Practices ("FHTP").

Key findings

Key findings from this fifth annual peer review include:

- As at 31 December 2020, almost 22 000 tax rulings in the scope of the transparency framework had been issued by the jurisdictions being reviewed. This is the cumulative figure, including certain past rulings issued since 2010. Over 1 700 tax rulings in scope of the transparency framework were issued in 2020 by the 131 jurisdictions reviewed.
- Over 41,000 exchanges of information took place by 31 December 2020, with approximately 5 000 exchanges undertaken in 2020, 7 000 exchanges undertaken during 2019, 9 000 exchanges undertaken during 2018, 14 000 exchanges undertaken during 2017 and 6,000 exchanges during 2016.
- Out of the 131 reviewed jurisdictions, 95 jurisdictions did not receive any recommendations, as they have met all the terms of reference. A further 10 jurisdictions received only one recommendation.
- 66 recommendations for improvement have been made for the year in review.
- 91 peer input questionnaires were submitted providing feedback on the conduct of the exchanges by Inclusive Framework members. Peer input is not mandatory, but in cases where it was provided it has in a number of cases allowed jurisdictions to revise their processes and improve the clarity and quality of information exchanged.
- In a number of cases, the peer review process has assisted jurisdictions in identifying areas where improvement is required, and jurisdictions have been able to take action to implement changes over 2021 while the peer review was ongoing. Where these changes were implemented in 2021, they are generally not taken into account in the recommendations issued for the year 2020. However, these changes would be reviewed in a subsequent peer review.

Table 1. Compilation of recommendations

Aspect of the implementation of the transparency framework that should be improved	Recommendation for improvement
Albania	
Albania does not yet have the necessary information gathering process in place.	Albania is recommended to put in place an effective information gathering process to identify all potential exchange jurisdictions for future rulings on preferential regimes and to implement a review and supervision mechanism, as soon as possible.
Albania does not yet have a process to complete the templates on relevant rulings, to make them available to the Competent Authority for exchange of information, and to exchange them with relevant jurisdictions.	Albania is recommended to develop a process to complete the templates for all relevant rulings and to ensure that the exchanges of information on rulings occur in accordance with the form and timelines under the transparency framework.
Andorra	
Andorra still experiences difficulties in identifying all potential exchange jurisdictions for future rulings.	Andorra is recommended to continue its efforts to ensure that all potential exchange jurisdictions are identified swiftly for all future rulings. This recommendation remains unchanged since the 2017, 2018 and 2019 peer review reports.
Andorra is still developing a process to ensure that the information is completed in the required form and exchanges are performed in accordance with the timelines.	Andorra is recommended to continue its efforts to put in place the necessary process to complete the information in the form of Annex C of the BEPS Action 5 Report, to ensure that information is submitted to the Competent Authority without undue delay and exchanges are performed in accordance with the timelines. These recommendations remain unchanged since the 2017, 2018 and 2019 peer review reports but since the 2019 peer review report they are targeted to specific aspects of the ToR that still need to be put in place.
Angola	
Angola has not yet finalised the steps to have in place its necessary information and gathering process.	Angola is recommended to finalise its information gathering process for identifying all past and future rulings and all potential exchange jurisdictions, with a review and supervision mechanism, as soon as possible. This recommendation remains unchanged since the 2017, 2018 and 2019 peer review reports.
Angola has not yet finalised the steps to have effective compulsory spontaneous exchange of information on the tax rulings within the scope of the transparency framework.	Angola is recommended to continue to put in place a domestic legal framework allowing spontaneous exchange of information on rulings and to continue its efforts to complete the templates for all relevant rulings and to ensure that the exchanges of information on rulings occur as soon as possible. This recommendation remains unchanged since the 2017, 2018 and 2019 peer review reports.
Antigua and Barbuda	
	No recommendations are made.
Argentina	
	No recommendations are made.
Armenia	
Armenia is in the process to finalise the information gathering process and to put in place a system for the identification and registration of issued tax rulings.	Armenia is recommended to finalise its information gathering process for identifying all future rulings and potential exchange jurisdictions, as soon as possible. This recommendation remains unchanged since the prior year peer review report.
Armenia does not have a process to complete the templates on relevant rulings, to make them available to the Competent Authority for exchange of information, and to exchange them with relevant jurisdictions.	Armenia is recommended to develop a process to complete the templates on relevant rulings and to ensure that the exchanges of information on rulings occur in accordance with the form and timelines under the transparency framework. This recommendation remains unchanged since the prior year peer review report.
Aruba	
	No recommendations are made.
Australia	
	No recommendations are made.
Austria	
	No recommendations are made.
Barbados	
Barbados did not identify or exchange information on new entrants to the	Barbados is recommended to identify and exchange information on all

grandfathered IP regime.	new entrants to the grandfathered IP regime as soon as possible. This recommendation remains unchanged since the 2017, 2018 and 2019 peer review reports.
Belgium	
	No recommendations are made.
Benin	
Benin has not yet finalised the steps to have in place its necessary information and gathering process.	Benin is recommended to finalise its information gathering process, with a review and supervision mechanism, as soon as possible. This recommendation remains unchanged since the 2018 and 2019 peer review reports.
Benin has not yet finalised the steps to have effective compulsory spontaneous exchange of information on the tax rulings within the scope of the transparency framework.	Benin is recommended to continue to put in place a domestic legal framework allowing spontaneous exchange of information on rulings and to continue its efforts to complete the templates for all relevant rulings and to ensure that the exchanges of information on rulings occur as soon as possible. This recommendation remains unchanged since the 2018 and 2019 peer review reports.
Bosnia and Herzegovina	
Bosnia and Herzegovina does not yet have the necessary information gathering process in place.	Bosnia and Herzegovina is recommended to ensure that it has put in place an effective information gathering process to identify all relevant past and future rulings and all potential exchange jurisdictions and to implement a review and supervision mechanism, as soon as possible.
Bosnia and Herzegovina does not yet have a domestic legal framework allowing spontaneous exchange of information on rulings and a process to complete the templates on relevant rulings, to make them available to the Competent Authority for exchange of information, and to exchange them with relevant jurisdictions.	Bosnia and Herzegovina is recommended to put in place the necessary domestic legal basis allowing spontaneous exchange of information on rulings, to develop a process to complete the templates for all relevant rulings and to ensure that the exchanges of information on rulings occur in accordance with the form and timelines under the transparency framework going forward.
Botswana	
Botswana does not have a review and supervision mechanism in place.	Botswana is recommended to put in place a review and supervision mechanism, as soon as possible. This recommendation remains unchanged since the 2018 and 2019 peer review reports.
Botswana does not yet have the necessary legal framework in place for exchanging information on rulings and a process in place to ensure the timely exchange of information on rulings in the form required by the transparency framework.	Botswana is recommended to continue to put in place a domestic legal framework allowing spontaneous exchange of information on rulings and to ensure the timely exchange of information on rulings in the form required by the transparency framework. This recommendation remains unchanged since the 2018 and 2019 peer review reports.
Brazil	
	No recommendations are made.
Brunei Darussalam	
	No recommendations are made.
Burkina Faso	
Burkina Faso has not put in place the necessary information gathering process.	Burkina Faso is recommended to finalise its information gathering process for identifying all future rulings and potential exchange jurisdictions, with a review and supervision mechanism, as soon as possible.
Burkina Faso does not have a process to complete the templates on relevant rulings, to make them available to the Competent Authority for exchange of information, and to exchange them with relevant jurisdictions.	Burkina Faso is recommended to develop a process to complete the templates on relevant rulings and to ensure that the exchanges of information on rulings occur in accordance with the form and timelines under the transparency framework.
Cabo Verde	
Cabo Verde does not have a process to complete the templates on relevant rulings and to make them available to the Competent Authority for exchange of information.	Cabo Verde is recommended to develop a process to complete the templates on relevant rulings and to ensure that the exchanges of information on rulings occur in accordance with the form and timelines under the transparency framework going forward.
Canada	
	No recommendations are made.
Chile	
	No recommendations are made.
China (People's Republic of)	
	No recommendations are made.

Colombia	
	No recommendations are made.
Congo	
It is not known whether Congo has finalised the steps to have in place its necessary information and gathering process.	Congo is recommended to finalise its information gathering process, with a review and supervision mechanism, as soon as possible. This recommendation remains unchanged since the 2017, 2018 and 2019 peer review reports.
It is not known whether Congo has finalised the steps to have effective compulsory spontaneous exchange of information on the tax rulings within the scope of the transparency framework.	Congo is recommended to continue to put in place a domestic legal framework allowing spontaneous exchange of information on rulings and to continue its efforts to complete the templates for all relevant rulings and to ensure that the exchanges of information on rulings occur as soon as possible. This recommendation remains unchanged since the 2017, 2018 and 2019 peer review reports.
Costa Rica	
	No recommendations are made.
Croatia	
	No recommendations are made.
Curaçao	
The information gathering process is still underway in Curaçao with respect to past and future rulings within the scope of the transparency framework and the classification of these rulings under each category.	Curaçao is recommended to finalise its information gathering process for identifying all past and future rulings within the scope of the transparency framework as soon as possible. This recommendation remains unchanged since the 2017, 2018 and 2019 peer review reports.
Curaçao experienced delays in exchanging information on past and future rulings.	Curaçao is recommended to continue its efforts to ensure that all information on past and future rulings is exchanged as soon as possible. This recommendation remains unchanged since the 2017, 2018 and 2019 peer review reports.
Czech Republic	
The Czech Republic experienced delays in the exchange of information on future rulings due to the application of the timelines set out in the EU Directive 2011/16/EU.	The Czech Republic is recommended to ensure that all information on future rulings is exchanged as soon as possible. The Czech Republic also received a recommendation on timely exchange of information on rulings in the 2017 and 2018 peer review reports.
Democratic Republic of Congo	
It is not known whether the Democratic Republic of the Congo has put in place the necessary information and gathering process.	The Democratic Republic of the Congo is recommended to finalise its information gathering process, with a review and supervision mechanism, as soon as possible.
It is not known whether the Democratic Republic of the Congo has put in place an effective compulsory spontaneous exchange of information on the tax rulings within the scope of the transparency framework.	The Democratic Republic of the Congo is recommended to continue to put in place a domestic legal framework allowing spontaneous exchange of information on rulings and to continue its efforts to complete the templates for all relevant rulings and to ensure that the exchanges of information on rulings occur as soon as possible.
Denmark	
	No recommendations are made.
Dominican Republic	
The Dominican Republic is still in the process of ensuring the timely exchange of information on rulings.	The Dominican Republic is recommended to ensure that the exchanges of information on rulings occur as soon as possible. This recommendation remains unchanged since the 2019 peer review report.
Egypt	
Egypt has not yet identified all potential exchange jurisdictions for both past and future rulings and does not have a review and supervision mechanism in place to ensure that all relevant information on the identification of rulings and potential exchange jurisdictions is captured adequately.	Egypt is recommended to continue its efforts to identify all potential exchange jurisdictions for both past and future rulings and to implement a review and supervision mechanism, as soon as possible. This recommendation remains unchanged since the 2018 and 2019 review reports.
Egypt does not have in place a process to ensure the timely exchange of information on rulings in the form required by the transparency framework.	Egypt is recommended to develop a process to complete the templates on relevant rulings and to ensure that the exchanges of information on rulings occur in accordance with the form and timelines under the transparency framework. This recommendation remains unchanged since the 2018 and 2019 peer review reports.
Estonia	
	No recommendations are made.

Eswatini	
It is not known whether Eswatini has put in place the necessary information gathering process.	Eswatini is recommended to finalise its information gathering process for identifying all future rulings and potential exchange jurisdictions, with a review and supervision mechanism, as soon as possible.
It is not known whether Eswatini has the necessary domestic legal basis allowing spontaneous exchange of information and whether Eswatini has a process to complete the templates on relevant rulings, to make them available to the Competent Authority for exchange of information, and to exchange them with relevant jurisdictions.	Eswatini is recommended to put in place a domestic legal framework allowing spontaneous exchange of information on rulings and to develop a process to complete the templates on relevant rulings and to ensure that the exchanges of information on rulings occur in accordance with the form and timelines under the transparency framework.
Faroe Islands	
The Faroe Islands does not yet have its necessary information and gathering process in place.	The Faroe Islands is recommended to put in place an effective information gathering process to identify all relevant past and future rulings and all potential exchange jurisdictions and to implement a review and supervision mechanism, as soon as possible. This recommendation remains unchanged since the prior year peer review report.
The Faroe Islands does not have a process to complete the templates on relevant rulings, to make them available to the Competent Authority for exchange of information, and to exchange them with relevant jurisdictions.	The Faroe Islands is recommended to develop a process to complete the templates for all relevant rulings and to ensure that the exchanges of information on rulings occur in accordance with the form and timelines under the transparency framework going forward. This recommendation remains unchanged since the prior year peer review report.
Finland	
	No recommendations are made.
France	
France did not identify or exchange information on new entrants to the IP regime or taxpayers benefitting from the third category of IP asset with respect to the former IP regime.	France is recommended to identify and exchange information on all new entrants to the IP regime, and to identify and exchange information on taxpayers benefitting from the third category of IP assets. This recommendation remains unchanged since the 2016, 2017, 2018 and 2019 peer review reports.
Gabon	
Gabon has not finalised the steps to have in place its necessary information gathering process, with a review and supervision mechanism.	Gabon is recommended to finalise its information gathering process, with a review and supervision mechanism, as soon as possible. This recommendation remains unchanged since the 2018 and 2019 peer review reports.
Gabon has not finalised the steps to have effective compulsory spontaneous exchange of information on the tax rulings within the scope of the transparency framework.	Gabon is recommended to continue its efforts to complete the templates for all relevant rulings and to ensure that the exchanges of information on rulings occur as soon as possible. This recommendation remains unchanged since the 2018 and 2019 peer review reports.
Georgia	
	No recommendations are made.
Germany	
	No recommendations are made.
Gibraltar	
	No recommendations are made.
Greece	
	No recommendations are made.
Grenada	
Grenada has not put in place the necessary information gathering process.	Grenada is recommended to finalise its information gathering process for identifying all future rulings and potential exchange jurisdictions, with a review and supervision mechanism, as soon as possible. This recommendation remains unchanged since the prior year peer review report.
Grenada does not have a process to complete the templates on relevant rulings, to make them available to the Competent Authority for exchange of information, and to exchange them with relevant jurisdictions.	Grenada is recommended to develop a process to complete the templates on relevant rulings and to ensure that the exchanges of information on rulings occur in accordance with the form and timelines under the transparency framework. This recommendation remains unchanged since the prior year peer review report.
Guernsey	
	No recommendations are made.
Hong Kong (China)	

	No recommendations are made.
Hungary	
Hungary did not yet apply the "best efforts approach" to identify potential exchange jurisdictions for all past rulings.	Hungary is recommended to continue to apply the "best efforts approach" to identify potential exchange jurisdictions for all past rulings. This recommendation remains unchanged since the 2016, 2017, 2018 and 2019 peer review reports.
Hungary experienced some delays for the exchange of future rulings.	Hungary is recommended to ensure that all information on future rulings is exchanged as soon as possible. This recommendation remains unchanged since the 2019 peer review report.
Hungary did not identify or exchange all information on new entrants to the grandfathered IP regime.	Hungary is recommended to continue its efforts to identify and exchange information on all new entrants to the grandfathered IP regime. This recommendation remains unchanged since the 2016, 2017, 2018 and 2019 peer review reports.
Iceland	
	No recommendations are made.
India	
India experienced delays in the exchange of information on future APAs.	India is recommended to continue its efforts to ensure that all information on future APAs is exchanged as soon as possible. This recommendation remains unchanged since the 2017, 2018 and 2019 peer review reports.
Indonesia	
	No recommendations are made.
Ireland	
	No recommendations are made.
Isle of Man	
	No recommendations are made.
Israel	
Israel identified additional future rulings that were not previously captured.	Israel is recommended to strengthen its information gathering process identifying all future rulings within the scope of the transparency framework and its review and supervision mechanism to ensure that the information gathering process is working effectively.
During the year in review, as well as in the 2019 peer review reports, concerns were raised regarding the completion of templates in accordance with the form agreed under the transparency framework.	Israel is recommended to develop a process to complete the templates on future rulings, and in particular, the summary section, in accordance with the form agreed under the transparency framework. This recommendation remains unchanged since the 2019 peer review report.
Italy	
	No recommendations are made.
Jamaica	
	No recommendations are made.
Japan	
	No recommendations are made.
Jersey	
	No recommendations are made.
Jordan	
Jordan does not have specific mechanisms in place for identifying future rulings and potential exchange jurisdictions within the scope of the transparency framework as well as for reviewing and supervising that all relevant information is captured adequately.	Jordan is recommended to ensure that it has put in place an effective information gathering process to identify all future rulings and potential exchange jurisdictions, with a review and supervision mechanism, as soon as possible. This recommendation remains unchanged since the prior year peer review report.
Jordan has not the necessary domestic legal basis to exchange information spontaneously and Jordan does not yet have a process to exchange information on rulings in the required format and timelines.	Jordan is recommended to put in place a domestic legal framework allowing spontaneous exchange of information on the relevant tax rulings and to ensure the timely exchange of information on rulings in the form required by the transparency framework. This recommendation remains unchanged since the prior year peer review report.
Jordan has not identified information on new entrants to the Development zone IP regime during the relevant period, and has not exchanged information on these taxpayers.	Jordan is recommended to identify information and to put in place a domestic legal framework allowing spontaneous exchange of information on all new entrants to the IP regime. This recommendation remains unchanged since the prior year peer review report.
Kazakhstan	
Kazakhstan has not yet finalised the steps to have in place its necessary	Kazakhstan is recommended to finalise its information gathering

information and gathering process.	process, with a review and supervision mechanism, as soon as possible. This recommendation remains unchanged since the 2018 and 2019 peer review reports.
Kazakhstan has not yet finalised the steps to have effective compulsory spontaneous exchange of information on the tax rulings within the scope of the transparency framework.	Kazakhstan is recommended to continue to put in place a domestic legal framework allowing spontaneous exchange of information on rulings and to continue its efforts to complete the templates for all relevant rulings and to ensure that the exchanges of information on rulings occur as soon as possible. This recommendation remains unchanged since the 2018 and 2019 peer review reports.
Kenya	
	No recommendations are made.
Korea	
	No recommendations are made.
Latvia	
	No recommendations are made.
Liechtenstein	
	No recommendations are made.
Lithuania	
	No recommendations are made.
Luxembourg	
	No recommendations are made.
Malaysia	
Malaysia experienced difficulties in identifying all potential exchange jurisdictions for future rulings.	Malaysia is recommended to continue its efforts to ensure that all potential exchange jurisdictions are identified swiftly for all future rulings. This recommendation remains unchanged since the prior year peer review report.
Malaysia experienced delays in the provision of rulings to the Competent Authority and did not undertake spontaneous exchange of information on all future tax rulings within the scope of the transparency framework during the year in review.	Malaysia is recommended to continue its efforts to reduce the timeliness for providing the information on rulings to the Competent Authority and to complete the templates for all relevant future rulings and to ensure that the exchanges of information on future rulings occur as soon as possible. This recommendation remains unchanged since the 2017, 2018 and 2019 peer review reports.
Malta	
	No recommendations are made.
Mauritius	
	No recommendations are made.
Mexico	
	No recommendations are made.
Morocco	
	No recommendations are made.
Namibia	
Namibia does not yet have the necessary information gathering process in place.	Namibia is recommended to ensure that it has put in place an effective information gathering process to identify all relevant past and future rulings and all potential exchange jurisdictions and to implement a review and supervision mechanism, as soon as possible.
Namibia does not yet have a process to complete the templates on relevant rulings, to make them available to the Competent Authority for exchange of information, and to exchange them with relevant jurisdictions.	Namibia is recommended to develop a process to complete the templates for all relevant rulings and to ensure that the exchanges of information on rulings occur in accordance with the form and timelines under the transparency framework going forward.
Netherlands	
The Netherlands experienced delays in the provision of rulings to the Competent Authority.	The Netherlands is recommended to ensure that information is made available to the Competent Authority without undue delay.
New Zealand	
	No recommendations are made.
Norway	
	No recommendations are made.
Peru	
	No recommendations are made.

Philippines	
The Philippines does not currently collect information on all potential exchange jurisdictions, particularly the ultimate parent company for past rulings.	The Philippines is recommended to apply the "best efforts approach" to identify potential exchange jurisdictions for all past rulings. This recommendation remains unchanged since the 2017, 2018 and 2019 peer review reports.
The Philippines does not currently collect information on all potential exchange jurisdictions, particularly the ultimate parent company for future rulings.	The Philippines is recommended to ensure that all potential exchange jurisdictions are identified swiftly for future rulings. This recommendation remains unchanged since the 2017, 2018 and 2019 peer review reports.
The Philippines does not yet have the necessary domestic legal framework in place for exchanging information on rulings or a process in place to ensure the timely exchange of information on rulings in the form required by the transparency framework.	The Philippines is recommended to continue to put in place a domestic legal framework allowing spontaneous exchange of information on rulings and to ensure the timely exchange of information on rulings in the form required by the transparency framework. This recommendation remains unchanged since the 2017, 2018 and 2019 peer review reports.
Poland	
	No recommendations are made.
Portugal	
	No recommendations are made.
Qatar	
	No recommendations are made.
Romania	
	No recommendations are made.
Russia	
	No recommendations are made.
Saint Kitts and Nevis	
	No recommendations are made.
Saint Lucia	
Saint Lucia does not require taxpayers to provide all necessary information to identify all potential exchange jurisdictions for future rulings.	Saint Lucia is recommended to ensure that all potential exchange jurisdictions are identified swiftly for all future rulings. This recommendation remains unchanged since the 2018 and 2019 peer review reports but it is now targeted to only this specific aspect that still needs to be put in place.
San Marino	
	No recommendations are made.
Senegal	
	No recommendations are made.
Seychelles	
	No recommendations are made.
Singapore	
	No recommendations are made.
Sint Maarten	
	No recommendations are made.
Slovak Republic	
	No recommendations are made.
Slovenia	
	No recommendations are made.
South Africa	
	No recommendations are made.
Spain	
Spain has not exchanged information on new assets of existing taxpayers benefitting from the grandfathered regime, as this information was not available during the year in review.	Spain is recommended to continue its efforts to identify and exchange relevant information on new assets of existing taxpayers benefitting from the grandfathered IP regime. This recommendation remains unchanged since the 2017, 2018 and 2019 peer review reports.
Sri Lanka	
It is not known whether Sri Lanka has put in place the necessary information gathering process.	Sri Lanka is recommended to finalise its information gathering process for identifying all future rulings and potential exchange jurisdictions, with a review and supervision mechanism, as soon as possible. This recommendation remains unchanged since the 2017, 2018 and 2019

	peer review reports.
It is not known whether Sri Lanka has a process to complete the templates on relevant rulings, to make them available to the Competent Authority for exchange of information, and to exchange them with relevant jurisdictions.	Sri Lanka is recommended to put in place a domestic legal framework allowing spontaneous exchange of information on rulings and to develop a process to complete the templates on relevant rulings and to ensure that the exchanges of information on rulings occur in accordance with the form and timelines under the transparency framework. This recommendation remains unchanged since the 2017, 2018 and 2019 peer review reports.
Sweden	
	No recommendations are made.
Switzerland	
Switzerland identified additional past rulings that were not previously captured.	Switzerland is recommended to strengthen its information gathering process by identifying all past rulings within the scope of the transparency framework and its review and supervision mechanism to ensure that the information gathering process is working effectively. This recommendation remains unchanged since the prior year peer review report.
Switzerland experienced delays in the exchange of information on past and future rulings.	Switzerland is recommended to continue to ensure that all information on past and future rulings is exchanged as soon as possible. This recommendation remains unchanged since the prior year peer review report.
Thailand	
Thailand found that the database for future rulings issued in 2019 and 2020 may be incomplete due to a technical issue when migrating data from paper into the database.	Thailand is recommended to strengthen its information gathering process identifying all future rulings within the scope of the transparency framework and its review and supervision mechanism to ensure that the information gathering process is working effectively.
Thailand does not yet have the necessary legal framework in place for exchanging information on rulings.	Thailand is recommended to finalise the amendments to put the domestic legal basis in place to commence exchanges as soon as possible. This recommendation remains unchanged since the prior year peer review report.
Thailand did not undertake spontaneous exchange of information on all tax rulings within the scope of the transparency framework during the year in review.	Thailand is recommended to ensure that all information on past and future rulings is exchanged as soon as possible after the domestic legal basis is in force. This recommendation remains unchanged since the 2018 and 2019 peer review reports.
Turkey	
	No recommendations are made.
Ukraine	
	No recommendations are made.
United Kingdom	
	No recommendations are made.
United States	
	No recommendations are made.
Uruguay	
	No recommendations are made.
Vietnam	
Viet Nam is currently putting in place a process for completion of templates and exchange of information on rulings.	Viet Nam is recommended to develop a process to complete the templates on relevant rulings and to ensure that the exchanges of information on rulings occur in accordance with the form and timelines under the transparency framework. This recommendation remains unchanged since the 2017, 2018 and 2019 peer review reports.

References

OECD (2015), *Countering Harmful Tax Practices More Effectively, Taking into Account Transparency and Substance, Action 5 - 2015 Final Report*, OECD/G20 Base Erosion and Profit Shifting Project, OECD Publishing, Paris, https://dx.doi.org/10.1787/9789264241190-en. [1]

Notes

[1] The Action 5 Report, *Countering Harmful Tax Practices More Effectively, Taking Into Account Transparency and Substance* (OECD, 2015) also provides that additional types of rulings could be added to the scope of the transparency framework in the future, where the FHTP and the Inclusive Framework agree that such a ruling could lead to BEPS concerns in the absence of spontaneous information exchange.

[2] The relevant jurisdictions that do not issue rulings in scope of the transparency framework are: Belize, Bulgaria, Cameroon, Cook Islands, Cote d'Ivoire, Djibouti, Dominica, Greenland, Haiti, Honduras, Liberia, Macau (China), Maldives, Monaco, Mongolia, Montenegro, Montserrat, Nigeria, North Macedonia, Oman, Pakistan, Panama, Papua New Guinea, Paraguay, Saint Vincent and the Grenadines, Saudi Arabia, Serbia, Sierra Leone, Trinidad and Tobago, Tunisia, Zambia.

1 Introduction

Overview of the peer review on the exchange of information on tax rulings

The Action 5 Report (OECD, 2015[1]) is one of the four BEPS minimum standards. It involves two distinct aspects: a review of certain preferential tax regimes and substantial activities in no or only nominal tax jurisdictions to ensure they are not harmful, and the transparency framework. Each of the four BEPS minimum standards is subject to peer review in order to ensure timely and accurate implementation and thus safeguard the level playing field. All members of the Inclusive Framework on BEPS commit to implementing the Action 5 minimum standard and to participating in the peer review, on an equal footing. The peer review of the Action 5 minimum standard is undertaken by the FHTP and approved by the Inclusive Framework on BEPS.

The purpose of a peer review is to ensure the effective and consistent implementation of an agreed standard and to recognise progress made by jurisdictions in this regard. The peer review evaluates the implementation of the standard against an agreed set of criteria. These criteria are set out in terms of reference, which include each of the elements that a jurisdiction needs to demonstrate it has fulfilled in order to show effective implementation of the standard.[1]

The peer review has been conducted in accordance with the agreed methodology. The methodology sets out the process for undertaking the peer review, including the process for collecting the relevant data, the preparation and approval of annual reports, the outputs of the review and the follow up process.

The terms of reference and agreed methodology do not alter the Action 5 minimum standard. Any terms used in the terms of reference or methodology take their meaning from the language and context of the Action 5 Report (OECD, 2015[1])and the references therein. Any terms in this report which are not included in the glossary take their meaning from the language and context of the Action 5 Report (OECD, 2015[1]).

Outline of the key aspects assessed in the annual report

This annual report contains the findings of the fifth annual peer review of jurisdictions' compliance with the transparency framework. It assesses the implementation of the transparency framework for the period 1 January 2020 - 31 December 2020.

The reports on each reviewed jurisdiction cover each of the aspects of the terms of reference. These capture the key elements of the transparency framework which are briefly described below. Where recommendations from prior years' peer review reports were not addressed, the report specifically notes this. Jurisdictions are urged to address these recommendations that have remained in place for more than one review.

A. The information gathering process

This involves assessing the processes in place in each of the jurisdictions for identifying past and future rulings that fall within the scope of the transparency framework, and for each of these rulings, identifying the jurisdictions with which the information should be exchanged. The review of the information gathering process also covers any supervision mechanism that the jurisdiction has in place to ensure that all relevant information is captured adequately.

B. The exchange of information

The exchange of information requires the legal and administrative framework to be in place to allow spontaneous exchange of information on the relevant tax rulings and subsequent exchange of the relevant rulings where a valid exchange of information request is received. Information on past rulings was to be spontaneously exchanged pursuant to the relevant deadline outlined in each jurisdiction's report.[2] Information on future rulings is to be spontaneously exchanged as soon as possible and no later than three months after the date on which the ruling becomes available to the Competent Authority for exchange of information. The exchange of information should occur in the agreed standardised form, either using the template contained in Annex C of the Action 5 Report (OECD, 2015[1]) or the OECD XML Schema. Adequate completion of the summary section in the Annex C template or the OECD XML Schema should be ensured through adherence to the instruction sheet to the summary section or the internal FHTP suggested guidance, or an alternate process that allows the summary section to contain sufficient detail for the receiving jurisdiction's tax administration to appropriately assess the potential base erosion and profit shifting risks posed by the ruling where applicable.

The peer review includes reviewing (i) that there is a sufficient domestic and international legal framework for the exchange information related to rulings; (ii) that the summary templates for information on rulings being exchanged are complete and in the appropriate form; and (iii) that the systems are in place to ensure that information on rulings is transmitted to the jurisdiction's Competent Authority for exchange of information without undue delay and exchanged with relevant jurisdictions in accordance with the appropriate timelines.

With respect to the international exchange of information, the terms of reference required jurisdictions to exchange information with Inclusive Framework members being reviewed for the same year, to the extent that an exchange of information agreement was in force for such exchanges and subject to the recipient jurisdiction demonstrating that it would keep the information received confidential.[3]

C. Statistics

Each jurisdiction is required to report statistics on the exchange of information under the transparency framework including (i) the total number of spontaneous exchanges sent, (ii) the number of spontaneous exchanges under each category of ruling and (iii) a list of jurisdictions with which the information was exchanged for each type of ruling.

D. Exchange of information on IP regimes

The review of the transparency framework also includes a review of the spontaneous exchanges of information which are required to occur in respect of certain features of IP regimes, as set out in the Action 5 "nexus approach." This includes, irrespective of whether a tax ruling is provided, identifying and exchanging information on taxpayers which benefit from the third category of IP assets (as defined in paragraph 37 of the Action 5 Report), and taxpayers making use of the option to treat the nexus ratio as a rebuttable presumption (as defined in paragraphs 67- 69 of the Action 5 Report). This aspect of the review is only relevant for those jurisdictions which offer IP regimes, and the minimum standard does not require any jurisdiction to introduce such a regime.

Spontaneous exchange of information is also required with respect to new entrants benefiting from grandfathered IP regimes (regardless of whether a ruling is provided). This applies with respect to IP regimes that were not compliant with the nexus approach, and where jurisdictions have taken steps to abolish the regime, or amend it, as part of the FHTP's regime review process. In some cases, when introducing those legislative changes, jurisdictions have chosen to provide grandfathering to existing taxpayers to provide time to transition to the new rules. Additional spontaneous exchange of information on the taxpayers benefiting from this grandfathering is required where taxpayers or new IP assets were transferred into a non-nexus IP regime in the period between the announcement of forthcoming changes and those changes taking place. The timelines for which these enhanced transparency vary according to the time at which the FHTP reviewed the regime, and are set out in Annex A of the 2017 Progress Report on Preferential Regimes (OECD, 2017b[2]).

Response to the report

In addition, jurisdictions had the option to include a response to the report and update on recent developments which occurred after the 2020 year in review. Where included, this reflects the individual jurisdiction's views, and not those of the FHTP or the OECD Secretariat.

References

OECD (2021), *BEPS Action 5 on Harmful Tax Practices - Terms of Reference and Methodology for the Conduct of the Peer Reviews of the Action 5 Transparency Framework*, OECD Publishing, Paris, http://www.oecd.org/tax/beps/beps-action-5-harmful-tax-practices-peer-review-transparency-framework.pdf. [3]

OECD (2015), *Countering Harmful Tax Practices More Effectively, Taking into Account Transparency and Substance, Action 5 - 2015 Final Report*, OECD/G20 Base Erosion and Profit Shifting Project, OECD Publishing, Paris, https://dx.doi.org/10.1787/9789264241190-en. [1]

OECD (ed.) (2017b), *Harmful Tax Practices - 2017 Progress Report on Preferential Regimes*, OECD Publishing, Paris, http://dx.doi.org/10.1787/9789264283954-en. [2]

OECD/Council of Europe (2011), *The Multilateral Convention on Mutual Administrative Assistance in Tax Matters: Amended by the 2010 Protocol*, OECD Publishing, Paris, https://dx.doi.org/10.1787/9789264115606-en. [4]

Notes

[1] Terms of Reference and Methodology for the review available at www.oecd.org/tax/beps/beps-action-5-harmful-tax-practices-peer-review-transparency-framework.pdf (OECD, 2021).

[2] The Action 5 Report (OECD, 2015) acknowledged that some jurisdictions may need to put in place the domestic or international legal framework in order to comply with the obligations under Action 5. In such cases the timelines for exchange of information on rulings are subject to a jurisdiction's legal framework.

[3] Where a ruling related only to tax years which were not covered by the relevant exchange of information agreement, no exchange of information would be required to occur in respect of that ruling. No negative inference is drawn in the peer review where an exchange was not permitted to occur because of the absence of, or the tax years covered by, an exchange of information agreement, although Inclusive Framework members are encouraged to expand their exchange of information agreements where relevant.

Albania

Albania has met all aspects of the terms of reference (OECD, 2021[3]) (ToR) for the calendar year 2020 (year in review), except for having the necessary information gathering process in place (ToR I.A), and having a domestic legal basis for spontaneous exchange of information and exchanging information on the tax rulings in accordance with the form and timelines under the transparency framework (ToR II.B). Albania receives two recommendations on these points for the year in review.

This is Albania's first review of implementation of the transparency framework.

Albania can legally issue five types of rulings within the scope of the transparency framework.

In practice, Albania issued no rulings within the scope of the transparency framework.

As no exchanges were required to take place, no peer input was received in respect of the exchanges of information on rulings received from Albania.

A. The information gathering process (ToR I.A)

1. Albania can legally issue the following two types of rulings within the scope of the transparency framework: (i) preferential regimes;[1] and (ii) cross-border unilateral APAs and any other cross-border unilateral tax rulings (such as an advance tax ruling) covering transfer pricing or the application of transfer pricing principles. Rulings in scope of the FHTP work are issued by the General Directorate of Taxation (GDT).

Past rulings (ToR I.A.1.1, I.A.1.2, I.A.2.1, I.A.2.2)

2. For Albania, past rulings are any tax rulings issued prior to 1 March 2020. However, there is no obligation for Albania to conduct spontaneous exchange information on past rulings.

Future rulings (ToR I.A.1.1, I.A.1.2, I.A.2.1)

3. For Albania, future rulings are any tax rulings within scope that are issued on or after 1 March 2020.

4. No rulings were issued by Albania during the future rulings period in the year in review. Albania indicated that rulings are issued based on legal provisions and will be immediately identified by the GDT. Albania also indicates that all relevant information in relation to APAs, including information on relevant exchange jurisdictions, are available to the GDT. In particular, for APAs, Albania confirms that based on Instruction no. 9 of 2015 on APAs, taxpayers are required to provide information on related parties, as well immediate and ultimate parent companies at the time the request for a ruling is submitted to the tax administration as well as additional information at the request of the tax administration. Regarding rulings on preferential regimes, there are no processes yet in place to ensure the identification of all relevant exchange jurisdictions and thus to ensure the implementation of the obligations relating to the transparency framework.

Review and supervision (ToR I.A.3)

5. Albania does not yet have a review and supervision mechanism under the transparency framework for the year in review.

Conclusion on section A

6. Albania is recommended to put in place an effective information gathering process to identify all potential exchange jurisdictions for future rulings on preferential regimes and to implement a review and supervision mechanism, as soon as possible (ToR I.A).

B. The exchange of information (ToR II.B)

Legal basis for spontaneous exchange of information (ToR II.B.1, II.B.2)

7. Albania has the necessary domestic legal basis to exchange information spontaneously. In this regard, Albania confirms Article 61/1 of the law on tax procedures allows spontaneous exchange of information on the implementation of international agreements. Albania notes that there are no legal or practical impediments that prevent the spontaneous exchange of information on rulings as contemplated in the Action 5 minimum standard.

8. Albania has international agreements permitting spontaneous exchange of information, including being a party to (i) the *Multilateral Convention on Mutual Administrative Assistance in Tax Matters: Amended by the 2010 Protocol* (OECD/Council of Europe, 2011[4]) ("the Convention") and (ii) bilateral agreements in force with 42 jurisdictions.[2]

Completion and exchange of templates (ToR II.B.3, II.B.4, II.B.5, II.B.6, II.B.7)

9. Albania does not yet have a process to complete the templates on all relevant rulings, to make them available to the Competent Authority for exchange of information, and to exchange them with relevant jurisdictions.

10. During the year in review, no exchanges were required to take place and no data on the timeliness of exchanges is reported.

Conclusion on section B

11. Albania is recommended to develop a process to complete the templates for all relevant rulings and to ensure that the exchanges of information on rulings occur in accordance with the form and timelines under the transparency framework going forward (ToR II.B).

C. Statistics (ToR IV)

12. As there was no information on rulings exchanged by Albania for the year in review, no statistics can be reported.

D. Matters related to intellectual property regimes (ToR I.A.1.3)

13. Albania does not offer an intellectual property regime for which transparency requirements under the Action 5 Report (OECD, 2015[1]) were imposed.

Summary of recommendations on implementation of the transparency framework

Aspect of implementation of the transparency framework that should be improved	Recommendation for improvement
Albania does not yet have the necessary information gathering process in place.	Albania is recommended to put in place an effective information gathering process to identify all potential exchange jurisdictions for future rulings on preferential regimes and to implement a review and supervision mechanism, as soon as possible.
Albania does not yet have a process to complete the templates on relevant rulings, to make them available to the Competent Authority for exchange of information, and to exchange them with relevant jurisdictions.	Albania is recommended to develop a process to complete the templates for all relevant rulings and to ensure that the exchanges of information on rulings occur in accordance with the form and timelines under the transparency framework.

Jurisdiction's response and recent developments

14. Albania notes that 2020 was the first year of implementation of the transparency framework for their tax administration. Albania is currently in the process of taking appropriate steps to implement the transparency and action the recommendations of this report.

References

OECD (2021), *BEPS Action 5 on Harmful Tax Practices - Terms of Reference and Methodology for the Conduct of the Peer Reviews of the Action 5 Transparency Framework*, OECD Publishing, Paris, http://www.oecd.org/tax/beps/beps-action-5-harmful-tax-practices-peer-review-transparency-framework.pdf. [3]

OECD (2015), *Countering Harmful Tax Practices More Effectively, Taking into Account Transparency and Substance, Action 5 - 2015 Final Report*, OECD/G20 Base Erosion and Profit Shifting Project, OECD Publishing, Paris, https://dx.doi.org/10.1787/9789264241190-en. [1]

OECD (ed.) (2017b), *Harmful Tax Practices - 2017 Progress Report on Preferential Regimes*, OECD Publishing, Paris, http://dx.doi.org/10.1787/9789264283954-en. [2]

OECD/Council of Europe (2011), *The Multilateral Convention on Mutual Administrative Assistance in Tax Matters: Amended by the 2010 Protocol*, OECD Publishing, Paris, https://dx.doi.org/10.1787/9789264115606-en. [4]

Notes

[1] Industry Incentive Regime.

[2] Participating jurisdictions to the Convention are available here: www.oecd.org/tax/exchange-of-tax-information/convention-on-mutual-administrative-assistance-in-tax-matters.htm. Albania also has bilateral agreements with Austria, Belgium, Bosnia and Herzegovina, Bulgaria, China (People's Republic of), Croatia, Czech Republic, Egypt, Estonia, France, Germany, Greece, Hungary, Iceland, India, Ireland, Italy, Korea, Kosovo, Kuwait, Latvia, Malaysia, Malta, Moldova, Montenegro, Netherlands, North Macedonia, Norway, Poland, Qatar, Romania, Russia, Saudi Arabia, Serbia, Singapore, Slovenia, Spain, Sweden, Switzerland, Turkey, United Arab Emirates, United Kingdom.

Andorra

Andorra has met all aspects of the terms of reference (OECD, 2021[3]) (ToR) for the calendar year 2020 (year in review), except for identifying all potential exchange jurisdictions for future rulings (ToR I.A.2.1) and for ensuring that the information is completed in the required form (II.B.4) and exchanges are performed in accordance with the timelines (ToR II.B.5 and II.B.6). Andorra receives two recommendations on these points for the year in review.

In the prior year report, as well as in the 2017 and 2018 peer reviews, Andorra had received the same two recommendations. As they have not been addressed, the recommendations remain in place.

Andorra can legally issue five types of rulings within the scope of the transparency framework.

In practice, Andorra issued no rulings within the scope of the transparency framework.[1]

As no exchanges were required to take place, no peer input was received in respect of the exchanges of information on rulings received from Andorra.

A. The information gathering process (ToR I.A)

15. Andorra can legally issue the following five types of rulings within the scope of the transparency framework: (i) preferential regimes;[2] (ii) cross-border unilateral APAs and any other cross-border unilateral tax rulings (such as an advance tax ruling) covering transfer pricing or the application of transfer pricing principles; (iii) rulings providing for unilateral downward adjustments; (iv) permanent establishment rulings; and (v) related party conduit rulings.

Past rulings (ToR I.A.1.1, I.A.1.2, I.A.2.1, I.A.2.2)

16. For Andorra, past rulings are any tax rulings within scope that are issued either (i) on or after 1 January 2015 but before 1 April 2017; and (ii) on or after 1 January 2012 but before 1 January 2015, provided they were still in effect as at 1 January 2015.

17. In the prior year peer review report, it was determined that Andorra's undertakings to identify past rulings and all potential exchange jurisdictions were sufficient to meet the minimum standard. Andorra's implementation in this regard remains unchanged, and therefore continues to meet the minimum standard.

Future rulings (ToR I.A.1.1, I.A.1.2, I.A.2.1)

18. For Andorra, future rulings are any tax rulings within scope that are issued on or after 1 April 2017.

19. In the prior years' peer review reports, it was determined future rulings were able to be identified, but that the information on potential exchange jurisdictions was not always being collected, and instead this was being performed by the application of the "best efforts approach." The prior years' reports noted that Andorra intended to amend the application process to require the taxpayer to identify all relevant jurisdictions when requesting the ruling. However, this amendment did not take place during the year in review. Andorra is therefore recommended to continue its efforts to ensure that all potential exchange jurisdictions are identified swiftly for all future rulings.

Review and supervision (ToR I.A.3)

20. In the prior years' peer review reports, it was determined that Andorra's review and supervision mechanism was sufficient to meet the minimum standard. Andorra's implementation in this regard remains unchanged, and therefore continues to meet the minimum standard.

Conclusion on section A

21. Andorra has met all of the ToR for the information gathering process except for identifying all potential exchange jurisdictions for future rulings (ToR I.A.2.1). Andorra is recommended to ensure that all potential exchange jurisdictions are identified swiftly for all future rulings.

B. The exchange of information (ToR II.B)

Legal basis for spontaneous exchange of information (ToR II.B.1, II.B.2)

22. Andorra has the necessary domestic legal basis to exchange information spontaneously. Andorra notes that there are no legal or practical impediments that prevent the spontaneous exchange of information on rulings as contemplated in the Action 5 minimum standard.

23. Andorra has international agreements permitting spontaneous exchange of information, including being a party to (i) the *Multilateral Convention on Mutual Administrative Assistance in Tax Matters:*

Amended by the 2010 Protocol (OECD/Council of Europe, 2011[4]) ("the Convention") and (ii) bilateral agreements in force with 28 jurisdictions.[3]

Completion and exchange of templates (ToR II.B.3, II.B.4, II.B.5, II.B.6, II.B.7)

24. In the prior years' peer review reports, it was determined that Andorra's process for the completion and exchange of templates met all the ToR, except for undertaking spontaneous exchange of information on tax rulings within the scope of the transparency framework (ToR II.B). Therefore, Andorra was recommended to complete the templates for all relevant rulings and to ensure that the exchanges of information on rulings occur as soon as possible.

25. In the prior year peer review report, it was determined that Andorra's previously issued rulings related to preferential regimes were related to wholly domestic taxpayers without any related parties in a foreign jurisdiction, and therefore, no exchange of information needed to take place. However, in the event that a relevant ruling is issued in future, Andorra will need to have the processes in place to complete the templates and conduct the exchanges in accordance with the transparency framework.

26. In the prior years' peer review reports, it was noted that Andorra intends to require taxpayers to provide all relevant information needed to complete the template contained in Annex C of the BEPS Action 5 Report (OECD, 2015[1]). Andorra intends to include such an obligation in future tax reforms.

27. As these issues have not been addressed, the recommendation remains in place. In particular, Andorra is recommended to ensure that the information on future rulings is completed in the form of the template contained in Annex C of the Action 5 Report (OECD, 2015[1]) (ToR II.B.4), to put in place appropriate systems to ensure that information on rulings is transmitted to the competent authority responsible for international exchange of information without undue delay (ToR II.B.5) and to ensure that the information to be exchanged is transmitted to the relevant jurisdictions in accordance with the agreed timelines (ToR II.B.6).

28. As there were no exchanges for the year in review, no data on the timeliness of exchanges can be reported.

Conclusion on section B

29. Andorra has met all of the ToR for the exchange of information process except for ensuring that the information is completed in the required form (II.B.4) and having a process in place to ensure any exchanges will be performed in accordance with the timelines (ToR II.B.5 and II.B.6). Andorra is recommended to continue its efforts to put in place the necessary process to complete the information in the form of Annex C of the Action 5 Report (OECD, 2015[1]), to ensure that information is submitted to the Competent Authority without undue delay and exchanges are performed in accordance with the timelines. These recommendations remain unchanged since the 2017, 2018 and 2019 peer review reports.

C. Statistics (ToR IV)

30. As no rulings were issued, no statistics can be reported.

D. Matters related to intellectual property regimes (ToR I.A.1.3)

31. Andorra offers an intellectual property regime (IP regime)[4] that is not subject to the transparency requirements under the Action 5 Report (OECD, 2015[1]), because:

- ***New entrants benefitting from the grandfathered IP regime***: no enhanced transparency requirements apply, as explained in the prior year peer review report.
- ***Third category of IP assets***: not applicable as the regime does not allow the third category of IP assets to qualify for the benefits.
- ***Taxpayers making the use of the option to treat the nexus ratio as a rebuttable presumption***: not applicable the regime does not allow the nexus ratio to be treated as a rebuttable presumption.

Summary of recommendations on implementation of the transparency framework

Aspect of implementation of the transparency framework that should be improved	Recommendation for improvement
Andorra still experiences difficulties in identifying all potential exchange jurisdictions for future rulings.	Andorra is recommended to continue its efforts to ensure that all potential exchange jurisdictions are identified swiftly for all future rulings. This recommendation remains unchanged since the 2017, 2018 and 2019 peer review reports.
Andorra is still developing a process to ensure that the information is completed in the required form and exchanges are performed in accordance with the timelines.	Andorra is recommended to continue its efforts to put in place the necessary process to complete the information in the form of Annex C of the BEPS Action 5 Report, to ensure that information is submitted to the Competent Authority without undue delay and exchanges are performed in accordance with the timelines. These recommendations remain unchanged since the 2017, 2018 and 2019 peer review reports but since the 2019 peer review report they are targeted to specific aspects of the ToR that still need to be put in place.

Jurisdiction's response and recent developments

32. Andorra notes that during the year 2021, it has drafted internal guidance on the steps that the Andorran Tax Administration must take when issuing a ruling within the scope of the transparency framework, including how to complete the Annex C template. This will be described in more detail in next year's peer review report. In addition, the Government of Andorra is working on a Law Draft on Direct Tax Reform Measures which includes a new additional disposition to Law 21/2014 on Taxation which relates specifically to the spontaneous exchange of rulings. It is expected that this Law Draft will enter into parliamentary procedure in the course of August or September, and that it will be approved before the end of the year.

References

OECD (2021), *BEPS Action 5 on Harmful Tax Practices - Terms of Reference and Methodology for the Conduct of the Peer Reviews of the Action 5 Transparency Framework*, OECD Publishing, Paris, http://www.oecd.org/tax/beps/beps-action-5-harmful-tax-practices-peer-review-transparency-framework.pdf. [3]

OECD (2015), *Countering Harmful Tax Practices More Effectively, Taking into Account Transparency and Substance, Action 5 - 2015 Final Report*, OECD/G20 Base Erosion and Profit Shifting Project, OECD Publishing, Paris, https://dx.doi.org/10.1787/9789264241190-en. [1]

OECD (ed.) (2017b), *Harmful Tax Practices - 2017 Progress Report on Preferential Regimes*, OECD Publishing, Paris, http://dx.doi.org/10.1787/9789264283954-en. [2]

OECD/Council of Europe (2011), *The Multilateral Convention on Mutual Administrative Assistance in Tax Matters: Amended by the 2010 Protocol*, OECD Publishing, Paris, https://dx.doi.org/10.1787/9789264115606-en. [4]

Notes

[1] In the prior years' peer review reports, it was noted that Andorra had issued 169 past and 58 future rulings. All those rulings were related to preferential regimes, but all taxpayers were domestic taxpayers (not part of a multinational group) and therefore no exchanges on these rulings were required for the Action 5 transparency framework.

[2] These regimes are: 1) Holding company regime and 2) Special regime for exploitation of certain intangibles.

[3] Participating jurisdictions to the Convention are available here: www.oecd.org/tax/exchange-of-tax-information/convention-on-mutual-administrative-assistance-in-tax-matters.htm. Andorra also has bilateral agreements with Argentina, Australia, Austria, Belgium, Cyprus, Czech Republic, Denmark, Faroe Islands, Finland, France, Germany, Greenland, Iceland, Italy, Korea, Liechtenstein, Luxembourg, Malta, Monaco, Netherlands, Norway, Poland, Portugal, San Marino, Spain, Sweden, Switzerland and United Arab Emirates.

[4] Special regime for exploitation of certain intangibles.

Angola

Angola has met all aspects of the terms of reference (OECD, 2021[3]) (ToR) for the calendar year 2020 (year in review), except for identifying all past and future rulings and all potential exchange jurisdictions with a review and supervision mechanism (ToR I.A) and exchanging information on the tax rulings in a timely manner (ToR II.B). Angola receives two recommendations on this point for the year in review.

In the prior year report, as well as in the 2017 and 2018 peer reviews, Angola had received the same recommendations. As they have not been addressed, the recommendations remain in place.

Angola can legally issue five types of rulings within the scope of the transparency framework.

In practice, Angola issued rulings within the scope of the transparency framework as follows:

Type of ruling	Number of rulings
Past rulings	0
Future rulings in the period 1 April 2017 – 31 December 2017	1
Future rulings in the calendar year 2018	0
Future rulings in the calendar year 2019	0
Future rulings in the year in review	0

As no exchanges took place, no peer input was received in respect of the exchanges of information on rulings received from Angola.

A. The information gathering process (ToR I.A)

33. Angola can legally issue the following five types of rulings within the scope of the transparency framework: (i) preferential regimes;[1] (ii) cross-border unilateral APAs and any other cross-border unilateral tax rulings (such as an advance tax ruling) covering transfer pricing or the application of transfer pricing principles; (iii) rulings providing for unilateral downward adjustments; (iv) permanent establishment rulings; and (v) related party conduit rulings.

Past rulings (ToR I.A.1.1, I.A.1.2, I.A.2.1, I.A.2.2)

34. For Angola, past rulings are any tax rulings within scope that are issued either (i) on or after 1 January 2015 but before 1 April 2017; and (ii) on or after 1 January 2012 but before 1 January 2015, provided they were still in effect as at 1 January 2015.

35. In the prior years' peer review reports, it was determined that Angola has not recorded the information on the tax rulings issued with the necessary level of detail to meet the standard of the transparency framework and that the necessary information on past rulings is unlikely to be found on the available records. Angola noted that they are not required to exchange past rulings but did not identify any past rulings. Therefore, Angola was recommended to finalise its information gathering process for identifying all past rulings and potential exchange jurisdictions.

36. During the year in review, no additional implementation steps were taken.

Future rulings (ToR I.A.1.1, I.A.1.2, I.A.2.1)

37. For Angola, future rulings are any tax rulings within scope that are issued on or after 1 April 2017.

38. In the prior years' peer review reports, it was determined that Angola was following guidelines covering which rulings would fall within the scope of the transparency framework and what information should be kept in order to meet the level of detail required by the transparency framework.

39. During the year in review, Angola started to identify all rulings that have been issued by the Angolan tax administration (AGT). In accordance with internal procedures, the different departments within AGT send the identified rulings to the International Cooperation Department. This department is responsible for analysing whether the rulings fall within the scope of the transparency framework. As this is still ongoing for rulings issued on or after 1 April 2017, the recommendation on this point remains in place.

Review and supervision (ToR I.A.3)

40. In the prior years' peer review reports, it was determined that Angola did not yet have a review and supervision mechanism for past rulings under the transparency framework. Angola implemented a review and supervision mechanism for future rulings by requiring that the information on tax rulings be recorded in hard copy and electronically in spreadsheets with the name, date and topic of the information requested or issue being complained or appealed. However, during the year in review, no additional implementation steps were taken.

Conclusion on section A

41. Angola is recommended to finalise its information gathering process for identifying all past and future rulings and all potential exchange jurisdictions, with a review and supervision mechanism, as soon as possible (ToR I.A).

B. The exchange of information (ToR II.B)

Legal basis for spontaneous exchange of information (ToR II.B.1, II.B.2)

42. Angola is currently in the process of putting in place the necessary domestic legal basis to exchange information spontaneously. During the prior year, Angola had already reviewed and approved its general tax code, which includes a clause that allows the Angolan Revenue Administration to gather information from taxpayers.

43. Angola has international agreements permitting spontaneous exchange of information, including bilateral agreements in force with two jurisdictions.[2] Angola is not a party to the *Multilateral Convention on Mutual Administrative Assistance in Tax Matters: Amended by the 2010 Protocol* (OECD/Council of Europe, 2011[4]) ("the Convention"). Angola is encouraged to continue its efforts to expand its international exchange of information instruments to be able to exchange information on tax rulings. It is noted, however, that jurisdictions are assessed on their compliance with the transparency framework in respect of the exchange of information network in effect for the year of the particular annual review.

Completion and exchange of templates (ToR II.B.3, II.B.4, II.B.5, II.B.6, II.B.7)

44. In the prior years' peer review reports, it was determined that Angola is still developing a process to complete the templates on relevant rulings, to make them available to the Competent Authority for exchange of information and to exchange them with relevant jurisdictions. During the prior year, an information exchange unit was created to assume the role of the Competent Authority. Angola's tax offices are henceforth required to send reports to this unit on a monthly basis, but in practice the unit has not yet received any reports.

45. During the year in review, as well as during the prior year, Angola was negotiating to obtain an electronic tool for the exchange of information.

46. As Angola did not have the necessary legal basis to conduct exchanges, no data on the timeliness of exchanges can be reported.

Conclusion on section B

47. Angola is recommended to continue its efforts to put in place a domestic legal framework allowing spontaneous exchange of information on rulings and to complete the templates for all relevant rulings and to ensure that the exchanges of information on rulings occur as soon as possible (ToR II.B).

C. Statistics (ToR IV)

48. As no rulings were issued, no statistics can be reported.

D. Matters related to intellectual property regimes (ToR I.A.1.3)

49. Angola does not offer an intellectual property regime for which transparency requirements under the Action 5 Report (OECD, 2015[1]) were imposed.

Summary of recommendations on implementation of the transparency framework

Aspect of implementation of the transparency framework that should be improved	Recommendation for improvement
Angola has not yet finalised the steps to have in place its necessary information and gathering process.	Angola is recommended to finalise its information gathering process for identifying all past and future rulings and all potential exchange jurisdictions, with a review and supervision mechanism, as soon as possible. This recommendation remains unchanged since the 2017, 2018 and 2019 peer review reports.
Angola has not yet finalised the steps to have effective compulsory spontaneous exchange of information on the tax rulings within the scope of the transparency framework.	Angola is recommended to continue to put in place a domestic legal framework allowing spontaneous exchange of information on rulings and to continue its efforts to complete the templates for all relevant rulings and to ensure that the exchanges of information on rulings occur as soon as possible. This recommendation remains unchanged since the 2017, 2018 and 2019 peer review reports.

References

OECD (2021), *BEPS Action 5 on Harmful Tax Practices - Terms of Reference and Methodology for the Conduct of the Peer Reviews of the Action 5 Transparency Framework*, OECD Publishing, Paris, http://www.oecd.org/tax/beps/beps-action-5-harmful-tax-practices-peer-review-transparency-framework.pdf. [3]

OECD (2015), *Countering Harmful Tax Practices More Effectively, Taking into Account Transparency and Substance, Action 5 - 2015 Final Report*, OECD/G20 Base Erosion and Profit Shifting Project, OECD Publishing, Paris, https://dx.doi.org/10.1787/9789264241190-en. [1]

OECD (ed.) (2017b), *Harmful Tax Practices - 2017 Progress Report on Preferential Regimes*, OECD Publishing, Paris, http://dx.doi.org/10.1787/9789264283954-en. [2]

OECD/Council of Europe (2011), *The Multilateral Convention on Mutual Administrative Assistance in Tax Matters: Amended by the 2010 Protocol*, OECD Publishing, Paris, https://dx.doi.org/10.1787/9789264115606-en. [4]

Notes

[1] A special tax regime for oil and gas.

[2] Angola has bilateral agreements with Portugal and the United Arab Emirates.

Antigua and Barbuda

Antigua and Barbuda has met all aspects of the terms of reference (OECD, 2021[3]) (ToR) for the calendar year 2020 (year in review) that can be met in the absence of rulings being issued in practice, and no recommendations are made.

Antigua and Barbuda can legally issue four types of rulings within the scope of the transparency framework.

In practice, Antigua and Barbuda issued no rulings within the scope of the transparency framework.

As no exchanges were required to take place, no peer input was received in respect of the exchanges of information on rulings received from Antigua and Barbuda.

A. The information gathering process (ToR I.A)

50. Antigua and Barbuda can legally issue the following four types of rulings within the scope of the transparency framework: (i) cross-border unilateral APAs and any other cross-border unilateral tax rulings (such as an advance tax ruling) covering transfer pricing or the application of transfer pricing principles; (ii) rulings providing for unilateral downward adjustments; (iii) permanent establishment rulings; and (iv) related party conduit rulings.

51. For Antigua and Barbuda, past rulings are any tax rulings issued prior to 1 March 2019. Future rulings are any tax rulings within scope that are issued on or after 1 March 2019.

52. In the prior year peer review report, it was determined that Antigua and Barbuda's undertakings to identify past and future rulings and all potential exchange jurisdictions were sufficient to meet the minimum standard. In the prior year, Antigua and Barbuda indicated the possibility to introduce an internal electronic repository of rulings issued. In the year in review, Antigua and Barbuda confirmed that rulings issued will be stored on the internal drive of the Competent Authority to facilitate electronic access to this information. In the year in review, Antigua and Barbuda has also advanced the drafting of the Tax Administration and Procedures Act (TAPA) Regulations to formally require that the necessary information to meet the requirements of the transparency framework would be obtained in all cases and indicated the intention to complete the regulations by the end of 2021. In addition, it was determined that Antigua and Barbuda's review and supervision mechanism was sufficient to meet the minimum standard. Antigua and Barbuda's implementation remains unchanged, and therefore continues to meet the minimum standard.

53. Antigua and Barbuda has met all of the ToR for the information gathering process that can be met in the absence of rulings being issued and no recommendations are made.

B. The exchange of information (ToR II.B)

54. Antigua and Barbuda has international agreements permitting spontaneous exchange of information, including being a party to (i) the *Multilateral Convention on Mutual Administrative Assistance in Tax Matters: Amended by the 2010 Protocol* (OECD/Council of Europe, 2011[4]) ("the Convention"), (ii) bilateral agreements in force with 11 jurisdictions and tax information exchange agreements in force with 11 jurisdictions.[1]

55. As Antigua and Barbuda did not issue any future rulings within the scope of the transparency framework in the relevant period, Antigua and Barbuda was not required to exchange any information on rulings in the year in review and no data on the timeliness of exchanges can be reported.

56. In the prior year peer review report, it was determined that Antigua and Barbuda's process for the completion and exchange of templates were sufficient to meet the minimum standard. With respect to past rulings, no further action was required. Antigua and Barbuda's implementation in this regard remains unchanged and therefore continues to meet the minimum standard.

57. Antigua and Barbuda has the necessary legal basis for spontaneous exchange of information. Antigua and Barbuda has met all of the ToR for the exchange of information process that can be met in the absence of rulings being issued and exchanged in practice and no recommendations are made.

C. Matters related to intellectual property regimes (ToR I.A.1.3)

58. Antigua and Barbuda does not offer an intellectual property regime for which transparency requirements under the Action 5 Report (OECD, 2015[1]) were imposed.

Summary of recommendations on implementation of the transparency framework

Aspect of implementation of the transparency framework that should be improved	Recommendation for improvement
	No recommendations are made.

References

OECD (2021), *BEPS Action 5 on Harmful Tax Practices - Terms of Reference and Methodology for the Conduct of the Peer Reviews of the Action 5 Transparency Framework*, OECD Publishing, Paris, http://www.oecd.org/tax/beps/beps-action-5-harmful-tax-practices-peer-review-transparency-framework.pdf. [3]

OECD (2015), *Countering Harmful Tax Practices More Effectively, Taking into Account Transparency and Substance, Action 5 - 2015 Final Report*, OECD/G20 Base Erosion and Profit Shifting Project, OECD Publishing, Paris, https://dx.doi.org/10.1787/9789264241190-en. [1]

OECD (ed.) (2017b), *Harmful Tax Practices - 2017 Progress Report on Preferential Regimes*, OECD Publishing, Paris, http://dx.doi.org/10.1787/9789264283954-en. [2]

OECD/Council of Europe (2011), *The Multilateral Convention on Mutual Administrative Assistance in Tax Matters: Amended by the 2010 Protocol*, OECD Publishing, Paris, https://dx.doi.org/10.1787/9789264115606-en. [4]

Notes

[1] Participating jurisdictions to the Convention are available here: www.oecd.org/tax/exchange-of-tax-information/convention-on-mutual-administrative-assistance-in-tax-matters.htm. Antigua and Barbuda also has bilateral agreements with Switzerland and jurisdictions party to the CARICOM agreement. Tax information exchange agreements with Aruba, Australia, Denmark, Finland, France, Germany, Ireland, Netherlands, Norway, United Kingdom and United States also permit for the spontaneous exchange of information.

Argentina

Argentina has met all aspects of the terms of reference (OECD, 2021[3]) (ToR) for the calendar year 2020 (year in review) and no recommendations are made.

Argentina can legally issue five types of rulings within the scope of the transparency framework.

In practice, Argentina issued rulings within the scope of the transparency framework as follows:

Type of ruling	Number of rulings
Past rulings	2
Future rulings in the period 1 April 2016 – 31 December 2016	0
Future rulings in the calendar year 2017	1
Future rulings in the calendar year 2018	0
Future rulings in the calendar year 2019	1
Future rulings in the year in review	0

As no exchanges were required to take place, no peer input was received in respect of the exchanges of information on rulings received from Argentina.

A. The information gathering process (ToR I.A)

59. Argentina can legally issue the following five types of rulings within the scope of the transparency framework: (i) preferential regimes;[1] (ii) cross-border unilateral APAs and any other cross-border unilateral tax rulings (such as an advance tax ruling) covering transfer pricing or the application of transfer pricing principles; (iii) rulings providing for unilateral downward adjustments; (iv) permanent establishment rulings; and (v) related party conduit rulings.

60. For Argentina, past rulings are any tax rulings within scope that are issued either: (i) on or after 1 January 2014 but before 1 April 2016; or (ii) on or after 1 January 2010 but before 1 January 2014, provided they were still in effect as at 1 January 2014. Future rulings are any tax rulings within scope that are issued on or after 1 April 2016.

61. In the prior years' peer review reports, it was determined that Argentina's undertakings to identify past and future rulings and all potential exchange jurisdictions were sufficient to meet the minimum standard. In addition, it was determined that Argentina's review and supervision mechanism was sufficient to meet the minimum standard. With respect to past rulings, Argentina's implementation remains unchanged, and therefore continues to meet the minimum standard.

62. Argentina has met all of the ToR for the information gathering process and no recommendations are made.

B. The exchange of information (ToR II.B)

63. Argentina has international agreements permitting spontaneous exchange of information, including being a party to (i) the *Multilateral Convention on Mutual Administrative Assistance in Tax Matters: Amended by the 2010 Protocol* (OECD/Council of Europe, 2011[4]) ("the Convention") and (ii) bilateral agreements in force with 24 jurisdictions.[2]

64. During the year in review, no exchanges were required to take place and no data on the timeliness of exchanges is reported.

65. In the prior years' peer review reports, it was determined that Argentina's process for the completion and exchange of templates were sufficient to meet the minimum standard. With respect to past rulings, no further action was required. Argentina's implementation in this regard remains unchanged and therefore continues to meet the minimum standard.

66. Argentina has the necessary legal basis for spontaneous exchange of information, a process for completing the templates in a timely way and has completed all exchanges. Argentina has met all of the ToR for the exchange of information process and no recommendations are made.

C. Statistics (ToR IV)

67. As no rulings were issued, no statistics can be reported.

D. Matters related to intellectual property regimes (ToR I.A.1.3)

68. Argentina does not offer an intellectual property regime for which transparency requirements under the Action 5 Report (OECD, 2015[1]) were imposed.

Summary of recommendations on implementation of the transparency framework

Aspect of implementation of the transparency framework that should be improved	Recommendation for improvement
	No recommendations are made.

References

OECD (2021), *BEPS Action 5 on Harmful Tax Practices - Terms of Reference and Methodology for the Conduct of the Peer Reviews of the Action 5 Transparency Framework*, OECD Publishing, Paris, http://www.oecd.org/tax/beps/beps-action-5-harmful-tax-practices-peer-review-transparency-framework.pdf. [3]

OECD (2015), *Countering Harmful Tax Practices More Effectively, Taking into Account Transparency and Substance, Action 5 - 2015 Final Report*, OECD/G20 Base Erosion and Profit Shifting Project, OECD Publishing, Paris, https://dx.doi.org/10.1787/9789264241190-en. [1]

OECD (ed.) (2017b), *Harmful Tax Practices - 2017 Progress Report on Preferential Regimes*, OECD Publishing, Paris, http://dx.doi.org/10.1787/9789264283954-en. [2]

OECD/Council of Europe (2011), *The Multilateral Convention on Mutual Administrative Assistance in Tax Matters: Amended by the 2010 Protocol*, OECD Publishing, Paris, https://dx.doi.org/10.1787/9789264115606-en. [4]

Notes

1 Promotional regime for software industry.

2 Participating jurisdictions to the Convention are available here: www.oecd.org/tax/exchange-of-tax-information/convention-on-mutual-administrative-assistance-in-tax-matters.htm. Argentina also has bilateral agreements with Aruba, Australia, Azerbaijan, Belgium, Bolivia, Brazil, Canada, Chile, Denmark, Ecuador, Finland, France, Italy, Mexico, Netherlands, Norway, Peru, Russia, Spain, Sweden, United Arab Emirates, United States, United Kingdom and Venezuela.

Armenia

Armenia is continuing to take steps to implement the legal basis for the transparency framework and to commence administrative preparations in line with the terms of reference (OECD, 2021[3]) (ToR) to ensure that it finalises its information gathering process for future rulings (ToR I.A) and that information on rulings will be identified and exchanged in a timely manner (ToR II.B). Armenia receives two recommendations on these points for the calendar year 2020 (year in review).

In the prior year report, Armenia had received the same recommendations. As they have not been addressed, the recommendations remain in place.

Armenia can legally issue two types of rulings within the scope of the transparency framework.

In practice, Armenia issued no rulings within the scope of the transparency framework.

As no exchanges were required to take place, no peer input was received in respect of the exchanges of information on rulings received from Armenia.

A. The information gathering process (ToR I.A)

69. Armenia can legally issue the following two types of rulings within the scope of the transparency framework: (i) preferential regimes;[1] and (ii) permanent establishment rulings.

Past rulings (ToR I.A.1.1, I.A.1.2, I.A.2.1, I.A.2.2)

70. For Armenia, past rulings are any tax rulings issued prior to 1 September 2019. However, there is no obligation for Armenia to conduct spontaneous exchange information on past rulings.

Future rulings (ToR I.A.1.1, I.A.1.2, I.A.2.1)

71. For Armenia, future rulings are any tax rulings within scope that are issued on or after 1 September 2019.

72. In the prior year peer review report, it was determined that processes to ensure the implementation of the obligations relating to the transparency framework with regard to the information gathering process were not yet in place (ToR I.A). Therefore, Armenia was recommended to finalise its information gathering process for identifying all future rulings and potential exchange jurisdictions, as soon as possible

73. During the year in review, Armenia indicates that a system is in the process of being finalised for the identification and registration of issued tax rulings. The information gathering process is centralised at the level of the International Cooperation Department (ICD) and steps will be taken to ensure efficient communication with the Administration Methodology and Procedures Department (AMPD) and to obtain information on the relevant exchange jurisdictions by taxpayers requesting a ruling. In this regard, Armenia indicated its intention to issue additional regulations (i.e. Chairman orders) to formalise the current information gathering process. It is also noted that Armenia intends to implement processes to make sure the necessary information to meet the requirements of the transparency framework is required in all cases. Armenia finally notes that the State Revenue Committee (SRC) has databases in place that will allow it to verify the accurateness of information provided by the taxpayer.

Review and supervision (ToR I.A.3)

74. In the prior year peer review report, it was determined that Armenia did not yet have a review and supervision mechanism under the transparency framework. Therefore, Armenia was recommended to put in place a review and supervision mechanism as soon as possible.

75. During the year in review, Armenia indicates that the competent authority for exchange of information (i.e. ICD) responsible for the issuance of tax rulings, is also responsible for the review and supervision mechanism and for ensuring that the information to be exchanged is accurate and complete. In addition, there are different layers of control within both AMPD and ICD, and the Internal Audit Department also verifies the accurateness of the process which is regulated by the statute of responsibility of each unit and department. The review and supervision process carried out by AMPD is finally approved by the relevant Deputy Chairmen of SRC.

Conclusion on section A

76. Armenia is recommended to finalise its information gathering process for identifying all future rulings and potential exchange jurisdictions, as soon as possible (ToR I.A).

B. The exchange of information (ToR II.B)

Legal basis for spontaneous exchange of information (ToR II.B.1, II.B.2)

77. Armenia has the necessary domestic legal basis to exchange information spontaneously. Armenia notes that there are no legal or practical impediments that prevent the spontaneous exchange of information on rulings as contemplated in the Action 5 minimum standard.

78. Armenia has international agreements permitting spontaneous exchange of information, including being a party to (i) the *Multilateral Convention on Mutual Administrative Assistance in Tax Matters: Amended by the 2010 Protocol* (OECD/Council of Europe, 2011[4]) ("the Convention") *and* (ii) bilateral agreements in force with 48 jurisdictions. Armenia ratified the Convention on 6 February 2020. The Convention entered into force on 1 June 2020 and will have effect for administrative assistance related to taxable periods beginning on or after 1 January 2021.[2]

Completion and exchange of templates (ToR II.B.3, II.B.4, II.B.5, II.B.6, II.B.7)

79. In the prior year peer review report, it was determined that Armenia's process for the completion and exchange of templates was not yet in place. Therefore, Armenia was recommended to develop a process to complete the templates on relevant rulings and to ensure that the exchanges of information on rulings occur in accordance with the form and timelines under the transparency framework.

80. During the year in review, Armenia indicates its intention to complete the templates according to Annex C of the BEPS Action 5 report (OECD, 2015[1]). However, Armenia is still developing a process to complete the templates on relevant rulings, to make them available without undue delay to the Competent Authority for exchange of information, and to exchange them with relevant jurisdictions according to the required timelines. To this end, Armenia is planning to issue internal regulations. As this process is still ongoing, the previous year recommendation remains in place.

81. During the year in review, no exchanges were required to take place and no data on the timeliness of exchanges is reported.

Conclusion on section B

82. Armenia has the necessary legal basis for spontaneous exchange of information. Armenia is recommended to develop a process to complete the templates on relevant rulings and to ensure that the exchanges of information on rulings occur in accordance with the form and timelines under the transparency framework going forward (ToR II.B).

C. Statistics (ToR IV)

83. As no rulings were issued, no statistics can be reported.

D. Matters related to intellectual property regimes (ToR I.A.1.3)

84. Armenia does not offer an intellectual property regime for which transparency requirements under the Action 5 Report (OECD, 2015[1]) were imposed.

Summary of recommendations on implementation of the transparency framework

Aspect of implementation of the transparency framework that should be improved	Recommendation for improvement
Armenia is in the process to finalise the information gathering process and to put in place a system for the identification and registration of issued tax rulings.	Armenia is recommended to finalise its information gathering process for identifying all future rulings and potential exchange jurisdictions, as soon as possible. This recommendation remains unchanged since the prior year peer review report.
Armenia does not have a process to complete the templates on relevant rulings, to make them available to the Competent Authority for exchange of information, and to exchange them with relevant jurisdictions.	Armenia is recommended to develop a process to complete the templates on relevant rulings and to ensure that the exchanges of information on rulings occur in accordance with the form and timelines under the transparency framework. This recommendation remains unchanged since the prior year peer review report.

References

OECD (2021), *BEPS Action 5 on Harmful Tax Practices - Terms of Reference and Methodology for the Conduct of the Peer Reviews of the Action 5 Transparency Framework*, OECD Publishing, Paris, http://www.oecd.org/tax/beps/beps-action-5-harmful-tax-practices-peer-review-transparency-framework.pdf. [3]

OECD (2015), *Countering Harmful Tax Practices More Effectively, Taking into Account Transparency and Substance, Action 5 - 2015 Final Report*, OECD/G20 Base Erosion and Profit Shifting Project, OECD Publishing, Paris, https://dx.doi.org/10.1787/9789264241190-en. [1]

OECD (ed.) (2017b), *Harmful Tax Practices - 2017 Progress Report on Preferential Regimes*, OECD Publishing, Paris, http://dx.doi.org/10.1787/9789264283954-en. [2]

OECD/Council of Europe (2011), *The Multilateral Convention on Mutual Administrative Assistance in Tax Matters: Amended by the 2010 Protocol*, OECD Publishing, Paris, https://dx.doi.org/10.1787/9789264115606-en. [4]

Notes

[1] With respect to the following preferential regimes: 1) Free economic zones and 2) Information technology projects.

[2] Participating jurisdictions to the Convention are available here: www.oecd.org/tax/exchange-of-tax-information/convention-on-mutual-administrative-assistance-in-tax-matters.htm. Armenia also has bilateral agreements with Austria, Belarus, Belgium, Bulgaria, Canada, China (People's Republic of), Croatia, Cyprus, Czech Republic, Denmark, Estonia, Finland, France, Georgia, Germany, Greece, Hungary, India, Indonesia, Iran, Ireland, Israel, Italy, Kazakhstan, Kuwait, Latvia, Lebanon, Lithuania, Luxembourg, Moldova, Netherlands, Poland, Qatar, Romania, Russia, Serbia, Slovak Republic, Slovenia, Spain, Sweden, Switzerland, Syrian Arab Republic, Thailand, Tajikistan, Turkmenistan, Ukraine, United Arab Emirates and United Kingdom.

Aruba

Aruba has met all aspects of the terms of reference (OECD, 2021[3]) (ToR) for the calendar year 2020 (year in review) that can be met in the absence of rulings being issued in practice, and no recommendations are made.

Aruba can legally issue five types of rulings within the scope of the transparency framework.

In practice, Aruba issued no rulings within the scope of the transparency framework.

As no exchanges were required to take place, no peer input was received in respect of the exchanges of information on rulings received from Aruba.

A. The information gathering process (ToR I.A)

85. Aruba can legally issue the following five types of rulings within the scope of the transparency framework: (i) preferential regimes;[1] (ii) cross-border unilateral APAs and any other cross-border unilateral tax rulings (such as an advance tax ruling) covering transfer pricing or the application of transfer pricing principles; (iii) rulings providing for unilateral downward adjustments; (iv) permanent establishment rulings; and (v) related party conduit rulings.

86. For Aruba, past rulings are any tax rulings issued prior to 1 September 2018. However, there is no obligation for Aruba to conduct spontaneous exchange information on past rulings. Future rulings are any tax rulings within scope that are issued on or after 1 September 2018.

87. In the prior year peer review report, it was determined that Aruba's undertakings to identify future rulings and all potential exchange jurisdictions were sufficient to meet the minimum standard. In addition, it was determined that Aruba's review and supervision mechanism was sufficient to meet the minimum standard. Aruba's implementation remains unchanged, and therefore continues to meet the minimum standard.

88. Aruba has met all of the ToR for the information gathering process and no recommendations are made.

B. The exchange of information (ToR II.B)

89. Aruba has international agreements permitting spontaneous exchange of information, including being a jurisdiction participating in (i) the *Multilateral Convention on Mutual Administrative Assistance in Tax Matters: Amended by the 2010 Protocol* (OECD/Council of Europe, 2011[4]) ("the Convention") and (ii) bilateral agreements in force with 25 jurisdictions.[2]

90. In the prior years' peer review reports, it was determined that Aruba's process for the completion and exchange of templates were sufficient to meet the minimum standard. Aruba's implementation in this regard remains unchanged and therefore continues to meet the minimum standard.

91. During the year in review, no exchanges were required to take place and no data on the timeliness of exchanges is reported.

92. Aruba has the necessary legal basis for spontaneous exchange of information, a process for completing the templates in a timely way and has completed all exchanges. Aruba has met all of the ToR for the exchange of information process and no recommendations are made.

C. Statistics (ToR IV)

93. As no rulings were issued, no statistics can be reported.

D. Matters related to intellectual property regimes (ToR I.A.1.3)

94. Aruba offers an intellectual property regime (IP regime)[3] that is not currently subject to the transparency requirements under the Action 5 Report (OECD, 2015[1]), because:

- ***New entrants benefitting from the grandfathered IP regime***: Aruba will idenfity companies benefitting from the grandfathered IP regime by 2021 and send letters to gather the necessary information by the end of July 2021.

- ***Third category of IP assets***: Aruba will identify companies benefitting from the third category of IP assets by 2021 and send letters to gather the necessary information by the end of July 2021.
- ***Taxpayers making the use of the option to treat the nexus ratio as a rebuttable presumption***: not applicable as the regime does not allow the nexus ratio to be treated as a rebuttable presumption.

Summary of recommendations on implementation of the transparency framework

Aspect of implementation of the transparency framework that should be improved	Recommendation for improvement
	No recommendations are made.

References

OECD (2021), *BEPS Action 5 on Harmful Tax Practices - Terms of Reference and Methodology for the Conduct of the Peer Reviews of the Action 5 Transparency Framework*, OECD Publishing, Paris, http://www.oecd.org/tax/beps/beps-action-5-harmful-tax-practices-peer-review-transparency-framework.pdf. [3]

OECD (2015), *Countering Harmful Tax Practices More Effectively, Taking into Account Transparency and Substance, Action 5 - 2015 Final Report*, OECD/G20 Base Erosion and Profit Shifting Project, OECD Publishing, Paris, https://dx.doi.org/10.1787/9789264241190-en. [1]

OECD (ed.) (2017b), *Harmful Tax Practices - 2017 Progress Report on Preferential Regimes*, OECD Publishing, Paris, http://dx.doi.org/10.1787/9789264283954-en. [2]

OECD/Council of Europe (2011), *The Multilateral Convention on Mutual Administrative Assistance in Tax Matters: Amended by the 2010 Protocol*, OECD Publishing, Paris, https://dx.doi.org/10.1787/9789264115606-en. [4]

Notes

[1] 1) Exempt companies, 2) Investment promotion, 3) Free zone, 4) Transparency regime and 5) Shipping regime.

[2] Participating jurisdictions to the Convention are available here: www.oecd.org/tax/exchange-of-tax-information/convention-on-mutual-administrative-assistance-in-tax-matters.htm. Aruba also has bilateral agreements with Antigua and Barbuda, Argentina, Australia, Bahamas, Bermuda, British Virgin Islands, Canada, Cayman Islands, Czech Republic, Denmark, Faroe Islands, Finland, France, Greenland, Iceland, Mexico, Netherlands, Norway, Saint Kitts and Nevis, Saint Lucia, Saint Vincent and the Grenadines, Spain, Sweden, United Kingdom and United States.

[3] Exempt company.

Australia

Australia has met all aspects of the terms of reference (OECD, 2021[3]) (ToR) for the calendar year 2020 (year in review), and no recommendations are made.

Australia can legally issue four types of rulings within the scope of the transparency framework.

In practice, Australia issued rulings within the scope of the transparency framework as follows:

Type of ruling	Number of rulings
Past rulings	202
Future rulings in the period 1 April 2016 – 31 December 2016	15
Future rulings in the calendar year 2017	13
Future rulings in the calendar year 2018	10
Future rulings in the calendar year 2019	15
Future rulings in the year in review	16

Peer input was received from six jurisdictions in respect of the exchanges of information on rulings received from Australia. The input was generally positive, noting that overall information was complete, in a correct format and received in a timely manner.

A. The information gathering process (ToR I.A)

95. Australia can legally issue the following four types of rulings within the scope of the transparency framework: (i) preferential regimes;[1] (ii) cross-border unilateral APAs and any other cross-border unilateral tax rulings (such as an advance tax ruling) covering transfer pricing or the application of transfer pricing principles; (iii) permanent establishment rulings; and (iv) related party conduit rulings.

96. For Australia, past rulings are any tax rulings within scope that are issued either: (i) on or after 1 January 2014 but before 1 April 2016; or (ii) on or after 1 January 2010 but before 1 January 2014, provided they were still in effect as at 1 January 2014. Future rulings are any tax rulings within scope that are issued on or after 1 April 2016.

97. In the prior years' peer review reports, it was determined that Australia's undertakings to identify past and future rulings and all potential exchange jurisdictions were sufficient to meet the minimum standard. In addition, it was determined that Australia's review and supervision mechanism was sufficient to meet the minimum standard. Australia's implementation remains unchanged, and therefore continues to meet the minimum standard.

98. Australia has met all of the ToR for the information gathering process and no recommendations are made.

B. The exchange of information (ToR II.B)

99. Australia has international agreements permitting spontaneous exchange of information, including being a party to (i) the *Multilateral Convention on Mutual Administrative Assistance in Tax Matters: Amended by the 2010 Protocol* (OECD/Council of Europe, 2011[4]) ("the Convention") and (ii) bilateral agreements in force with 45 jurisdictions.[2]

100. For the year in review, the timeliness of exchanges is as follows:

Future rulings within the scope of the transparency framework	Number of exchanges transmitted within three months of the information becoming available to the competent authority or immediately after legal impediments have been lifted	Delayed exchanges		
		Number of exchanges transmitted later than three months of the information on rulings becoming available to the competent authority	Reasons for the delays	Any other comments
	85	0	N/A	N/A
Total	85	0		

Follow up requests received for exchange of the ruling	Number	Average time to provide response	Number of requests not answered
	1	15 days	0

101. In the prior years' peer review reports, it was determined that Australia's process for the completion and exchange of templates were sufficient to meet the minimum standard. With respect to past rulings, no further action was required. Australia's implementation in this regard remains unchanged and therefore continues to meet the minimum standard.

102. Australia has the necessary legal basis for spontaneous exchange of information, a process for completing the templates in a timely way and has completed all exchanges. Australia has met all of the ToR for the exchange of information process and no recommendations are made.

C. Statistics (ToR IV)

103. The statistics for the year in review are as follows:

Category of ruling	Number of exchanges	Jurisdictions exchanged with
Ruling related to a preferential regime	0	N/A
Cross-border unilateral APAs and any other cross-border unilateral tax rulings (such as an advance tax ruling) covering transfer pricing or the application of transfer pricing principles	77	Argentina, Austria, Belgium, Brazil, Bulgaria, Canada, Chile, China (People's Republic of), Colombia, Costa Rica, Croatia, Czech Republic, Denmark, Estonia, Finland, France, Germany, Greece, Hong Kong (China), Hungary, India, Indonesia, Italy, Japan, Korea, Latvia, Lithuania, Malaysia, Mexico, Morocco, Netherlands, New Zealand, Norway, Peru, Poland, Portugal, Romania, Russia, Saudi Arabia, Serbia, Singapore, Slovakia, Slovenia, South Africa, Spain, Sweden, Switzerland, Thailand, Turkey, United Kingdom, Uruguay, United States
Permanent establishment rulings	8	Finland, New Zealand, Singapore, United Kingdom, United States
Related party conduit rulings	0	N/A
Total	85	

D. Matters related to intellectual property regimes (ToR I.A.1.3)

104. Australia does not offer an intellectual property regime for which transparency requirements under the Action 5 Report (OECD, 2015[1]) were imposed.

Summary of recommendations on implementation of the transparency framework

Aspect of implementation of the transparency framework that should be improved	Recommendation for improvement
	No recommendations are made.

References

OECD (2021), *BEPS Action 5 on Harmful Tax Practices - Terms of Reference and Methodology for the Conduct of the Peer Reviews of the Action 5 Transparency Framework*, OECD Publishing, Paris, http://www.oecd.org/tax/beps/beps-action-5-harmful-tax-practices-peer-review-transparency-framework.pdf. [3]

OECD (2015), *Countering Harmful Tax Practices More Effectively, Taking into Account Transparency and Substance, Action 5 - 2015 Final Report*, OECD/G20 Base Erosion and Profit Shifting Project, OECD Publishing, Paris, https://dx.doi.org/10.1787/9789264241190-en. [1]

OECD (ed.) (2017b), *Harmful Tax Practices - 2017 Progress Report on Preferential Regimes*, OECD Publishing, Paris, http://dx.doi.org/10.1787/9789264283954-en. [2]

OECD/Council of Europe (2011), *The Multilateral Convention on Mutual Administrative Assistance in Tax Matters: Amended by the 2010 Protocol*, OECD Publishing, Paris, https://dx.doi.org/10.1787/9789264115606-en. [4]

Notes

[1] With respect to the following preferential regimes: 1) Offshore banking unit regime and 2) Conduit foreign income regime.

[2] Participating jurisdictions to the Convention are available here: www.oecd.org/tax/exchange-of-tax-information/convention-on-mutual-administrative-assistance-in-tax-matters.htm. Australia also has bilateral agreements with Argentina, Austria, Belgium, Canada, Chile, China (People's Republic of), Czech Republic, Denmark, Fiji, Finland, France, Germany, Hungary, India, Indonesia, Ireland, Israel, Italy, Japan, Kiribati, Korea, Malaysia, Malta, Mexico, Netherlands, New Zealand, Norway, Papua New Guinea, Philippines, Poland, Romania, Russia, Singapore, Slovak Republic, South Africa, Spain, Sri Lanka, Sweden, Switzerland, Chinese Taipei, Thailand, Turkey, United Kingdom, United States and Viet Nam.

Austria

Austria has met all aspects of the terms of reference (OECD, 2021[3]) (ToR) for the calendar year 2020 (year in review), and no recommendations are made.

Austria can legally issue three types of rulings within the scope of the transparency framework.

In practice, Austria issued rulings within the scope of the transparency framework as follows:

Type of ruling	Number of rulings
Past rulings	59
Future rulings in the period 1 April 2016 – 31 December 2016	13
Future rulings in the calendar year 2017	10
Future rulings in the calendar year 2018	9
Future rulings in the calendar year 2019	14
Future rulings in the year in review	23

No peer input was received in respect of the exchanges of information on rulings received from Austria.

A. The information gathering process (ToR I.A)

105. Austria can legally issue three types of rulings within the scope of the transparency framework: (i) cross-border unilateral APAs and any other cross-border unilateral tax rulings (such as an advance tax ruling) covering transfer pricing or the application of transfer pricing principles, (ii) permanent establishment rulings, and (iii) related party conduit rulings.

106. For Austria, past rulings are any tax rulings within scope that are issued either: (i) on or after 1 January 2014 but before 1 April 2016; or (ii) on or after 1 January 2010 but before 1 January 2014, provided they were still in effect as at 1 January 2014. Future rulings are any tax rulings within scope that are issued on or after 1 April 2016.

107. In the prior years' peer review reports, it was determined that Austria's undertakings to identify past and future rulings and all potential exchange jurisdictions were sufficient to meet the minimum standard. In addition, it was determined that Austria's review and supervision mechanism was sufficient to meet the minimum standard. Austria's implementation remains unchanged, and therefore continues to meet the minimum standard.

108. Austria has met all of the ToR for the information gathering process and no recommendations are made.

B. The exchange of information (ToR II.B)

109. Austria has international agreements permitting spontaneous exchange of information, including being a party to (i) the *Multilateral Convention on Mutual Administrative Assistance in Tax Matters: Amended by the 2010 Protocol* (OECD/Council of Europe, 2011[4]) ("the Convention"), (ii) the Directive 2011/16/EU with all other European Union Member States and (iii) bilateral agreements in force with 89 jurisdictions.[1]

110. For the year in review, the timeliness of exchanges is as follows:

Future rulings within the scope of the transparency framework	Number of exchanges transmitted within three months of the information becoming available to the competent authority or immediately after legal impediments have been lifted	Delayed exchanges		
		Number of exchanges transmitted later than three months of the information on rulings becoming available to the competent authority	Reasons for the delays	Any other comments
	19	0	N/A	N/A

Follow up requests received for exchange of the ruling	Number	Average time to provide response	Number of requests not answered
	0	N/A	N/A

111. During the year in review, Austria recorded less exchanges than rulings because rulings issued in late 2020 were exchanged in a timely manner in early 2021.

112. In the prior years' peer review reports, it was determined that Austria's process for the completion and exchange of templates were sufficient to meet the minimum standard. With respect to past rulings, no further action was required. Austria's implementation in this regard remains unchanged and therefore continues to meet the minimum standard.

113. Austria has the necessary legal basis for spontaneous exchange of information, a process for completing the templates in a timely way and has completed all exchanges. Austria has met all of the ToR for the exchange of information process and no recommendations are made.

C. Statistics (ToR IV)

114. The statistics for the year in review are as follows:

Category of ruling	Number of exchanges	Jurisdictions exchanged with
Cross-border unilateral APAs and any other cross-border unilateral tax rulings (such as an advance tax ruling) covering transfer pricing or the application of transfer pricing principles	19	Brazil, Czech Republic, Germany, Luxembourg, Russia, South Africa, Switzerland, United States
Permanent establishment rulings	0	N/A
Related party conduit rulings	0	N/A

D. Matters related to intellectual property regimes (ToR I.A.1.3)

115. Austria does not offer an intellectual property regime for which transparency requirements under the Action 5 Report (OECD, 2015[1]) were imposed.

Summary of recommendations on implementation of the transparency framework

Aspect of implementation of the transparency framework that should be improved	Recommendation for improvement
	No recommendations are made.

References

OECD (2021), *BEPS Action 5 on Harmful Tax Practices - Terms of Reference and Methodology for the Conduct of the Peer Reviews of the Action 5 Transparency Framework*, OECD Publishing, Paris, http://www.oecd.org/tax/beps/beps-action-5-harmful-tax-practices-peer-review-transparency-framework.pdf. [3]

OECD (2015), *Countering Harmful Tax Practices More Effectively, Taking into Account Transparency and Substance, Action 5 - 2015 Final Report*, OECD/G20 Base Erosion and Profit Shifting Project, OECD Publishing, Paris, https://dx.doi.org/10.1787/9789264241190-en. [1]

OECD (ed.) (2017b), *Harmful Tax Practices - 2017 Progress Report on Preferential Regimes*, OECD Publishing, Paris, http://dx.doi.org/10.1787/9789264283954-en. [2]

OECD/Council of Europe (2011), *The Multilateral Convention on Mutual Administrative Assistance in Tax Matters: Amended by the 2010 Protocol*, OECD Publishing, Paris, https://dx.doi.org/10.1787/9789264115606-en. [4]

Notes

[1] Participating jurisdictions to the Convention are available here: www.oecd.org/tax/exchange-of-tax-information/convention-on-mutual-administrative-assistance-in-tax-matters.htm. Austria also has bilateral agreements with Albania, Algeria, Andorra, Armenia, Australia, Azerbaijan, Bahrain, Barbados, Bosnia and Herzegovina, Belarus, Belgium, Belize, Brazil, Bulgaria, Canada, Chile, China (People's Republic of), Croatia, Cyprus, Czech Republic, Denmark, Egypt, Estonia, Finland, North Macedonia, France, Georgia, Germany, Gibraltar, Greece, Guernsey, Hong Kong (China), Hungary, Iceland, India, Indonesia, Ireland, Israel, Italy, Japan, Jersey, Kazakhstan, Korea, Kuwait, Latvia, Liechtenstein, Lithuania, Luxembourg, Malaysia, Malta, Mauritius, Mexico, Moldova, Monaco, Montenegro, Morocco, Netherlands, New Zealand, Norway, Pakistan, Philippines, Poland, Portugal, Qatar, Romania, Russia, Saint Vincent and the Grenadines, San Marino, Saudi Arabia, Serbia, Singapore, Slovak Republic, Slovenia, South Africa, Spain, Sweden, Switzerland, Chinese Taipei, Tajikistan, Thailand, Tunisia, Turkey, Turkmenistan, Ukraine, United Arab Emirates, United Kingdom, United States, Venezuela and Viet Nam.

Barbados

Barbados has met all aspects of the terms of reference (OECD, 2021[3]) (ToR) for the calendar year 2020 (year in review), except for identifying and exchanging information on all new entrants to the grandfathered IP regime (ToR I.A.1.3). Barbados receives one recommendation on this point for the year in review.

In the prior year report, as well as in the 2017 and 2018 peer reviews, Barbados had received the same recommendation. As this issue has not been fully addressed, this recommendation remains in place.

Barbados can legally issue five types of rulings within the scope of the transparency framework.

In practice, Barbados issued rulings within the scope of the transparency framework as follows:

Type of ruling	Number of rulings
Past rulings	2
Future rulings in the period 1 September 2017 – 31 December 2017	0
Future rulings in the calendar year 2018	1
Future rulings in the calendar year 2019	0
Future rulings in the year in review	1

No peer input was received in respect of the exchanges of information on rulings received from Barbados.

A. The information gathering process (ToR I.A)

116. Barbados can legally issue the following five types of rulings within the scope of the transparency framework: (i) preferential regimes;[1] (ii) cross-border unilateral APAs and any other cross-border unilateral tax rulings (such as an advance tax ruling) covering transfer pricing or the application of transfer pricing principles; (iii) rulings providing for unilateral downward adjustments; (iv) permanent establishment rulings; and (v) related party conduit rulings.

117. For Barbados, past rulings are any tax rulings within scope that are issued either: (i) on or after 1 January 2015 but before 1 September 2017; or (ii) on or after 1 January 2012 but before 1 January 2015, provided they were still in effect as at 1 January 2015. Future rulings are any tax rulings within scope that are issued on or after 1 September 2017.

118. In the prior years' peer review reports, it was determined that Barbados's undertakings to identify past and future rulings and all potential exchange jurisdictions were sufficient to meet the minimum standard. In addition, it was determined that Barbados's review and supervision mechanism was sufficient to meet the minimum standard. Barbados's implementation remains unchanged, and therefore continues to meet the minimum standard.

119. Barbados has met all of the ToR for the information gathering process and no recommendations are made.

B. The exchange of information (ToR II.B)

120. Barbados has international agreements permitting spontaneous exchange of information, including being a party to (i) the *Multilateral Convention on Mutual Administrative Assistance in Tax Matters: Amended by the 2010 Protocol* (OECD/Council of Europe, 2011[4]) ("the Convention") and (ii) bilateral agreements in force with 40 jurisdictions.[2]

121. For the year in review, the timeliness of exchanges is as follows:

Future rulings within the scope of the transparency framework	Number of exchanges transmitted within three months of the information becoming available to the competent authority or immediately after legal impediments have been lifted	Delayed exchanges		
		Number of exchanges transmitted later than three months of the information on rulings becoming available to the competent authority	Reasons for the delays	Any other comments
	1	0	N/A	N/A

Follow up requests received for exchange of the ruling	Number	Average time to provide response	Number of requests not answered
	0	N/A	N/A

122. In the prior year's peer review report, it was determined that Barbados's process for the completion and exchange of templates were sufficient to meet the minimum standard. With respect to past rulings, no further action was required. Barbados's implementation in this regard remains unchanged and therefore continues to meet the minimum standard.

123. Barbados has the necessary legal basis for spontaneous exchange of information, a process for completing the templates in a timely way and has completed all exchanges. Barbados has met all of the ToR for the exchange of information process and no recommendations are made.

C. Statistics (ToR IV)

124. The statistics for the year in review are as follows:

Category of ruling	Number of exchanges	Jurisdictions exchanged with
Ruling related to a preferential regime	0	N/A
Cross-border unilateral APAs and any other cross-border unilateral tax rulings (such as an advance tax ruling) covering transfer pricing or the application of transfer pricing principles	0	N/A
Cross-border rulings providing for a unilateral downward adjustment to the taxpayer's taxable profits that is not directly reflected in the taxpayer's financial / commercial accounts	0	N/A
Permanent establishment rulings	*De minimis* rule applies	N/A
Related party conduit rulings	0	N/A
De minimis rule	1	N/A
IP regimes: total exchanges on taxpayers benefitting from the third category of IP assets, new entrants benefitting from grandfathered IP regimes; and taxpayers making use of the option to treat the nexus ratio as a rebuttable presumption	0	N/A
Total	1	

D. Matters related to intellectual property regimes (ToR I.A.1.3)

125. Barbados offered two intellectual property regimes (IP regime)[3] that were abolished as of 1 July 2018 and are subject to transparency requirements under the Action 5 Report (OECD, 2015[1]). It states that the identification of the benefitting taxpayers will occur as follows:

- ***New entrants benefitting from the grandfathered IP regime***: Transparency obligations apply for the two regimes, because grandfathering is provided to entrants that entered the regime after the relevant date from which enhanced transparency obligations apply. During the year in review, Barbados changed its law to require taxpayers to declare IP property and additional information to identify related party transactions. In parallel, the Barbados Revenue Authority (BRA) conducted an assessment based on the financial statements of newly formed International Business Companies and International Societies with Restricted Liability. As a result, the BRA identified two new entrants that potentially benefitted from the grandfathered IP regime, but is still auditing these entities. Therefore, Barbados has made relevant progress in the identification process, but it is not yet completely finalised. Barbados is therefore recommended to identify and exchange information on all new entrants to the grandfathered IP regime as soon as possible (ToR I.A.1.3).
- ***Third category of IP assets***: not applicable as the IP regimes has been abolished.
- ***Taxpayers making use of the option to treat the nexus ratio as a rebuttable presumption***: not applicable as the IP regimes has been abolished.

Summary of recommendations on implementation of the transparency framework

Aspect of implementation of the transparency framework that should be improved	Recommendation for improvement

Barbados did not identify or exchange information on new entrants to the grandfathered IP regime.	Barbados is recommended to identify and exchange information on all new entrants to the grandfathered IP regime as soon as possible. This recommendation remains unchanged since the 2017, 2018 and 2019 peer review reports.

References

OECD (2021), *BEPS Action 5 on Harmful Tax Practices - Terms of Reference and Methodology for the Conduct of the Peer Reviews of the Action 5 Transparency Framework*, OECD Publishing, Paris, http://www.oecd.org/tax/beps/beps-action-5-harmful-tax-practices-peer-review-transparency-framework.pdf. [3]

OECD (2015), *Countering Harmful Tax Practices More Effectively, Taking into Account Transparency and Substance, Action 5 - 2015 Final Report*, OECD/G20 Base Erosion and Profit Shifting Project, OECD Publishing, Paris, https://dx.doi.org/10.1787/9789264241190-en. [1]

OECD (ed.) (2017b), *Harmful Tax Practices - 2017 Progress Report on Preferential Regimes*, OECD Publishing, Paris, http://dx.doi.org/10.1787/9789264283954-en. [2]

OECD/Council of Europe (2011), *The Multilateral Convention on Mutual Administrative Assistance in Tax Matters: Amended by the 2010 Protocol*, OECD Publishing, Paris, https://dx.doi.org/10.1787/9789264115606-en. [4]

Notes

1 Credit for foreign currency earnings.

2 Participating jurisdictions to the Convention are available here: www.oecd.org/tax/exchange-of-tax-information/convention-on-mutual-administrative-assistance-in-tax-matters.htm. Barbados also has bilateral agreements with Antigua and Barbuda, Austria, Bahrain, Belize, Botswana, Canada, China (People's Republic of), Cyprus, Cuba, Czech Republic, Dominica, Finland, Grenada, Guyana, Iceland, Italy, Jamaica, Luxembourg, Malta, Mauritius, Mexico, Netherlands, Norway, Panama, Portugal, Saint Kitts and Nevis, Saint Lucia, Saint Vincent and the Grenadines, San Marino, Seychelles, Singapore, Spain, Sweden, Switzerland, Trinidad & Tobago, Qatar, United Arab Emirates, United Kingdom, United States and Venezuela.

3 1) International business companies and 2) International societies with restricted liability.

Belgium

Belgium has met all aspects of the terms of reference (OECD, 2021[3]) (ToR) for the calendar year 2020 (year in review), and no recommendations are made.

Belgium can legally issue four types of rulings within the scope of the transparency framework.

In practice, Belgium issued rulings within the scope of the transparency framework as follows:

Type of ruling	Number of rulings
Past rulings	586
Future rulings in the period 1 April 2016 – 31 December 2016	57
Future rulings in the calendar year 2017	107
Future rulings in the calendar year 2018	103
Future rulings in the calendar year 2019	73
Future rulings in the year in review	74

Peer input was received from two jurisdictions in respect of the exchanges of information on rulings received from Belgium. The input was positive, noting that information was complete, in a correct format and all received in a timely manner.

A. The information gathering process (ToR I.A)

126. Belgium can legally issue four types of rulings within the scope of the transparency framework: (i) preferential regimes;[1] (ii) cross-border unilateral APAs and any other cross-border unilateral tax rulings (such as an advance tax ruling) covering transfer pricing or the application of transfer pricing principles; (iii) rulings providing for unilateral downward adjustments; and (iv) permanent establishment rulings.

127. For Belgium, past rulings are any tax rulings within scope that are issued either: (i) on or after 1 January 2014 but before 1 April 2016; or (ii) on or after 1 January 2010 but before 1 January 2014, provided they were still in effect as at 1 January 2014. Future rulings are any tax rulings within scope that are issued on or after 1 April 2016.

128. In the prior years' peer review reports, it was determined that Belgium's undertakings to identify past and future rulings and all potential exchange jurisdictions were sufficient to meet the minimum standard. In addition, it was determined that Belgium's review and supervision mechanism was sufficient to meet the minimum standard. Belgium's implementation remains unchanged, and therefore continues to meet the minimum standard.

129. Belgium has met all of the ToR for the information gathering process and no recommendations are made.

B. The exchange of information (ToR II.B)

130. Belgium has international agreements permitting spontaneous exchange of information, including being a party to (i) the *Multilateral Convention on Mutual Administrative Assistance in Tax Matters: Amended by the 2010 Protocol* (OECD/Council of Europe, 2011[4]) ("the Convention"), (ii) the Directive 2011/16/EU with all other European Union Member States and (iii) bilateral agreements in force 77 jurisdictions.[2]

131. For the year in review, the timeliness of exchanges is as follows:

Future rulings within the scope of the transparency framework	Number of exchanges transmitted within three months of the information becoming available to the competent authority or immediately after legal impediments have been lifted	Delayed exchanges		
		Number of exchanges transmitted later than three months of the information on rulings becoming available to the competent authority	Reasons for the delays	Any other comments
	268	0	N/A	N/A

Follow up requests received for exchange of the ruling	Number	Average time to provide response	Number of requests not answered
	0	N/A	N/A

132. In the prior years' peer review reports, it was determined that Belgium's process for the completion and exchange of templates were sufficient to meet the minimum standard. With respect to past rulings, no further action was required. Belgium's implementation in this regard remains unchanged and therefore continues to meet the minimum standard.

133. Belgium has the necessary legal basis for spontaneous exchange of information, a process for completing the templates in a timely way and has completed all exchanges. Belgium has met all of the ToR for the exchange of information process and no recommendations are made.

C. Statistics (ToR IV)

134. The statistics for the year in review are as follows:

Category of ruling	Number of exchanges	Jurisdictions exchanged with
Ruling related to a preferential regime	*De minimis* rule applies	N/A
Cross-border unilateral APAs and any other cross-border unilateral tax rulings (such as an advance tax ruling) covering transfer pricing or the application of transfer pricing principles	228	Argentina, Australia, Austria, Barbados, Brazil, Bulgaria, Canada, Chile, China (People's Republic of), Colombia, Curaçao, Cyprus, Czech Republic, Denmark, Finland, France, Germany, Greece, Guernsey, Hong Kong (China), Hungary, India, Indonesia, Ireland, Israel, Italy, Japan, Jersey, Liechtenstein, Lithuania, Luxembourg, Malaysia, Malta, Mauritius, Mexico, Monaco, Netherlands, New Zealand, Norway, Pakistan, Panama, Poland, Portugal, Korea, Romania, Russia, Saudi Arabia, Singapore, Slovakia, South Africa, Spain, Sweden, Switzerland, Turkey, United Kingdom, United States
Cross-border rulings providing for a unilateral downward adjustment to the taxpayer's taxable profits that is not directly reflected in the taxpayer's financial / commercial accounts	0	N/A
Permanent establishment rulings	55	Austria, Cyprus, Czech Republic, Denmark, Finland, France, Germany, Hungary, Ireland, Italy, Lithuania, Luxembourg, Malta, Monaco, Netherlands, Poland, Portugal, Russia, Slovakia, Spain, Sweden, Switzerland, United Kingdom
De minimis rule	3	N/A
IP regimes: total exchanges on taxpayers benefitting from the third category of IP assets, new entrants benefitting from grandfathered IP regimes; and taxpayers making use of the option to treat the nexus ratio as a rebuttable presumption	0	N/A
Total	268[3]	

D. Matters related to intellectual property regimes (ToR I.A.1.3)

135. Belgium offers an intellectual property regime (IP regime)[4] that is subject to the transparency requirements under the Action 5 Report (OECD, 2015[1]). It states that the identification of the benefitting taxpayers will occur as follows:

- ***New entrants benefitting from the grandfathered IP regime***: In the prior year peer review report, it was determined that Belgium's process for identifying and exchanging information on new entrants to the grandfathered IP regime were sufficient to meet the minimum standard. Belgium's implementation in this regard remains unchanged and therefore continues to meet the minimum standard.
- ***Third category of IP assets***: not applicable as the regime does not allow the third category of IP assets to qualify for the benefits.
- ***Taxpayers making use of the option to treat the nexus ratio as a rebuttable presumption***: Belgium confirms that no taxpayer elected to treat the nexus approach as a rebuttable presumption.

Summary of recommendations on implementation of the transparency framework

Aspect of implementation of the transparency framework that should be improved	Recommendation for improvement
	No recommendations are made.

References

OECD (2021), *BEPS Action 5 on Harmful Tax Practices - Terms of Reference and Methodology for the Conduct of the Peer Reviews of the Action 5 Transparency Framework*, OECD Publishing, Paris, http://www.oecd.org/tax/beps/beps-action-5-harmful-tax-practices-peer-review-transparency-framework.pdf. [3]

OECD (2015), *Countering Harmful Tax Practices More Effectively, Taking into Account Transparency and Substance, Action 5 - 2015 Final Report*, OECD/G20 Base Erosion and Profit Shifting Project, OECD Publishing, Paris, https://dx.doi.org/10.1787/9789264241190-en. [1]

OECD (ed.) (2017b), *Harmful Tax Practices - 2017 Progress Report on Preferential Regimes*, OECD Publishing, Paris, http://dx.doi.org/10.1787/9789264283954-en. [2]

OECD/Council of Europe (2011), *The Multilateral Convention on Mutual Administrative Assistance in Tax Matters: Amended by the 2010 Protocol*, OECD Publishing, Paris, https://dx.doi.org/10.1787/9789264115606-en. [4]

Notes

[1] With respect to the following preferential regimes: 1) Patent income deduction, 2) tax shelter regime for maritime exploitation and 3) excess profits.

[2] Participating jurisdictions to the Convention are available here: www.oecd.org/tax/exchange-of-tax-information/convention-on-mutual-administrative-assistance-in-tax-matters.htm. Belgium also has bilateral agreements with Albania, Algeria, Andorra, Antigua and Barbuda, Argentina, Armenia, Australia, Azerbaijan, Bahrain, Bangladesh, Belarus, Brazil, Belize, Bosnia and Herzegovina, Canada, Chile, China (People's Republic of), Côte d'Ivoire, Democratic Republic of the Congo, Ecuador, Egypt, Gabon, Georgia, Ghana, Hong Kong (China), Iceland, India, Indonesia, Israel, Japan, Kazakhstan, Korea, Kosovo, Kyrgyzstan, Kuwait, Malaysia, Mauritius, Mexico, Moldova, Mongolia, Montenegro, Morocco, New Zealand, Nigeria, North Macedonia, Norway, Pakistan, Philippines, Russia, Rwanda, San Marino, Senegal, Serbia, Seychelles, Singapore, South Africa, Sri Lanka, Switzerland, Tajikistan, Chinese Taipei, Thailand, Tunisia, Turkey, Turkmenistan, Ukraine, United Arab Emirates, United States, Uruguay, Uzbekistan, Venezuela and Viet Nam.

[3] There were 268 unique exchanges. The total of number of exchanges given in this table, 286, is higher due to the fact that some exchanges relate to rulings that fall under more than one category.

[4] Innovation income deduction.

Benin

Benin is taking steps to implement the legal basis for the transparency framework and to commence administrative preparations (in line with the terms of reference (OECD, 2021[3]) (ToR)) to ensure that it finalises its information gathering process (ToR I.A) and that information on rulings will be identified and exchanged in a timely manner (ToR II.B). Benin receives two recommendations on this point for the calendar year 2020 (year in review).

In the prior year report, as well as in the 2018 peer review, Benin had received the same recommendations. As they have not been addressed, the recommendations remain in place.

Benin can legally issue one type of rulings within the scope of the transparency framework.

In practice, Benin issued no rulings within the scope of the transparency framework.

As no exchanges were required to take place, no peer input was received in respect of the exchanges of information on rulings received from Benin.

A. The information gathering process (ToR I.A)

136. Benin can legally issue the following type of rulings within the scope of the transparency framework: permanent establishment rulings.

Past rulings (ToR I.A.1.1, I.A.1.2, I.A.2.1, I.A.2.2)

137. For Benin, past rulings are any tax rulings within scope that are issued either (i) on or after 1 January 2015 but before 1 April 2017; and (ii) on or after 1 January 2012 but before 1 January 2015, provided they were still in effect as at 1 January 2015.

138. In the prior year's peer review report, it was determined that Benin reviewed its files on rulings and confirmed that no past rulings have been issued. As such, Benin indicated no past rulings within the scope of the transparency framework have been issued and there was no need to identify potential exchange jurisdictions.

Future rulings (ToR I.A.1.1, I.A.1.2, I.A.2.1)

139. For Benin, future rulings are any tax rulings within scope that are issued on or after 1 April 2017.

140. In the prior years' peer review reports, Benin indicated that there was no process in place to keep records of rulings for the purposes of the transparency framework. It was also noted that Benin intended to implement guidelines to ensure the necessary information to meet the requirements of the transparency framework is required in all cases, but there have been no developments during the year in review. Benin is therefore recommended to finalise its information gathering process as soon as possible.

Review and supervision (ToR I.A.3)

141. In the prior years' peer review reports, it was determined that Benin did not yet have a review and supervision mechanism under the transparency framework and was still in the process of considering the implementation of such a mechanism. As there have been no developments on this issue, the recommendation remains in place.

Conclusion on section A

142. Benin is recommended to finalise its information gathering process, with a review and supervision mechanism as soon as possible (ToR I.A).

B. The exchange of information (ToR II.B)

Legal basis for spontaneous exchange of information (ToR II.B.1, II.B.2)

143. Benin is still in the process of putting in place the necessary domestic legal basis to exchange information spontaneously.

144. Benin does not have currently in effect an agreement that would allow for spontaneous exchange of information under the transparency framework. Benin signed the *Multilateral Convention on Mutual Administrative Assistance in Tax Matters: Amended by the 2010 Protocol* (OECD/Council of Europe, 2011[4]) ("the Convention") in November 2019, but Benin has not yet ratified the Convention. Benin is therefore encouraged to continue its efforts to ratify the Convention and expand its international exchange of information instruments to be able to exchange information on rulings. It is noted, however, that

jurisdictions are assessed on their compliance with the transparency framework in respect of the exchange of information network in effect for the year of the particular annual review.

Completion and exchange of templates (ToR II.B.3, II.B.4, II.B.5, II.B.6, II.B.7)

145. Benin is still developing a process to complete the templates on relevant rulings, to make them available to the Competent Authority for exchange of information, and to exchange them with relevant jurisdictions.

146. As no exchanges were required to take place no data on the timeliness of exchanges can be reported.

Conclusion on section B

147. Benin is recommended to put in place a domestic legal framework allowing spontaneous exchange of information on rulings and to continue its efforts to complete the templates for all relevant rulings and to ensure that the exchanges of information on rulings occur as soon as possible (ToR II.B).

C. Statistics (ToR IV)

148. As no rulings were issued, no statistics can be reported.

D. Matters related to intellectual property regimes (ToR I.A.1.3)

149. Benin does not offer an intellectual property regime for which transparency requirements under the Action 5 Report (OECD, 2015[1]) were imposed.

Summary of recommendations on implementation of the transparency framework

Aspect of implementation of the transparency framework that should be improved	Recommendation for improvement
Benin has not yet finalised the steps to have in place its necessary information and gathering process.	Benin is recommended to finalise its information gathering process, with a review and supervision mechanism, as soon as possible. This recommendation remains unchanged since the 2018 and 2019 peer review reports.
Benin has not yet finalised the steps to have effective compulsory spontaneous exchange of information on the tax rulings within the scope of the transparency framework.	Benin is recommended to continue to put in place a domestic legal framework allowing spontaneous exchange of information on rulings and to continue its efforts to complete the templates for all relevant rulings and to ensure that the exchanges of information on rulings occur as soon as possible. This recommendation remains unchanged since the 2018 and 2019 peer review reports.

References

OECD (2021), *BEPS Action 5 on Harmful Tax Practices - Terms of Reference and Methodology for the Conduct of the Peer Reviews of the Action 5 Transparency Framework*, OECD Publishing, Paris, http://www.oecd.org/tax/beps/beps-action-5-harmful-tax-practices-peer-review-transparency-framework.pdf. [3]

OECD (2015), *Countering Harmful Tax Practices More Effectively, Taking into Account Transparency and Substance, Action 5 - 2015 Final Report*, OECD/G20 Base Erosion and Profit Shifting Project, OECD Publishing, Paris, https://dx.doi.org/10.1787/9789264241190-en. [1]

OECD (ed.) (2017b), *Harmful Tax Practices - 2017 Progress Report on Preferential Regimes*, OECD Publishing, Paris, http://dx.doi.org/10.1787/9789264283954-en. [2]

OECD/Council of Europe (2011), *The Multilateral Convention on Mutual Administrative Assistance in Tax Matters: Amended by the 2010 Protocol*, OECD Publishing, Paris, https://dx.doi.org/10.1787/9789264115606-en. [4]

Bosnia and Herzegovina

Bosnia and Herzegovina is taking steps to implement the legal basis for the transparency framework and to commence administrative preparations to ensure that information on rulings will be exchanged in a timely manner, in line with the terms of reference (OECD, 2021[3]) (ToR). Bosnia and Herzegovina receives two recommendations covering the information gathering process (ToR I.A) and exchange of information (ToR II.B) for the calendar year 2020 (year in review).

This is Bosnia and Herzegovina's first review of implementation of the transparency framework.

Bosnia and Herzegovina can legally issue five types of rulings within the scope of the transparency framework.

In practice, Bosnia and Herzegovina issued no rulings within the scope of the transparency framework.

As no exchanges were required to take place, no peer input was received in respect of the exchanges of information on rulings received from Bosnia and Herzegovina.

A. The information gathering process (ToR I.A)

150. Bosnia and Herzegovina can legally issue the following five types of rulings within the scope of the transparency framework: (i) cross-border unilateral APAs and any other cross-border unilateral tax rulings (such as an advance tax ruling) covering transfer pricing or the application of transfer pricing principles; (ii) rulings providing for unilateral downward adjustments; (iii) permanent establishment rulings; and (iv) related party conduit rulings. It is noted that the Tax Administration in the Bosnia and Herzegovina entity of Republic of Srpska is the only authority issuing rulings in scope of the FHTP work.

Past rulings (ToR I.A.1.1, I.A.1.2, I.A.2.1, I.A.2.2)

151. For Bosnia and Herzegovina, past rulings are any tax rulings issued prior to 1 March 2020. However, there is no obligation for Bosnia and Herzegovina to conduct spontaneous exchange information on past rulings.

Future rulings (ToR I.A.1.1, I.A.1.2, I.A.2.1)

152. For Bosnia and Herzegovina, future rulings are any tax rulings within scope that are issued on or after 1 March 2020.

153. No rulings were issued by Bosnia and Herzegovina during the future rulings period in the year in review. However, Bosnia and Herzegovina indicates that there are not yet processes in place to ensure the implementation of the obligations relating to the transparency framework.

Review and supervision (ToR I.A.3)

154. Bosnia and Herzegovina did not yet have a review and supervision mechanism under the transparency framework for the year in review.

Conclusion on section A

155. Bosnia and Herzegovina is recommended to ensure that it has put in place an effective information gathering process to identify all relevant future rulings and all potential exchange jurisdictions and to implement a review and supervision mechanism, as soon as possible (ToR I.A).

B. The exchange of information (ToR II.B)

Legal basis for spontaneous exchange of information (ToR II.B.1, II.B.2)

156. Bosnia and Herzegovina does not have the necessary domestic legal basis to exchange information spontaneously. Bosnia and Herzegovina can only exchange information on request.

157. Bosnia and Herzegovina has international agreements permitting spontaneous exchange of information, including bilateral agreements in force with 38 jurisdictions.[1] Bosnia and Herzegovina signed the *Multilateral Convention on Mutual Administrative Assistance in Tax Matters: Amended by the 2010 Protocol* (OECD/Council of Europe, 2011[4]) ("the Convention") on 26 November 2019 and ratified on 21 September 2020. The Convention entered into force on 1 January 2021. No exchanges could occur under the Convention for the year in review.[2]

Completion and exchange of templates (ToR II.B.3, II.B.4, II.B.5, II.B.6, II.B.7)

158. Bosnia and Herzegovina does not yet have a process to complete the templates on all relevant rulings, to make them available to the Competent Authority for exchange of information, and to exchange them with relevant jurisdictions.

159. During the year in review, no exchanges were required to take place and no data on the timeliness of exchanges is reported.

Conclusion on section B

160. Bosnia and Herzegovina is recommended to put in place the necessary domestic legal basis allowing spontaneous exchange of information on rulings, to develop a process to complete the templates for all relevant rulings and to ensure that the exchanges of information on rulings occur in accordance with the form and timelines under the transparency framework going forward (ToR II.B).

C. Statistics (ToR IV)

161. As there was no information on rulings exchanged by Bosnia and Herzegovina for the year in review, no statistics can be reported.

D. Matters related to intellectual property regimes (ToR I.A.1.3)

162. Bosnia and Herzegovina does not offer an intellectual property regime for which transparency requirements under the Action 5 Report (OECD, 2015[1]) were imposed.

Summary of recommendations on implementation of the transparency framework

Aspect of implementation of the transparency framework that should be improved	Recommendation for improvement
Bosnia and Herzegovina does not yet have the necessary information gathering process in place.	Bosnia and Herzegovina is recommended to ensure that it has put in place an effective information gathering process to identify all relevant past and future rulings and all potential exchange jurisdictions and to implement a review and supervision mechanism, as soon as possible.
Bosnia and Herzegovina does not yet have a domestic legal framework allowing spontaneous exchange of information on rulings and a process to complete the templates on relevant rulings, to make them available to the Competent Authority for exchange of information, and to exchange them with relevant jurisdictions.	Bosnia and Herzegovina is recommended to put in place the necessary domestic legal basis allowing spontaneous exchange of information on rulings, to develop a process to complete the templates for all relevant rulings and to ensure that the exchanges of information on rulings occur in accordance with the form and timelines under the transparency framework going forward.

Jurisdiction's response and recent developments

163. Bosnia and Herzegovina notes that 2020 was the first year of implementation of the transparency framework for their tax administration. Bosnia and Herzegovina is currently in the process of taking appropriate steps to implement the transparency and action the recommendations of this report.

References

OECD (2021), *BEPS Action 5 on Harmful Tax Practices - Terms of Reference and Methodology for the Conduct of the Peer Reviews of the Action 5 Transparency Framework*, OECD Publishing, Paris, http://www.oecd.org/tax/beps/beps-action-5-harmful-tax-practices-peer-review-transparency-framework.pdf. [3]

OECD (2015), *Countering Harmful Tax Practices More Effectively, Taking into Account Transparency and Substance, Action 5 - 2015 Final Report*, OECD/G20 Base Erosion and Profit Shifting Project, OECD Publishing, Paris, https://dx.doi.org/10.1787/9789264241190-en. [1]

OECD (ed.) (2017b), *Harmful Tax Practices - 2017 Progress Report on Preferential Regimes*, OECD Publishing, Paris, http://dx.doi.org/10.1787/9789264283954-en. [2]

OECD/Council of Europe (2011), *The Multilateral Convention on Mutual Administrative Assistance in Tax Matters: Amended by the 2010 Protocol*, OECD Publishing, Paris, https://dx.doi.org/10.1787/9789264115606-en. [4]

Notes

[1] Bosnia and Herzegovina has bilateral agreements with Albania, Algeria, Austria, Azerbaijan, Belgium, Czech Republic, Finland, France, Germany, Greece, Croatia, Iran, Ireland, Italy, Jordan, Kuwait, Qatar, China (People's Republic of), Cyprus, Hungary, Malaysia, Montenegro, Moldova, Netherlands, North Macedonia, Norway, Pakistan, Poland, Romania, Slovak Republic, Slovenia, Serbia, Spain, Sweden, Sri Lanka, Turkey, United Arab Emirates, United Kingdom.

[2] Participating jurisdictions to the Convention are available here: www.oecd.org/tax/exchange-of-tax-information/convention-on-mutual-administrative-assistance-in-tax-matters.htm.

Botswana

Botswana has met all aspects of the terms of reference (OECD, 2021[3]) (ToR) for the calendar year 2020 (year in review), except for having in place a review and supervision mechanism (ToR I.A.3) and having in place a domestic legal framework allowing spontaneous exchange of information on rulings by ensuring the timely exchange of information on rulings in the form required by the transparency framework (ToR II.B). Botswana receives two recommendations on these points for the year in review.

In the prior year report, as well as in the 2018 peer review, Botswana had received two recommendations. One of these recommendations has been partially addressed, but remains in place for the other part. The other recommendation has not been addressed and remains in place.

Botswana can legally issue three types of rulings within the scope of the transparency framework.

In practice, Botswana issued rulings within the scope of the transparency framework as follows:

Type of ruling	Number of rulings
Past rulings	10
Future rulings in the period 1 April 2018 – 31 December 2018	1
Future rulings in the calendar year 2019	3
Future rulings in the year in review	2

As no exchanges took place, no peer input was received in respect of the exchanges of information on rulings received from Botswana.

A. The information gathering process (ToR I.A)

164. Botswana can legally issue the following three types of rulings within the scope of the transparency framework: (i) preferential regimes;[1] (ii) cross-border unilateral APAs and any other cross-border unilateral tax rulings (such as an advance tax ruling) covering transfer pricing or the application of transfer pricing principles; and (iii) permanent establishment rulings.

Past rulings (ToR I.A.1.1, I.A.1.2, I.A.2.1, I.A.2.2)

165. For Botswana, past rulings are any tax rulings within scope that are issued either (i) on or after 1 January 2016 but before 1 April 2018; and (ii) on or after 1 January 2014 but before 1 January 2016, provided still in effect as at 1 January 2016.

166. In the prior year peer review report, it was noted that Botswana did not have a process in place for identifying the potential exchange jurisdictions for APAs and permanent establishment rulings and did not yet apply the best efforts approach. Therefore, Botswana was recommended to apply the best efforts approach to identify all potential exchange jurisdictions for APA and permanent establishment rulings, as soon as possible.

167. During the year in review, Botswana used documentation that they taxpayer submitted when applying for a ruling, annual reports and tax returns and other available information to identify the potential exchange jurisdictions. Botswana confirms that this process has now been completed and this part of the recommendation can be removed.

Future rulings (ToR I.A.1.1, I.A.1.2, I.A.2.1)

168. For Botswana, future rulings are any tax rulings within scope that are issued on or after 1 April 2018.

169. In the prior year peer review report, it was determined that Botswana's undertakings to identify future rulings and all potential exchange jurisdictions was sufficient to meet the minimum standard. Botswana's implementation in this regard remains unchanged, and therefore continues to meet the minimum standard.

Review and supervision (ToR I.A.3)

170. In the prior year peer review report, it was noted that Botswana did not yet have a review and supervision mechanism for past or future rulings under the transparency framework for the year in review. Therefore, Botswana was recommended to put in place a review and supervision mechanism, as soon as possible.

171. During the year in review, no additional work was undertaken and therefore, the prior year recommendation remains.

Conclusion on section A

172. Botswana is recommended to put in place a review and supervision mechanism, as soon as possible (ToR I.A.3).

B. The exchange of information (ToR II.B)

Legal basis for spontaneous exchange of information (ToR II.B.1, II.B.2)

173. Botswana does not have the necessary domestic legal basis to exchange information spontaneously. Botswana can only exchange information on request. Botswana is undergoing a comprehensive reform of its tax laws. Botswana notes that it has commenced a review of the exchange of information legislative framework with the support of the African Tax Administration Forum (ATAF) with a view to correcting identified shortcomings in this area. Due to the Covid-19 pandemic, this review has been delayed.

174. Botswana has international agreements permitting spontaneous exchange of information, including bilateral agreements in force with 27 jurisdictions.[2] Botswana signed the *Multilateral Convention on Mutual Administrative Assistance in Tax Matters: Amended by the 2010 Protocol* (OECD/Council of Europe, 2011[4]) ("the Convention") on 29 September 2020 and ratified on 15 June 2021. The Convention entered into force on 1 October 2021. No exchanges could occur under the Convention for the year in review.[3]

Completion and exchange of templates (ToR II.B.3, II.B.4, II.B.5, II.B.6, II.B.7)

175. Botswana is currently developing a process to complete the templates on relevant rulings, to make them available to the Competent Authority for exchange of information, and to exchange them with relevant jurisdictions.

176. As no exchanges took place for the year in review, no data on the timeliness of exchanges can be reported.

Conclusion on section B

177. Botswana is recommended to continue to put in place a domestic legal framework allowing spontaneous exchange of information on rulings and to ensure the timely exchange of information on rulings in the form required by the transparency framework (ToR II.B).

C. Statistics (ToR IV)

178. As there was no information on rulings exchanged by Botswana for the year in review, no statistics can be reported.

D. Matters related to intellectual property regimes (ToR I.A.1.3)

179. Botswana offered an intellectual property regime (IP regime)[4] that was abolished as of 1 January 2019 and that is not subject to the transparency requirements under the Action 5 Report (OECD, 2015[1]), as described in the prior year peer review report.

Summary of recommendations on implementation of the transparency framework

Aspect of implementation of the transparency framework that should be improved	Recommendation for improvement
Botswana does not have a review and supervision mechanism in place.	Botswana is recommended to put in place a review and supervision mechanism, as soon as possible. This

	recommendation remains unchanged since the 2018 and 2019 peer review reports.
Botswana does not yet have the necessary legal framework in place for exchanging information on rulings and a process in place to ensure the timely exchange of information on rulings in the form required by the transparency framework.	Botswana is recommended to continue to put in place a domestic legal framework allowing spontaneous exchange of information on rulings and to ensure the timely exchange of information on rulings in the form required by the transparency framework. This recommendation remains unchanged since the 2018 and 2019 peer review reports.

References

OECD (2021), *BEPS Action 5 on Harmful Tax Practices - Terms of Reference and Methodology for the Conduct of the Peer Reviews of the Action 5 Transparency Framework*, OECD Publishing, Paris, http://www.oecd.org/tax/beps/beps-action-5-harmful-tax-practices-peer-review-transparency-framework.pdf. [3]

OECD (2015), *Countering Harmful Tax Practices More Effectively, Taking into Account Transparency and Substance, Action 5 - 2015 Final Report*, OECD/G20 Base Erosion and Profit Shifting Project, OECD Publishing, Paris, https://dx.doi.org/10.1787/9789264241190-en. [1]

OECD (ed.) (2017b), *Harmful Tax Practices - 2017 Progress Report on Preferential Regimes*, OECD Publishing, Paris, http://dx.doi.org/10.1787/9789264283954-en. [2]

OECD/Council of Europe (2011), *The Multilateral Convention on Mutual Administrative Assistance in Tax Matters: Amended by the 2010 Protocol*, OECD Publishing, Paris, https://dx.doi.org/10.1787/9789264115606-en. [4]

Notes

[1] With respect to the following preferential regime: International financial services company.

[2] Botswana has bilateral agreements with Barbados, China (People's Republic of), Czech Republic, Denmark, Eswatini, Faroe Islands, Finland, France, Greenland, Iceland, India, Ireland, Isle of Man, Lesotho, Luxembourg, Malta, Mauritius, Mozambique, Namibia, Norway, Russia, Seychelles, South Africa, Sweden, United Kingdom, Zambia and Zimbabwe.

[3] Participating jurisdictions to the Convention are available here: www.oecd.org/tax/exchange-of-tax-information/convention-on-mutual-administrative-assistance-in-tax-matters.htm.

[4] International financial services company.

Brazil

Brazil has met all aspects of the terms of reference (OECD, 2021[3]) (ToR) for the calendar year 2020 (year in review), and no recommendations are made.

Brazil can legally issue two types of rulings within the scope of the transparency framework.

In practice, Brazil issued rulings within the scope of the transparency framework as follows:

Type of ruling	Number of rulings
Past rulings	10
Future rulings in the period 1 April 2016 – 31 December 2016	1
Future rulings in the calendar year 2017	2
Future rulings in the calendar year 2018	5
Future rulings in the calendar year 2019	0
Future rulings in the year of review	0

No peer input was received in respect of the exchanges of information on rulings received from Brazil.

A. The information gathering process (ToR I.A)

180. Brazil can legally issue the following two types of rulings within the scope of the transparency framework: (i) preferential regimes[1] and (ii) cross-border unilateral APAs and any other cross-border unilateral tax rulings (such as an advance tax ruling) covering transfer pricing or the application of transfer pricing principles.

181. For Brazil, past rulings are any tax rulings within scope that are issued either: (i) on or after 1 January 2014 but before 1 April 2016; or (ii) on or after 1 January 2010 but before 1 January 2014, provided they were still in effect as at 1 January 2014. Future rulings are any tax rulings within scope that are issued on or after 1 April 2016.

182. In the prior years' peer review reports, it was determined that Brazil's undertakings to identify past and future rulings and all potential exchange jurisdictions were sufficient to meet the minimum standard. In addition, it was determined that Brazil's review and supervision mechanism was sufficient to meet the minimum standard.

183. During the year in review, Brazil undertook a full review of all tax rulings issued both by the central taxation unit and the local taxation units and experienced difficulties in the identification of future rulings issued by local taxation units. As a result of the review, Brazil identified two additional rulings issued by the local taxation units in 2018 that were not otherwise identified in the prior year. Brazil also corrected some errors made in the communication of the dates of issuance of future rulings in the previous peer review reports with regard to the years 2016, 2017 and 2018, as shown in the summary table.

184. For those future rulings, Brazil was able to identify all the relevant exchange jurisdictions. For the sake of completeness, it is noted that for each ruling the immediate parent entity, ultimate parent entity, and the countries of residence of all related parties with whom the taxpayer enters into transactions that are covered by the rulings are all resident in the same jurisdiction.

185. As Brazil has quickly taken steps to identify and remedy the issue and this is not expected to be a recurring issue, no recommendations are made, however if this issue persists it will be noted and addressed in the next annual peer review. Brazil has met all of the ToR for the information gathering process and no recommendations are made.

B. The exchange of information (ToR II.B)

186. Brazil has international agreements permitting spontaneous exchange of information, including being a party to the (i) *Multilateral Convention on Mutual Administrative Assistance in Tax Matters: Amended by the 2010 Protocol* (OECD/Council of Europe, 2011[4]) ("the Convention"), (ii) bilateral agreements in force with 33 jurisdictions, and (iii) tax information exchange agreements in force with three jurisdictions.[2]

187. For the year in review, the timeliness of exchanges is as follows:

Future rulings in the scope of the transparency framework	Number of exchanges transmitted within three months of the information becoming available to the competent authority or immediately after legal impediments have been lifted	Delayed exchanges		
		Number of exchanges transmitted later than three months of the information on rulings becoming available to the competent authority	Reasons for the delays	Any other comments
	3		See below	These exchanges pertain to rulings that were issued in 2017 and

				2018 by the local taxation units and transmitted to the Competent Authority in 2020 and for which the relevant exchange of information agreement came into force in 2018.

Follow up requests received for exchange of the ruling	Number	Average time to provide response	Number of requests not answered
	0	N/A	N/A

188. In the prior years' peer review reports, it was determined that Brazil's process for the completion and exchange of templates were sufficient to meet the minimum standard. With respect to past rulings, no further action was required. Brazil's implementation in this regard remains unchanged and therefore continues to meet the minimum standard.

189. During the year in review, Brazil identified two additional rulings issued by the local taxation units in 2018 that were not otherwise identified in the prior year and therefore not previously transmitted to the Competent Authority for the exchanges with the relevant jurisdiction(s). The two rulings issued by the local taxation units in 2018 also referred to a ruling issued by the central taxation unit in 2017 that contained the comprehensive analysis of the tax matter. Brazil noted that the relevant exchange jurisdiction with regard to the three rulings was the same jurisdiction with which the relevant tax treaty providing for the spontaneous exchange of information only came into force in 2018. Given the relevance of the information included in the ruling issued in 2017, Brazil performed the exchange even though in 2017 there was no legal basis for the exchange of information for that ruling. During the year in review, Brazil also amended their exchange of rulings mechanism to ensure that all rulings issued by local taxation units were transmitted in a timely manner to the Competent Authority responsible for the exchanges. Brazil experienced some delays in exchanging information on two future rulings due to the lack of coordination between the central taxation unit, the local taxation units and the Competent Authority as well as the misunderstanding regarding the entry into force of the relevant exchange of information agreement for the exchanges. However, as soon as the additional rulings were identified, Brazil took steps to immediately inform the Competent Authority, which then performed the exchanges shortly after receiving the information. Therefore no recommendations are made as Brazil completed the exchanges on the additional future rulings as soon as the issues were identified and resolved, and this is not expected to be a recurring issue, however if this issue persists it will be noted and addressed in the next annual peer review.

190. Brazil has the necessary legal basis for spontaneous exchange of information, a process for completing the templates in a timely way and has completed all exchanges. Brazil has met all of the ToR for the exchange of information process and no recommendations are made.

C. Statistics (ToR IV)

191. The statistics for the year in review are as follows:

Category of ruling	Number of exchanges	Jurisdictions exchanged with
Ruling related to a preferential regime	0	N/A
Cross-border unilateral advance pricing agreements (APAs) and any other cross-border unilateral tax rulings (such as an advance tax ruling) covering transfer pricing or the	*De minimis* rule applies	N/A

application of transfer pricing principles		
De minimis rule	3	N/A
Total	3	

D. Matters related to intellectual property regimes (ToR I.A.1.3)

192. Brazil does not offer an intellectual property regime for which transparency requirements under the Action 5 Report (OECD, 2015[1]) were imposed.

Summary of recommendations on implementation of the transparency framework

Aspect of implementation of the transparency framework that should be improved	Recommendation for improvement
	No recommendations are made.

References

OECD (2021), *BEPS Action 5 on Harmful Tax Practices - Terms of Reference and Methodology for the Conduct of the Peer Reviews of the Action 5 Transparency Framework*, OECD Publishing, Paris, http://www.oecd.org/tax/beps/beps-action-5-harmful-tax-practices-peer-review-transparency-framework.pdf. [3]

OECD (2015), *Countering Harmful Tax Practices More Effectively, Taking into Account Transparency and Substance, Action 5 - 2015 Final Report*, OECD/G20 Base Erosion and Profit Shifting Project, OECD Publishing, Paris, https://dx.doi.org/10.1787/9789264241190-en. [1]

OECD (ed.) (2017b), *Harmful Tax Practices - 2017 Progress Report on Preferential Regimes*, OECD Publishing, Paris, http://dx.doi.org/10.1787/9789264283954-en. [2]

OECD/Council of Europe (2011), *The Multilateral Convention on Mutual Administrative Assistance in Tax Matters: Amended by the 2010 Protocol*, OECD Publishing, Paris, https://dx.doi.org/10.1787/9789264115606-en. [4]

Notes

1 With respect to the following preferential regime: PADIS – Semiconductors Industry.

2 Participating jurisdictions to the Convention are available here: www.oecd.org/tax/exchange-of-tax-information/convention-on-mutual-administrative-assistance-in-tax-matters.htm. Brazil also has bilateral agreements with Argentina, Austria, Belgium, Canada, Chile, China (People's Republic of), Czech Republic, Denmark, Equator, Finland, France, Hungary, India, Israel, Italy, Japan, Korea, Luxembourg, Mexico, Norway, Netherlands, Peru, Portugal, Philippines, Slovak Republic, Russia, South Africa, Spain,

Sweden, Trinidad and Tobago, Turkey, Ukraine and Venezuela. The TIEAs with Jersey, Switzerland and the United Kingdom also permit for the spontaneous exchange of information.

Brunei Darussalam

Brunei Darussalam has met all aspects of the terms of reference (OECD, 2021[3]) (ToR) for the calendar year 2020 (year in review) that can be met in the absence of rulings being issued in practice, and no recommendations are made.

Brunei Darussalam can legally issue five types of rulings within the scope of the transparency framework.

In practice, Brunei Darussalam issued no rulings within the scope of the transparency framework.

As no exchanges were required to take place, no peer input was received in respect of the exchanges of information on rulings received from Brunei Darussalam.

A. The information gathering process (ToR I.A)

193. Brunei Darussalam can legally issue the following five types of rulings within the scope of the transparency framework: (i) preferential regimes;[1] (ii) cross-border unilateral APAs and any other cross-border unilateral tax rulings (such as an advance tax ruling) covering transfer pricing or the application of transfer pricing principles; (iii) rulings providing for unilateral downward adjustments; (iv) permanent establishment rulings; and (v) related party conduit rulings.

194. For Brunei Darussalam, past rulings are any tax rulings within scope that are issued either: (i) on or after 1 January 2015 but before 1 April 2017; or (ii) on or after 1 January 2012 but before 1 January 2015, provided they were still in effect as at 1 January 2015. Future rulings are any tax rulings within scope that are issued on or after 1 April 2017.

195. In the prior years' peer review reports, it was determined that Brunei Darussalam's undertakings to identify past and future rulings and all potential exchange jurisdictions were sufficient to meet the minimum standard. In addition, it was determined that Brunei Darussalam's review and supervision mechanism was sufficient to meet the minimum standard. Brunei Darussalam's implementation remains unchanged, and therefore continues to meet the minimum standard.

196. Brunei Darussalam has met all of the ToR for the information gathering process and no recommendations are made.

B. The exchange of information (ToR II.B)

197. Brunei Darussalam has international agreements permitting spontaneous exchange of information, including being a party to (i) the *Multilateral Convention on Mutual Administrative Assistance in Tax Matters: Amended by the 2010 Protocol* (OECD/Council of Europe, 2011[4]) ("the Convention") and (ii) bilateral agreements in force with 18 jurisdictions.[2]

198. As Brunei Darussalam did not issue any future rulings within the scope of the transparency framework in the relevant period, Brunei Darussalam was not required to exchange any information on rulings in the year in review and no data on the timeliness of exchanges can be reported.

199. In the prior years' peer review reports, it was determined that Brunei Darussalam's process for the completion and exchange of templates were sufficient to meet the minimum standard. With respect to past rulings, no further action was required. Brunei Darussalam's implementation in this regard remains unchanged and therefore continues to meet the minimum standard.

200. Brunei Darussalam has the necessary legal basis for spontaneous exchange of information. Brunei Darussalam has met all of the ToR for the exchange of information process that can be met in the absence of rulings being issued and exchanged in practice and no recommendations are made.

C. Statistics (ToR IV)

201. As no rulings were issued, no statistics can be reported.

D. Matters related to intellectual property regimes (ToR I.A.1.3)

202. Brunei Darussalam does not offer an intellectual property regime for which transparency requirements under the Action 5 Report (OECD, 2015[1]) were imposed.

Summary of recommendations on implementation of the transparency framework

Aspect of implementation of the transparency framework that should be improved	Recommendation for improvement
	No recommendations are made.

References

OECD (2021), *BEPS Action 5 on Harmful Tax Practices - Terms of Reference and Methodology for the Conduct of the Peer Reviews of the Action 5 Transparency Framework*, OECD Publishing, Paris, http://www.oecd.org/tax/beps/beps-action-5-harmful-tax-practices-peer-review-transparency-framework.pdf. [3]

OECD (2015), *Countering Harmful Tax Practices More Effectively, Taking into Account Transparency and Substance, Action 5 - 2015 Final Report*, OECD/G20 Base Erosion and Profit Shifting Project, OECD Publishing, Paris, https://dx.doi.org/10.1787/9789264241190-en. [1]

OECD (ed.) (2017b), *Harmful Tax Practices - 2017 Progress Report on Preferential Regimes*, OECD Publishing, Paris, http://dx.doi.org/10.1787/9789264283954-en. [2]

OECD/Council of Europe (2011), *The Multilateral Convention on Mutual Administrative Assistance in Tax Matters: Amended by the 2010 Protocol*, OECD Publishing, Paris, https://dx.doi.org/10.1787/9789264115606-en. [4]

Notes

[1] Investment incentive order.

[2] Participating jurisdictions to the Convention are available here: www.oecd.org/tax/exchange-of-tax-information/convention-on-mutual-administrative-assistance-in-tax-matters.htm. Brunei Darussalam also has bilateral agreements with Bahrain, Cambodia, China (People's Republic of), Hong Kong (China), Indonesia, Japan, Korea, Kuwait, Lao People's Democratic Republic, Luxembourg, Malaysia, Oman, Pakistan, Qatar, Singapore, United Arab Emirates, United Kingdom and Viet Nam.

Burkina Faso

Burkina Faso is taking steps to implement the legal basis for the transparency framework and to commence administrative preparations to ensure that information on future rulings will be exchanged in a timely manner, in line with the terms of reference (OECD, 2021[3]) (ToR). Burkina Faso receives two recommendations covering the information gathering process (ToR I.A) and exchange of information (ToR II.B) for the calendar year 2020 (year in review).

This is Burkina Faso's first review of implementation of the transparency framework. During the prior year peer review, as well as for the 2017 and 2018 peer reviews, it was determined that Burkina Faso could not issue rulings within the scope of the transparency framework.

Burkina Faso can legally issue five types of ruling within the scope of the transparency framework.

In practice, it is not known whether Burkina Faso issued any rulings within the scope of the transparency framework.

No peer input was received in respect of the exchanges of information on rulings received from Burkina Faso.

A. The information gathering process (ToR I.A)

203. Burkina Faso can legally issue the following five types of rulings within the scope of the transparency framework: (i) preferential regimes, (ii) cross-border unilateral APAs and any other cross-border unilateral tax rulings (such as an advance tax ruling) covering transfer pricing or the application of transfer pricing principles; (iii) rulings providing for unilateral downward adjustments; (iv) permanent establishment rulings; and (v) related party conduit rulings.

Past rulings (ToR I.A.1.1, I.A.1.2, I.A.2.1, I.A.2.2)

204. For Burkina Faso, past rulings are any tax rulings within scope that are issued either (i) on or after 1 January 2015 but before 1 April 2017; and (ii) on or after 1 January 2012 but before 1 January 2015, provided they were still in effect as at 1 January 2015.

205. As it was determined that Burkina Faso could not issue rulings within the scope of the transparency framework prior to the year in review, Burkina Faso is not required to ensure the implementation of the obligations relating to the transparency framework for past rulings.

Future rulings (ToR I.A.1.1, I.A.1.2, I.A.2.1)

206. For Burkina Faso, future rulings are any tax rulings within scope that are issued on or after 1 April 2017.

207. No future rulings were identified by Burkina Faso during the year in review. Burkina Faso does not yet have a process in place to ensure the implementation of the obligations relating to the transparency framework.

Review and supervision (ToR I.A.3)

208. Burkina Faso did not yet have a review and supervision mechanism under the transparency framework for the year in review.

Conclusion on section A

209. Burkina Faso is recommended to ensure that it has put in place an effective information gathering process to identify all relevant future rulings and all potential exchange jurisdictions and to implement a review and supervision mechanism, as soon as possible (ToR I.A).

B. The exchange of information (ToR II.B)

Legal basis for spontaneous exchange of information (ToR II.B.1, II.B.2)

210. Burkina Faso has the necessary domestic legal basis to exchange information spontaneously. Burkina Faso notes that there are no legal or practical impediments that prevent the spontaneous exchange of information on rulings as contemplated in the Action 5 minimum standard.

211. Burkina Faso has international agreements permitting spontaneous exchange of information, including bilateral agreements in force with 16 jurisdictions.[1] Burkina Faso signed the *Multilateral Convention on Mutual Administrative Assistance in Tax Matters: Amended by the 2010 Protocol* (OECD/Council of Europe, 2011[4]) ("the Convention"). Burkina Faso is encouraged to continue its efforts to ratify the Convention and expand its international exchange of information instruments to be able to exchange information on rulings. It is noted, however, that jurisdictions are assessed on their compliance

with the transparency framework in respect of the exchange of information network in effect for the year of the particular annual review.

Completion and exchange of templates (ToR II.B.3, II.B.4, II.B.5, II.B.6, II.B.7)

212. Burkina Faso does not yet have a process to complete the templates on all relevant future rulings, to make them available to the Competent Authority for exchange of information, and to exchange them with relevant jurisdictions.

Conclusion on section B

213. Burkina Faso is recommended to develop a process to complete the templates for all relevant future rulings and to ensure that the exchanges of information on rulings occur in accordance with the form and timelines under the transparency framework going forward (ToR II.B).

C. Statistics (ToR IV)

214. As the Secretariat is not aware whether information on rulings was exchanged by Burkina Faso for the year in review, no statistics can be reported.

D. Matters related to intellectual property regimes (ToR I.A.1.3)

215. Burkina Faso does not offer an intellectual property regime for which transparency requirements under the Action 5 Report (OECD, 2015[1]) were imposed.

Summary of recommendations on implementation of the transparency framework

Aspect of implementation of the transparency framework that should be improved	Recommendation for improvement
Burkina Faso has not put in place the necessary information gathering process.	Burkina Faso is recommended to finalise its information gathering process for identifying all future rulings and potential exchange jurisdictions, with a review and supervision mechanism, as soon as possible.
Burkina Faso does not have a process to complete the templates on relevant rulings, to make them available to the Competent Authority for exchange of information, and to exchange them with relevant jurisdictions.	Burkina Faso is recommended to develop a process to complete the templates on relevant rulings and to ensure that the exchanges of information on rulings occur in accordance with the form and timelines under the transparency framework.

References

OECD (2021), *BEPS Action 5 on Harmful Tax Practices - Terms of Reference and Methodology for the Conduct of the Peer Reviews of the Action 5 Transparency Framework*, OECD Publishing, Paris, http://www.oecd.org/tax/beps/beps-action-5-harmful-tax-practices-peer-review-transparency-framework.pdf. [3]

OECD (2015), *Countering Harmful Tax Practices More Effectively, Taking into Account Transparency and Substance, Action 5 - 2015 Final Report*, OECD/G20 Base Erosion and Profit Shifting Project, OECD Publishing, Paris, https://dx.doi.org/10.1787/9789264241190-en. [1]

OECD (ed.) (2017b), *Harmful Tax Practices - 2017 Progress Report on Preferential Regimes*, OECD Publishing, Paris, http://dx.doi.org/10.1787/9789264283954-en. [2]

OECD/Council of Europe (2011), *The Multilateral Convention on Mutual Administrative Assistance in Tax Matters: Amended by the 2010 Protocol*, OECD Publishing, Paris, https://dx.doi.org/10.1787/9789264115606-en. [4]

Notes

[1] Burkina Faso has bilateral agreements with Benin, Cabo Verde, Cote d'Ivoire, France, Gambia, Ghana, Guinea, Guinea-Bissau, Liberia, Mali, Niger, Nigeria, Senegal, Sierra Leone, Togo, Tunisia.

Cabo Verde

Cabo Verde has met all aspects of the terms of reference (OECD, 2021[3]) (ToR) for the calendar year 2020 (year in review) that can be met in the absence of rulings being issued in practice, except for exchanging information on the tax rulings in a timely manner (ToR II.B). Cabo Verde receives one recommendation on these points for the year in review.

In the prior year report, Cabo Verde had received the same recommendation. As it has not been addressed, the recommendation remains in place.

Cabo Verde can legally issue one type of ruling within the scope of the transparency framework.

In practice, Cabo Verde issued no rulings within the scope of the transparency framework.

As no exchanges were required to take place, no peer input was received in respect of the exchanges of information on rulings received from Cabo Verde.

A. The information gathering process (ToR I.A)

216. Cabo Verde can legally issue the following one type of rulings within the scope of the transparency framework: permanent establishment (PE) rulings.

217. For Cabo Verde, past rulings are any tax rulings issued prior to 1 March 2019. However, there is no obligation for Cabo Verde to conduct spontaneous exchange of information on past rulings. Future rulings are any tax rulings within scope that are issued on or after 1 March 2019.

218. In the prior year peer review report, it was determined that Cabo Verde's undertakings to identify past and future rulings and all potential exchange jurisdictions were sufficient to meet the minimum standard. In addition, it was determined that Cabo Verde's review and supervision mechanism was sufficient to meet the minimum standard. During the year in review, Cabo Verde indicated its intention to formalise these processes aimed at capturing the information adequately by developing guidance covering the information gathering process as well as the implementation of a revision and supervision mechanism for future rulings, including appropriate training for the relevant tax officers. Cabo Verde's implementation remains unchanged, and therefore continues to meet the minimum standard.

219. Cabo Verde has met all of the ToR for the information gathering process that can be met in the absence of rulings being issued in practice and no recommendations are made.

B. The exchange of information (ToR II.B)

Legal basis for spontaneous exchange of information (ToR II.B.1, II.B.2)

220. Cabo Verde has the necessary domestic legal basis to exchange information spontaneously. Cabo Verde notes that there are no legal or practical impediments that prevent the spontaneous exchange of information on rulings as contemplated in the Action 5 minimum standard.

221. Cabo Verde has international agreements permitting spontaneous exchange of information, including being a party to (i) the *Multilateral Convention on Mutual Administrative Assistance in Tax Matters: Amended by the 2010 Protocol* (OECD/Council of Europe, 2011[4]) ("the Convention") and (ii) bilateral agreements in force with two jurisdictions.[1]

Completion and exchange of templates (ToR II.B.3, II.B.4, II.B.5, II.B.6, II.B.7)

222. In the prior year peer review report, it was determined that Cabo Verde did not have a process in place to complete the templates on relevant rulings in the agreed form, to make them available to the Competent Authority for exchange of information without undue delay, and to exchange them with relevant jurisdictions in accordance with the agreed timelines. Therefore, Cabo Verde was recommended to develop a process to complete the templates on relevant rulings and to ensure that the exchanges of information on rulings occur in accordance with the form and timelines under the transparency framework going forward. With respect to past rulings, no action was required. During the year in review, Cabo Verde indicated that this process is not yet in place and internal guidance is going to be developed to address this issue. Therefore, the prior year recommendation remains.

223. During the year in review, no exchanges were required to take place and no data on the timeliness of exchanges is reported.

Conclusion on section B

224. Cabo Verde has the necessary legal basis for spontaneous exchange of information. Cabo Verde does not have a process to complete the templates on relevant rulings and to make them available to the Competent Authority for exchange of information.

225. Cabo Verde is recommended to develop a process to complete the templates on relevant rulings and to ensure that the exchanges of information on rulings occur in accordance with the form and timelines under the transparency framework going forward (ToR II.B).

C. Statistics (ToR IV)

226. As no rulings were issued, no statistics can be reported.

D. Matters related to intellectual property regimes (ToR I.A.1.3)

227. Cabo Verde does not offer an intellectual property regime for which transparency requirements under the Action 5 Report (OECD, 2015[1]) were imposed.

Summary of recommendations on implementation of the transparency framework

Aspect of implementation of the transparency framework that should be improved	Recommendation for improvement
Cabo Verde does not have a process to complete the templates on relevant rulings and to make them available to the Competent Authority for exchange of information.	Cabo Verde is recommended to develop a process to complete the templates on relevant rulings and to ensure that the exchanges of information on rulings occur in accordance with the form and timelines under the transparency framework going forward. This recommendation remains unchanged since the prior year peer review report.

References

OECD (2021), *BEPS Action 5 on Harmful Tax Practices - Terms of Reference and Methodology for the Conduct of the Peer Reviews of the Action 5 Transparency Framework*, OECD Publishing, Paris, http://www.oecd.org/tax/beps/beps-action-5-harmful-tax-practices-peer-review-transparency-framework.pdf. [3]

OECD (2015), *Countering Harmful Tax Practices More Effectively, Taking into Account Transparency and Substance, Action 5 - 2015 Final Report*, OECD/G20 Base Erosion and Profit Shifting Project, OECD Publishing, Paris, https://dx.doi.org/10.1787/9789264241190-en. [1]

OECD (ed.) (2017b), *Harmful Tax Practices - 2017 Progress Report on Preferential Regimes*, OECD Publishing, Paris, http://dx.doi.org/10.1787/9789264283954-en. [2]

OECD/Council of Europe (2011), *The Multilateral Convention on Mutual Administrative Assistance in Tax Matters: Amended by the 2010 Protocol*, OECD Publishing, Paris, https://dx.doi.org/10.1787/9789264115606-en. [4]

Notes

[1] Parties to the Convention are available here: www.oecd.org/tax/exchange-of-tax-information/convention-on-mutual-administrative-assistance-in-tax-matters.htm. Cabo Verde also has bilateral agreements with Portugal and Spain.

Canada

Canada has met all aspects of the terms of reference (OECD, 2021[3]) (ToR) for the calendar year 2020 (year in review), and no recommendations are made.

Canada can legally issue four types of rulings within the scope of the transparency framework.

In practice, Canada issued rulings within the scope of the transparency framework as follows:

Type of ruling	Number of rulings
Past rulings	12
Future rulings in the period 1 April 2016 – 31 December 2016	2
Future rulings in the calendar year 2017	2
Future rulings in the calendar year 2018	1
Future rulings in the calendar year 2019	1
Future rulings in the year in review	1

As no exchanges were required to take place during the year in review, no peer input was received in respect of the exchanges of information on rulings received from Canada.

A. The information gathering process (ToR I.A)

228. Canada can legally issue four types of rulings within the scope of the transparency framework: (i) preferential regimes;[1] (ii) cross-border unilateral APAs and any other cross-border unilateral tax rulings (such as an advance tax ruling) covering transfer pricing or the application of transfer pricing principles; (iii) permanent establishment rulings; and (iv) related party conduit rulings.

229. For Canada, past rulings are any tax rulings within scope that are issued either: (i) on or after 1 January 2014 but before 1 April 2016; or (ii) on or after 1 January 2010 but before 1 January 2014, provided they were still in effect as at 1 January 2014. Future rulings are any tax rulings within scope that are issued on or after 1 April 2016.

230. In the prior years' peer review reports, it was determined that Canada's undertakings to identify past and future rulings and all potential exchange jurisdictions were sufficient to meet the minimum standard. In addition, it was determined that Canada's review and supervision mechanism was sufficient to meet the minimum standard. Canada's implementation remains unchanged, and therefore continues to meet the minimum standard.

231. Canada has met all of the ToR for the information gathering process and no recommendations are made.

B. The exchange of information (ToR II.B)

232. Canada has international agreements permitting spontaneous exchange of information, including being a party to (i) the *Multilateral Convention on Mutual Administrative Assistance in Tax Matters: Amended by the 2010 Protocol* (OECD/Council of Europe, 2011[4]) ("the Convention") and (ii) bilateral agreements in force with 95 jurisdictions.[2]

233. During the year in review, no exchanges were required to take place and no data on the timeliness of exchanges is reported. Canada notes that one ruling was submitted to the Competent Authority in late December 2020 and subsequently exchanged in January 2021. This will be reflected in next year's report.

234. In the prior years' peer review reports, it was determined that Canada's process for the completion and exchange of templates were sufficient to meet the minimum standard. With respect to past rulings, no further action was required. Canada's implementation in this regard remains unchanged and therefore continues to meet the minimum standard.

235. Canada has the necessary legal basis for spontaneous exchange of information, a process for completing the templates in a timely way and has completed all exchanges. Canada has met all of the ToR for the exchange of information process and no recommendations are made.

C. Statistics (ToR IV)

236. As no exchanges were required to take place during the year in review, no statistics can be reported.

D. Matters related to intellectual property regimes (ToR I.A.1.3)

237. Canada does not offer an intellectual property regime for which transparency requirements under the Action 5 Report (OECD, 2015[1]) were imposed.

Summary of recommendations on implementation of the transparency framework

Aspect of implementation of the transparency framework that should be improved	Recommendation for improvement
	No recommendations are made.

References

OECD (2021), *BEPS Action 5 on Harmful Tax Practices - Terms of Reference and Methodology for the Conduct of the Peer Reviews of the Action 5 Transparency Framework*, OECD Publishing, Paris, http://www.oecd.org/tax/beps/beps-action-5-harmful-tax-practices-peer-review-transparency-framework.pdf. [3]

OECD (2015), *Countering Harmful Tax Practices More Effectively, Taking into Account Transparency and Substance, Action 5 - 2015 Final Report*, OECD/G20 Base Erosion and Profit Shifting Project, OECD Publishing, Paris, https://dx.doi.org/10.1787/9789264241190-en. [1]

OECD (ed.) (2017b), *Harmful Tax Practices - 2017 Progress Report on Preferential Regimes*, OECD Publishing, Paris, http://dx.doi.org/10.1787/9789264283954-en. [2]

OECD/Council of Europe (2011), *The Multilateral Convention on Mutual Administrative Assistance in Tax Matters: Amended by the 2010 Protocol*, OECD Publishing, Paris, https://dx.doi.org/10.1787/9789264115606-en. [4]

Notes

[1] With respect to the following preferential regimes: 1) Life insurance business and 2) International shipping.

[2] Participating jurisdictions to the Convention are available here: www.oecd.org/tax/exchange-of-tax-information/convention-on-mutual-administrative-assistance-in-tax-matters.htm. Canada also has bilateral agreements with Algeria, Argentina, Armenia, Australia, Austria, Azerbaijan, Bangladesh, Barbados, Belgium, Brazil, Bulgaria, Cameroon, Chile, China (People's Republic of), Colombia, Cote d'Ivoire, Croatia, Cyprus, Czech Republic, Denmark, Dominican Republic, Ecuador, Egypt, Estonia, Finland, France, Gabon, Germany, Greece, Guyana, Hong Kong (China), Hungary, Iceland, India, Indonesia, Ireland, Israel, Italy, Jamaica, Japan, Jordan, Kazakhstan, Kenya, Korea, Kuwait, Kyrgyzstan, Latvia, Lithuania, Luxembourg, Madagascar, Malaysia, Malta, Mexico, Moldova, Mongolia, Morocco, Netherlands, New Zealand, Nigeria, Norway, Oman, Pakistan, Papua New Guinea, Peru, Philippines, Poland, Portugal, Romania, Russia, Senegal, Serbia, Singapore, Slovak Republic, Slovenia, South Africa, Spain, Sri Lanka, Sweden, Switzerland, Chinese Taipei, Tanzania, Thailand, Trinidad & Tobago, Tunisia, Turkey, Ukraine, United Arab Emirates, United Kingdom, United States, Uzbekistan, Venezuela, Viet Nam, Zambia and Zimbabwe. The Tax Information Exchange Agreement with Aruba also permits spontaneous exchange of information.

Chile

Chile has met all aspects of the terms of reference (OECD, 2021[3]) (ToR) for the calendar year 2020 (year in review), and no recommendations are made.

Chile can legally issue two types of rulings within the scope of the transparency framework.

In practice, Chile issued rulings within the scope of the transparency framework as follows:

Type of ruling	Number of rulings
Past rulings	0
Future rulings in the period 1 April 2016 – 31 December 2016	0
Future rulings in the calendar year 2017	0
Future rulings in the calendar year 2018	0
Future rulings in the calendar year 2019	2
Future rulings in the year in review	0

Peer input was received from one jurisdiction in respect of the exchanges of information on rulings received from Chile. The input was generally positive, noting that overall information was complete, in a correct format and received in a timely manner.

A. The information gathering process (ToR I.A)

238. Chile can legally issue the following two types of rulings within the scope of the transparency framework: (i) cross-border unilateral APAs and any other cross-border unilateral tax rulings (such as an advance tax ruling) covering transfer pricing or the application of transfer pricing principles; and (ii) related party conduit rulings.

239. For Chile, past rulings are any tax rulings within scope that are issued either: (i) on or after 1 January 2014 but before 1 April 2016; or (ii) on or after 1 January 2010 but before 1 January 2014, provided they were still in effect as at 1 January 2014. Future rulings are any tax rulings within scope that are issued on or after 1 April 2016.

240. In the prior years' peer review reports, it was determined that Chile's undertakings to identify past and future rulings and all potential exchange jurisdictions were sufficient to meet the minimum standard, noting however that they had not yet exchanged information on rulings within the scope of the standard. In addition, it was determined that Chile's review and supervision mechanism was sufficient to meet the minimum standard. Chile's implementation remains unchanged, and therefore continues to meet the minimum standard.

241. Chile has met all of the ToR for the information gathering process and no recommendations are made.

B. The exchange of information (ToR II.B)

242. Chile has international agreements permitting spontaneous exchange of information, including being a party to (i) the *Multilateral Convention on Mutual Administrative Assistance in Tax Matters: Amended by the 2010 Protocol* (OECD/Council of Europe, 2011[4]) ("the Convention") and (ii) bilateral agreements in force with 33 jurisdictions.[1]

243. During the year in review, Chile exchanged information for the first time. Chile reported seven exchanges during the year in review for two future rulings issued in December 2019.

244. For the year in review, the timeliness of exchanges is as follows:

Future rulings within the scope of the transparency framework	Number of exchanges transmitted within three months of the information becoming available to the competent authority or immediately after legal impediments have been lifted	Delayed exchanges		
		Number of exchanges transmitted later than three months of the information on rulings becoming available to the competent authority	Reasons for the delays	Any other comments
	7	0	N/A	N/A
Total	7	0		

Follow up requests received for exchange of the ruling	Number	Average time to provide response	Number of requests not answered
	1	N/A	1

245. Chile notes that it did not respond to the follow-up request because the request related to underlying information regarding the taxpayer's accounts rather than to the specific content of the ruling. Subsequently, the request was closed as the country confirmed that they had obtained the information directly from the taxpayer.

246. In the prior years' peer review reports, it was determined that Chile's process for the completion and exchange of templates were sufficient to meet the minimum standard. With respect to past rulings, no further action was required. Chile's implementation in this regard remains unchanged and therefore continues to meet the minimum standard. It should be noted that for the peer input, one peer indicated that the information in the summary box of the template could be more detailed.

247. Chile has the necessary legal basis for spontaneous exchange of information, a process for completing the templates in a timely way and has completed all exchanges. Chile has met all of the ToR for the exchange of information process and no recommendations are made.

C. Statistics (ToR IV)

248. The statistics for the year in review are as follows:

Category of ruling	Number of exchanges	Jurisdictions exchanged with
Cross-border unilateral APAs and any other cross-border unilateral tax rulings (such as an advance tax ruling) covering transfer pricing or the application of transfer pricing principles	*De minimis rule* applies	N/A
Related party conduit rulings	0	N/A
De minimis rule	7	N/A
Total	7	

D. Matters related to intellectual property regimes (ToR I.A.1.3)

249. Chile does not offer an intellectual property regime for which transparency requirements under the Action 5 Report (OECD, 2015[1]) were imposed.

Summary of recommendations on implementation of the transparency framework

Aspect of implementation of the transparency framework that should be improved	Recommendation for improvement
	No recommendations are made.

References

OECD (2021), *BEPS Action 5 on Harmful Tax Practices - Terms of Reference and Methodology for the Conduct of the Peer Reviews of the Action 5 Transparency Framework*, OECD Publishing, Paris, http://www.oecd.org/tax/beps/beps-action-5-harmful-tax-practices-peer-review-transparency-framework.pdf. [3]

OECD (2015), *Countering Harmful Tax Practices More Effectively, Taking into Account Transparency and Substance, Action 5 - 2015 Final Report*, OECD/G20 Base Erosion and Profit Shifting Project, OECD Publishing, Paris, https://dx.doi.org/10.1787/9789264241190-en. [1]

OECD (ed.) (2017b), *Harmful Tax Practices - 2017 Progress Report on Preferential Regimes*, OECD Publishing, Paris, http://dx.doi.org/10.1787/9789264283954-en. [2]

OECD/Council of Europe (2011), *The Multilateral Convention on Mutual Administrative Assistance in Tax Matters: Amended by the 2010 Protocol*, OECD Publishing, Paris, https://dx.doi.org/10.1787/9789264115606-en. [4]

Notes

[1] Participating jurisdictions to the Convention are available here: www.oecd.org/tax/exchange-of-tax-information/convention-on-mutual-administrative-assistance-in-tax-matters.htm. Chile also has bilateral agreements with Argentina, Australia, Austria, Belgium, Brazil, Canada, China (People's Republic of), Colombia, Croatia, Czech Republic, Denmark, Ecuador, France, Ireland, Italy, Japan, Korea, Malaysia, Mexico, Norway, New Zealand, Paraguay, Peru, Poland, Portugal, Russia, Spain, South Africa, Sweden, Switzerland, Thailand, United Kingdom and Uruguay.

China (People's Republic of)

China has met all aspects of the terms of reference (OECD, 2021[3]) (ToR) for the calendar year 2020 (year in review), and no recommendations are made.

China can legally issue one type of ruling within the scope of the transparency framework.

In practice, China issued rulings within the scope of the transparency framework as follows:

Type of ruling	Number of rulings
Past rulings	11
Future rulings in the period 1 April 2016 – 31 December 2016	6
Future rulings in the calendar year 2017	3
Future rulings in the calendar year 2018	2
Future rulings in the calendar year 2019	4
Future rulings in the year in review	15

No peer input was received in respect of the exchanges of information on rulings received from China.

A. The information gathering process (ToR I.A)

250. China can legally issue one type of ruling within the scope of the transparency framework: cross-border unilateral APAs and any other cross-border unilateral tax rulings (such as an advance tax ruling) covering transfer pricing or the application of transfer pricing principles.

251. There was previously a legal barrier to the exchange of information on rulings in China, which did not allow the exchange of past rulings. The legal framework in China was subsequently amended to allow exchanges on future rulings. Future rulings are any tax rulings within scope that are issued on or after 1 April 2016.

252. In the prior years' peer review reports, it was determined that China's undertakings to identify past and future rulings and all potential exchange jurisdictions were sufficient to meet the minimum standard. In addition, it was determined that China's review and supervision mechanism was sufficient to meet the minimum standard. China's implementation remains unchanged, and therefore continues to meet the minimum standard.

253. China has met all of the ToR for the information gathering process and no recommendations are made.

B. The exchange of information (ToR II.B)

254. China has international agreements permitting spontaneous exchange of information, including being a party to (i) the *Multilateral Convention on Mutual Administrative Assistance in Tax Matters: Amended by the 2010 Protocol* (OECD/Council of Europe, 2011[4]) ("the Convention") and (ii) bilateral agreements in force with 107 jurisdictions.[1]

255. For the year in review, the timeliness of exchanges is as follows:

Future rulings within the scope of the transparency framework	Number of exchanges transmitted within three months of the information becoming available to the competent authority or immediately after legal impediments have been lifted	Delayed exchanges		
		Number of exchanges transmitted later than three months of the information on rulings becoming available to the competent authority	Reasons for the delays	Any other comments
	27	0	N/A	N/A

Follow up requests received for exchange of the ruling	Number	Average time to provide response	Number of requests not answered
	0	N/A	N/A

256. In the prior years' peer review reports, it was determined that China's process for the completion and exchange of templates were sufficient to meet the minimum standard. With respect to past rulings, no further action was required. China's implementation in this regard remains unchanged and therefore continues to meet the minimum standard.

257. China has the necessary legal basis for spontaneous exchange of information, a process for completing the templates in a timely way and has completed all exchanges. China has met all of the ToR for the exchange of information process and no recommendations are made.

C. Statistics (ToR IV)

258. The statistics for the year in review are as follows:

Category of ruling	Number of exchanges	Jurisdictions exchanged with
Cross-border unilateral APAs and any other cross-border unilateral tax rulings (such as an advance tax ruling) covering transfer pricing or the application of transfer pricing principles	27	Hong Kong (China), Japan, Macau (China), Russia, Singapore, United States

D. Matters related to intellectual property regimes (ToR I.A.1.3)

259. China does not offer an intellectual property regime for which transparency requirements under the Action 5 Report (OECD, 2015[1]) were imposed.

Summary of recommendations on implementation of the transparency framework

Aspect of implementation of the transparency framework that should be improved	Recommendation for improvement
	No recommendations are made.

References

OECD (2021), *BEPS Action 5 on Harmful Tax Practices - Terms of Reference and Methodology for the Conduct of the Peer Reviews of the Action 5 Transparency Framework*, OECD Publishing, Paris, http://www.oecd.org/tax/beps/beps-action-5-harmful-tax-practices-peer-review-transparency-framework.pdf. [3]

OECD (2015), *Countering Harmful Tax Practices More Effectively, Taking into Account Transparency and Substance, Action 5 - 2015 Final Report*, OECD/G20 Base Erosion and Profit Shifting Project, OECD Publishing, Paris, https://dx.doi.org/10.1787/9789264241190-en. [1]

OECD (ed.) (2017b), *Harmful Tax Practices - 2017 Progress Report on Preferential Regimes*, OECD Publishing, Paris, http://dx.doi.org/10.1787/9789264283954-en. [2]

OECD/Council of Europe (2011), *The Multilateral Convention on Mutual Administrative Assistance in Tax Matters: Amended by the 2010 Protocol*, OECD Publishing, Paris, https://dx.doi.org/10.1787/9789264115606-en. [4]

Notes

[1] Participating jurisdictions to the Convention are available here: www.oecd.org/tax/exchange-of-tax-information/convention-on-mutual-administrative-assistance-in-tax-matters.htm. China also has bilateral agreements with Albania, Algeria, Armenia, Australia, Austria, Azerbaijan, Bahrain, Bangladesh, Barbados, Belarus, Belgium, Bosnia and Herzegovina, Brazil, Brunei Darussalam, Bulgaria, Cambodia, Canada, Chile, Croatia, Cuba, Cyprus, Czech Republic, Denmark, Ecuador, Egypt, Estonia, Ethiopia, Finland, France, Georgia, Germany, Greece, Hungary, Iceland, India, Indonesia, Iran, Ireland, Israel, Italy, Jamaica, Japan, Kazakhstan, Korea, Kuwait, Kyrgyzstan, Lao People's Democratic Republic, Latvia, Lithuania, Luxembourg, Malaysia, Malta, Mauritius, Mexico, Moldova, Mongolia, Montenegro, Morocco, Nepal, Netherlands, New Zealand, Nigeria, North Macedonia, Norway, Oman, Pakistan, Papua New Guinea, Philippines, Poland, Portugal, Qatar, Romania, Russia, Saudi Arabia, Serbia, Seychelles, Singapore, Slovenia, South Africa, Spain, Sri Lanka, Sudan, Sweden, Switzerland, Syrian Arab Republic, Tajikistan, Thailand, Trinidad and Tobago, Tunisia, Turkey, Turkmenistan, Ukraine, United Arab Emirates, United Kingdom, United States, Uzbekistan, Venezuela, Viet Nam, Zambia and Zimbabwe.

Colombia

Colombia has met all aspects of the terms of reference (OECD, 2021[3]) (ToR) for the calendar year 2020 (year in review), and no recommendations are made.

Colombia can legally issue one type of ruling within the scope of the transparency framework.

In practice, Colombia issued rulings within the scope of the transparency framework as follows:

Type of ruling	Number of rulings
Past rulings	1
Future rulings in the period 1 April 2016 – 31 December 2016	0
Future rulings in the calendar year 2017	0
Future rulings in the calendar year 2018	0
Future rulings in the calendar year 2019	0
Future rulings in the year in review	0

As no exchanges were required to take place, no peer input was received in respect of the exchanges of information on rulings received from Colombia.

A. The information gathering process (ToR I.A)

260. Colombia can legally issue one type of rulings within the scope of the transparency framework: cross-border unilateral APAs and any other cross-border unilateral tax rulings (such as an advance tax ruling) covering transfer pricing or the application of transfer pricing principles.

261. For Colombia, past rulings are any tax rulings within scope that are issued either: (i) on or after 1 January 2014 but before 1 April 2016; or (ii) on or after 1 January 2010 but before 1 January 2014, provided they were still in effect as at 1 January 2014. Future rulings are any tax rulings within scope that are issued on or after 1 April 2016.

262. In the prior years' peer review reports, it was determined that Colombia's undertakings to identify past and future rulings and all potential exchange jurisdictions were sufficient to meet the minimum standard. Colombia's implementation remains unchanged, and therefore continues to meet the minimum standard. In addition, it was determined that Colombia's review and supervision mechanism was sufficient to meet the minimum standard. Furthermore, during the year in review, a decree was issued providing the new International Taxation Office of the Colombian Tax Administration (DIAN) with the legal competence to assess and conclude APAs (Decree 1742 of 22 December 2020).

263. Colombia has met all of the ToR for the information gathering process and no recommendations are made.

B. The exchange of information (ToR II.B)

264. Colombia has international agreements permitting spontaneous exchange of information, including being a party to (i) the *Multilateral Convention on Mutual Administrative Assistance in Tax Matters: Amended by the 2010 Protocol* (OECD/Council of Europe, 2011[4]) ("the Convention"), (ii) bilateral agreements in force with 10 jurisdictions, (iii) multilateral tax agreements in force with three jurisdictions and (iv) tax information exchange agreements with one jurisdiction.[1]

265. As Colombia was not required to exchange any information on rulings for the year in review, no data on the timeliness of exchanges can be reported.

266. In the prior years' peer review reports, it was determined that Colombia's process for the completion and exchange of templates were sufficient to meet the minimum standard. With respect to past rulings, no further action was required. Colombia's implementation in this regard remains unchanged and therefore continues to meet the minimum standard.

267. Colombia has the necessary legal basis for spontaneous exchange of information, a process for completing the templates in a timely way and complete all exchanges. Colombia has met all of the ToR for the exchange of information process and no recommendations are made.

C. Statistics (ToR IV)

268. As no rulings were issued, no statistics can be reported.

D. Matters related to intellectual property regimes (ToR I.A.1.3)

269. Colombia does not offer an intellectual property regime for which transparency requirements under the Action 5 Report (OECD, 2015[1]) were imposed.

Summary of recommendations on implementation of the transparency framework

Aspect of implementation of the transparency framework that should be improved	Recommendation for improvement
	No recommendations are made.

References

OECD (2021), *BEPS Action 5 on Harmful Tax Practices - Terms of Reference and Methodology for the Conduct of the Peer Reviews of the Action 5 Transparency Framework*, OECD Publishing, Paris, http://www.oecd.org/tax/beps/beps-action-5-harmful-tax-practices-peer-review-transparency-framework.pdf. [3]

OECD (2015), *Countering Harmful Tax Practices More Effectively, Taking into Account Transparency and Substance, Action 5 - 2015 Final Report*, OECD/G20 Base Erosion and Profit Shifting Project, OECD Publishing, Paris, https://dx.doi.org/10.1787/9789264241190-en. [1]

OECD (ed.) (2017b), *Harmful Tax Practices - 2017 Progress Report on Preferential Regimes*, OECD Publishing, Paris, http://dx.doi.org/10.1787/9789264283954-en. [2]

OECD/Council of Europe (2011), *The Multilateral Convention on Mutual Administrative Assistance in Tax Matters: Amended by the 2010 Protocol*, OECD Publishing, Paris, https://dx.doi.org/10.1787/9789264115606-en. [4]

Notes

[1] Participating jurisdictions to the Convention are available here: www.oecd.org/tax/exchange-of-tax-information/convention-on-mutual-administrative-assistance-in-tax-matters.htm. Colombia also has bilateral agreements with Canada, Chile, Czech Republic, India, Korea, Mexico, Portugal, Spain, Switzerland and United Kingdom; multilateral tax agreements with Bolivia, Ecuador and Peru; and a tax information exchange agreement with the United States.

Congo

Congo[1] did not provide a completed peer review questionnaire to the Secretariat. It is not known whether Congo has implemented the transparency framework in line with the terms of reference (OECD, 2021[3]) (ToR) for the calendar year 2020 (year in review). Congo receives two recommendations covering the information gathering process (ToR I.A) and exchange of information (ToR II.B) for the year in review.

In the prior year report, as well as in the 2017 and 2018 peer reviews, Congo received the same recommendations. As they have not been addressed, the recommendations remain in place.

Congo can legally issue two types of rulings within the scope of the transparency framework.

In practice, Congo did not issue any type of rulings within the scope of the transparency framework in previous years. For the year in review, as well as for the prior year, it is not known whether Congo issued any type of rulings within the scope of the transparency framework.

No peer input was received in respect of the exchanges of information on rulings received from Congo.

A. The information gathering process (ToR I.A)

270. Congo can legally issue the following two types of rulings within the scope of the transparency framework: (i) cross-border unilateral APAs and any other cross-border unilateral tax rulings (such as an advance tax ruling) covering transfer pricing or the application of transfer pricing principles and (ii) permanent establishment rulings.

Past rulings (ToR I.A.1.1, I.A.1.2, I.A.2.1, I.A.2.2)

271. For Congo, past rulings are any tax rulings within scope that are issued either (i) on or after 1 January 2015 but before 1 April 2017; and (ii) on or after 1 January 2012 but before 1 January 2015, provided they were still in effect as at 1 January 2015.

272. In the 2018 peer review report, it was determined that Congo issued no past rulings in scope of the transparency framework. As such, there was no need to identify potential exchange jurisdictions.

Future rulings (ToR I.A.1.1, I.A.1.2, I.A.2.1)

273. For Congo, future rulings are any tax rulings within scope that are issued on or after 1 April 2017.

274. In the 2018 peer review report, Congo indicated that there were no processes in place for the record keeping of rulings for the purposes of the transparency framework. It was noted that Congo intended to implement guidelines and practices to make sure the necessary information to meet the requirements of the transparency framework is required in all cases. Congo was recommended to finalise its information gathering process as soon as possible.

275. During the year in review, as it is not known whether Congo has finalised its information gathering process, the recommendation remains in place.

Review and supervision (ToR I.A.3)

276. In the 2018 peer review report, it was determined that Congo did not yet have a review and supervision mechanism under the transparency framework. Congo was in the process of considering the implementation of a revision and supervision mechanism for ensuring implementation of the transparency framework. As it is not known whether Congo has put in place a review and supervision mechanism under the transparency framework for the year in review, the recommendation remains in place.

Conclusion on section A

277. Congo is recommended to finalise its information gathering process, with a review and supervision mechanism, as soon as possible (ToR I.A).

B. The exchange of information (ToR II.B)

Legal basis for spontaneous exchange of information (ToR II.B.1, II.B.2)

278. In the 2018 peer review report, it was determined that Congo was in the process of putting in place the necessary domestic legal basis to exchange information spontaneously. It is not known whether Congo has already put in place the necessary domestic legal basis to exchange information spontaneously for the year in review.

279. Congo has international agreements permitting spontaneous exchange of information, including bilateral agreements in force with 3 jurisdictions.[2] Congo is not a party to the *Multilateral Convention on Mutual Administrative Assistance in Tax Matters: Amended by the 2010 Protocol* (OECD/Council of Europe, 2011[4]) ("the Convention"). Congo is encouraged to continue its efforts to expand its international exchange of information instruments to be able to exchange information on rulings. It is noted, however, that jurisdictions are assessed on their compliance with the transparency framework in respect of the exchange of information network in effect for the year of the particular annual review.

Completion and exchange of templates (ToR II.B.3, II.B.4, II.B.5, II.B.6, II.B.7)

280. In the 2018 peer review report, it was determined that Congo was developing a process to complete the templates on relevant rulings, to make them available to the Competent Authority for exchange of information, and to exchange them with relevant jurisdictions. It is not known whether Congo has already put in place such a process for the year in review.

281. As it is not known whether exchanges took place in the year of review, no data on the timeliness of exchanges can be reported.

Conclusion on section B

282. Congo is recommended to put in place a domestic legal framework allowing spontaneous exchange of information on rulings and to continue its efforts to complete the templates for all relevant rulings and to ensure that the exchanges of information on rulings occur as soon as possible (ToR II.B).

C. Statistics (ToR IV)

283. As the Secretariat is not aware whether information on rulings was exchanged by Congo for the year in review, no statistics can be reported.

D. Matters related to intellectual property regimes (ToR I.A.1.3)

284. Congo does not offer an intellectual property regime for which transparency requirements under the Action 5 Report (OECD, 2015[1]) were imposed.

Summary of recommendations on implementation of the transparency framework

Aspect of implementation of the transparency framework that should be improved	Recommendation for improvement
It is not known whether Congo has finalised the steps to have in place its necessary information and gathering process.	Congo is recommended to finalise its information gathering process, with a review and supervision mechanism, as soon as possible. This recommendation remains unchanged since the 2017, 2018 and 2019 peer review reports.
It is not known whether Congo has finalised the steps to have effective compulsory spontaneous exchange of information on the tax rulings within the scope of the transparency framework.	Congo is recommended to continue to put in place a domestic legal framework allowing spontaneous exchange of information on rulings and to continue its efforts to complete the templates for all relevant rulings and to ensure that the exchanges of information on rulings occur as soon as possible. This recommendation remains unchanged since the 2017, 2018 and 2019 peer review reports.

References

OECD (2021), *BEPS Action 5 on Harmful Tax Practices - Terms of Reference and Methodology for the Conduct of the Peer Reviews of the Action 5 Transparency Framework*, OECD Publishing, Paris, http://www.oecd.org/tax/beps/beps-action-5-harmful-tax-practices-peer-review-transparency-framework.pdf. [3]

OECD (2015), *Countering Harmful Tax Practices More Effectively, Taking into Account Transparency and Substance, Action 5 - 2015 Final Report*, OECD/G20 Base Erosion and Profit Shifting Project, OECD Publishing, Paris, https://dx.doi.org/10.1787/9789264241190-en. [1]

OECD (ed.) (2017b), *Harmful Tax Practices - 2017 Progress Report on Preferential Regimes*, OECD Publishing, Paris, http://dx.doi.org/10.1787/9789264283954-en. [2]

OECD/Council of Europe (2011), *The Multilateral Convention on Mutual Administrative Assistance in Tax Matters: Amended by the 2010 Protocol*, OECD Publishing, Paris, https://dx.doi.org/10.1787/9789264115606-en. [4]

Notes

[1] Congo was not yet in a position to provide written comments on the draft report.

[2] Congo has bilateral agreements with France, Italy and Mauritius.

Costa Rica

Costa Rica has met all aspects of the terms of reference (OECD, 2021[3]) (ToR) for the calendar year 2020 (year in review), and no recommendations are made.

Costa Rica can legally issue two types of rulings within the scope of the transparency framework.

In practice, Costa Rica issued rulings within the scope of the transparency framework as follows:

Type of ruling	Number of rulings
Past rulings	6
Future rulings in the calendar year 2017	3
Future rulings in the calendar year 2018	4
Future rulings in the calendar year 2019	0
Future rulings in the year in review	3

No peer input was received in respect of the exchanges of information on rulings received from Costa Rica.

A. The information gathering process (ToR I.A)

285. Costa Rica can legally issue the following two types of rulings within the scope of the transparency framework: (i) cross-border unilateral APAs and any other cross-border unilateral tax rulings (such as an advance tax ruling) covering transfer pricing or the application of transfer pricing principles and (ii) permanent establishment (PE) rulings. To date, Costa Rica has issued only PE rulings given the resolution that establishes the requirements related to the issuance of APAs rulings has been issued on 16 March 2021 and published on 24 March 2021. As such, this report assesses the implementation with respect to PE rulings. The implementation with respect to APA rulings will be assessed in the next year's peer review.

286. For Costa Rica, past rulings are any tax rulings within scope that are issued either: (i) on or after 1 January 2015 but before 1 April 2017; or (ii) on or after 1 January 2012 but before 1 January 2015, provided they were still in effect as at 1 January 2015. Future rulings are any tax rulings within scope that are issued on or after 1 April 2017.

287. In the prior years' peer review reports, it was determined that Costa Rica's undertakings to identify past and future rulings and all potential exchange jurisdictions were sufficient to meet the minimum standard. In addition, it was determined that Costa Rica's review and supervision mechanism was sufficient to meet the minimum standard. Whilst Costa Rica's actions already meet the minimum standard under the transparency framework, Costa Rica continued to develop a shareholder register to further enhance Costa Rica's information gathering abilities for the standard. The functionality of the shareholder register has been scheduled in stages aimed to cover companies in 2020 and trusts, foundations and associations in 2021.

288. Costa Rica's implementation remains unchanged, and therefore continues to meet the minimum standard.

289. Costa Rica has met all of the ToR for the information gathering process and no recommendations are made.

B. The exchange of information (ToR II.B)

290. Costa Rica has international agreements permitting spontaneous exchange of information, including being a party to (i) the *Multilateral Convention on Mutual Administrative Assistance in Tax Matters: Amended by the 2010 Protocol* (OECD/Council of Europe, 2011[4]) ("the Convention"), (ii) the Convention on Mutual Assistance and Technical Cooperation between Tax and Customs Administrations of Central America, (iii) bilateral agreements in force with three jurisdictions, and (iv) tax information exchange agreements in force with two jurisdictions.[1]

291. For the year in review, the timeliness of exchanges is as follows:

Future rulings within the scope of the transparency framework	Number of exchanges transmitted within three months of the information becoming available to the competent authority or immediately after legal impediments have been lifted	Delayed exchanges		
		Number of exchanges transmitted later than three months of the information on rulings becoming available to the competent authority	Reasons for the delays	Any other comments
	4	0	N/A	N/A

Follow up requests received for exchange of the ruling	Number	Average time to provide response	Number of requests not answered
	0	N/A	N/A

292. In the prior years' peer review reports, it was determined that Costa Rica's process for the completion and exchange of templates were sufficient to meet the minimum standard. With respect to past rulings, no further action was required. Costa Rica's implementation in this regard remains unchanged and therefore continues to meet the minimum standard.

293. Costa Rica has the necessary legal basis for spontaneous exchange of information, a process for completing the templates in a timely way and has completed all exchanges. Costa Rica has met all of the ToR for the exchange of information process and no recommendations are made.

C. Statistics (ToR IV)

294. The statistics for the year in review are as follows:

Category of ruling	Number of exchanges	Jurisdictions exchanged with
Cross-border unilateral APAs and any other cross-border unilateral tax rulings (such as an advance tax ruling) covering transfer pricing or the application of transfer pricing principles	N/A	N/A
Permanent establishment rulings	*De minimis* rule applies	N/A
De minimis rule	4	N/A
Total	4	

D. Matters related to intellectual property regimes (ToR I.A.1.3)

295. Costa Rica does not offer an intellectual property regime for which transparency requirements under the Action 5 Report (OECD, 2015[1]) were imposed.

Summary of recommendations on implementation of the transparency framework

Aspect of implementation of the transparency framework that should be improved	Recommendation for improvement
	No recommendations are made.

References

OECD (2021), *BEPS Action 5 on Harmful Tax Practices - Terms of Reference and Methodology for the Conduct of the Peer Reviews of the Action 5 Transparency Framework*, OECD Publishing, Paris, http://www.oecd.org/tax/beps/beps-action-5-harmful-tax-practices-peer-review-transparency-framework.pdf. [3]

OECD (2015), *Countering Harmful Tax Practices More Effectively, Taking into Account Transparency and Substance, Action 5 - 2015 Final Report*, OECD/G20 Base Erosion and Profit Shifting Project, OECD Publishing, Paris, https://dx.doi.org/10.1787/9789264241190-en. [1]

OECD (ed.) (2017b), *Harmful Tax Practices - 2017 Progress Report on Preferential Regimes*, OECD Publishing, Paris, http://dx.doi.org/10.1787/9789264283954-en. [2]

OECD/Council of Europe (2011), *The Multilateral Convention on Mutual Administrative Assistance in Tax Matters: Amended by the 2010 Protocol*, OECD Publishing, Paris, https://dx.doi.org/10.1787/9789264115606-en. [4]

Notes

1 Participating jurisdictions to the Convention are available here: www.oecd.org/tax/exchange-of-tax-information/convention-on-mutual-administrative-assistance-in-tax-matters.htm. Costa Rica is also party to the Convention on Mutual Assistance and Technical Cooperation between Tax and Customs Administrations of Central America including El Salvador, Guatemala, Honduras and Nicaragua. Costa Rica has bilateral tax agreements with Germany, Mexico and Spain, and tax information exchange agreements with Argentina and the United States, the latter renewed in September 2020. All these agreements allow spontaneous exchange of information.

Croatia

Croatia has met all aspects of the terms of reference (OECD, 2021[3]) (ToR) for the calendar year 2020 (year in review), and no recommendations are made.

Croatia can legally issue four types of rulings within the scope of the transparency framework.

In practice, Croatia issued rulings within the scope of the transparency framework as follows:

Type of ruling	Number of rulings
Past rulings	0
Future rulings in the period 1 April 2017 – 31 December 2017	0
Future rulings in the calendar year 2018	1
Future rulings in the calendar year 2019	0
Future rulings in the year in review	0

As no exchanges were required to take place, no peer input was received in respect of the exchanges of information on rulings received from Croatia.

A. The information gathering process (ToR I.A)

296. Croatia can legally issue the following four types of rulings within the scope of the transparency framework: (i) cross-border unilateral APAs and any other cross-border unilateral tax rulings (such as an advance tax ruling) covering transfer pricing or the application of transfer pricing principles; (ii) rulings providing for unilateral downward adjustments; (iii) permanent establishment rulings; and (iv) related party conduit rulings.

297. For Croatia, past rulings are any tax rulings within scope that are issued either: (i) on or after 1 January 2015 but before 1 April 2017; or (ii) on or after 1 January 2012 but before 1 January 2015, provided they were still in effect as at 1 January 2014. Future rulings are any tax rulings within scope that are issued on or after 1 April 2017.

298. In the prior years' peer review reports, it was determined that Croatia's undertakings to identify past and future rulings and all potential exchange jurisdictions were sufficient to meet the minimum standard. In addition, it was determined that Croatia's review and supervision mechanism was sufficient to meet the minimum standard. Croatia's implementation remains unchanged, and therefore continues to meet the minimum standard.

299. Croatia has met all of the ToR for the information gathering process and no recommendations are made.

B. The exchange of information (ToR II.B)

300. Croatia has international agreements permitting spontaneous exchange of information, including being a party to (i) the *Multilateral Convention on Mutual Administrative Assistance in Tax Matters: Amended by the 2010 Protocol* (OECD/Council of Europe, 2011[4]) ("the Convention"), (ii) the Directive 2011/16/EU with all other European Union Member States and (iii) bilateral agreements in force with 66 jurisdictions.[1]

301. As Croatia did not issue any rulings within the scope of the transparency framework in the relevant period, Croatia was not required to exchange any information on rulings in the year in review and no data on the timeliness of exchanges can be reported.

302. In the prior years' peer review reports, it was determined that Croatia's process for the completion and exchange of templates were sufficient to meet the minimum standard. With respect to past rulings, no further action was required. Croatia's implementation in this regard remains unchanged and therefore continues to meet the minimum standard.

303. Croatia has the necessary legal basis for spontaneous exchange of information, a process for completing the templates in a timely way and has completed all exchanges. Croatia has met all of the ToR for the exchange of information process and no recommendations are made.

C. Statistics (ToR IV)

304. As no rulings were issued, no statistics can be reported.

D. Matters related to intellectual property regimes (ToR I.A.1.3)

305. Croatia does not offer an intellectual property regime for which transparency requirements under the Action 5 Report (OECD, 2015[1]) were imposed.

Summary of recommendations on implementation of the transparency framework

Aspect of implementation of the transparency framework that should be improved	Recommendation for improvement
	No recommendations are made.

References

OECD (2021), *BEPS Action 5 on Harmful Tax Practices - Terms of Reference and Methodology for the Conduct of the Peer Reviews of the Action 5 Transparency Framework*, OECD Publishing, Paris, http://www.oecd.org/tax/beps/beps-action-5-harmful-tax-practices-peer-review-transparency-framework.pdf. [3]

OECD (2015), *Countering Harmful Tax Practices More Effectively, Taking into Account Transparency and Substance, Action 5 - 2015 Final Report*, OECD/G20 Base Erosion and Profit Shifting Project, OECD Publishing, Paris, https://dx.doi.org/10.1787/9789264241190-en. [1]

OECD (ed.) (2017b), *Harmful Tax Practices - 2017 Progress Report on Preferential Regimes*, OECD Publishing, Paris, http://dx.doi.org/10.1787/9789264283954-en. [2]

OECD/Council of Europe (2011), *The Multilateral Convention on Mutual Administrative Assistance in Tax Matters: Amended by the 2010 Protocol*, OECD Publishing, Paris, https://dx.doi.org/10.1787/9789264115606-en. [4]

Notes

[1] Participating jurisdictions to the Convention are available here: www.oecd.org/tax/exchange-of-tax-information/convention-on-mutual-administrative-assistance-in-tax-matters.htm. Croatia also has bilateral agreements with Albania, Armenia, Austria, Azerbaijan, Belarus, Belgium, Bosnia and Herzegovina, Bulgaria, Canada, Chile, China (People's Republic of), Czech Republic, Denmark, Estonia, Finland, France, Georgia, Germany, Greece, Hungary, Iceland, India, Indonesia, Iran, Ireland, Israel, Italy, Japan, Jordan, Kazakhstan, Korea, Kosovo, Kuwait, Latvia, Lithuania, Luxembourg, Malaysia, Malta, Mauritius, Morocco, Moldova, Montenegro, Netherlands, North Macedonia, Norway, Oman, Poland, Portugal, Qatar, Romania, Russia, San Marino, Serbia, Slovak Republic, Slovenia, South Africa, Spain, Syrian Arab Republic, Sweden, Switzerland, Turkey, Turkmenistan, Ukraine, United Arab Emirates, United Kingdom and Viet Nam.

Curaçao

Curaçao has met all aspects of the terms of reference (OECD, 2021[3]) (ToR) for the calendar year 2020 (year in review) except for identifying rulings within the scope of the transparency framework and under which category of rulings they fall (ToR I.A.1) and completing exchanges of information on rulings in accordance with the timelines (ToR II.B.5 and II.B.6). Curaçao receives two recommendations on these points for the year in review.

In the prior year report, as well as in the 2017 and 2018 peer reviews, Curaçao received three recommendations. Curaçao has resolved one of these issues, however two recommendations have not been addressed and remain in place.

Curaçao can legally issue five types of rulings within the scope of the transparency framework.

In practice, Curaçao issued rulings that are potentially within the scope of the transparency framework as follows:

Type of ruling	Number of rulings
Past rulings	3 621
Future rulings in the period 1 April 2017 – 31 December 2017	320
Future rulings in the calendar year 2018	48
Future rulings in the calendar year 2019	40
Future rulings in the year of review	20

As no exchanges took place, no peer input was received in respect of the exchanges of information on rulings received from Curaçao.

A. The information gathering process (ToR I.A)

306. Curaçao can legally issue the following five types of rulings within the scope of the transparency framework: (i) preferential regimes;[1] (ii) cross-border unilateral APAs and any other cross-border unilateral tax rulings (such as an advance tax ruling) covering transfer pricing or the application of transfer pricing principles; (iii) rulings providing for unilateral downward adjustments; (iv) permanent establishment rulings; and (v) related party conduit rulings.

Past rulings (ToR I.A.1.1, I.A.1.2, I.A.2.1, I.A.2.2)

307. For Curaçao, past rulings are any tax rulings within scope that are issued either (i) on or after 1 January 2015 but before 1 April 2017; and (ii) on or after 1 January 2012 but before 1 January 2015, provided they were still in effect as at 1 January 2015.

308. In the prior years' peer review reports, it was determined that Curaçao's undertakings to identify past rulings and all potential exchange jurisdictions have met all the ToR, except for completing the process of reviewing the templates to confirm that all past rulings identified are cross-border rulings and therefore within the scope of the transparency framework, and to identify which category of rulings they fall under (ToR I.4.1.2). Therefore, Curaçao was recommended to continue its work to complete its information gathering process on past rulings as soon as possible.

309. Due to the Covid-19 pandemic, during the year in review, Curaçao was not able to fully continue its work to accurately identify and categorise past rulings. Therefore, this process is still ongoing given the large number of rulings, many of which fall into more than one category. As Curaçao completes the identification and categorisation process, they are also identifying the potential exchange jurisdictions. Curaçao anticipates that this process will be completed by the end of March 2022. Therefore, the prior years' recommendation remains.

Future rulings (ToR I.A.1.1, I.A.1.2, I.A.2.1)

310. For Curaçao, future rulings are any tax rulings within scope that are issued on or after 1 April 2017.

311. In the prior years' peer review reports, it was determined that Curaçao's undertakings to identify future rulings and all potential exchange jurisdictions have met all the ToR, except for completing the process of reviewing the templates to confirm that all future rulings identified are cross border rulings and therefore within the scope of the transparency framework, and to identify which category each ruling falls into (ToR I.4.1.2). Therefore, Curaçao was recommended to continue its work to complete its information-gathering process on future rulings as soon as possible.

312. Due to the Covid-19 pandemic, during the year in review, Curaçao was not able to fully continue its work on reviewing future rulings in order to identify all rulings within the scope of the transparency framework and assess the definitive number of rulings per category. As Curaçao completes the identification and categorisation process, they are also identifying the potential exchange jurisdictions. This process is still ongoing with respect to future rulings issued before July 2018, when a new procedure requiring future rulings and potential exchange jurisdictions to be immediately identified at the point of issue was put in place. This process will be completed by the end of March 2022. Therefore, the prior year recommendation remains.

313. Curaçao is also working on the development of an electronic online system to digitalise the ruling request process. This new electronic procedure is intended to further increase the speed and accuracy of the information gathering process in future. Curaçao noted that this electronic system is expected to be in place in 2023.

Review and supervision (ToR I.A.3)

314. In the prior years' peer review reports, it was determined that Curaçao's review and supervision mechanism was sufficient to meet the minimum standard. Curaçao's implementation in this regard remains unchanged, and therefore continues to meet the minimum standard.

Conclusion on section A

315. Curaçao has met all of the ToR for the information gathering process except for identifying rulings within the scope of the transparency framework and under which category of rulings they fall (ToR I.A.1). Curaçao is recommended to finalise its information gathering process for identifying all past and future rulings within the scope of the transparency framework as soon as possible.

B. The exchange of information (ToR II.B)

Legal basis for spontaneous exchange of information (ToR II.B.1, II.B.2)

316. Curaçao has the necessary domestic legal basis to exchange information spontaneously. Curaçao notes that there are no legal or practical impediments that prevent the spontaneous exchange of information on rulings as contemplated in the Action 5 minimum standard.

317. Curaçao has international agreements permitting spontaneous exchange of information, including being a jurisdiction participating in (i) the *Multilateral Convention on Mutual Administrative Assistance in Tax Matters: Amended by the 2010 Protocol* (OECD/Council of Europe, 2011[4]) ("the Convention") and (ii) bilateral agreements in force with two jurisdictions.[2]

Completion and exchange of templates (ToR II.B.3, II.B.4, II.B.5, II.B.6, II.B.7)

318. In the prior years' peer review reports, it was determined that Curaçao's process for the completion and exchange of templates met all the ToR, except for the timely exchange of information on past and future rulings (ToR II.5.6). Therefore, Curaçao was recommended to continue its work to continue its efforts to ensure all information on past and future rulings is exchanged as soon as possible.

319. During the year in review, Curaçao continued its work on exchanging information on past and future rulings as soon as they were identified, but experienced delays because of the Covid-19 pandemic. Curaçao still needs to identify which of the approximately 3 500 rulings issued from previous years, meet the conditions to be exchanged. This process is expected to be completed by the end of March 2022. In addition, no exchanges have taken place for any of the rulings issued in the year of review. Therefore, the prior year recommendation remains.

Conclusion on section B

320. Curaçao has met all of the ToR for the information gathering process except for completing exchanges of information on rulings in accordance with the timelines (ToR II.B.5 and II.B.6) and Curaçao is recommended to continue its efforts to ensure that all information on past and future rulings is exchanged as soon as possible.

C. Statistics (ToR IV)

321. As there was no information on rulings exchanged by Curaçao for the year in review, no statistics can be reported.

D. Matters related to intellectual property regimes (ToR I.A.1.3)

322. Curaçao offered an intellectual property regime (IP regime)[3] that was abolished from 30 June 2018 and not subject to the transparency requirements under the Action 5 Report (OECD, 2015[1]), because:

- ***New entrants benefitting from the grandfathered IP regime:*** the IP regimes has been abolished without grandfathering for taxpayers entering after the relevant date from which enhanced transparency obligations apply. As such, no enhanced transparency requirements apply.
- ***Third category of IP assets***: not applicable as the IP regime has been abolished.
- ***Taxpayers making use of the option to treat the nexus ratio as a rebuttable presumption***: not applicable as the IP regime has been abolished.

323. In addition, Curaçao offers two IP regimes[4] that are subject to the transparency requirements under the Action 5 Report (OECD, 2015[1]). It states that the identification of the benefitting taxpayers will occur as follows:

- ***New entrants benefitting from the grandfathered IP regime***: no enhanced transparency requirements apply, as explained in the prior year peer review.
- ***Third category of IP assets***: the regimes allow the third category of IP assets to qualify for the benefits. Therefore, enhanced transparency requirements apply and Curaçao has a process in place for the identification and exchange of information, as described in the prior year report. For the year in review, no taxpayers have applied to benefit from the third category of IP assets under both regimes, and therefore no information on these taxpayers needed to be exchanged.
- ***Taxpayers making use of the option to treat the nexus ratio as a rebuttable presumption***: not applicable as the regimes do not allow the nexus ratio to be treated as a rebuttable presumption.

Summary of recommendations on implementation of the transparency framework

Aspect of implementation of the transparency framework that should be improved	Recommendation for improvement
The information gathering process is still underway in Curaçao with respect to past and future rulings within the scope of the transparency framework and the classification of these rulings under each category.	Curaçao is recommended to finalise its information gathering process for identifying all past and future rulings within the scope of the transparency framework as soon as possible. This recommendation remains unchanged since the 2017, 2018 and 2019 peer review reports.
Curaçao experienced delays in exchanging information on past and future rulings.	Curaçao is recommended to continue its efforts to ensure that all information on past and future rulings is exchanged as soon as possible. This recommendation remains unchanged since the 2017, 2018 and 2019 peer review reports.

Jurisdiction's response and recent developments

324. Curaçao indicates that it is fully committed to ensure that all past rulings are being identified and exchanged. Therefore, the dedicated team will continue to identify the rulings, by going through the files manually and completing and exchanging the templates for the rulings in scope. Curaçao notes that it plans to have this work completed by March 2022.

References

OECD (2021), *BEPS Action 5 on Harmful Tax Practices - Terms of Reference and Methodology for the Conduct of the Peer Reviews of the Action 5 Transparency Framework*, OECD Publishing, Paris, http://www.oecd.org/tax/beps/beps-action-5-harmful-tax-practices-peer-review-transparency-framework.pdf. [3]

OECD (2015), *Countering Harmful Tax Practices More Effectively, Taking into Account Transparency and Substance, Action 5 - 2015 Final Report*, OECD/G20 Base Erosion and Profit Shifting Project, OECD Publishing, Paris, https://dx.doi.org/10.1787/9789264241190-en. [1]

OECD (ed.) (2017b), *Harmful Tax Practices - 2017 Progress Report on Preferential Regimes*, OECD Publishing, Paris, http://dx.doi.org/10.1787/9789264283954-en. [2]

OECD/Council of Europe (2011), *The Multilateral Convention on Mutual Administrative Assistance in Tax Matters: Amended by the 2010 Protocol*, OECD Publishing, Paris, https://dx.doi.org/10.1787/9789264115606-en. [4]

Notes

1 With respect to the following preferential regimes: 1) Export facility; 2) Tax exempt entity; 3) Free zone; and 4) Offshore regime. The offshore regime has been abolished in 2001 and is grandfathered for fiscal years preceding 30 June 2019.

2 Participating jurisdictions to the Convention are available here: www.oecd.org/tax/exchange-of-tax-information/convention-on-mutual-administrative-assistance-in-tax-matters.htm. Curaçao also has bilateral agreements with the Netherlands and Norway.

3 This regime is the Export facility.

4 These regimes are: 1) Curaçao investment company (formerly Tax exempt entity); and 2) Innovation box.

Czech Republic

The Czech Republic has met all aspects of the terms of reference (OECD, 2021[3]) (ToR) for the calendar year 2020 (year in review), except for the timely exchange of information on rulings (ToR II.B.6). The Czech Republic receives one recommendation on this point for the year in review.

In the prior year report, no recommendations were made. However, in the 2017 and 2018 peer reviews, the Czech Republic had received the same recommendation. As the issue has now recurred, the recommendation has been reinstated.

The Czech Republic can legally issue two types of rulings within the scope of the transparency framework.

In practice, the Czech Republic issued rulings within the scope of the transparency framework as follows:

Type of ruling	Number of rulings
Past rulings	48
Future rulings in the period 1 April 2016 – 31 December 2016	5
Future rulings in the calendar year 2017	11
Future rulings in the calendar year 2018	7
Future rulings in the calendar year 2019	19
Future rulings in the year in review	15

Peer input was received from one jurisdiction in respect of the exchanges of information on rulings received from the Czech Republic. The input was positive, noting that information was complete, in a correct format and received in a timely manner.

A. The information gathering process (ToR I.A)

325. The Czech Republic can legally issue the following two types of rulings within the scope of the transparency framework: (i) cross-border unilateral APAs and any other cross-border unilateral tax rulings (such as an advance tax ruling) covering transfer pricing or the application of transfer pricing principles and (ii) permanent establishment rulings.

326. For the Czech Republic, past rulings are any tax rulings within scope that are issued either: (i) on or after 1 January 2014 but before 1 April 2016; or (ii) on or after 1 January 2010 but before 1 January 2014, provided they were still in effect as at 1 January 2014. Future rulings are any tax rulings within scope that are issued on or after 1 April 2016.

327. In the prior years' peer review reports, it was determined that the Czech Republic's undertakings to identify past and future rulings and all potential exchange jurisdictions were sufficient to meet the minimum standard. In addition, it was determined that the Czech Republic's review and supervision mechanism was sufficient to meet the minimum standard. The Czech Republic's implementation remains unchanged, and therefore continues to meet the minimum standard.

328. The Czech Republic has met all of the ToR for the information gathering process and no recommendations are made.

B. The exchange of information (ToR II.B)

Legal basis for spontaneous exchange of information (ToR II.B.1, II.B.2)

329. The Czech Republic has the necessary domestic legal basis to exchange information spontaneously. The Czech Republic notes that there are no legal or practical impediments that prevent the spontaneous exchange of information on rulings as contemplated in the Action 5 minimum standard.

330. The Czech Republic has international agreements permitting spontaneous exchange of information, including being a party to (i) the *Multilateral Convention on Mutual Administrative Assistance in Tax* Matters*: Amended by the 2010 Protocol* (OECD/Council of Europe, 2011[4]) ("the Convention"), (ii) the Directive 2011/16/EU with all other European Union Member States and (iii) bilateral agreements in force with 92 jurisdictions.[1]

Completion and exchange of templates (ToR II.B.3, II.B.4, II.B.5, II.B.6, II.B.7)

331. In the prior years' peer review reports, it was determined that the Czech Republic's process for the completion and exchange of templates were sufficient to meet the minimum standard. With respect to past rulings, no further action was required. The Czech Republic continues to apply the European Union (EU) timelines for the exchange of information on future rulings (EU Directive 2011/16/EU), i.e. exchanges of information on future rulings are carried out within three months after the end of the calendar half-year in which these rulings were issued, regardless of whether the exchange is transmitted to EU Member States or other jurisdictions. Despite the best efforts to meet the FHTP timelines (and to therefore exchange faster than the domestic legislation and EU Directive would require), during the year in review the Czech Republic experienced delays in the exchange of information on future rulings and as a consequence, exchanges were performed later than three months after the tax ruling became available to the competent authority. The Czech Republic noted that this delay was also a result of the limited activities carried out by the Czech Tax Authorities due to the COVID-19 pandemic. The issue will be reviewed again in the subsequent year's peer review to monitor whether the Czech Republic meets the FHTP timelines despite the obligation to comply with the EU Directive.

332. For the year in review, the timeliness of exchanges is as follows:

Future rulings within the scope of the transparency framework	Number of exchanges transmitted within three months of the information becoming available to the competent authority or immediately after legal impediments have been lifted	Delayed exchanges		
		Number of exchanges transmitted later than three months of the information on rulings becoming available to the competent authority	Reasons for the delays	Any other comments
	0	30	Application of the EU DAC3 timelines and constraints due to the COVID-19 pandemic	N/A

Follow up requests received for exchange of the ruling	Number	Average time to provide response	Number of requests not answered
	0	N/A	N/A

Conclusion on section B

333. The Czech Republic has met all of the ToR for the exchange of information process except for ensuring that the information to be exchanged is transmitted to the relevant jurisdictions in accordance with the agreed timelines. The Czech Republic is recommended to ensure that all information on future rulings is exchanged as soon as possible (ToR II.B.6).

C. Statistics (ToR IV)

334. The statistics for the year in review are as follows:

Category of ruling	Number of exchanges	Jurisdictions exchanged with
Cross-border unilateral APAs and any other cross-border unilateral tax rulings (such as an advance tax ruling) covering transfer pricing or the application of transfer pricing principles	24	Albania, Belgium, Bosnia and Herzegovina, France, Germany, Hungary, Italy, Liechtenstein, Luxembourg, Morocco, North Macedonia, Romania, Serbia, Slovak Republic, Spain, Switzerland, United Kingdom
Permanent establishment rulings	6	Belgium, Germany, Japan, Malta, Mauritius
Total	30	

D. Matters related to intellectual property regimes (ToR I.A.1.3)

335. Czech Republic does not offer an intellectual property regime for which transparency requirements under the Action 5 Report (OECD, 2015[1]) were imposed.

Summary of recommendations on implementation of the transparency framework

Aspect of implementation of the transparency framework that should be improved	Recommendation for improvement
The Czech Republic experienced delays in the exchange of information on future rulings due to the application of the timelines set out in the EU Directive 2011/16/EU.	The Czech Republic is recommended to ensure that all information on future rulings is exchanged as soon as possible. The Czech Republic also received a recommendation on timely exchange of information on rulings in the 2017 and 2018 peer review reports.

References

OECD (2021), *BEPS Action 5 on Harmful Tax Practices - Terms of Reference and Methodology for the Conduct of the Peer Reviews of the Action 5 Transparency Framework*, OECD Publishing, Paris, http://www.oecd.org/tax/beps/beps-action-5-harmful-tax-practices-peer-review-transparency-framework.pdf. [3]

OECD (2015), *Countering Harmful Tax Practices More Effectively, Taking into Account Transparency and Substance, Action 5 - 2015 Final Report*, OECD/G20 Base Erosion and Profit Shifting Project, OECD Publishing, Paris, https://dx.doi.org/10.1787/9789264241190-en. [1]

OECD (ed.) (2017b), *Harmful Tax Practices - 2017 Progress Report on Preferential Regimes*, OECD Publishing, Paris, http://dx.doi.org/10.1787/9789264283954-en. [2]

OECD/Council of Europe (2011), *The Multilateral Convention on Mutual Administrative Assistance in Tax Matters: Amended by the 2010 Protocol*, OECD Publishing, Paris, https://dx.doi.org/10.1787/9789264115606-en. [4]

Notes

[1] Participating jurisdictions to the Convention are available here: www.oecd.org/tax/exchange-of-tax-information/convention-on-mutual-administrative-assistance-in-tax-matters.htm. The Czech Republic also has bilateral agreements with Albania, Azerbaijan, Armenia, Australia, Austria, Bahrain, Barbados, Belarus, Belgium, Bosnia and Herzegovina, Botswana, Brazil, Bulgaria, Canada, Chile, China (People's Republic of), Colombia, Croatia, Cyprus, Democratic People's Republic of Korea, Denmark, Egypt, Estonia, Ethiopia, Finland, France, Georgia, Germany, Ghana, Greece, Hong Kong (China), Hungary, Iceland, India, Indonesia, Iran, Ireland, Israel, Italy, Japan, Jordan, Kazakhstan, Korea, Kuwait, Kyrgyzstan, Latvia, Lebanon, Liechtenstein, Lithuania, Luxembourg, Malaysia, Malta, Mexico, Moldovia, Mongolia, Montenegro, Morocco, Netherlands, New Zealand, Nigeria, North Macedonia, Norway, Pakistan, Panama, Philippines, Poland, Portugal, Romania, Russia, Saudi Arabia, Serbia, Singapore, Slovak Republic, Slovenia, South Africa, Spain, Sri Lanka, Sweden, Switzerland, Syrian Arab Republic, Tajikistan, Thailand, Tunisia, Turkey, Turkmenistan, Ukraine, United Arab Emirates, United Kingdom, United States, Uzbekistan, Venezuela and Viet Nam.

Democratic Republic of Congo[1]

The Democratic Republic of the Congo did not provide a completed peer review questionnaire to the Secretariat. It is not known whether the Democratic Republic of the Congo has implemented the transparency framework in line with the terms of reference (OECD, 2021[3]) (ToR) for the calendar year 2020 (year in review). The Democratic Republic of the Congo receives two recommendations covering the information gathering process (ToR I.A) and exchange of information (ToR II.B) for the year in review.

In the prior year report, as well as in the 2017 and 2018 peer reviews, it was established that the Democratic Republic of the Congo does not issue any type of rulings within the scope of the transparency framework in practice.

For the year in review, it is not known whether the Democratic Republic of the Congo put in place the administrative process or developed the administrative capacity to issue such rulings.

In practice, the Democratic Republic of the Congo did not issue any type of rulings within the scope of the transparency framework in previous years. For the year in review, it is not known whether the Democratic Republic of the Congo issued any such rulings.

No peer input was received in respect of the exchanges of information on rulings received from the Democratic Republic of the Congo.

A. The information gathering process (ToR I.A)

336. In previous years, the Democratic Republic of the Congo indicated that it does not issue any type of rulings within the scope of the transparency framework. Theoretically, there was no impediment for the Democratic Republic of the Congo to issue rulings, but in practice Democratic Republic of the Congo did not issue any rulings.

337. For the year in review, it is not known whether the Democratic Republic of the Congo put in place the administrative process or developed the administrative capacity to issue such rulings.

Past rulings (ToR I.A.1.1, I.A.1.2, I.A.2.1, I.A.2.2)

338. For the Democratic Republic of the Congo, past rulings are any tax rulings within scope that are issued either (i) on or after 1 January 2015 but before 1 April 2017; and (ii) on or after 1 January 2012 but before 1 January 2015, provided they were still in effect as at 1 January 2015.

339. In the prior years' peer review reports, it was determined that the Democratic Republic of the Congo did not issue rulings in scope of the transparency framework. As such, no past rulings have been issued and this section is not assessed.

Future rulings (ToR I.A.1.1, I.A.1.2, I.A.2.1)

340. For the Democratic Republic of the Congo, future rulings are any tax rulings within scope that are issued on or after 1 April 2017.

341. In prior years' peer review reports, it was established that the Democratic Republic of the Congo met all aspects of the ToR that can be met in the absence of rulings being issued.

342. For the year in review, as it is not known whether the Democratic Republic of the Congo can issue rulings in practice, the Democratic Republic of the Congo is recommended to put in place an information gathering process for future rulings as soon as possible.

Review and supervision (ToR I.A.3)

343. In prior years' peer review reports, it was established that the Democratic Republic of the Congo met all aspects of the ToR that can be met in the absence of rulings being issued.

344. For the year in review, as it is not known whether the Democratic Republic of the Congo can issue rulings in practice, the Democratic Republic of the Congo is recommended to put in place a review and supervision mechanism as soon as possible.

Conclusion on section A

345. The Democratic Republic of the Congo is recommended to put in place an information gathering process, with a review and supervision mechanism, as soon as possible (ToR I.A).

B. The exchange of information (ToR II.B)

Legal basis for spontaneous exchange of information (ToR II.B.1, II.B.2)

346. It is not known whether the Democratic Republic of the Congo has the necessary domestic legal basis to exchange information spontaneously. The Democratic Republic of the Congo is not a party to the *Multilateral Convention on Mutual Administrative Assistance in Tax Matters: Amended by the 2010*

Protocol (OECD/Council of Europe, 2011[4]) ("the Convention"). The Democratic Republic of the Congo is encouraged to continue its efforts to expand its international exchange of information instruments to be able to exchange information on rulings. It is noted, however, that jurisdictions are assessed on their compliance with the transparency framework in respect of the exchange of information network in effect for the year of the particular annual review.

Completion and exchange of templates (ToR II.B.3, II.B.4, II.B.5, II.B.6, II.B.7)

347. In prior years' peer review reports, it was established that the Democratic Republic of the Congo met all aspects of the ToR that can be met in the absence of rulings being issued.

348. For the year in review, as it is not known whether the Democratic Republic of the Congo can issue rulings in practice, the Democratic Republic of the Congo is recommended to put in place a process to complete the templates for all relevant rulings and to ensure that the exchanges of information on rulings occur as soon as possible.

349. As it is not known whether exchanges took place in the year of review, no data on the timeliness of exchanges can be reported.

Conclusion on section B

350. The Democratic Republic of the Congo is recommended to put in place a domestic legal framework allowing spontaneous exchange of information on rulings and to put in place a process to complete the templates for all relevant rulings and to ensure that the exchanges of information on rulings occur as soon as possible (ToR II.B).

C. Statistics (ToR IV)

351. As the Secretariat is not aware whether information on rulings was exchanged by the Democratic Republic of the Congo for the year in review, no statistics can be reported.

D. Matters related to intellectual property regimes (ToR I.A.1.3)

352. The Democratic Republic of the Congo does not offer an intellectual property regime for which transparency requirements under the Action 5 Report (OECD, 2015[1]) were imposed.

Summary of recommendations on implementation of the transparency framework

Aspect of implementation of the transparency framework that should be improved	Recommendation for improvement
It is not known whether the Democratic Republic of the Congo has put in place the necessary information and gathering process.	The Democratic Republic of the Congo is recommended to finalise its information gathering process, with a review and supervision mechanism, as soon as possible.
It is not known whether the Democratic Republic of the Congo has put in place an effective compulsory spontaneous exchange of information on the tax rulings within the scope of the transparency framework.	The Democratic Republic of the Congo is recommended to continue to put in place a domestic legal framework allowing spontaneous exchange of information on rulings and to continue its efforts to complete the templates for all relevant rulings and to ensure that the exchanges of information on rulings occur as soon as possible.

References

OECD (2021), *BEPS Action 5 on Harmful Tax Practices - Terms of Reference and Methodology for the Conduct of the Peer Reviews of the Action 5 Transparency Framework*, OECD Publishing, Paris, http://www.oecd.org/tax/beps/beps-action-5-harmful-tax-practices-peer-review-transparency-framework.pdf. [3]

OECD (2015), *Countering Harmful Tax Practices More Effectively, Taking into Account Transparency and Substance, Action 5 - 2015 Final Report*, OECD/G20 Base Erosion and Profit Shifting Project, OECD Publishing, Paris, https://dx.doi.org/10.1787/9789264241190-en. [1]

OECD (ed.) (2017b), *Harmful Tax Practices - 2017 Progress Report on Preferential Regimes*, OECD Publishing, Paris, http://dx.doi.org/10.1787/9789264283954-en. [2]

OECD/Council of Europe (2011), *The Multilateral Convention on Mutual Administrative Assistance in Tax Matters: Amended by the 2010 Protocol*, OECD Publishing, Paris, https://dx.doi.org/10.1787/9789264115606-en. [4]

Notes

[1] Democratic Republic of Congo was not yet in a position to provide written comments on the draft report.

Denmark

Denmark has met all aspects of the terms of reference (OECD, 2021[3]) (ToR) for the calendar year 2020 (year in review), and no recommendations are made.

Denmark can legally issue five types of rulings within the scope of the transparency framework.

In practice, Denmark issued rulings within the scope of the transparency framework as follows:

Type of ruling	Number of rulings
Past rulings	43
Future rulings in the period 1 April 2016 – 31 December 2016	7
Future rulings in the calendar year 2017	17
Future rulings in the calendar year 2018	13
Future rulings in the calendar year 2019	14
Future rulings in the year in review	9

No peer input was received in respect of the exchanges of information on rulings received from Denmark.

A. The information gathering process (ToR I.A)

353. Denmark can legally issue the following five types of rulings within the scope of the transparency framework: (i) preferential regimes;[1] (ii) cross-border unilateral APAs and any other cross-border unilateral tax rulings (such as an advance tax ruling) covering transfer pricing or the application of transfer pricing principles; (iii) rulings providing for unilateral downward adjustments; (iv) permanent establishment rulings; and (v) related party conduit rulings.

354. For Denmark, past rulings are any tax rulings within scope that are issued either: (i) on or after 1 January 2014 but before 1 April 2016; or (ii) on or after 1 January 2010 but before 1 January 2014, provided they were still in effect as at 1 January 2014. Future rulings are any tax rulings within scope that are issued on or after 1 April 2016.

355. In the prior years' peer review reports, it was determined that Denmark's undertakings to identify past and future rulings and all potential exchange jurisdictions were sufficient to meet the minimum standard. In addition, it was determined that Denmark's review and supervision mechanism was sufficient to meet the minimum standard. Denmark's implementation remains unchanged, and therefore continues to meet the minimum standard.

356. Denmark has met all of the ToR for the information gathering process and no recommendations are made.

B. The exchange of information (ToR II.B)

357. Denmark has international agreements permitting spontaneous exchange of information, including being a party to (i) the *Multilateral Convention on Mutual Administrative Assistance in Tax Matters: Amended by the 2010 Protocol* (OECD/Council of Europe, 2011[4]) ("the Convention"), (ii) the Directive 2011/16/EU with all other European Union Member States and (iii) bilateral agreements in force with 71 jurisdictions.[2]

358. For the year in review, the timeliness of exchanges is as follows:

Future rulings within the scope of the transparency framework	Number of exchanges transmitted within three months of the information becoming available to the competent authority or immediately after legal impediments have been lifted	Delayed exchanges		
		Number of exchanges transmitted later than three months of the information on rulings becoming available to the competent authority	Reasons for the delays	Any other comments
	9	0	N/A	N/A

Follow up requests received for exchange of the ruling	Number	Average time to provide response	Number of requests not answered
	0	N/A	N/A

359. In the prior years' peer review reports, it was determined that Denmark's process for the completion and exchange of templates were sufficient to meet the minimum standard. With respect to past rulings, no further action was required. Denmark's implementation in this regard remains unchanged and therefore continues to meet the minimum standard.

360. Denmark has the necessary legal basis for spontaneous exchange of information, a process for completing the templates in a timely way and has completed all exchanges. Denmark has met all of the ToR for the exchange of information process and no recommendations are made.

C. Statistics (ToR IV)

361. The statistics for the year in review are as follows:

Category of ruling	Number of exchanges	Jurisdictions exchanged with
Ruling related to a preferential regime	0	N/A
Cross-border unilateral APAs and any other cross-border unilateral tax rulings (such as an advance tax ruling) covering transfer pricing or the application of transfer pricing principles	0	N/A
Cross-border rulings providing for a unilateral downward adjustment to the taxpayer's taxable profits that is not directly reflected in the taxpayer's financial / commercial accounts	0	N/A
Permanent establishment rulings	8	Germany, Ireland, Norway, Thailand, United Kingdom, United States
Related party conduit rulings	1	*De minimis* rule applies
Total	9	

D. Matters related to intellectual property regimes (ToR I.A.1.3)

362. Denmark does not offer an intellectual property regime for which transparency requirements under the Action 5 Report (OECD, 2015[1]) were imposed.

Summary of recommendations on implementation of the transparency framework

Aspect of implementation of the transparency framework that should be improved	Recommendation for improvement
	No recommendations are made.

References

OECD (2021), *BEPS Action 5 on Harmful Tax Practices - Terms of Reference and Methodology for the Conduct of the Peer Reviews of the Action 5 Transparency Framework*, OECD Publishing, Paris, http://www.oecd.org/tax/beps/beps-action-5-harmful-tax-practices-peer-review-transparency-framework.pdf. [3]

OECD (2015), *Countering Harmful Tax Practices More Effectively, Taking into Account Transparency and Substance, Action 5 - 2015 Final Report*, OECD/G20 Base Erosion and Profit Shifting Project, OECD Publishing, Paris, https://dx.doi.org/10.1787/9789264241190-en. [1]

OECD (ed.) (2017b), *Harmful Tax Practices - 2017 Progress Report on Preferential Regimes*, OECD Publishing, Paris, http://dx.doi.org/10.1787/9789264283954-en. [2]

OECD/Council of Europe (2011), *The Multilateral Convention on Mutual Administrative Assistance in Tax Matters: Amended by the 2010 Protocol*, OECD Publishing, Paris, https://dx.doi.org/10.1787/9789264115606-en. [4]

Notes

[1] With respect to the following preferential regime: tonnage tax.

[2] Participating jurisdictions to the Convention are available here: www.oecd.org/tax/exchange-of-tax-information/convention-on-mutual-administrative-assistance-in-tax-matters.htm. Denmark also has bilateral agreements with Argentina, Armenia, Aruba, Australia, Austria, Azerbaijan, Bangladesh, Belarus, Belgium, Brazil, Bulgaria, Canada, Chile, China (People's Republic of), Croatia, Cyprus, Czech Republic, Egypt, Estonia, Georgia, Germany, Ghana, Greece, Hungary, India, Indonesia, Ireland, Israel, Italy, Jamaica, Japan, Kenya, Korea, Kuwait, Latvia, Lithuania, Luxembourg, Malaysia, Malta, Mexico, Montenegro, Morocco, Netherlands, New Zealand, Pakistan, Philippines, Poland, Portugal, North Macedonia, Romania, Russia, Serbia, Singapore, Slovak Republic, Slovenia, South Africa, Sri Lanka, Switzerland, Chinese Taipei, Tanzania, Thailand, Trinidad and Tobago, Tunisia, Turkey, Uganda, Ukraine, United Kingdom, United States, Venezuela, Viet Nam and Zambia.

Dominican Republic

The Dominican Republic has met all aspects of the terms of reference (OECD, 2021[3]) (ToR) for the calendar year 2020 (year in review), except the timely exchange of information on rulings (ToR II.B). The Dominican Republic receives one recommendation on this point for the year in review.

In the prior year report, the Dominican Republic had received the same recommendation. As it has not been addressed, the recommendation remains in place.

The Dominican Republic can legally issue five types of rulings within the scope of the transparency framework.

In practice, the Dominican Republic issued rulings within the scope of the transparency framework as follows:

Type of ruling	Number of rulings
Future rulings in the period 1 March 2019 – 31 December 2019	23
Future rulings in the year in review	57

Peer input was received from two jurisdictions in respect of the exchanges of information on rulings received from the Dominican Republic. The input was generally positive, noting that overall information was complete, in a correct format and almost all received in a timely manner. However, one peer indicated that exchanges on rulings were not timely.

A. The information gathering process (ToR I.A)

363. The Dominican Republic can legally issue the following five types of rulings within the scope of the transparency framework: (i) preferential regimes;[1] (ii) cross-border unilateral APAs and any other cross-border unilateral tax rulings (such as an advance tax ruling) covering transfer pricing or the application of transfer pricing principles; (iii) rulings providing for unilateral downward adjustments; (iv) permanent establishment rulings; and (v) related party conduit rulings.

364. For the Dominican Republic, past rulings are any tax rulings within scope that are issued prior to 1 March 2019. However, there is no obligation for the Dominican Republic to conduct spontaneous exchange information on past rulings. Future rulings are any tax rulings within scope that are issued on or after 1 March 2019.

365. In the prior years' peer review reports, it was determined that the Dominican Republic's undertakings to identify past and future rulings and all potential exchange jurisdictions were sufficient to meet the minimum standard. In addition, it was determined that the Dominican Republic's review and supervision mechanism was sufficient to meet the minimum standard. The Dominican Republic's implementation remains unchanged, and therefore continues to meet the minimum standard.

366. The Dominican Republic has met all of the ToR for the information gathering process and no recommendations are made.

B. The exchange of information (ToR II.B)

Legal basis for spontaneous exchange of information (ToR II.B.1, II.B.2)

367. The Dominican Republic has the necessary domestic legal basis to exchange information spontaneously. The Dominican Republic notes that there are no legal or practical impediments that prevent the spontaneous exchange of information on rulings as contemplated in the Action 5 minimum standard.

368. The Dominican Republic has international agreements permitting spontaneous exchange of information, including being a party to (i) the *Multilateral Convention on Mutual Administrative Assistance in Tax Matters: Amended by the 2010 Protocol* (OECD/Council of Europe, 2011[4]) ("the Convention") and (ii) bilateral agreements in force with three jurisdictions.[2]

Completion and exchange of templates (ToR II.B.3, II.B.4, II.B.5, II.B.6, II.B.7)

369. In the prior year peer review report, it was determined that the Dominican Republic's process for the completion and exchange of templates met all the ToR, except for the timely exchange of information on rulings (ToR II.B). During the year in review, the Dominican Republic still experienced delays for the exchange of information on rulings, which was also related to the fact that the relevant officials needed to telework because of the Covid-19 pandemic. The Dominican Republic is recommended to ensure that the exchanges of information on rulings occur as soon as possible.

370. For the year in review, the timeliness of exchanges is as follows:

Future rulings within the scope of the transparency framework	Number of exchanges transmitted within three months of the information becoming available to the competent authority or immediately after legal impediments have been lifted	Delayed exchanges		
		Number of exchanges transmitted later than three months of the information on rulings becoming available to the competent authority	Reasons for the delays	Any other comments
	0	100	See previous paragraph.	N/A

Follow up requests received for exchange of the ruling	Number	Average time to provide response	Number of requests not answered
	0	N/A	N/A

Conclusion on section B

371. The Dominican Republic has met all of the ToR for the exchange of information process except for the timely exchange of information on rulings (ToR II.B) and the Dominican Republic is recommended to ensure that the exchanges of information on rulings occur as soon as possible.

C. Statistics (ToR IV)

372. The statistics for the year in review are as follows:

Category of ruling	Number of exchanges	Jurisdictions exchanged with
Ruling related to a preferential regime	0	N/A
Cross-border unilateral APAs and any other cross-border unilateral tax rulings (such as an advance tax ruling) covering transfer pricing or the application of transfer pricing principles	100	Barbados, Canada, Costa Rica, Curaçao, France, Ireland, Luxembourg, Mexico, Netherlands, Panama, Saint Kitts and Nevis, Spain, Switzerland, United States
Cross-border rulings providing for a unilateral downward adjustment to the taxpayer's taxable profits that is not directly reflected in the taxpayer's financial / commercial accounts	0	N/A
Permanent establishment rulings	0	N/A
Related party conduit rulings	0	N/A
Total	100	

D. Matters related to intellectual property regimes (ToR I.A.1.3)

373. The Dominican Republic does not offer an intellectual property regime for which transparency requirements under the Action 5 Report (OECD, 2015[1]) were imposed.

Summary of recommendations on implementation of the transparency framework

Aspect of implementation of the transparency framework that should be improved	Recommendation for improvement
The Dominican Republic is still in the process of ensuring the timely exchange of information on rulings.	The Dominican Republic is recommended to ensure that the exchanges of information on rulings occur as soon as possible. This recommendation remains unchanged since the 2019 peer review report.

References

OECD (2021), *BEPS Action 5 on Harmful Tax Practices - Terms of Reference and Methodology for the Conduct of the Peer Reviews of the Action 5 Transparency Framework*, OECD Publishing, Paris, http://www.oecd.org/tax/beps/beps-action-5-harmful-tax-practices-peer-review-transparency-framework.pdf. [3]

OECD (2015), *Countering Harmful Tax Practices More Effectively, Taking into Account Transparency and Substance, Action 5 - 2015 Final Report*, OECD/G20 Base Erosion and Profit Shifting Project, OECD Publishing, Paris, https://dx.doi.org/10.1787/9789264241190-en. [1]

OECD (ed.) (2017b), *Harmful Tax Practices - 2017 Progress Report on Preferential Regimes*, OECD Publishing, Paris, http://dx.doi.org/10.1787/9789264283954-en. [2]

OECD/Council of Europe (2011), *The Multilateral Convention on Mutual Administrative Assistance in Tax Matters: Amended by the 2010 Protocol*, OECD Publishing, Paris, https://dx.doi.org/10.1787/9789264115606-en. [4]

Notes

[1] These regimes are: i) Border development and ii) Logistics centres. It should be noted that FHTP has not yet concluded if these regimes are in scope. If the FHTP decides that these regimes are out of scope for the FHTP, then exchange of information on rulings with respect to these regimes would no longer be required under the Action 5 transparency framework. However, until then, the Dominican Republic has committed to do the spontaneous exchange of information on rulings related to these regimes.

[2] Participating jurisdictions to the Convention are available here: www.oecd.org/tax/exchange-of-tax-information/convention-on-mutual-administrative-assistance-in-tax-matters.htm. The Dominican Republic also has bilateral agreements with Canada, Spain and United States.

Egypt

Egypt is taking steps to implement the legal basis for exchange of information under the transparency framework, and has commenced administrative preparations to ensure that information on rulings will be exchanged. Egypt has met all aspects of the terms of reference (OECD, 2021[3]) (ToR) for the calendar year 2020 (year in review), except for identifying all potential exchange jurisdictions for both past and future rulings (ToR I.A.2.1 and ToR I.A.2.2), having in place a review and supervision mechanism (ToR I.A.3) and having in place a process to ensure the timely exchange of information on rulings in the form required by the transparency framework (ToR II.B). Egypt receives two recommendations on these points for the year in review.

In the prior year report, as well as in the 2018 peer review, Egypt had received the same recommendations. As they have not been addressed, the recommendations remain in place.

Egypt can legally issue three types of rulings within the scope of the transparency framework.

In practice, Egypt issued rulings within the scope of the transparency framework as follows:

Type of ruling	Number of rulings
Past rulings	31
Future rulings in the period 1 April 2018 – 31 December 2018	3
Future rulings in the calendar year 2019	11
Future rulings in the year in review	2

As no exchanges took place, no peer input was received in respect of the exchanges of information on rulings received from Egypt.

A. The information gathering process (ToR I.A)

374. Egypt can legally issue the following three types of rulings within the scope of the transparency framework: (i) cross-border unilateral APAs and any other cross-border unilateral tax rulings (such as an advance tax ruling) covering transfer pricing or the application of transfer pricing principles; (ii) permanent establishment rulings; and (iii) related party conduit rulings.

Past rulings (ToR I.A.1.1, I.A.1.2, I.A.2.1, I.A.2.2)

375. For Egypt, past rulings are any tax rulings within scope that are issued either (i) on or after 1 January 2016 but before 1 April 2018; and (ii) on or after 1 January 2014 but before 1 January 2016, provided still in effect as at 1 January 2016.

376. In the prior year peer review report, it was determined that Egypt's undertakings to identify past rulings and all potential exchange jurisdictions have met all the ToR, except for identifying all potential exchange jurisdictions for past rulings (ToR I.A.2.2). Therefore, Egypt was recommended to apply the "best efforts approach" to identify potential exchange jurisdictions for past rulings.

377. During the year in review, Egypt has not yet identified the potential exchange jurisdictions for all past rulings, and therefore the recommendation remains in place.

Future rulings (ToR I.A.1.1, I.A.1.2, I.A.2.1)

378. For Egypt, future rulings are any tax rulings within scope that are issued on or after 1 April 2018.

379. In the prior year peer review report, Egypt's process to identify rulings within the scope of the transparency framework was described, and in addition its process for identifying potential exchange jurisdictions for APAs. However, it was also noted that Egypt did not yet have a process in place for the identification of potential exchange jurisdictions for future rulings other than APAs. Therefore, it was determined that Egypt's undertakings to identify future rulings and all potential exchange jurisdictions have met all the ToR, except for identifying all potential exchange jurisdictions for future rulings other than APAs (ToR I.A.2.1). Egypt was recommended to ensure that all potential exchange jurisdictions are identified swiftly for all future rulings other than APAs.

380. During the year in review, Egypt has not yet put in place a process to identify the potential exchange jurisdictions for all future rulings other than APAs, and therefore the recommendation remains in place.

Review and supervision (ToR I.A.3)

381. Egypt does not yet have in place a review and supervision mechanism for the identification of rulings and potential exchange jurisdictions (ToR I.A.3), and therefore the recommendation remains in place.

382. As noted in the prior year peer review report, Egypt envisages that supervision on the identification of rulings and potential exchange jurisdictions will take place by the managers of the relevant departments. Egypt also intends to issue internal guidance for staff on the identification process.

Conclusion on section A

383. Egypt has met the ToR for the information gathering process except for identifying all potential exchange jurisdictions for past and future rulings (ToR I.A.2.1 and ToR I.A.2.2) and having in place a review and supervision mechanism (ToR I.A.3). Egypt is recommended to continue its efforts to identify all

potential exchange jurisdictions for both past and future rulings and to implement a review and supervision mechanism, as soon as possible.

B. The exchange of information (ToR II.B)

Legal basis for spontaneous exchange of information (ToR II.B.1, II.B.2)

384. Egypt has the necessary domestic legal basis to exchange information spontaneously. Egypt notes that there are no legal or practical impediments that prevent the spontaneous exchange of information on rulings as contemplated in the Action 5 minimum standard.

385. Egypt has international agreements permitting spontaneous exchange of information, including bilateral agreements in force with 58 jurisdictions.[1] Egypt is not a party to the *Multilateral Convention on Mutual Administrative Assistance in Tax Matters: Amended by the 2010 Protocol* (OECD/Council of Europe, 2011[4]) ("the Convention"). Egypt is encouraged to continue its efforts to expand its international exchange of information instruments to be able to exchange information on tax rulings. It is noted, however, that jurisdictions are assessed on their compliance with the transparency framework in respect of the exchange of information network in effect for the year of the particular annual review

Completion and exchange of templates (ToR II.B.3, II.B.4, II.B.5, II.B.6, II.B.7)

386. In the prior year peer review report, it was determined that Egypt did not have a process for the completion and exchange of templates. Therefore, Egypt was recommended to develop a process to complete the templates on relevant rulings and to ensure that the exchanges of information on rulings occur in accordance with the form and timelines under the transparency framework (ToR II.B). As no action has been undertaken on this aspect during the year in review, the recommendation remains in place.

387. During the year in review, no exchanges took place and therefore no data on the timeliness of exchanges is reported.

Conclusion on section B

388. Egypt has the necessary legal basis for spontaneous exchange of information, a process for completing the templates in a timely way and has completed all exchanges. Egypt is recommended to swiftly implement its process to complete the templates on relevant rulings and to ensure that the exchanges of information on rulings occur in accordance with the form and timelines under the transparency framework (ToR II.B).

C. Statistics (ToR IV)

389. As there was no information on rulings exchanged by Egypt for the year in review, no statistics can be reported.

D. Matters related to intellectual property regimes (ToR I.A.1.3)

390. Egypt does not offer an intellectual property regime for which transparency requirements under the Action 5 Report (OECD, 2015[1]) were imposed.

Summary of recommendations on implementation of the transparency framework

Aspect of implementation of the transparency framework that should be improved	Recommendation for improvement
Egypt has not yet identified all potential exchange jurisdictions for both past and future rulings and does not have a review and supervision mechanism in place to ensure that all relevant information on the identification of rulings and potential exchange jurisdictions is captured adequately.	Egypt is recommended to continue its efforts to identify all potential exchange jurisdictions for both past and future rulings and to implement a review and supervision mechanism, as soon as possible. This recommendation remains unchanged since the 2018 and 2019 review reports.
Egypt does not have in place a process to ensure the timely exchange of information on rulings in the form required by the transparency framework.	Egypt is recommended to develop a process to complete the templates on relevant rulings and to ensure that the exchanges of information on rulings occur in accordance with the form and timelines under the transparency framework. This recommendation remains unchanged since the 2018 and 2019 peer review reports.

References

OECD (2021), *BEPS Action 5 on Harmful Tax Practices - Terms of Reference and Methodology for the Conduct of the Peer Reviews of the Action 5 Transparency Framework*, OECD Publishing, Paris, http://www.oecd.org/tax/beps/beps-action-5-harmful-tax-practices-peer-review-transparency-framework.pdf. [3]

OECD (2015), *Countering Harmful Tax Practices More Effectively, Taking into Account Transparency and Substance, Action 5 - 2015 Final Report*, OECD/G20 Base Erosion and Profit Shifting Project, OECD Publishing, Paris, https://dx.doi.org/10.1787/9789264241190-en. [1]

OECD (ed.) (2017b), *Harmful Tax Practices - 2017 Progress Report on Preferential Regimes*, OECD Publishing, Paris, http://dx.doi.org/10.1787/9789264283954-en. [2]

OECD/Council of Europe (2011), *The Multilateral Convention on Mutual Administrative Assistance in Tax Matters: Amended by the 2010 Protocol*, OECD Publishing, Paris, https://dx.doi.org/10.1787/9789264115606-en. [4]

Notes

[1] Albania, Algeria, Austria, Bahrain, Belarus, Belgium, Bulgaria, Canada, China (People's Republic of), Cyprus, Czech Republic, Denmark, Ethiopia, Finland, France, Georgia, Germany, Greece, Hungary, India, Indonesia, Iraq, Ireland, Italy, Japan, Jordan, Korea, Kuwait, Lebanon, Libya, Malaysia, Malta, Mauritius, Morocco, Netherlands, Norway, Pakistan, Palestinian Authority, Poland, Romania, Russia, Saudi Arabia, Serbia, Singapore, Spain, South Africa, Sudan, Sweden, Syrian Arab Republic, Tunisia, Turkey, Ukraine, United Arab Emirates, United Kingdom, United States, Uzbekistan and Yemen. Egypt also has an agreement with the Council of Arab Economic Unity permitting spontaneous exchange of information.

Estonia

Estonia has met all aspects of the terms of reference (OECD, 2021[3]) (ToR) for the calendar year 2020 (year in review), and no recommendations are made.

Estonia can legally issue two types of rulings within the scope of the transparency framework.

In practice, Estonia issued rulings within the scope of the transparency framework as follows:

Type of ruling	Number of rulings
Past rulings	20
Future rulings in the period 1 April 2016 – 31 December 2016	8
Future rulings in the calendar year 2017	11
Future rulings in the calendar year 2018	9
Future rulings in the calendar year 2019	9
Future rulings in the year in review	7

No peer input was received in respect of the exchanges of information on rulings received from Estonia.

A. The information gathering process (ToR I.A)

391. Estonia can legally issue the following two types of rulings within the scope of the transparency framework: (i) permanent establishment rulings and (ii) related party conduit rulings.

392. For Estonia, past rulings are any tax rulings within scope that are issued either: (i) on or after 1 January 2014 but before 1 April 2016; or (ii) on or after 1 January 2010 but before 1 January 2014, provided they were still in effect as at 1 January 2014. Future rulings are any tax rulings within scope that are issued on or after 1 April 2016.

393. In the prior years' peer review reports, it was determined that Estonia's undertakings to identify past and future rulings and all potential exchange jurisdictions were sufficient to meet the minimum standard. In addition, it was determined that Estonia's review and supervision mechanism was sufficient to meet the minimum standard. Estonia's implementation remains unchanged, and therefore continues to meet the minimum standard.

394. Estonia has met all of the ToR for the information gathering process and no recommendations are made.

B. The exchange of information (ToR II.B)

395. Estonia has international agreements permitting spontaneous exchange of information, including being a party to (i) the *Multilateral Convention on Mutual Administrative Assistance in Tax Matters: Amended by the 2010 Protocol* (OECD/Council of Europe, 2011[4]) ("the Convention"), (ii) the Directive 2011/16/EU with all other European Union Member States and (iii) bilateral agreements in force with 60 jurisdictions.[1]

396. For the year in review, the timeliness of exchanges is as follows:

Future rulings within the scope of the transparency framework	Number of exchanges transmitted within three months of the information becoming available to the competent authority or immediately after legal impediments have been lifted	Delayed exchanges		
		Number of exchanges transmitted later than three months of the information on rulings becoming available to the competent authority	Reasons for the delays	Any other comments
	8	0	N/A	N/A

Follow up requests received for exchange of the ruling	Number	Average time to provide response	Number of requests not answered
	0	N/A	N/A

397. In the prior years' peer review reports, it was determined that Estonia's process for the completion and exchange of templates were sufficient to meet the minimum standard. With respect to past rulings, no further action was required from Estonia. Estonia's implementation in this regard remains unchanged and therefore continues to meet the minimum standard.

398. Estonia has the necessary legal basis for spontaneous exchange of information, a process for completing the templates in a timely way and has completed all exchanges. Estonia has met all of the ToR for the exchange of information process and no recommendations are made.

C. Statistics (ToR IV)

399. The statistics for the year in review are as follows:

Category of ruling	Number of exchanges	Jurisdictions exchanged with
Permanent establishment rulings	2	*De minimis* rule applies
Related party conduit rulings	6	Finland, France, Germany, Luxembourg, Sweden, United Kingdom
Total	8	

D. Matters related to intellectual property regimes (ToR I.A.1.3)

400. Estonia does not offer an intellectual property regime for which transparency requirements under the Action 5 Report (OECD, 2015[1]) were imposed.

Summary of recommendations on implementation of the transparency framework

Aspect of implementation of the transparency framework that should be improved	Recommendation for improvement
	No recommendations are made.

References

OECD (2021), *BEPS Action 5 on Harmful Tax Practices - Terms of Reference and Methodology for the Conduct of the Peer Reviews of the Action 5 Transparency Framework*, OECD Publishing, Paris, http://www.oecd.org/tax/beps/beps-action-5-harmful-tax-practices-peer-review-transparency-framework.pdf. [3]

OECD (2015), *Countering Harmful Tax Practices More Effectively, Taking into Account Transparency and Substance, Action 5 - 2015 Final Report*, OECD/G20 Base Erosion and Profit Shifting Project, OECD Publishing, Paris, https://dx.doi.org/10.1787/9789264241190-en. [1]

OECD (ed.) (2017b), *Harmful Tax Practices - 2017 Progress Report on Preferential Regimes*, OECD Publishing, Paris, http://dx.doi.org/10.1787/9789264283954-en. [2]

OECD/Council of Europe (2011), *The Multilateral Convention on Mutual Administrative Assistance in Tax Matters: Amended by the 2010 Protocol*, OECD Publishing, Paris, https://dx.doi.org/10.1787/9789264115606-en. [4]

Notes

[1] Participating jurisdictions to the Convention are available here: www.oecd.org/tax/exchange-of-tax-information/convention-on-mutual-administrative-assistance-in-tax-matters.htm. Estonia also has bilateral agreements with Albania, Armenia, Azerbaijan, Austria, Bahrain, Belarus, Belgium, Bulgaria, Canada, China (People's Republic of), Croatia, Cyprus, Czech Republic, Denmark, Finland, France, Georgia, Germany, Greece, Hungary, Hong Kong (China), Iceland, India, Ireland, Isle of Man, Israel, Italy, Japan, Jersey, Kazakhstan, Korea, Kyrgyzstan, Latvia, Lithuania, Luxembourg, Malta, Mexico, Moldova, Netherlands, North Macedonia, Norway, Poland, Portugal, Romania, Serbia, Singapore, Slovak Republic, Slovenia, Spain, Sweden, Switzerland, Thailand, Turkey, Turkmenistan, Ukraine, United Arab Emirates, United Kingdom, United States, Uzbekistan and Viet Nam.

Eswatini

Eswatini did not provide a completed peer review questionnaire to the Secretariat.[1] It is not known whether Eswatini has implemented the transparency framework in line with the terms of reference (OECD, 2021[3]) (ToR) for the calendar year 2020 (year in review). Eswatini receives two recommendations covering the information gathering process (ToR I.A) and exchange of information (ToR II.B) for the year in review.

This is Eswatini's first review of implementation of the transparency framework.

It is not known whether Eswatini can legally issue any types of ruling within the scope of the transparency framework, or whether in practice Eswatini issued any such rulings.

No peer input was received in respect of the exchanges of information on rulings received from Eswatini.

A. The information gathering process (ToR I.A)

401. Eswatini was not yet able to complete the peer review questionnaire. It is not known whether Eswatini has implemented the transparency framework during the year in review.

Conclusion on section A

402. Eswatini is recommended to ensure that it has put in place an effective information gathering process to identify all relevant past and future rulings and all potential exchange jurisdictions and to implement a review and supervision mechanism, as soon as possible (ToR I.A).

B. The exchange of information (ToR II.B)

Legal basis for spontaneous exchange of information (ToR II.B.1, II.B.2)

403. It is not known whether Eswatini has the necessary domestic legal basis to exchange information spontaneously. Eswatini is recommended to put in place a domestic legal framework allowing spontaneous exchange of information on rulings if needed.

404. Eswatini has international agreements permitting spontaneous exchange of information, including bilateral agreements in force with 7 jurisdictions and tax information exchange agreements in force with 2 jurisdictions.[2] Eswatini signed the *Multilateral Convention on Mutual Administrative Assistance in Tax Matters: Amended by the 2010 Protocol* (OECD/Council of Europe, 2011[4]) ("the Convention") on 29 September 2020 and ratified on 16 March 2021. The Convention entered into force on 1 July 2021. No exchanges could occur under the Convention for the year in review.[3]

Completion and exchange of templates (ToR II.B.3, II.B.4, II.B.5, II.B.6, II.B.7)

405. It is not known whether Eswatini has put in place a process to exchange information on rulings in accordance with the form and timelines required by the transparency framework. Eswatini is recommended to ensure the timely exchange of information on rulings in the form required by the transparency framework.

Conclusion on section B

406. Eswatini is recommended to put in place a domestic legal framework allowing spontaneous exchange of information on rulings and develop a process to complete the templates on relevant rulings and to ensure that the exchanges of information on rulings occur in accordance with the form and timelines under the transparency framework (ToR II.B).

C. Statistics (ToR IV)

407. As the Secretariat is not aware whether information on rulings was exchanged by Eswatini for the year in review, no statistics can be reported.

D. Matters related to intellectual property regimes (ToR I.A.1.3)

408. Eswatini does not offer an intellectual property regime for which transparency requirements under the Action 5 Report (OECD, 2015[1]) were imposed.

Summary of recommendations on implementation of the transparency framework

Aspect of implementation of the transparency framework that should be improved	Recommendation for improvement
It is not known whether Eswatini has put in place the necessary information gathering process.	Eswatini is recommended to finalise its information gathering process for identifying all future rulings and potential exchange jurisdictions, with a review and supervision mechanism, as soon as possible.
It is not known whether Eswatini has the necessary domestic legal basis allowing spontaneous exchange of information and whether Eswatini has a process to complete the templates on relevant rulings, to make them available to the Competent Authority for exchange of information, and to exchange them with relevant jurisdictions.	Eswatini is recommended to put in place a domestic legal framework allowing spontaneous exchange of information on rulings and to develop a process to complete the templates on relevant rulings and to ensure that the exchanges of information on rulings occur in accordance with the form and timelines under the transparency framework.

Jurisdiction's response and recent developments

409. Eswatini provided a completed peer review questionnaire to the Secretariat beyond the timelines set in the methodology for the conduct of the peer reviews of the Action 5 transparency framework. Eswatini notes that 2020 is the first year of implementation of the transparency framework according to the FHTP timelines. Eswatini is currently assessing their internal process in order to take appropriate steps to implement the transparency framework and action the recommendations of this report as needed. Input received and further steps undertaken by Eswatini will be taken into account in the 2022 peer review process.

References

OECD (2021), *BEPS Action 5 on Harmful Tax Practices - Terms of Reference and Methodology for the Conduct of the Peer Reviews of the Action 5 Transparency Framework*, OECD Publishing, Paris, http://www.oecd.org/tax/beps/beps-action-5-harmful-tax-practices-peer-review-transparency-framework.pdf. [3]

OECD (2015), *Countering Harmful Tax Practices More Effectively, Taking into Account Transparency and Substance, Action 5 - 2015 Final Report*, OECD/G20 Base Erosion and Profit Shifting Project, OECD Publishing, Paris, https://dx.doi.org/10.1787/9789264241190-en. [1]

OECD (ed.) (2017b), *Harmful Tax Practices - 2017 Progress Report on Preferential Regimes*, OECD Publishing, Paris, http://dx.doi.org/10.1787/9789264283954-en. [2]

OECD/Council of Europe (2011), *The Multilateral Convention on Mutual Administrative Assistance in Tax Matters: Amended by the 2010 Protocol*, OECD Publishing, Paris, https://dx.doi.org/10.1787/9789264115606-en. [4]

Notes

[1] An update is provided in the jurisdiction's response and recent developments section.

[2] Eswatini has bilateral agreements with Botswana, Lesotho, Mauritius, Seychelles, South Africa, Chinese Taipei, United Kingdom. The TIEAs with Isle of Man and Guernsey also permit for the spontaneous exchange of information.

[3] Participating jurisdictions to the Convention are available here: www.oecd.org/tax/exchange-of-tax-information/convention-on-mutual-administrative-assistance-in-tax-matters.htm.

Faroe Islands

The Faroe Islands is taking steps to implement the legal basis for the transparency framework and to commence administrative preparations to ensure that information on rulings will be exchanged in a timely manner, in line with the terms of reference (OECD, 2021[3]) (ToR). For the calendar year 2020 (year in review), the Faroe Islands receives two recommendations covering the information gathering process (ToR I.A) and exchange of information (ToR II.B).

In the prior year report, the Faroe Islands had received the same two recommendations. As they have not been addressed, the recommendations remain in place.

The Faroe Islands can legally issue two types of rulings within the scope of the transparency framework.

In practice, the Faroe Islands issued rulings within the scope of the transparency framework as follows:

Type of ruling	Number of rulings
Past rulings	0
Future rulings in the period 1 September 2019 – 31 December 2019	0
Future rulings in the year in review	1

As no exchanges took place, no peer input was received in respect of the exchanges of information on rulings received from the Faroe Islands.

A. The information gathering process (ToR I.A)

410. The Faroe Islands can legally issue the following five types of rulings within the scope of the transparency framework: (i) preferential regimes[1] and (ii) permanent establishment rulings.

Past rulings (ToR I.A.1.1, I.A.1.2, I.A.2.1, I.A.2.2)

411. For the Faroe Islands, past rulings are any tax rulings issued prior to 1 September 2019.

412. In the prior year peer review report, it was determined that there is no obligation for the Faroe Islands to conduct spontaneous exchange information on past rulings. Therefore, the Faroe Islands was recommended to put in place an effective information gathering process to identify all relevant past rulings and all potential exchange jurisdictions as soon as possible.

413. During the year in review, the Faroe Islands did not implement steps to identify past rulings or to identify potential exchange jurisdictions, and therefore the recommendation remains in place.

Future rulings (ToR I.A.1.1, I.A.1.2, I.A.2.1)

414. For the Faroe Islands, future rulings are any tax rulings within scope that are issued on or after 1 September 2019.

415. In the prior year peer review report, it was determined that the Faroe Islands had no processes in place for the record keeping of rulings for the purposes of the transparency framework. Therefore, the Faroe Islands was recommended to put in place an effective information gathering process to identify all relevant future rulings and all potential exchange jurisdictions as soon as possible. The Faroe Islands intended to implement guidelines and practices to make sure the necessary information to meet the requirements of the transparency framework is required in all cases.

416. During the year in review, the Faroe Islands identified one future ruling but it did not implement steps to identify past rulings or to identify potential exchange jurisdictions, and therefore the recommendation remains in place.

Review and supervision (ToR I.A.3)

417. In the prior year peer review report, it was determined that the Faroe Islands did not yet have a review and supervision mechanism under the transparency framework. During the year in review, the Faroe Islands did not implement such a review and supervision mechanism, and therefore the recommendation remains in place.

Conclusion on section A

418. The Faroe Islands is recommended to put in place an effective information gathering process to identify all relevant past and future rulings and all potential exchange jurisdictions and to implement a review and supervision mechanism, as soon as possible (ToR I.A).

B. The exchange of information (ToR II.B)

Legal basis for spontaneous exchange of information (ToR II.B.1, II.B.2)

419. The Faroe Islands has the necessary domestic legal basis to exchange information spontaneously. The Faroe Islands notes that there are no legal or practical impediments that prevent the spontaneous exchange of information on rulings as contemplated in the Action 5 minimum standard.

420. The Faroe Islands has international agreements permitting spontaneous exchange of information, including being a participating jurisdiction to (i) the *Multilateral Convention on Mutual Administrative Assistance in Tax Matters: Amended by the 2010 Protocol* (OECD/Council of Europe, 2011[4]) ("the Convention"), (ii) the Nordic Convention on Assistance in Tax Matters and (iii) bilateral agreements in force with four jurisdictions.[2]

Completion and exchange of templates (ToR II.B.3, II.B.4, II.B.5, II.B.6, II.B.7)

421. In the prior year peer review report, it was determined that the Faroe Islands is still developing a process to complete the templates on relevant rulings, to make them available to the Competent Authority for exchange of information, and to exchange them with relevant jurisdictions. Therefore, the Faroe Islands was recommended to develop a process to complete the templates for all relevant rulings and to ensure that the exchanges of information on rulings occur in accordance with the form and timelines under the transparency framework going forward.

422. During the year in review, the Faroe Islands did not implement such a process, and therefore the recommendation remains in place.

423. As no exchanges took place in the year of review, no data on the timeliness of exchanges can be reported.

Conclusion on section B

424. The Faroe Islands is recommended to develop a process to complete the templates for all relevant rulings and to ensure that the exchanges of information on rulings occur in accordance with the form and timelines under the transparency framework going forward (ToR II.B).

C. Statistics (ToR IV)

425. As there was no information on rulings exchanged by the Faroe Islands for the year in review, no statistics can be reported.

D. Matters related to intellectual property regimes (ToR I.A.1.3)

426. The Faroe Islands does not offer an intellectual property regime for which transparency requirements under the Action 5 Report (OECD, 2015[1]) were imposed.

Summary of recommendations on implementation of the transparency framework

Aspect of implementation of the transparency framework that should be improved	Recommendation for improvement
The Faroe Islands does not yet have its necessary	The Faroe Islands is recommended to put in place an

information and gathering process in place.	effective information gathering process to identify all relevant past and future rulings and all potential exchange jurisdictions and to implement a review and supervision mechanism, as soon as possible. This recommendation remains unchanged since the prior year peer review report.
The Faroe Islands does not have a process to complete the templates on relevant rulings, to make them available to the Competent Authority for exchange of information, and to exchange them with relevant jurisdictions.	The Faroe Islands is recommended to develop a process to complete the templates for all relevant rulings and to ensure that the exchanges of information on rulings occur in accordance with the form and timelines under the transparency framework going forward. This recommendation remains unchanged since the prior year peer review report.

References

OECD (2021), *BEPS Action 5 on Harmful Tax Practices - Terms of Reference and Methodology for the Conduct of the Peer Reviews of the Action 5 Transparency Framework*, OECD Publishing, Paris, http://www.oecd.org/tax/beps/beps-action-5-harmful-tax-practices-peer-review-transparency-framework.pdf. [3]

OECD (2015), *Countering Harmful Tax Practices More Effectively, Taking into Account Transparency and Substance, Action 5 - 2015 Final Report*, OECD/G20 Base Erosion and Profit Shifting Project, OECD Publishing, Paris, https://dx.doi.org/10.1787/9789264241190-en. [1]

OECD (ed.) (2017b), *Harmful Tax Practices - 2017 Progress Report on Preferential Regimes*, OECD Publishing, Paris, http://dx.doi.org/10.1787/9789264283954-en. [2]

OECD/Council of Europe (2011), *The Multilateral Convention on Mutual Administrative Assistance in Tax Matters: Amended by the 2010 Protocol*, OECD Publishing, Paris, https://dx.doi.org/10.1787/9789264115606-en. [4]

Notes

[1] With respect to the following preferential regimes: 1) Tonnage tax regime; 2) International shipping regime.

[2] Parties to the Convention are available here: www.oecd.org/tax/exchange-of-tax-information/convention-on-mutual-administrative-assistance-in-tax-matters.htm. Parties to the Nordic Convention on Assistance in Tax Matters are Denmark, Finland, Iceland, Norway and Sweden. The Faroe Islands also has bilateral agreements with Greenland, India, Switzerland and the United Kingdom. The bilateral agreements with Switzerland and India are the Danish tax treaties, which are territorially extended to include the Faroe Islands.

Finland

Finland has met all aspects of the terms of reference (OECD, 2021[3]) (ToR) for the calendar year 2020 (year in review), and no recommendations are made.

Finland can legally issue four types of rulings within the scope of the transparency framework.

In practice, Finland issued rulings within the scope of the transparency framework as follows:

Type of ruling	Number of rulings
Past rulings	42
Future rulings in the period 1 April 2016 – 31 December 2016	13
Future rulings in the calendar year 2017	19
Future rulings in the calendar year 2018	8
Future rulings in the calendar year 2019	32
Future rulings in the year in review	27

Peer input was received from three jurisdictions in respect of the exchanges of information on rulings received from Finland. The input was generally positive, noting that information was complete, in a correct format and received in a timely manner.

A. The information gathering process (ToR I.A)

427. Finland can legally issue the following four types of rulings within the scope of the transparency framework: (i) preferential regimes;[1] (ii) cross-border unilateral APAs and any other cross-border unilateral tax rulings (such as an advance tax ruling) covering transfer pricing or the application of transfer pricing principles; (iii) permanent establishment rulings; and (iv) related party conduit rulings.

428. For Finland, past rulings are any tax rulings within scope that are issued either: (i) on or after 1 January 2014 but before 1 April 2016; or (ii) on or after 1 January 2010 but before 1 January 2014, provided they were still in effect as at 1 January 2014. Future rulings are any tax rulings within scope that are issued on or after 1 April 2016.

429. In the prior years' peer review reports, it was determined that Finland's undertakings to identify past and future rulings and all potential exchange jurisdictions were sufficient to meet the minimum standard. In addition, it was determined that Finland's review and supervision mechanism was sufficient to meet the minimum standard. Finland's implementation remains unchanged, and therefore continues to meet the minimum standard.

430. Finland has met all of the ToR for the information gathering process and no recommendations are made.

B. The exchange of information (ToR II.B)

431. Finland has international agreements permitting spontaneous exchange of information, including being a party to (i) the *Multilateral Convention on Mutual Administrative Assistance in Tax Matters: Amended by the 2010 Protocol* (OECD/Council of Europe, 2011[4]) ("the Convention"), (ii) the Directive 2011/16/EU with all other European Union Member States and (iii) bilateral agreements in force with 89 jurisdictions.[2]

432. For the year in review, the timeliness of exchanges is as follows:

Future rulings within the scope of the transparency framework	Number of exchanges transmitted within three months of the information becoming available to the competent authority or immediately after legal impediments have been lifted	Delayed exchanges		
		Number of exchanges transmitted later than three months of the information on rulings becoming available to the competent authority	Reasons for the delays	Any other comments
	87	0	N/A	N/A

Follow up requests received for exchange of the ruling	Number	Average time to provide response	Number of requests not answered
	0	N/A	N/A

433. In the prior years' peer review reports, it was determined that Finland's process for the completion and exchange of templates were sufficient to meet the minimum standard. With respect to past rulings, no further action was required. Finland's implementation in this regard remains unchanged and therefore continues to meet the minimum standard.

434. Finland has the necessary legal basis for spontaneous exchange of information, a process for completing the templates in a timely way and has completed all exchanges. Finland has met all of the ToR for the exchange of information process and no recommendations are made.

C. Statistics (ToR IV)

435. The statistics for the year in review are as follows:

Category of ruling	Number of exchanges	Jurisdictions exchanged with
Ruling related to a preferential regime	0	N/A
Cross-border unilateral APAs and any other cross-border unilateral tax rulings (such as an advance tax ruling) covering transfer pricing or the application of transfer pricing principles	85	Australia, Austria, Brazil, Bulgaria, Canada, China (People's Republic of), Cyprus, Denmark, Estonia, France, Germany, Hong Kong (China), India, Indonesia, Ireland, Japan, Korea, Latvia, Lithuania, Luxembourg, Malta, Mexico, Netherlands, New Zealand, Norway, Poland, Romania, Russia, Singapore, Slovak Republic, Spain, Sweden, Switzerland, United Kingdom, United States
Permanent establishment rulings	1	*De minimis* rule applies
Related party conduit rulings	0	N/A
Total	87	

D. Matters related to intellectual property regimes (ToR I.A.1.3)

436. Finland does not offer an intellectual property regime for which transparency requirements under the Action 5 Report (OECD, 2015[1]) were imposed.

Summary of recommendations on implementation of the transparency framework

Aspect of implementation of the transparency framework that should be improved	Recommendation for improvement
	No recommendations are made.

References

OECD (2021), *BEPS Action 5 on Harmful Tax Practices - Terms of Reference and Methodology for the Conduct of the Peer Reviews of the Action 5 Transparency Framework*, OECD Publishing, Paris, http://www.oecd.org/tax/beps/beps-action-5-harmful-tax-practices-peer-review-transparency-framework.pdf. [3]

OECD (2015), *Countering Harmful Tax Practices More Effectively, Taking into Account Transparency and Substance, Action 5 - 2015 Final Report*, OECD/G20 Base Erosion and Profit Shifting Project, OECD Publishing, Paris, https://dx.doi.org/10.1787/9789264241190-en. [1]

OECD (ed.) (2017b), *Harmful Tax Practices - 2017 Progress Report on Preferential Regimes*, OECD Publishing, Paris, http://dx.doi.org/10.1787/9789264283954-en. [2]

OECD/Council of Europe (2011), *The Multilateral Convention on Mutual Administrative Assistance in Tax Matters: Amended by the 2010 Protocol*, OECD Publishing, Paris, https://dx.doi.org/10.1787/9789264115606-en. [4]

Notes

[1] With respect to the following preferential regime: shipping regime.

[2] Participating jurisdictions to the Convention are available here: www.oecd.org/tax/exchange-of-tax-information/convention-on-mutual-administrative-assistance-in-tax-matters.htm. Finland also has bilateral agreements with Argentina, Armenia, Aruba, Australia, Austria, Azerbaijan, Bailiwick of Jersey, Barbados, Belarus, Belgium Bermuda, Bosnia and Herzegovina, Brazil, British Virgin Islands, Bulgaria, Canada, Cayman Islands, China (People's Republic of), Cook Islands, Croatia, Cyprus, Czech Republic, Denmark, Egypt, Estonia, Faroe Islands, France, Georgia, Germany, Greece, Guatemala, Guernsey, Hungary, India, Indonesia, Ireland, Isle of Man, Israel, Italy, Japan, Kazakhstan, Korea, Kosovo, Kyrgyzstan, Latvia, Lebanon, Lithuania, Luxembourg, Malaysia, Malta, Mexico, Moldova, Monaco, Montenegro, Morocco, Netherlands, Netherlands Antilles, New Zealand, North Macedonia, Norway, Pakistan, Panama, Philippines, Poland, Portugal, Romania, Russia, Serbia, Singapore, Slovak Republic, Slovenia, South Africa, Spain, Sri Lanka, Sweden, Switzerland, Tajikistan, Tanzania, Thailand, Turkey, Turkmenistan, Ukraine, United Arab Emirates, United Kingdom, United States, Uruguay, Uzbekistan, Viet Nam and Zambia.

France

France has met all aspects of the terms of reference (OECD, 2021[3]) (ToR) for the calendar year 2020 (year in review), except for identifying and exchanging information on new entrants to the grandfathered IP regime and or taxpayers benefitting from the third category of IP assets (ToR I.A.1.3). France receives one recommendation on this point for the year in review.

In the prior year report, as well as in the 2016, 2017 and 2018 peer reviews, France had received the same recommendation. As it has not been addressed, the recommendation remains in place.

France can legally issue three types of rulings within the scope of the transparency framework.

In practice, France issued rulings within the scope of the transparency framework as follows:

Type of ruling	Number of rulings
Past rulings	45
Future rulings in the period 1 April 2016 – 31 December 2016	4
Future rulings in the calendar year 2017	6
Future rulings in the calendar year 2018	6
Future rulings in the calendar year 2019	16
Future rulings in the year of review	8

No peer input was received in respect of the exchanges of information on rulings received from France.

A. The information gathering process (ToR I.A)

437. France can legally issue the following three types of rulings within the scope of the transparency framework: (i) preferential regimes;[1] (ii) cross-border unilateral APAs and any other cross-border unilateral tax rulings (such as an advance tax ruling) covering transfer pricing or the application of transfer pricing principles; and (iii) permanent establishment rulings.

438. For France, past rulings are any tax rulings within scope that are issued either: (i) on or after 1 January 2014 but before 1 April 2016; or (ii) on or after 1 January 2010 but before 1 January 2014, provided they were still in effect as at 1 January 2014. Future rulings are any tax rulings within scope that are issued on or after 1 April 2016.

439. In the prior years' peer review reports, it was determined that France's undertakings to identify past and future rulings and all potential exchange jurisdictions were sufficient to meet the minimum standard. In addition, it was determined that France's review and supervision mechanism was sufficient to meet the minimum standard. France's implementation remains unchanged, and therefore continues to meet the minimum standard.

440. France has met all of the ToR for the information gathering process and no recommendations are made.

B. The exchange of information (ToR II.B)

441. France has international agreements permitting spontaneous exchange of information, including being a party to the (i) *Multilateral Convention on Mutual Administrative Assistance in Tax Matters: Amended by the 2010 Protocol* (OECD/Council of Europe, 2011[4]) ("the Convention"), (ii) the Directive 2011/16/EU with all other European Union Member States and (iii) bilateral agreements in force with 125 jurisdictions.[2]

442. For the year in review, the timeliness of exchanges is as follows:

Future rulings in the scope of the transparency framework	Number of exchanges transmitted within three months of the information becoming available to the competent authority or immediately after legal impediments have been lifted	Delayed exchanges		
		Number of exchanges transmitted later than three months of the information on rulings becoming available to the competent authority	Reasons for the delays	Any other comments
	8	0	N/A	N/A

Follow up requests received for exchange of the ruling	Number	Average time to provide response	Number of requests not answered
	0	N/A	N/A

443. In the prior years' peer review reports, it was determined that France's process for the completion and exchange of templates were sufficient to meet the minimum standard. With respect to past rulings, no further action was required. France's implementation in this regard remains unchanged and therefore continues to meet the minimum standard.

444. France has the necessary legal basis for spontaneous exchange of information, a process for completing the templates in a timely way and has completed all exchanges. France has met all of the ToR for the exchange of information process and no recommendations are made.

C. Statistics (ToR IV)

445. The statistics for the year in review are as follows:

Category of ruling	Number of exchanges	Jurisdictions exchanged with
Ruling related to a preferential regime	4	*De minimis* rule applies
Cross-border unilateral advance pricing agreements (APAs) and any other cross-border unilateral tax rulings (such as an advance tax ruling) covering transfer pricing or the application of transfer pricing principles	2	*De minimis* rule applies
Permanent establishment rulings	2	*De minimis* rule applies
IP regimes: total exchanges on taxpayers benefitting from the third category of IP assets, new entrants benefitting from grandfathered IP regimes; and taxpayers making use of the option to treat the nexus ratio as a rebuttable presumption	0	N/A
Total	8	

D. Matters related to intellectual property regimes (ToR I.A.1.3)

446. France offers an intellectual property regimes (IP regime)[3] that is subject to the transparency requirements under the Action 5 Report (OECD, 2015[1]). This regime was amended with effect from 1 January 2019 and is compliant with the nexus approach. It states that the identification of the benefitting taxpayers will occur as follows:

- ***New entrants benefitting from the grandfathered IP regime***: With respect to the previous form of the regime that existed until 31 December 2018, France should have information available and exchanged on new entrants after the relevant date from which enhanced transparency obligations apply. France has not identified information on new entrants to the previous IP regime, and as such has not exchanged information on these taxpayers. Therefore, France is recommended to identify and exchange information on all new entrants to the IP regime. This recommendation was included in the 2016, 2017, 2018 and 2019 peer review reports, and has not yet been acted upon. The recommendation is therefore retained.
- ***Third category of IP assets***: The previous form of the regime provided benefits to income from patentable inventions, which appear to be a type of the "third category of IP asset" described in paragraph 37 of the Action 5 report (OECD, 2015[1]). France has not implemented all of the requirements associated with this category of IP assets, thus the transparency requirements described in paragraph 37 would still apply to this case. France did not identify taxpayers benefiting from the third category of IP assets, and as such, has not exchanged information on these taxpayers. This recommendation was included in the 2016, 2017, 2018 and 2019 peer review reports, and has not been acted upon. The recommendation is therefore retained.

  In addition, the amended IP regime will allow benefits for the third category of IP assets.[4] Taxpayers benefiting from the regime have to provide a list of relevant assets in their tax return. Based on the tax return, France can identify the taxpayers benefiting from the third category of IP assets.
- ***Taxpayers making use of the option to treat the nexus ratio as a rebuttable presumption***: The amended IP regime allows for the option to treat the nexus ratio as a rebuttable presumption. Taxpayers opting to do so must obtain a ruling from the tax administration, and are required to list the specific assets for which the presumption was rebutted in their tax return. France confirms that no taxpayer elected to treat the nexus approach as a rebuttable presumption.

Summary of recommendations on implementation of the transparency framework

Aspect of implementation of the transparency framework that should be improved	Recommendation for improvement
France did not identify or exchange information on new entrants to the IP regime or taxpayers benefitting from the third category of IP asset with respect to the former IP regime.	France is recommended to identify and exchange information on all new entrants to the IP regime, and to identify and exchange information on taxpayers benefitting from the third category of IP assets. This recommendation remains unchanged since the 2016, 2017, 2018 and 2019 peer review reports.

Jurisdiction's response and recent developments

447. France notes that it is currently undertaking actions in order to address the recommendation concerning the identification and exchange of information on new entrants to the old IP regime. France has identified all new entrants for the years 2015-2018 and the competent services are currently in the process of identifying for which of those taxpayers, exchanges should take place. Once those taxpayers are identified, the competent services will proceed with the exchange of information with the relevant jurisdictions. However, France notes that it is not able to identify and exchange information on taxpayers benefitting from the third category of IP assets, as the reporting formalities of the old IP regime were not calibrated to collect such information.

References

OECD (2021), *BEPS Action 5 on Harmful Tax Practices - Terms of Reference and Methodology for the Conduct of the Peer Reviews of the Action 5 Transparency Framework*, OECD Publishing, Paris, http://www.oecd.org/tax/beps/beps-action-5-harmful-tax-practices-peer-review-transparency-framework.pdf. [3]

OECD (2015), *Countering Harmful Tax Practices More Effectively, Taking into Account Transparency and Substance, Action 5 - 2015 Final Report*, OECD/G20 Base Erosion and Profit Shifting Project, OECD Publishing, Paris, https://dx.doi.org/10.1787/9789264241190-en. [1]

OECD (ed.) (2017b), *Harmful Tax Practices - 2017 Progress Report on Preferential Regimes*, OECD Publishing, Paris, http://dx.doi.org/10.1787/9789264283954-en. [2]

OECD/Council of Europe (2011), *The Multilateral Convention on Mutual Administrative Assistance in Tax Matters: Amended by the 2010 Protocol*, OECD Publishing, Paris, https://dx.doi.org/10.1787/9789264115606-en. [4]

Notes

[1] With respect to the following preferential regime: Shipping regime.

[2] Participating jurisdictions to the Convention are available here: www.oecd.org/tax/exchange-of-tax-information/convention-on-mutual-administrative-assistance-in-tax-matters.htm. France also has bilateral agreements with: Albania, Algeria, Andorra, Argentina, Armenia, Australia, Austria, Azerbaijan, Bahrain, Bangladesh, Belarus, Belgium, Benin, Bolivia, Bosnia and Herzegovina, Botswana, Brazil, Bulgaria, Burkina Faso, Cameroon, Canada, Central African Republic, Chile, China (People's Republic of), Congo, Côte d'Ivoire, Croatia, Cyprus, Czech Republic, Ecuador, Egypt, Estonia, Ethiopia, Finland, French Polynesia, Gabon, Georgia, Germany, Ghana, Greece, Guinea, Hong Kong (China), Hungary, Iceland, India, Indonesia, Iran, Ireland, Israel, Italy, Jamaica, Japan, Jordan, Kazakhstan, Kenya, Korea, Kosovo, Kuwait, Kyrgyzstan, Latvia, Lebanon, Libya, Lithuania, Luxembourg, Madagascar, Malawi, Malaysia, Mali, Malta, Mauritania, Mauritius, Mexico, Monaco, Mongolia, Montenegro, Morocco, Namibia, Netherlands, New Caledonia, New Zealand, Niger, Nigeria, North Macedonia, Norway, Oman, Pakistan, Panama, Philippines, Poland, Portugal, Qatar, Romania, Russia, Saudi Arabia, Senegal, Serbia, Singapore, Slovak Republic, Slovenia, South Africa, Spain, Sri Lanka, Sint Maarten, Saint Pierre and Miquelon, Sweden, Switzerland, Syrian Arab Republic, Chinese Taipei, Thailand, Togo, Trinidad and Tobago, Tunisia, Turkey, Turkmenistan, Ukraine, United Arab Emirates, United Kingdom, United States, Uzbekistan, Venezuela, Viet Nam, Zambia and Zimbabwe.

[3] Reduced corporation tax rate on IP income, formerly known as Reduced rate for long term capital gains and profits from the licensing of IP rights.

[4] The regime provides for the third category of IP assets (article 238(I)(5) of the French General Tax Code), but will only entry into force by a decree (article 37(III)(2) of the 2020 Finance Law) that was not yet published in 2019.

Gabon

Gabon is taking steps to implement the transparency framework and to commence administrative preparations to ensure that information on rulings will be exchanged in a timely manner, in line with the terms of reference (OECD, 2021[3]) (ToR) for the calendar year 2020 (year in review). Gabon receives two recommendations covering the information gathering process (ToR I.A), exchange of information (ToR II.B) for the year in review.

In the prior year report, as well as in the 2018 peer review, Gabon received the same recommendations. As they have not been addressed, the recommendations remain in place.

Gabon can legally issue two types of rulings within the scope of the transparency framework.

In practice, Gabon issued no rulings within the scope of the transparency framework.

As no exchanges were required to take place, no peer input was received in respect of the exchanges of information on rulings received from Gabon.

A. The information gathering process (ToR I.A)

448. Gabon can legally issue the following two types of rulings within the scope of the transparency framework: (i) rulings related to a preferential regime,[1] and (ii) cross-border unilateral APAs any other cross-border unilateral tax rulings (such as an advance tax ruling) covering transfer pricing or the application of transfer pricing principles.

Past rulings (ToR I.A.1.1, I.A.1.2, I.A.2.1, I.A.2.2)

449. For Gabon, past rulings are any tax rulings within scope that are issued either (i) on or after 1 January 2016 but before 1 April 2018; and (ii) on or after 1 January 2014 but before 1 January 2016, provided they were still in effect as at 1 January 2016.

450. In the 2018 peer review report, it was determined that Gabon issued no past rulings within the scope of the transparency framework. As such, there was no need to identify potential exchange jurisdictions.

Future rulings (ToR I.A.1.1, I.A.1.2, I.A.2.1)

451. For Gabon, future rulings are any tax rulings within scope that are issued on or after 1 April 2018.

452. In the 2018 peer review report, Gabon indicated that there were no processes in place for the record keeping of rulings for the purposes of the transparency framework. It was noted that Gabon intended to implement guidelines and practices to make sure the necessary information to meet the requirements of the transparency framework is required in all cases. Gabon was recommended to finalise its information gathering process as soon as possible.

453. During the year in review, Gabon established the "Cellule Prix de Transfert" which is not yet fully operational and its activities are still limited to tax audits. Gabon is also negotiating with taxpayers with a view to concluding APAs. No additional steps to finalise its information gathering process were taken, and therefore the prior year recommendation remains.

Review and supervision (ToR I.A.3)

454. In the 2018 peer review report, it was determined that Gabon did not yet have a review and supervision mechanism under the transparency framework. Gabon was in the process of considering the implementation of a revision and supervision mechanism for ensuring implementation of the transparency framework.

455. During the year in review, no additional steps were taken, and therefore the prior year recommendation remains.

Conclusion on section A

456. Gabon is recommended to finalise its information gathering process, with a review and supervision mechanism, as soon as possible (ToR I.A).

B. The exchange of information (ToR II.B)

Legal basis for spontaneous exchange of information (ToR II.B.1, II.B.2)

457. During the year in review, Gabon has put in place the necessary domestic legal basis to exchange information spontaneously. Gabon has international agreements permitting spontaneous exchange of information, including bilateral agreements in force with 5 jurisdictions.[2] Gabon signed the *Multilateral Convention on Mutual Administrative Assistance in Tax Matters: Amended by the 2010 Protocol* (OECD/Council of Europe, 2011[4]) ("the Convention").[3] Gabon is encouraged to continue its efforts to expand its international exchange of information instruments to be able to exchange information on rulings. It is noted, however, that jurisdictions are assessed on their compliance with the transparency framework in respect of the exchange of information network in effect for the year of the particular annual review.

Completion and exchange of templates (ToR II.B.3, II.B.4, II.B.5, II.B.6, II.B.7)

458. In the 2018 peer review report, it was determined that Gabon was developing a process to complete the templates on relevant rulings, to make them available to the Competent Authority for exchange of information, and to exchange them with relevant jurisdictions.

459. During the year in review, no additional steps were taken, and therefore the prior year recommendation remains.

460. As no exchanges took place for the year in review, no data on the timeliness of exchanges can be reported.

Conclusion on section B

461. Gabon is recommended to put in place a domestic legal framework allowing spontaneous exchange of information on rulings and to continue its efforts to complete the templates for all relevant rulings and to ensure that the exchanges of information on rulings occur as soon as possible (ToR II.B).

C. Statistics (ToR IV)

462. As no rulings were issued, no statistics can be reported.

D. Matters related to intellectual property regimes (ToR I.A.1.3)

463. Gabon does not offer an intellectual property regime for which transparency requirements under the Action 5 Report (OECD, 2015[1]) were imposed.

Summary of recommendations on implementation of the transparency framework

Aspect of implementation of the transparency framework that should be improved	Recommendation for improvement
Gabon has not finalised the steps to have in place its necessary information gathering process, with a review and supervision mechanism.	Gabon is recommended to finalise its information gathering process, with a review and supervision mechanism, as soon as possible. This recommendation remains unchanged since the 2018 and 2019 peer review reports.
Gabon has not finalised the steps to have effective compulsory spontaneous exchange of information on the tax rulings within the scope of the transparency framework.	Gabon is recommended to continue its efforts to complete the templates for all relevant rulings and to ensure that the exchanges of information on rulings occur as soon as

	possible. This recommendation remains unchanged since the 2018 and 2019 peer review reports.

References

OECD (2021), *BEPS Action 5 on Harmful Tax Practices - Terms of Reference and Methodology for the Conduct of the Peer Reviews of the Action 5 Transparency Framework*, OECD Publishing, Paris, http://www.oecd.org/tax/beps/beps-action-5-harmful-tax-practices-peer-review-transparency-framework.pdf. [3]

OECD (2015), *Countering Harmful Tax Practices More Effectively, Taking into Account Transparency and Substance, Action 5 - 2015 Final Report*, OECD/G20 Base Erosion and Profit Shifting Project, OECD Publishing, Paris, https://dx.doi.org/10.1787/9789264241190-en. [1]

OECD (ed.) (2017b), *Harmful Tax Practices - 2017 Progress Report on Preferential Regimes*, OECD Publishing, Paris, http://dx.doi.org/10.1787/9789264283954-en. [2]

OECD/Council of Europe (2011), *The Multilateral Convention on Mutual Administrative Assistance in Tax Matters: Amended by the 2010 Protocol*, OECD Publishing, Paris, https://dx.doi.org/10.1787/9789264115606-en. [4]

Notes

[1] With respect to the following preferential regime: Special economic zone.

[2] Gabon has bilateral agreements in force with Belgium, Canada, France, Korea and Morocco.

[3] Participating jurisdictions to the Convention are available here: www.oecd.org/tax/exchange-of-tax-information/convention-on-mutual-administrative-assistance-in-tax-matters.htm.

Georgia

Georgia has met all aspects of the terms of reference (OECD, 2021[3]) (ToR) for the calendar year 2020 (year in review), and no recommendations are made.

Georgia can legally issue four types of rulings within the scope of the transparency framework.

In practice, Georgia issued no rulings within the scope of the transparency framework.

As no exchanges were required to take place, no peer input was received in respect of the exchanges of information on rulings received from Georgia.

A. The information gathering process (ToR I.A)

464. Georgia can legally issue the following four types of rulings within the scope of the transparency framework: (i) preferential regimes;[1] (ii) cross-border unilateral APAs and any other cross-border unilateral tax rulings (such as an advance tax ruling) covering transfer pricing or the application of transfer pricing principles; (iii) permanent establishment rulings; and (iv) related party conduit rulings.

465. For Georgia, past rulings are any tax rulings within scope that are issued either: (i) on or after 1 January 2016 but before 1 April 2018; or (ii) on or after 1 January 2014 but before 1 January 2016, provided they were still in effect as at 1 January 2016. Future rulings are any tax rulings within scope that are issued on or after 1 April 2018.

466. In the prior years' peer review reports, it was determined that Georgia's undertakings to identify past and future rulings and all potential exchange jurisdictions were sufficient to meet the minimum standard. In addition, it was determined that Georgia's review and supervision mechanism was sufficient to meet the minimum standard. Georgia's implementation remains unchanged, and therefore continues to meet the minimum standard.

467. Georgia has met all of the ToR for the information gathering process and no recommendations are made.

B. The exchange of information (ToR II.B)

468. Georgia has international agreements permitting spontaneous exchange of information, including being a party to (i) the *Multilateral Convention on Mutual Administrative Assistance in Tax Matters: Amended by the 2010 Protocol* (OECD/Council of Europe, 2011[4]) ("the Convention") and (ii) bilateral agreements in force with 57 jurisdictions.[2]

469. As Georgia did not issue any rulings within the scope of the transparency framework in the relevant period, Georgia was not required to exchange any information on rulings in the year in review and no data on the timeliness of exchanges can be reported.

470. In the prior years' peer review reports, it was determined that Georgia's process for the completion and exchange of templates were sufficient to meet the minimum standard. With respect to past rulings, no further action was required. Georgia's implementation in this regard remains unchanged and therefore continues to meet the minimum standard.

471. Georgia has the necessary legal basis for spontaneous exchange of information, a process for completing the templates in a timely way and has completed all exchanges. Georgia has met all of the ToR for the exchange of information process and no recommendations are made.

C. Statistics (ToR IV)

472. As no rulings were issued, no statistics can be reported.

D. Matters related to intellectual property regimes (ToR I.A.1.3)

473. Georgia does not offer an intellectual property regime for which transparency requirements under the Action 5 Report (OECD, 2015[1]) were imposed.

Summary of recommendations on implementation of the transparency framework

Aspect of implementation of the transparency framework that should be improved	Recommendation for improvement
	No recommendations are made.

References

OECD (2021), *BEPS Action 5 on Harmful Tax Practices - Terms of Reference and Methodology for the Conduct of the Peer Reviews of the Action 5 Transparency Framework*, OECD Publishing, Paris, http://www.oecd.org/tax/beps/beps-action-5-harmful-tax-practices-peer-review-transparency-framework.pdf. [3]

OECD (2015), *Countering Harmful Tax Practices More Effectively, Taking into Account Transparency and Substance, Action 5 - 2015 Final Report*, OECD/G20 Base Erosion and Profit Shifting Project, OECD Publishing, Paris, https://dx.doi.org/10.1787/9789264241190-en. [1]

OECD (ed.) (2017b), *Harmful Tax Practices - 2017 Progress Report on Preferential Regimes*, OECD Publishing, Paris, http://dx.doi.org/10.1787/9789264283954-en. [2]

OECD/Council of Europe (2011), *The Multilateral Convention on Mutual Administrative Assistance in Tax Matters: Amended by the 2010 Protocol*, OECD Publishing, Paris, https://dx.doi.org/10.1787/9789264115606-en. [4]

Notes

[1] With respect to the following preferential regimes: 1) International financial company and 2) Virtual zone person.

[2] Participating jurisdictions to the Convention are available here: www.oecd.org/tax/exchange-of-tax-information/convention-on-mutual-administrative-assistance-in-tax-matters.htm. Georgia also has bilateral agreements with Armenia, Austria, Azerbaijan, Bahamas, Bahrain, Belarus, Belgium, Bulgaria, China (People's Republic of), Croatia, Cyprus, Czech Republic, Denmark, Egypt, Estonia, Finland, France, Germany, Greece, Hungary, Iceland, India, Iran, Ireland, Israel, Italy, Japan, Kazakhstan, Korea, Kuwait, Latvia, Liechtenstein, Lithuania, Luxembourg, Malta, Moldova, Netherlands, Norway, Poland, Portugal, Qatar, Romania, San Marino, Saudi Arabia, Serbia, Singapore, Slovak Republic, Slovenia, Spain, Sweden, Switzerland, Turkey, Turkmenistan, Ukraine, United Arab Emirates, United Kingdom and Uzbekistan.

Germany

Germany has met all aspects of the terms of reference (OECD, 2021[3]) (ToR) for the calendar year 2020 (year in review), and no recommendations are made.

Germany can legally issue five types of rulings within the scope of the transparency framework.

In practice, Germany issued rulings within the scope of the transparency framework as follows:

Type of ruling	Number of rulings
Past rulings	30
Future rulings in the period 1 April 2016 – 31 December 2016	7
Future rulings in the calendar year 2017	10
Future rulings in the calendar year 2018	10
Future rulings in the calendar year 2019	8
Future rulings in the year in review	13

No peer input was received in respect of the exchanges of information on rulings received from Germany.

A. The information gathering process (ToR II.A)

474. Germany can legally issue five types of rulings within the scope of the transparency framework: (i) preferential regimes;[1] (ii) cross-border unilateral APAs and any other cross-border unilateral tax rulings (such as an advance tax ruling) covering transfer pricing or the application of transfer pricing principles; (iii) rulings providing for unilateral downward adjustments; (iv) permanent establishment rulings; and (v) related party conduit rulings.

475. For Germany, past rulings are any tax rulings within scope that are issued either: (i) on or after 1 January 2014 but before 1 April 2016; or (ii) on or after 1 January 2010 but before 1 January 2014, provided they were still in effect as at 1 January 2014. Future rulings are any tax rulings within scope that are issued on or after 1 April 2016.

476. In the prior years' peer review reports, it was determined that Germany's undertakings to identify past and future rulings and all potential exchange jurisdictions were sufficient to meet the minimum standard. In addition, it was determined that Germany's review and supervision mechanism was sufficient to meet the minimum standard. Germany's implementation remains unchanged, and therefore continues to meet the minimum standard.

477. Germany has met all of the ToR for the information gathering process and no recommendations are made.

B. The exchange of information (ToR II.B)

478. Germany has international agreements permitting spontaneous exchange of information, including being a party to (i) the *Multilateral Convention on Mutual Administrative Assistance in Tax Matters: Amended by the 2010 Protocol* (OECD/Council of Europe, 2011[4]) ("the Convention"), (ii) the Directive 2011/16/EU with all other European Union Member States and (iii) bilateral agreements in force with 95 jurisdictions.[2]

479. For the year in review, the timeliness of exchanges is as follows:

Future rulings within the scope of the transparency framework	Number of exchanges transmitted within three months of the information becoming available to the competent authority or immediately after legal impediments have been lifted	Delayed exchanges		
		Number of exchanges transmitted later than three months of the information on rulings becoming available to the competent authority	Reasons for the delays	Any other comments
	11	2	See below	N/A

Follow up requests received for exchange of the ruling	Number	Average time to provide response	Number of requests not answered
	0	N/A	N/A

480. With respect to the two delayed exchanges, Germany notes that these were due to an addition of more information and objections to the exchange by the domestic taxpayer respectively. In particular, these exchanges relate to rulings issued by local tax authorities, who wrongly carried out hearings for domestic parties affected by these rulings before exchanging the information. As such, the Competent Authority experienced delays. Germany notes that this goes counter to the BMF letter of 17 August 2017 on Tax Rulings which instructs local tax authorities not to hold a hearing for future rulings prior to the exchange of information. Consequently, as the local tax authorities should not have heard the parties involved, the

necessary notifications for future rulings should already have taken place before the ruling is issued. Therefore, it is not expected that these will be a recurring issue, and this will be monitored in next year's peer review report.

481. In the prior years' peer review reports, it was determined that Germany's process for the completion and exchange of templates were sufficient to meet the minimum standard. With respect to past rulings, no further action was required. Germany's implementation in this regard remains unchanged and therefore continues to meet the minimum standard.

482. Germany has the necessary legal basis for spontaneous exchange of information, a process for completing the templates in a timely way and has completed all exchanges. Germany has met all of the ToR for the exchange of information process and no recommendations are made.

C. Statistics (ToR IV)

483. The statistics for the year in review are as follows:

Category of ruling	Number of exchanges	Jurisdictions exchanged with
Ruling related to a preferential regime	0	N/A
Cross-border unilateral APAs and any other cross-border unilateral tax rulings (such as an advance tax ruling) covering transfer pricing or the application of transfer pricing principles	5	Canada, Netherlands, United States
Cross-border rulings providing for a unilateral downward adjustment to the taxpayer's taxable profits that is not directly reflected in the taxpayer's financial / commercial accounts	1	*De minimis* rule applies
Permanent establishment rulings	7	Belgium, Netherlands, Switzerland, United States
Related party conduit rulings	0	N/A
Total	13	

D. Matters related to intellectual property regimes (ToR I.A.1.3)

484. Germany does not offer an intellectual property regime for which transparency requirements under the Action 5 Report (OECD, 2015[1]) were imposed.

Summary of recommendations on implementation of the transparency framework

Aspect of implementation of the transparency framework that should be improved	Recommendation for improvement
	No recommendations are made.

References

OECD (2021), *BEPS Action 5 on Harmful Tax Practices - Terms of Reference and Methodology for the Conduct of the Peer Reviews of the Action 5 Transparency Framework*, OECD Publishing, Paris, http://www.oecd.org/tax/beps/beps-action-5-harmful-tax-practices-peer-review-transparency-framework.pdf. [3]

OECD (2015), *Countering Harmful Tax Practices More Effectively, Taking into Account Transparency and Substance, Action 5 - 2015 Final Report*, OECD/G20 Base Erosion and Profit Shifting Project, OECD Publishing, Paris, https://dx.doi.org/10.1787/9789264241190-en. [1]

OECD (ed.) (2017b), *Harmful Tax Practices - 2017 Progress Report on Preferential Regimes*, OECD Publishing, Paris, http://dx.doi.org/10.1787/9789264283954-en. [2]

OECD/Council of Europe (2011), *The Multilateral Convention on Mutual Administrative Assistance in Tax Matters: Amended by the 2010 Protocol*, OECD Publishing, Paris, https://dx.doi.org/10.1787/9789264115606-en. [4]

Notes

[1] With respect to the following preferential regimes: 1) Tonnage tax regime.

[2] Participating jurisdictions to the Convention are available here: www.oecd.org/tax/exchange-of-tax-information/convention-on-mutual-administrative-assistance-in-tax-matters.htm. Germany also has bilateral agreements with Albania, Algeria, Argentina, Armenia, Australia, Austria, Bangladesh, Belarus, Belgium, Bolivia, Bosnia and Herzegovina, Bulgaria, Canada, China (People's Republic of), Costa Rica, Côte d'Ivoire, Croatia, Cyprus, Czech Republic, Denmark, Ecuador, Egypt, Estonia, Finland, France, Georgia, Ghana, Greece, Hungary, Iceland, India, Indonesia, Iran, Ireland, Israel, Italy, Jamaica, Japan, Jersey, Kazakhstan, Kenia, Korea, Kosovo, Kuwait, Kyrgyzstan, Latvia, Liberia, Liechtenstein, Lithuania, Luxembourg, Malaysia, Malta, Morocco, Mauritius, Mexico, Moldavia, Mongolia, Montenegro, Namibia, Netherlands, New Zealand, North Macedonia, Norway, Pakistan, Philippines, Poland, Portugal, Romania, Russia, Serbia, Singapore, Slovak Republic, Slovenia, South Africa, Spain, Sri Lanka, Sweden, Switzerland, Syrian Arab Republic, Tajikistan, Thailand, Trinidad and Tobago, Tunisia, Turkey, Turkmenistan, Ukraine, United Arab Emirates, United Kingdom, United States, Uruguay, Uzbekistan, Venezuela, Viet Nam, Zambia, Zimbabwe.

Gibraltar

Gibraltar has met all aspects of the terms of reference (OECD, 2021[3]) (ToR) for the calendar year 2020 (year in review) that can be met in the absence of rulings being issued in practice and no recommendations are made.

This is Gibraltar's first review of implementation of the transparency framework.

Gibraltar can legally issue four types of rulings within the scope of the transparency framework.

In practice, Gibraltar issued no rulings within the scope of the transparency framework.

As no rulings were issued, no exchanges were required to take place, and no peer input was received in respect of the exchanges of information on rulings received from Gibraltar.

A. The information gathering process (ToR I.A)

485. Gibraltar can legally issue the following four types of rulings within the scope of the transparency framework: (i) cross-border unilateral APAs and any other cross-border unilateral tax rulings (such as an advance tax ruling) covering transfer pricing or the application of transfer pricing principles; (ii) rulings providing for unilateral downward adjustments; (iii) permanent establishment rulings; and (iv) related party conduit rulings. Rulings are issued by the Commissioner of Income Tax (hereafter "the Commissioner"), under the domestic procedure set out in the Income Tax Rules (Tax Rulings) of 2018 (hereafter "the Rules").

Past rulings (ToR I.A.1.1, I.A.1.2, I.A.2.1, I.A.2.2)

486. For Gibraltar, past rulings are any tax rulings issued prior to 1 March 2020. However, there is no obligation for Gibraltar to conduct spontaneous exchange information on past rulings.

Future rulings (ToR I.A.1.1, I.A.1.2, I.A.2.1)

487. For Gibraltar, future rulings are any tax rulings within scope that are issued on or after 1 March 2020.

488. The ruling process in Gibraltar encompasses an assessment of whether the ruling issued by the Commissioner is within the scope of the transparency framework. All relevant information, including information on relevant exchange jurisdictions, needs to be provided by the taxpayer at the time the request for a ruling is submitted to the ITO. In this regard, Gibraltar notes that the Rules requires extensive documentation to be submitted with any ruling application including, but not limited to: i) a comprehensive description of the facts and circumstances which give rise to the request; ii) a description of the underlying business activities to which the tax ruling relates including the nature and place of the activities, the place of effective management of the business, the human and technical means used (or intended to be used) by the applicant in pursuing the business activities and the classes of customers at which the business activities are targeted or intended to be targeted; and iii) sufficient evidence to support any assertion made in the application, including benchmarks or thresholds applied for determining arms-length equivalence or other matters. If the ruling is identified as within the scope of the transparency framework, information on the jurisdiction of residence of related parties, ultimate and immediate parent entities, head office charged with effective management and ultimate beneficial owners covered by the ruling would also be sought. The Commissioner can request any additional information deemed necessary for the exchange of information directly to the applicant or through the issuance of a statutory notice for gathering such information.

489. To date no rulings within the scope of the transparency framework have been issued as no applications have been submitted by taxpayers requiring the issuance of such rulings. As such, there was no need to identify potential exchange jurisdictions.

Review and supervision (ToR I.A.3)

490. The accuracy of the information gathering process and the identification of rulings within the scope of the transparency framework is supervised by the corporate tax team within ITO. Taxpayers can send their ruling applications electronically to a dedicated email address. Applications are reviewed by the corporate tax team with the oversight of both the head of the corporate tax section and a senior counsel, who advise on technical and substantive matters relating to procedural aspects of the domestic process, requirements under the transparency framework, adherence to legislative timeframes and requirements, and finally the content of the ruling applications. Prior to the issuance of any ruling, an internal control is in place to ensure that all relevant information needed for the purpose of the exchange of information under the transparency framework is adequately captured. If needed, requests for further information can be

made in accordance with the Rules. Given the expected small volumes of ruling applications in the jurisdiction, Gibraltar is able to ensure a meticulous supervision and monitoring process of all ruling applications made.

Conclusion on section A

491. Gibraltar has met all of the ToR for the information gathering process that can be met in the absence of rulings being issued in practice and no recommendations are made.

B. The exchange of information (ToR II.B)

Legal basis for spontaneous exchange of information (ToR II.B.1, II.B.2)

492. Gibraltar has the necessary domestic legal basis to exchange information spontaneously. Gibraltar notes that there are no legal or practical impediments that prevent the spontaneous exchange of information on rulings as contemplated in the Action 5 minimum standard.

493. Gibraltar has international agreements permitting spontaneous exchange of information, including participating in (i) the *Multilateral Convention on Mutual Administrative Assistance in Tax Matters: Amended by the 2010 Protocol* (OECD/Council of Europe, 2011[4]) ("the Convention") following the territorial extension of this convention to Gibraltar by the United Kingdom, (ii) bilateral agreements in force with one jurisdiction and iii) tax information exchange agreements in force with four jurisdictions.[1]

Completion and exchange of templates (ToR II.B.3, II.B.4, II.B.5, II.B.6, II.B.7)

494. Although Gibraltar issued no future rulings, Gibraltar has indicated that the Commissioner is the competent authority for Gibraltar for the purposes of exchanging information under the transparency framework. In the event that a relevant ruling is issued, the rulings team within ITO is in charge of the preparation of the information exchanges with the supervision and guidance by both the head of the corporate tax section and a senior counsel and in close coordination with the Commissioner. Exchanges would either be sent via encrypted email to the corresponding competent authority of the relevant exchange jurisdiction(s) or made available for download by the same jurisdiction(s) via Her Majesty's Government of Gibraltar's cloud facility. Gibraltar indicated its intention to complete the templates in the form of Annex C of the BEPS Action 5 Report (OECD, 2015[1]) and to exchange them in PDF template format. The various levels of supervision and monitoring would ensure that the summary section of the template is completed in line with the internal FHTP suggested guidance and each of the mandatory fields of information required in the Annex C template are present in the information exchanged. Given the expected small volumes of ruling applications in the jurisdiction, Gibraltar is able to ensure a meticulous supervision and monitoring process of applicable procedures and timelines. To this end, internal communication functions, including email-based reminders and diary functions, are used as well. Finally, the close coordination between the rulings team and the Commissioner ensures that information is readily available to the Competent Authority (i.e. the Commissioner) to be exchanged according to the FHTP agreed timelines and in any case within a period of 3 months from the date of issue of the ruling.

495. As Gibraltar did not issue any rulings within the scope of the transparency framework in the relevant period, Gibraltar was not required to exchange any information on rulings in the year in review and no data on the timeliness of exchanges can be reported.

Conclusion on section B

496. Gibraltar has the necessary legal basis for spontaneous exchange of information and a process for completing the templates in a timely way. Gibraltar has met all of the ToR for the exchange of information process that can be met in the absence of rulings being issued and exchanged in practice and no recommendations are made.

C. Statistics (ToR IV)

497. As no rulings were issued, no statistics can be reported.

D. Matters related to intellectual property regimes (ToR I.A.1.3)

498. Gibraltar does not offer an intellectual property regime for which transparency requirements under the Action 5 Report (OECD, 2015[1]) were imposed.

Summary of recommendations on implementation of the transparency framework

Aspect of implementation of the transparency framework that should be improved	Recommendation for improvement
	No recommendations are made.

References

OECD (2021), *BEPS Action 5 on Harmful Tax Practices - Terms of Reference and Methodology for the Conduct of the Peer Reviews of the Action 5 Transparency Framework*, OECD Publishing, Paris, http://www.oecd.org/tax/beps/beps-action-5-harmful-tax-practices-peer-review-transparency-framework.pdf. [3]

OECD (2015), *Countering Harmful Tax Practices More Effectively, Taking into Account Transparency and Substance, Action 5 - 2015 Final Report*, OECD/G20 Base Erosion and Profit Shifting Project, OECD Publishing, Paris, https://dx.doi.org/10.1787/9789264241190-en. [1]

OECD (ed.) (2017b), *Harmful Tax Practices - 2017 Progress Report on Preferential Regimes*, OECD Publishing, Paris, http://dx.doi.org/10.1787/9789264283954-en. [2]

OECD/Council of Europe (2011), *The Multilateral Convention on Mutual Administrative Assistance in Tax Matters: Amended by the 2010 Protocol*, OECD Publishing, Paris, https://dx.doi.org/10.1787/9789264115606-en. [4]

Notes

[1] Participating jurisdictions to the Convention are available here: www.oecd.org/tax/exchange-of-tax-information/convention-on-mutual-administrative-assistance-in-tax-matters.htm. Gibraltar also has a bilateral agreement with the United Kingdom and tax information exchange agreements with Guernsey, Isle of Man, United Kingdom and United States.

Greece

Greece has met all aspects of the terms of reference (OECD, 2021[3]) (ToR) for the calendar year 2020 (year in review), and no recommendations are made.

Greece can legally issue one type of rulings within the scope of the transparency framework.

In practice, Greece issued rulings within the scope of the transparency framework as follows:

Type of ruling	Number of rulings
Past rulings	1
Future rulings in the period 1 April 2016 – 31 December 2016	0
Future rulings in the calendar year 2017	0
Future rulings in the calendar year 2018	2
Future rulings in the calendar year 2019	0
Future rulings in the year in review	1

No peer input was received in respect of the exchanges of information on rulings received from Greece.

A. The information gathering process (ToR I.A)

499. Greece can legally issue one type of ruling within the scope of the transparency framework: cross-border unilateral APAs and any other cross-border unilateral tax rulings (such as an advance tax ruling) covering transfer pricing or the application of transfer pricing principles.

500. For Greece, past rulings are any tax rulings within scope that are issued either: (i) on or after 1 January 2014 but before 1 April 2016; or (ii) on or after 1 January 2010 but before 1 January 2014, provided they were still in effect as at 1 January 2014. Future rulings are any tax rulings within scope that are issued on or after 1 April 2016.

501. In the prior years' peer review reports, it was determined that Greece's undertakings to identify past and future rulings and all potential exchange jurisdictions were sufficient to meet the minimum standard. In addition, it was determined that Greece's review and supervision mechanism was sufficient to meet the minimum standard. Greece's implementation remains unchanged, and therefore continues to meet the minimum standard.

502. Greece has met all of the ToR for the information gathering process and no recommendations are made.

B. The exchange of information (ToR II.B)

503. Greece has international agreements permitting spontaneous exchange of information, including being a party to (i) the *Multilateral Convention on Mutual Administrative Assistance in Tax Matters: Amended by the 2010 Protocol* (OECD/Council of Europe, 2011[4]) ("the Convention"), (ii) the Directive 2011/16/EU with all other European Union Member States and (iii) bilateral agreements in force 57 jurisdictions.[1]

504. During the year in review, no exchanges were required to take place and no data on the timeliness of exchanges is reported. Greece notes that one ruling was issued in December 2020 and subsequently exchanged in early 2021. This will be reflected in next year's report.

505. In the prior years' peer review reports, it was determined that Greece's process for the completion and exchange of templates were sufficient to meet the minimum standard. With respect to past rulings, no further action was required. Greece's implementation in this regard remains unchanged and therefore continues to meet the minimum standard.

506. Greece has the necessary legal basis for spontaneous exchange of information, a process for completing the templates in a timely way and has completed all exchanges. Greece has met all of the ToR for the exchange of information process and no recommendations are made.

C. Statistics (ToR IV)

507. As there was no information on rulings exchanged by Greece for the year in review, no statistics can be reported.

D. Matters related to intellectual property regimes (ToR I.A.1.3)

508. Greece does not offer an intellectual property regime for which transparency requirements under the Action 5 Report (OECD, 2015[1]) were imposed.

Summary of recommendations on implementation of the transparency framework

Aspect of implementation of the transparency framework that should be improved	Recommendation for improvement
	No recommendations are made.

References

OECD (2021), *BEPS Action 5 on Harmful Tax Practices - Terms of Reference and Methodology for the Conduct of the Peer Reviews of the Action 5 Transparency Framework*, OECD Publishing, Paris, http://www.oecd.org/tax/beps/beps-action-5-harmful-tax-practices-peer-review-transparency-framework.pdf. [3]

OECD (2015), *Countering Harmful Tax Practices More Effectively, Taking into Account Transparency and Substance, Action 5 - 2015 Final Report*, OECD/G20 Base Erosion and Profit Shifting Project, OECD Publishing, Paris, https://dx.doi.org/10.1787/9789264241190-en. [1]

OECD (ed.) (2017b), *Harmful Tax Practices - 2017 Progress Report on Preferential Regimes*, OECD Publishing, Paris, http://dx.doi.org/10.1787/9789264283954-en. [2]

OECD/Council of Europe (2011), *The Multilateral Convention on Mutual Administrative Assistance in Tax Matters: Amended by the 2010 Protocol*, OECD Publishing, Paris, https://dx.doi.org/10.1787/9789264115606-en. [4]

Notes

[1] Participating jurisdictions to the Convention are available here: www.oecd.org/tax/exchange-of-tax-information/convention-on-mutual-administrative-assistance-in-tax-matters.htm. Greece also has bilateral agreements with Albania, Armenia, Austria, Azerbaijan, Belgium, Bosnia and Herzegovina, Bulgaria, Canada, China (People's Republic of), Qatar, Croatia, Cyprus, Czech Republic, Denmark, Egypt, Estonia, Finland, France, Germany, Georgia, Hungary, Iceland, India, Ireland, Israel, Italy, Korea, Kuwait, Latvia, Lithuania, Luxembourg, Malta, Mexico, Moldova, Morocco, Netherlands, Norway, Poland, Portugal, Romania, Russia, San Marino, Saudi Arabia, Serbia, Slovak Republic, Slovenia, Spain, South Africa, Sweden, Switzerland, Tunisia, Turkey, Ukraine, United Arab Emirates, United Kingdom, Uzbekistan and United States.

Grenada

Grenada is taking steps to implement the aspects of the terms of reference (OECD, 2021[3]) (ToR) for the transparency framework and to commence administrative preparations to ensure that it establishes an information gathering process (ToR I.A) and that information on rulings will be identified and exchanged in a timely manner (ToR II.B). Grenada receives two recommendations on these points for the calendar year 2020 (year in review).

In the prior year report, Grenada had received three recommendations. One issue has been resolved and therefore the prior year recommendation is removed. As the other two recommendations have not been addressed, they remain in place.

Grenada can legally issue five types of rulings within the scope of the transparency framework.

In practice, Grenada issued no rulings within the scope of the transparency framework.

As no exchanges were required to take place, no peer input was received in respect of the exchanges of information on rulings received from Grenada.

A. The information gathering process (ToR I.A)

509. Grenada can legally issue the following five types of rulings within the scope of the transparency framework: (i) preferential regimes; (ii) cross-border unilateral APAs and any other cross-border unilateral tax rulings (such as an advance tax ruling) covering transfer pricing or the application of transfer pricing principles; (iii) rulings providing for unilateral downward adjustments; (iv) permanent establishment rulings; and (v) related party conduit rulings.

Past rulings (ToR I.A.1.1, I.A.1.2, I.A.2.1, I.A.2.2)

510. For Grenada, past rulings are any tax rulings issued prior to 1 March 2019. However, there is no obligation for Grenada to conduct spontaneous exchange information on past rulings.

Future rulings (ToR I.A.1.1, I.A.1.2, I.A.2.1)

511. For Grenada, future rulings are any tax rulings within scope that are issued on or after 1 March 2019.

512. No rulings were issued by Grenada during the period in review. Grenada indicates that there are not yet processes in place to ensure the implementation of the obligations relating to the transparency framework such as the record keeping of rulings. It is noted that Grenada intends to implement appropriate processes to ensure the necessary information to meet the requirements of the transparency framework is required in all cases.

Review and supervision (ToR I.A.3)

513. Grenada did not yet have a review and supervision mechanism under the transparency framework for the year in review. Grenada is discussing the implementation of a revision and supervision mechanism for ensuring implementation of the transparency framework.

Conclusion on section A

514. Grenada is recommended to finalise its information gathering process for identifying all future rulings and potential exchange jurisdictions, with a review and supervision mechanism, as soon as possible (ToR I.A).

B. The exchange of information (ToR II.B)

Legal basis for spontaneous exchange of information (ToR II.B.1, II.B.2)

515. Grenada has the necessary domestic legal basis to exchange information spontaneously. Grenada notes that there are no legal or practical impediments that prevent the spontaneous exchange of information on rulings as contemplated in the Action 5 minimum standard.

516. Grenada has international agreements permitting spontaneous exchange of information, including being a party to (i) the *Multilateral Convention on Mutual Administrative Assistance in Tax Matters: Amended by the 2010 Protocol* (OECD/Council of Europe, 2011[4]) ("the Convention") and (ii) bilateral agreements in force with 15 jurisdictions.[1]

Completion and exchange of templates (ToR II.B.3, II.B.4, II.B.5, II.B.6, II.B.7)

517. Grenada is still developing a process to complete the templates on relevant rulings, to make them available to the Competent Authority for exchange of information, and to exchange them with relevant jurisdictions.

518. During the year in review, no exchanges were required to take place and no data on the timeliness of exchanges is reported.

Conclusion on section B

519. Grenada is recommended to develop a process to complete the templates on relevant rulings and to ensure that the exchanges of information on rulings occur in accordance with the form and timelines under the transparency framework (ToR II.B).

C. Statistics (ToR IV)

520. As no rulings were issued, no statistics can be reported.

D. Matters related to intellectual property regimes (ToR I.A.1.3)

521. Grenada does not offer an intellectual property regime for which transparency requirements under the Action 5 Report (OECD, 2015[1]) were imposed.

Summary of recommendations on implementation of the transparency framework

Aspect of implementation of the transparency framework that should be improved	Recommendation for improvement
Grenada has not put in place the necessary information gathering process.	Grenada is recommended to finalise its information gathering process for identifying all future rulings and potential exchange jurisdictions, with a review and supervision mechanism, as soon as possible. This recommendation remains unchanged since the prior year peer review report.
Grenada does not have a process to complete the templates on relevant rulings, to make them available to the Competent Authority for exchange of information, and to exchange them with relevant jurisdictions.	Grenada is recommended to develop a process to complete the templates on relevant rulings and to ensure that the exchanges of information on rulings occur in accordance with the form and timelines under the transparency framework. This recommendation remains unchanged since the prior year peer review report.

References

OECD (2021), *BEPS Action 5 on Harmful Tax Practices - Terms of Reference and Methodology for the Conduct of the Peer Reviews of the Action 5 Transparency Framework*, OECD Publishing, Paris, http://www.oecd.org/tax/beps/beps-action-5-harmful-tax-practices-peer-review-transparency-framework.pdf. [3]

OECD (2015), *Countering Harmful Tax Practices More Effectively, Taking into Account Transparency and Substance, Action 5 - 2015 Final Report*, OECD/G20 Base Erosion and Profit Shifting Project, OECD Publishing, Paris, https://dx.doi.org/10.1787/9789264241190-en. [1]

OECD (ed.) (2017b), *Harmful Tax Practices - 2017 Progress Report on Preferential Regimes*, OECD Publishing, Paris, http://dx.doi.org/10.1787/9789264283954-en. [2]

OECD/Council of Europe (2011), *The Multilateral Convention on Mutual Administrative Assistance in Tax Matters: Amended by the 2010 Protocol*, OECD Publishing, Paris, https://dx.doi.org/10.1787/9789264115606-en. [4]

Notes

[1] Participating jurisdictions to the Convention are available here: www.oecd.org/tax/exchange-of-tax-information/convention-on-mutual-administrative-assistance-in-tax-matters.htm. Grenada also has bilateral agreements with South Africa, the United Kingdom, and jurisdictions party to the CARICOM agreement.

Guernsey

Guernsey has met all aspects of the terms of reference (OECD, 2021[3]) (ToR) for the calendar year 2020 (year in review), and no recommendations are made.

Guernsey can legally issue four types of rulings within the scope of the transparency framework.

In practice, Guernsey issued rulings within the scope of the transparency framework as follows:

Type of ruling	Number of rulings
Past rulings	5
Future rulings in the period 1 April 2017 – 31 December 2017	3
Future rulings in the calendar year 2018	2
Future rulings in the calendar year 2019	1
Future rulings in the year in review	0

Peer input was received from one jurisdiction in respect of the exchanges of information on rulings received from Guernsey. The input was positive, noting that information was complete, in a correct format and received in a timely manner.

A. The information gathering process (ToR I.A)

522. Guernsey can legally issue four types of rulings within the scope of the transparency framework: (i) cross-border unilateral APAs and any other cross-border unilateral tax rulings (such as an advance tax ruling) covering transfer pricing or the application of transfer pricing principles; (ii) rulings providing for unilateral downward adjustments; (iii) permanent establishment rulings; and (iv) related party conduit rulings.

523. For Guernsey, past rulings are any tax rulings within scope that are issued either: (i) on or after 1 January 2015 but before 1 April 2017; or (ii) on or after 1 January 2012 but before 1 January 2015, provided they were still in effect as at 1 January 2015. Future rulings are any tax rulings within scope that are issued on or after 1 April 2017.

524. In the prior years' peer review reports, it was determined that Guernsey's undertakings to identify past and future rulings and all potential exchange jurisdictions were sufficient to meet the minimum standard. In addition, it was determined that Guernsey's review and supervision mechanism was sufficient to meet the minimum standard. Guernsey's implementation remains unchanged, and therefore continues to meet the minimum standard.

525. Guernsey has met all of the ToR for the information gathering process and no recommendations are made.

B. The exchange of information (ToR II.B)

526. Guernsey has international agreements permitting spontaneous exchange of information, including being a jurisdiction participating in (i) the *Multilateral Convention on Mutual Administrative Assistance in Tax Matters: Amended by the 2010 Protocol* (OECD/Council of Europe, 2011[4]) ("the Convention") and (ii) bilateral agreements in force with 18 jurisdictions.[1]

527. For the year in review, the timeliness of exchanges is as follows:

Future rulings within the scope of the transparency framework	Number of exchanges transmitted within three months of the information becoming available to the competent authority or immediately after legal impediments have been lifted	Delayed exchanges		
		Number of exchanges transmitted later than three months of the information on rulings becoming available to the competent authority	Reasons for the delays	Any other comments
	2[2]	0	N/A	N/A

Follow up requests received for exchange of the ruling	Number	Average time to provide response	Number of requests not answered
	0	N/A	N/A

528. In the prior years' peer review reports, it was determined that Guernsey's process for the completion and exchange of templates were sufficient to meet the minimum standard. With respect to past rulings, no further action was required. Guernsey's implementation in this regard remains unchanged and therefore continues to meet the minimum standard.

529. Guernsey has the necessary legal basis for spontaneous exchange of information, a process for completing the templates in a timely way and has completed all exchanges. Guernsey has met all of the ToR for the exchange of information process and no recommendations are made.

C. Statistics (ToR IV)

530. The statistics for the year in review are as follows:

Category of ruling	Number of exchanges	Jurisdictions exchanged with
Cross-border unilateral APAs and any other cross-border unilateral tax rulings (such as an advance tax ruling) covering transfer pricing or the application of transfer pricing principles	0	N/A
Cross-border rulings providing for a unilateral downward adjustment to the taxpayer's taxable profits that is not directly reflected in the taxpayer's financial / commercial accounts	*De minimis* rule applies	N/A
Permanent establishment rulings	0	N/A
Related party conduit rulings	0	N/A
De minimis rule	2	
Total	2	

D. Matters related to intellectual property regimes (ToR I.A.1.3)

531. Guernsey does not offer an intellectual property regime for which transparency requirements under the Action 5 Report (OECD, 2015[1]) were imposed.

Summary of recommendations on implementation of the transparency framework

Aspect of implementation of the transparency framework that should be improved	Recommendation for improvement
	No recommendations are made.

References

OECD (2021), *BEPS Action 5 on Harmful Tax Practices - Terms of Reference and Methodology for the Conduct of the Peer Reviews of the Action 5 Transparency Framework*, OECD Publishing, Paris, http://www.oecd.org/tax/beps/beps-action-5-harmful-tax-practices-peer-review-transparency-framework.pdf. [3]

OECD (2015), *Countering Harmful Tax Practices More Effectively, Taking into Account Transparency and Substance, Action 5 - 2015 Final Report*, OECD/G20 Base Erosion and Profit Shifting Project, OECD Publishing, Paris, https://dx.doi.org/10.1787/9789264241190-en. [1]

OECD (ed.) (2017b), *Harmful Tax Practices - 2017 Progress Report on Preferential Regimes*, OECD Publishing, Paris, http://dx.doi.org/10.1787/9789264283954-en. [2]

OECD/Council of Europe (2011), *The Multilateral Convention on Mutual Administrative Assistance in Tax Matters: Amended by the 2010 Protocol*, OECD Publishing, Paris, https://dx.doi.org/10.1787/9789264115606-en. [4]

Notes

[1] Participating jurisdictions to the Convention are available here: www.oecd.org/tax/exchange-of-tax-information/convention-on-mutual-administrative-assistance-in-tax-matters.htm. Guernsey also has bilateral agreements with British Virgin Islands, Cayman Islands, Cyprus, Gibraltar, Hong Kong (China), Isle of Man, Jersey, Liechtenstein, Luxembourg, Malta, Mauritius, Monaco, Qatar, Seychelles, Singapore, Turks and Caicos Islands, United Kingdom and United States.

[2] Guernsey clarified that the two exchanges reported in the 2019 peer review report were only performed in January 2020. As such, this year's peer review report also includes these same exchanges. The ruling issued in late 2019 only resulted in two exchanges in early 2020 within FHTP guidelines.

Hong Kong (China)

Hong Kong (China) ("Hong Kong") has met all aspects of the terms of reference (OECD, 2021[3]) (ToR) for the calendar year 2020 (year in review), and no recommendations are made.

Hong Kong can legally issue four types of rulings within the scope of the transparency framework.

In practice, Hong Kong issued rulings within the scope of the transparency framework as follows:

Type of ruling	Number of rulings
Past rulings	1
Future rulings in the calendar year 2017	0
Future rulings in the calendar year 2018	0
Future rulings in the calendar year 2019	2
Future rulings in the year in review	1

No peer input was received in respect of the exchanges of information on rulings received from Hong Kong.

A. The information gathering process (ToR I.A)

532. Hong Kong can legally issue the following four types of rulings within the scope of the transparency framework: (i) preferential regimes;[1] (ii) cross-border unilateral APAs and any other cross-border unilateral tax rulings (such as an advance tax ruling) covering transfer pricing or the application of transfer pricing principles; (iii) permanent establishment rulings; and (iv) related party conduit rulings.

533. For Hong Kong, past rulings are any tax rulings within scope that are issued either: (i) on or after 1 January 2015 but before 1 April 2017; or (ii) on or after 1 January 2012 but before 1 January 2015, provided they were still in effect as at 1 January 2015. Future rulings are any tax rulings within scope that are issued on or after 1 April 2017.

534. In the prior years' peer review reports, it was determined that Hong Kong's undertakings to identify past and future rulings and all potential exchange jurisdictions were sufficient to meet the minimum standard. In addition, it was determined that Hong Kong's review and supervision mechanism was sufficient to meet the minimum standard. Hong Kong's implementation remains unchanged, and therefore continues to meet the minimum standard.

535. Hong Kong has met all of the ToR for the information gathering process and no recommendations are made.

B. The exchange of information (ToR II.B)

536. Hong Kong has international agreements permitting spontaneous exchange of information, including being a jurisdiction participating in (i) the *Multilateral Convention on Mutual Administrative Assistance in Tax Matters: Amended by the 2010 Protocol* (OECD/Council of Europe, 2011[4]) ("the Convention") and (ii) bilateral agreements in force with 38 jurisdictions.[2]

537. For the year in review, the timeliness of exchanges is as follows:

Future rulings within the scope of the transparency framework	Number of exchanges transmitted within three months of the information becoming available to the competent authority or immediately after legal impediments have been lifted	Delayed exchanges		
		Number of exchanges transmitted later than three months of the information on rulings becoming available to the competent authority	Reasons for the delays	Any other comments
	1	0	N/A	N/A

Follow up requests received for exchange of the ruling	Number	Average time to provide response	Number of requests not answered
	0	N/A	N/A

538. In the prior years' peer review reports, it was determined that Hong Kong's process for the completion and exchange of templates were sufficient to meet the minimum standard. With respect to past rulings, no further action was required. Hong Kong's implementation in this regard remains unchanged and therefore continues to meet the minimum standard.

539. Hong Kong has the necessary legal basis for spontaneous exchange of information, a process for completing the templates in a timely way and has completed all exchanges. Hong Kong has met all of the ToR for the exchange of information process and no recommendations are made.

C. Statistics (ToR IV)

540. The statistics for the year in review are as follows:

Category of ruling	Number of exchanges	Jurisdictions exchanged with
Ruling related to a preferential regime	*De minimis* rule applies	N/A
Cross-border unilateral APAs and any other cross-border unilateral tax rulings (such as an advance tax ruling) covering transfer pricing or the application of transfer pricing principles	0	N/A
Cross-border rulings providing for a unilateral downward adjustment to the taxpayer's taxable profits that is not directly reflected in the taxpayer's financial / commercial accounts	0	N/A
Permanent establishment rulings	0	N/A
De minimis rule	1	N/A
Total	1	

D. Matters related to intellectual property regimes (ToR I.A.1.3)

541. Hong Kong does not offer an intellectual property regime for which transparency requirements under the Action 5 Report (OECD, 2015[1]) were imposed.

Summary of recommendations on implementation of the transparency framework

Aspect of implementation of the transparency framework that should be improved	Recommendation for improvement
	No recommendations are made.

References

OECD (2021), *BEPS Action 5 on Harmful Tax Practices - Terms of Reference and Methodology for the Conduct of the Peer Reviews of the Action 5 Transparency Framework*, OECD Publishing, Paris, http://www.oecd.org/tax/beps/beps-action-5-harmful-tax-practices-peer-review-transparency-framework.pdf. [3]

OECD (2015), *Countering Harmful Tax Practices More Effectively, Taking into Account Transparency and Substance, Action 5 - 2015 Final Report*, OECD/G20 Base Erosion and Profit Shifting Project, OECD Publishing, Paris, https://dx.doi.org/10.1787/9789264241190-en. [1]

OECD (ed.) (2017b), *Harmful Tax Practices - 2017 Progress Report on Preferential Regimes*, OECD Publishing, Paris, http://dx.doi.org/10.1787/9789264283954-en. [2]

OECD/Council of Europe (2011), *The Multilateral Convention on Mutual Administrative Assistance in Tax Matters: Amended by the 2010 Protocol*, OECD Publishing, Paris, https://dx.doi.org/10.1787/9789264115606-en. [4]

Notes

[1] With respect to the following preferential regimes: 1) profits tax concession for corporate treasury centres; 2) profits tax concession for professional reinsurers; 3) profits tax concession for captive insurers; 4) profits tax exemptions for ship operators; 5) profits tax concessions for aircraft lessors and aircraft leasing managers; and 6) profits tax concession for ship lessors and ship leasing managers.

[2] Participating jurisdictions to the Convention are available here: www.oecd.org/tax/exchange-of-tax-information/convention-on-mutual-administrative-assistance-in-tax-matters.htm. Hong Kong also has bilateral agreements with Austria, Belarus, Belgium, Cambodia, Canada, China (People's Republic of), Estonia, Finland, France, Guernsey, Hungary, India, Indonesia, Ireland, Italy, Japan, Jersey, Korea, Latvia, Macau (China), Malaysia, Malta, Mexico, Netherlands, New Zealand, Pakistan, Portugal, Qatar, Romania, Saudi Arabia, Serbia, South Africa, Spain, Switzerland, Thailand, United Arab Emirates, United Kingdom and Viet Nam.

Hungary

Hungary has met all aspects of the terms of reference (OECD, 2021[3]) (ToR) for the calendar year 2020 (year in review), except for applying the "best efforts approach" to identify potential exchange jurisdictions for all past rulings (ToR I.A.2.2), the timely exchange of information on future rulings (ToR II.B.6) and identifying or exchanging information on new entrants to the grandfathered IP regime (ToR I.A.1.3). Hungary receives three recommendations on these points for the year in review.

In the prior year report, as well as in the 2016, 2017 and 2018 peer reviews, Hungary had received the same recommendations with respect to the identification of exchange jurisdictions for past rulings and the grandfathered IP regime. In the prior year report, Hungary had received the same recommendation with respect to the exchange on future rulings. As they have not been addressed, the recommendations remain in place.

Hungary can legally issue four types of rulings within the scope of the transparency framework.

In practice, Hungary issued rulings within the scope of the transparency framework as follows:

Type of ruling	Number of rulings
Past rulings	77
Future rulings in the period 1 April 2016 – 31 December 2016	4
Future rulings in the calendar year 2017	9
Future rulings in the calendar year 2018	11
Future rulings in the calendar year 2019	21
Future rulings in the year in review	18

Peer input was received from one jurisdiction in respect of the exchanges of information on rulings received from Hungary. The input was positive, noting that information was complete, in a correct format and received in a timely manner.

A. The information gathering process (ToR I.A)

542. Hungary can legally issue the following four types of rulings within the scope of the transparency framework: (i) preferential regimes;[1] (ii) cross-border unilateral APAs and any other cross-border unilateral tax rulings (such as an advance tax ruling) covering transfer pricing or the application of transfer pricing principles; (iii) permanent establishment rulings; and (iv) related party conduit rulings.

Past rulings (ToR I.A.1.1, I.A.1.2, I.A.2.1, I.A.2.2)

543. For Hungary, past rulings are any tax rulings within scope that are issued either: (i) on or after 1 January 2014 but before 1 April 2016; or (ii) on or after 1 January 2010 but before 1 January 2014, provided they were still in effect as at 1 January 2014.

544. In the prior years' peer review reports, it was determined that Hungary had not used the "best efforts approach" to identify potential exchange jurisdictions, meaning that Hungary had only identified potential exchange jurisdictions for around half of the past ATRs, although it had identified most potential exchange jurisdictions for APAs but not necessarily the ultimate parent company jurisdiction. Therefore, Hungary was recommended to continue to apply the "best efforts approach" to identify potential exchange jurisdictions for all past rulings.

545. During the year in review, Hungary has not been able to take additional steps. As such, the recommendation remains.

Future rulings (ToR I.A.1.1, I.A.1.2, I.A.2.1)

546. For Hungary, future rulings are any tax rulings within scope that are issued on or after 1 April 2016.

547. In the prior year peer review report, it was determined that Hungary's undertakings to identify future rulings and all potential exchange jurisdictions was sufficient to meet the minimum standard. Hungary's implementation in this regard remains unchanged, and therefore continues to meet the minimum standard.

Review and supervision (ToR I.A.3)

548. In the prior years' peer review reports, it was determined that Hungary's review and supervision mechanism was sufficient to meet the minimum standard. Hungary's implementation in this regard remains unchanged, and therefore continues to meet the minimum standard.

Conclusion on section A

549. Hungary has met all of the ToR for the information gathering process except for applying the "best efforts approach" for past rulings (ToR I.A.2.2) and Hungary is recommended to continue to apply the "best efforts approach" to identify potential exchange jurisdictions for all past rulings.

B. The exchange of information (ToR II.B)

Legal basis for spontaneous exchange of information (ToR II.B.1, II.B.2)

550. Hungary has the necessary domestic legal basis to exchange information spontaneously. Hungary notes that there are no legal or practical impediments that prevent the spontaneous exchange of information on rulings as contemplated in the Action 5 minimum standard.

551. Hungary has international agreements permitting spontaneous exchange of information, including being a party to (i) the *Multilateral Convention on Mutual Administrative Assistance in Tax Matters: Amended by the 2010 Protocol* (OECD/Council of Europe, 2011[4]) ("the Convention"), (ii) the Directive 2011/16/EU with all other European Union Member States and (iii) bilateral agreements in force with 81 jurisdictions.[2]

Completion and exchange of templates (ToR II.B.3, II.B.4, II.B.5, II.B.6, II.B.7)

552. In the prior year peer review report, it was determined that Hungary's process for the completion and exchange of templates was sufficient to meet the minimum standard. Hungary's implementation in this regard remains unchanged and therefore continues to meet the minimum standard.

553. For the year in review, the timeliness of exchanges is as follows:

Future rulings within the scope of the transparency framework	Number of exchanges transmitted within three months of the information becoming available to the competent authority or immediately after legal impediments have been lifted	Delayed exchanges		
		Number of exchanges transmitted later than three months of the information on rulings becoming available to the competent authority	Reasons for the delays	Any other comments
	42	15	See below	N/A

Follow up requests received for exchange of the ruling	Number	Average time to provide response	Number of requests not answered
	0	N/A	N/A

554. During the year in review, Hungary still experienced some delays in exchanging future rulings. Hungary conducted these outstanding exchanges in April 2021. Hungary is recommended to ensure that all information on future rulings is exchanged as soon as possible.

Conclusion on section B

555. Hungary has the necessary legal basis for spontaneous exchange of information, a process for completing the templates in a timely way and has completed all exchanges. Hungary has met all of the ToR for the exchange of information process except for the timely exchange of information on future rulings (ToR II.B.6) and Hungary is recommended to ensure that all information on future rulings is exchanged as soon as possible.

C. Statistics (ToR IV)

556. The statistics for the year in review are as follows:

Category of ruling	Number of exchanges	Jurisdictions exchanged with
Ruling related to a preferential regime	0	N/A
Cross-border unilateral APAs and any other cross-border unilateral tax rulings (such as an advance tax ruling) covering transfer pricing or the application of transfer pricing principles	42	Austria, Belgium, Canada, Czech Republic, Finland, France, Germany, Italy, Luxembourg, Netherlands, Norway, Poland, Portugal, Spain, Sweden, Switzerland, United Kingdom, United States, Uruguay
Permanent establishment rulings	15	Canada, Germany, Ireland, Luxembourg, Switzerland, United States, Uruguay
Related party conduit rulings	0	N/A
IP regimes: total exchanges on taxpayers benefitting from the third category of IP assets, new entrants benefitting from grandfathered IP regimes; and taxpayers making use of the option to treat the nexus ratio as a rebuttable presumption	0	
Total	57	

D. Matters related to intellectual property regimes (ToR I.A.1.3)

557. Hungary offers an intellectual property regime (IP regime)[3] that is subject to the transparency requirements under the Action 5 Report (OECD, 2015[1]). It states that the identification of the benefitting taxpayers will occur as follows:

- ***New entrants benefitting from the grandfathered IP regime***: Taxpayers that are new entrants to the IP regime can be identified in the tax return. The first tax returns containing information on new entrants have been filed after the relevant date from which enhanced transparency obligations apply. In the prior year, Hungary identified new entrants resulting in 14 exchanges. For the year in review, Hungary does not report any exchanges resulting from identifications of new entrants.
- ***Third category of IP assets***: not applicable as the regime does not allow the third category of IP assets to qualify for the benefits.
- ***Taxpayers making use of the option to treat the nexus ratio as a rebuttable presumption***: not applicable as the regime does not allow the nexus ratio to be treated as a rebuttable presumption.

558. Hungary is recommended to continue its efforts to identify and exchange information on all new entrants to the grandfathered IP regime as soon as possible (ToR I.A.1.3).

Summary of recommendations on implementation of the transparency framework

Aspect of implementation of the transparency framework that should be improved	Recommendation for improvement
Hungary did not yet apply the "best efforts approach" to identify potential exchange jurisdictions for all past rulings.	Hungary is recommended to continue to apply the "best efforts approach" to identify potential exchange jurisdictions for all past rulings. This recommendation remains unchanged since the 2016, 2017, 2018 and 2019 peer review reports.
Hungary experienced some delays for the exchange of future rulings.	Hungary is recommended to ensure that all information on future rulings is exchanged as soon as possible. This recommendation remains unchanged since the 2019 peer review report.
Hungary did not identify or exchange all information on new	Hungary is recommended to continue its efforts to identify

entrants to the grandfathered IP regime.	and exchange information on all new entrants to the grandfathered IP regime. This recommendation remains unchanged since the 2016, 2017, 2018 and 2019 peer review reports.

References

OECD (2021), *BEPS Action 5 on Harmful Tax Practices - Terms of Reference and Methodology for the Conduct of the Peer Reviews of the Action 5 Transparency Framework*, OECD Publishing, Paris, http://www.oecd.org/tax/beps/beps-action-5-harmful-tax-practices-peer-review-transparency-framework.pdf. [3]

OECD (2015), *Countering Harmful Tax Practices More Effectively, Taking into Account Transparency and Substance, Action 5 - 2015 Final Report*, OECD/G20 Base Erosion and Profit Shifting Project, OECD Publishing, Paris, https://dx.doi.org/10.1787/9789264241190-en. [1]

OECD (ed.) (2017b), *Harmful Tax Practices - 2017 Progress Report on Preferential Regimes*, OECD Publishing, Paris, http://dx.doi.org/10.1787/9789264283954-en. [2]

OECD/Council of Europe (2011), *The Multilateral Convention on Mutual Administrative Assistance in Tax Matters: Amended by the 2010 Protocol*, OECD Publishing, Paris, https://dx.doi.org/10.1787/9789264115606-en. [4]

Notes

[1] With respect to the following preferential regime: IP regime for royalties and capital gains.

[2] Participating jurisdictions to the Convention are available here: www.oecd.org/tax/exchange-of-tax-information/convention-on-mutual-administrative-assistance-in-tax-matters.htm. Hungary also has bilateral agreements with Albania, Armenia, Australia, Austria, Azerbaijan, Bahrain, Belarus, Belgium, Bosnia and Herzegovina, Brazil, Bulgaria, Canada, China (People's Republic of), Chinese Taipei, Croatia, Cyprus, Czech Republic, Denmark, Egypt, Estonia, Finland, France, Georgia, Germany, Greece, Hong Kong (China), Iceland, India, Indonesia, Iran, Ireland, Israel, Italy, Japan, Kazakhstan, Korea, Kosovo, Kuwait, Latvia, Liechtenstein, Lithuania, Luxembourg, Malaysia, Malta, Mexico, Moldova, Mongolia, Montenegro, Morocco, Netherlands, North Macedonia, Norway, Oman, Pakistan, Philippines, Poland, Portugal, Qatar, Romania, Russia, San Marino, Saudi Arabia, Serbia, Singapore, Slovak Republic, Slovenia, South Africa, Spain, Sweden, Switzerland, Thailand, Tunisia, Turkey, Turkmenistan, Ukraine, United Arab Emirates, United Kingdom, United States, Uruguay, Uzbekistan and Viet Nam.

[3] IP regime for royalties and capital gains.

Iceland

Iceland has met all aspects of the terms of reference (OECD, 2021[3]) (ToR) for the calendar year 2020 (year in review), and no recommendations are made.

Iceland can legally issue two types of rulings within the scope of the transparency framework.

In practice, Iceland issued rulings within the scope of the transparency framework as follows:

Type of ruling	Number of rulings
Past rulings	1
Future rulings in the period 1 April 2016 – 31 December 2016	0
Future rulings in the calendar year 2017	0
Future rulings in the calendar year 2018	0
Future rulings in the calendar year 2019	0
Future rulings in the year in review	0

As no exchanges were required to take place, no peer input was received in respect of the exchanges of information on rulings received from Iceland.

A. The information gathering process (ToR I.A)

559. Iceland can legally issue the following two types of rulings within the scope of the transparency framework: (i) permanent establishment rulings and (ii) related party conduit rulings.

560. For Iceland, past rulings are any tax rulings within scope that are issued either: (i) on or after 1 January 2014 but before 1 April 2016; or (ii) on or after 1 January 2010 but before 1 January 2014, provided they were still in effect as at 1 January 2014. Future rulings are any tax rulings within scope that are issued on or after 1 April 2016.

561. In the prior years' peer review reports, it was determined that Iceland's undertakings to identify past and future rulings and all potential exchange jurisdictions were sufficient to meet the minimum standard. In addition, it was determined that Iceland's review and supervision mechanism was sufficient to meet the minimum standard. Iceland's implementation remains unchanged, and therefore continues to meet the minimum standard.

562. Iceland has met all of the ToR for the information gathering process and no recommendations are made.

B. The exchange of information (ToR II.B)

563. Iceland has international agreements permitting spontaneous exchange of information, including being a party to (i) the *Multilateral Convention on Mutual Administrative Assistance in Tax Matters: Amended by the 2010 Protocol* (OECD/Council of Europe, 2011[4]) ("the Convention"), (ii) the Nordic Convention with Denmark, Faroe Islands, Finland, Norway and Sweden and (iii) bilateral agreements in force with 40 jurisdictions.[1]

564. As Iceland was not required to exchange any information on rulings for the year in review and no data on the timeliness of exchanges can be reported.

565. In the prior years' peer review reports, it was determined that Iceland's process for the completion and exchange of templates were sufficient to meet the minimum standard. With respect to past rulings, no further action was required. Iceland's implementation in this regard remains unchanged and therefore continues to meet the minimum standard.

566. Iceland has the necessary legal basis for spontaneous exchange of information, a process for completing the templates in a timely way and has completed all exchanges. Iceland has met all of the ToR for the exchange of information process and no recommendations are made.

C. Statistics (ToR IV)

567. As no rulings were issued, no statistics can be reported.

D. Matters related to intellectual property regimes (ToR I.A.1.3)

568. Iceland does not offer an intellectual property regime for which transparency requirements under the Action 5 Report (OECD, 2015[1]) were imposed.

Summary of recommendations on implementation of the transparency framework

Aspect of implementation of the transparency framework that should be improved	Recommendation for improvement
	No recommendations are made.

References

OECD (2021), *BEPS Action 5 on Harmful Tax Practices - Terms of Reference and Methodology for the Conduct of the Peer Reviews of the Action 5 Transparency Framework*, OECD Publishing, Paris, http://www.oecd.org/tax/beps/beps-action-5-harmful-tax-practices-peer-review-transparency-framework.pdf. [3]

OECD (2015), *Countering Harmful Tax Practices More Effectively, Taking into Account Transparency and Substance, Action 5 - 2015 Final Report*, OECD/G20 Base Erosion and Profit Shifting Project, OECD Publishing, Paris, https://dx.doi.org/10.1787/9789264241190-en. [1]

OECD (ed.) (2017b), *Harmful Tax Practices - 2017 Progress Report on Preferential Regimes*, OECD Publishing, Paris, http://dx.doi.org/10.1787/9789264283954-en. [2]

OECD/Council of Europe (2011), *The Multilateral Convention on Mutual Administrative Assistance in Tax Matters: Amended by the 2010 Protocol*, OECD Publishing, Paris, https://dx.doi.org/10.1787/9789264115606-en. [4]

Notes

[1] Participating jurisdictions to the Convention are available here: www.oecd.org/tax/exchange-of-tax-information/convention-on-mutual-administrative-assistance-in-tax-matters.htm. Iceland also has bilateral agreements with Albania, Austria, Barbados, Belgium, Canada, China (People's Republic of), Croatia, Cyprus, Czech Republic, Estonia, France, Georgia, Greece, Greenland, Germany, Hungary, India, Ireland, Italy, Japan, Korea, Latvia, Liechtenstein, Lithuania, Luxembourg, Malta, Mexico, Netherlands, Poland, Portugal, Romania, Russia, Slovak Republic, Slovenia, Spain, Switzerland, Ukraine, United Kingdom, United States, Viet Nam.

India

India has met all aspects of the terms of reference (OECD, 2021[3]) (ToR) for the calendar year 2020 (year in review), except for ensuring that information on future rulings is exchanged as soon as possible (ToR II.B.6). India receives one recommendation on this point for the year in review.

In the prior year report, as well as in the 2017 and 2018 peer reviews, India had received the same recommendation. During the year in review, a number of exchanges remained delayed, and therefore the recommendation remains in place.

India can legally issue two types of rulings within the scope of the transparency framework.

In practice, India issued rulings within the scope of the transparency framework as follows:

Type of ruling	Number of rulings
Past rulings	69
Future rulings in the period 1 April 2016 – 31 December 2016	55
Future rulings in the calendar year 2017	73
Future rulings in the calendar year 2018	44
Future rulings in the calendar year 2019	137
Future rulings in the year in review	28

Peer input was received from four jurisdictions in respect of the exchanges of information on rulings received from India. The input was positive, noting that information was complete and in a correct format. However, peer input indicated that not all exchanges of information on rulings were conducted in a timely manner.

A. The information gathering process (ToR I.A)

569. India can legally issue the following two types of rulings within the scope of the transparency framework: (i) cross-border unilateral APAs and any other cross-border unilateral tax rulings (such as an advance tax ruling) covering transfer pricing or the application of transfer pricing principles; and (ii) permanent establishment rulings.

570. For India, past rulings are any tax rulings within scope that are issued either: (i) on or after 1 January 2014 but before 1 April 2016; or (ii) on or after 1 January 2010 but before 1 January 2014, provided they were still in effect as at 1 January 2014. Future rulings are any tax rulings within scope that are issued on or after 1 April 2016.

571. In the prior year peer review report, it was determined that India's undertakings to identify past and future rulings and all potential exchange jurisdictions were sufficient to meet the minimum standard. In addition, it was determined that India's review and supervision mechanism was sufficient to meet the minimum standard. India's implementation remains unchanged, and therefore continues to meet the minimum standard.

572. India has met all of the ToR for the information gathering process and no recommendations are made.

B. The exchange of information (ToR II.B)

Legal basis for spontaneous exchange of information (ToR II.B.1, II.B.2)

573. India has the necessary domestic legal basis to exchange information spontaneously. India notes that there are no legal or practical impediments that prevent the spontaneous exchange of information on rulings as contemplated in the Action 5 minimum standard.

574. India has international agreements permitting spontaneous exchange of information, including being a party to (i) the *Multilateral Convention on Mutual Administrative Assistance in Tax Matters: Amended by the 2010 Protocol* (OECD/Council of Europe, 2011[4]) ("the Convention"), (ii) the South Asian Association for Regional Cooperation (SAARC) Agreement and (iii) bilateral agreements in force with 100 jurisdictions.[1]

Completion and exchange of templates (ToR II.B.3, II.B.4, II.B.5, II.B.6, II.B.7)

575. In the prior years' peer review reports, it was determined that India's process for the completion and exchange of templates met all the ToR, except for ensuring that information on future APA rulings is exchanged as soon as possible (ToR II.B.6). Therefore, India was recommended to ensure the timely exchange of information on future APA rulings. With respect to past rulings, no further action was required.

576. For the year in review, the timeliness of exchanges is as follows:

Future rulings within the scope of the transparency framework	Number of exchanges transmitted within three months of the information becoming available to the competent authority or immediately after legal impediments have been lifted	Delayed exchanges		
		Number of exchanges transmitted later than three months of the information on rulings becoming available to the competent authority	Reasons for the delays	Any other comments
	68	83	See below	N/A

Follow up requests received for exchange of the ruling	Number	Average time to provide response	Number of requests not answered
	0	N/A	N/A

577. During the year in review, India continued to encounter delays with respect to the exchange of information on future APAs. This was mostly due to the fact that India had to use the "best efforts approach" to identify potential exchange jurisdictions for APAs filed before 16 June 2017. It is noted that new ruling application templates requiring this information came into effect from 16 June 2017 for APAs filed on or after that date. In addition, India faced difficulties in carrying out exchanges due to the Covid-19 pandemic. Therefore, India is still recommended to continue to ensure the timely exchange of information on future APA rulings (ToR II.B.6).

Conclusion on section B

578. India has met all of the ToR for the information gathering process except for ensuring that information on future APA rulings is exchanged as soon as possible (ToR II.B.6). India is recommended to continue to ensure the timely exchange of information on future APA rulings.

C. Statistics (ToR IV)

579. The statistics for the year in review are as follows:

Category of ruling	Number of exchanges	Jurisdictions exchanged with
Cross-border unilateral APAs and any other cross-border unilateral tax rulings (such as an advance tax ruling) covering transfer pricing or the application of transfer pricing principles	148	Australia, Belgium, Brazil, Canada, China (People's Republic of), Denmark, France, Germany, Greece, Guernsey, Hong Kong (China), Hungary, Indonesia, Ireland, Italy, Japan, Jersey, Korea, Luxembourg, Mexico, Netherlands, New Zealand, Norway, Poland, Portugal, Russia, Singapore, Spain, Sweden, Switzerland, United Kingdom, United States
Permanent establishment rulings	3	*De minimis* rule applies
Total	151	

D. Matters related to intellectual property regimes (ToR I.A.1.3)

580. India offers an intellectual property regime (IP regime)[2] that is not subject to the transparency requirements under the Action 5 Report (OECD, 2015[1]), because:

- ***New entrants benefitting from the grandfathered IP regime***: the regime is a new nexus-compliant regime and therefore there is no grandfathered IP regime for which enhanced transparency requirements will apply.
- ***Third category of IP assets***: not applicable as the regime does not allow the third category of IP assets to qualify for the benefits.
- ***Taxpayers making the use of the option to treat the nexus ratio as a rebuttable presumption***: not applicable the regime does not allow the nexus ratio to be treated as a rebuttable presumption.

Summary of recommendations on implementation of the transparency framework

Aspect of implementation of the transparency framework that should be improved	Recommendation for improvement
India experienced delays in the exchange of information on future APAs.	India is recommended to continue its efforts to ensure that all information on future APAs is exchanged as soon as possible. This recommendation remains unchanged since the 2017, 2018 and 2019 peer review reports.

References

OECD (2021), *BEPS Action 5 on Harmful Tax Practices - Terms of Reference and Methodology for the Conduct of the Peer Reviews of the Action 5 Transparency Framework*, OECD Publishing, Paris, http://www.oecd.org/tax/beps/beps-action-5-harmful-tax-practices-peer-review-transparency-framework.pdf. [3]

OECD (2015), *Countering Harmful Tax Practices More Effectively, Taking into Account Transparency and Substance, Action 5 - 2015 Final Report*, OECD/G20 Base Erosion and Profit Shifting Project, OECD Publishing, Paris, https://dx.doi.org/10.1787/9789264241190-en. [1]

OECD (ed.) (2017b), *Harmful Tax Practices - 2017 Progress Report on Preferential Regimes*, OECD Publishing, Paris, http://dx.doi.org/10.1787/9789264283954-en. [2]

OECD/Council of Europe (2011), *The Multilateral Convention on Mutual Administrative Assistance in Tax Matters: Amended by the 2010 Protocol*, OECD Publishing, Paris, https://dx.doi.org/10.1787/9789264115606-en. [4]

Notes

[1] Participating jurisdictions to the Convention are available here: www.oecd.org/tax/exchange-of-tax-information/convention-on-mutual-administrative-assistance-in-tax-matters.htm. India also has bilateral agreements with Albania, Armenia, Australia, Austria, Azerbaijan, Bahamas, Bangladesh, Belarus, Belgium, Bhutan, Botswana, Brazil, Brunei Darussalam, Bulgaria, Canada, China (People's Republic of), Colombia, Croatia, Cyprus, Czech Republic, Denmark, Egypt, Estonia, Ethiopia, Faroe Islands, Fiji, Finland, France, Georgia, Germany, Greece, Grenada, Hungary, Iceland, Indonesia, Ireland, Israel, Italy, Japan, Jordan, Kazakhstan, Kenya, Korea, Kuwait, Kyrgyzstan, Latvia, Libya, Lithuania, Luxembourg, Malaysia, Malta, Mauritius, Mexico, Moldova, Mongolia, Morocco, Montenegro, Mozambique, Myanmar, Namibia, Nepal, Netherlands, New Zealand, North Macedonia, Norway, Oman, Philippines, Poland, Portugal, Qatar, Romania, Russia, Saudi Arabia, Serbia, Singapore, Slovak Republic, Slovenia, South Africa, Spain, Sri Lanka, Sudan, Sweden, Switzerland, Syrian Arab Republic, Chinese Taipei, Tajikistan, Tanzania, Thailand, Trinidad and Tobago, Turkey, Turkmenistan, Uganda, Ukraine, United Arab Emirates, United Kingdom, United States, Uruguay, Uzbekistan, Vanuatu and Zambia. The SAARC was entered into force on 19 May 2010 and provides for exchanges with Bangladesh, Bhutan, Maldives, Nepal, Pakistan and Sri Lanka.

[2] Tax on income from patent.

Indonesia

Indonesia has met all aspects of the terms of reference (OECD, 2021[3]) (ToR) for the calendar year 2020 (year in review), and no recommendations are made.

Indonesia can legally issue one type of rulings within the scope of the transparency framework.

In practice, Indonesia issued rulings within the scope of the transparency framework as follows:

Type of ruling	Number of rulings
Past rulings	0
Future rulings in the period 1 April 2016 – 31 December 2016	0
Future rulings in the calendar year 2017	0
Future rulings in the calendar year 2018	0
Future rulings in the calendar year 2019	1
Future rulings in the year in review	1

No peer input was received in respect of the exchanges of information on rulings received from Indonesia.

A. The information gathering process (ToR I.A)

581. Indonesia can legally issue one type of ruling within the scope of the transparency framework: (i) cross-border unilateral APAs and any other cross-border unilateral tax rulings (such as an advance tax ruling) covering transfer pricing or the application of transfer pricing principles.

582. For Indonesia, past rulings are any tax rulings within scope that are issued either: (i) on or after 1 January 2014 but before 1 April 2016; or (ii) on or after 1 January 2010 but before 1 January 2014, provided they were still in effect as at 1 January 2014. Future rulings are any tax rulings within scope that are issued on or after 1 April 2016.

583. In the prior years' peer review reports, it was determined that Indonesia's undertakings to identify past and future rulings and all potential exchange jurisdictions were sufficient to meet the minimum standard. In addition, it was determined that Indonesia's review and supervision mechanism was sufficient to meet the minimum standard. Indonesia's implementation remains unchanged, and therefore continues to meet the minimum standard.

584. Indonesia has met all of the ToR for the information gathering process and no recommendations are made.

B. The exchange of information (ToR II.B)

585. Indonesia has international agreements permitting spontaneous exchange of information, including being a party to (i) the *Multilateral Convention on Mutual Administrative Assistance in Tax Matters: Amended by the 2010 Protocol* (OECD/Council of Europe, 2011[4]) ("the Convention") and (ii) bilateral agreements in force with 69 jurisdictions.[1]

586. For the year in review, the timeliness of exchanges is as follows:

Future rulings within the scope of the transparency framework	Number of exchanges transmitted within three months of the information becoming available to the competent authority or immediately after legal impediments have been lifted	Delayed exchanges		
		Number of exchanges transmitted later than three months of the information on rulings becoming available to the competent authority	Reasons for the delays	Any other comments
	1	0	N/A	N/A

Follow up requests received for exchange of the ruling	Number	Average time to provide response	Number of requests not answered
	0	N/A	N/A

587. In the prior years' peer review reports, it was determined that Indonesia's process for the completion and exchange of templates were sufficient to meet the minimum standard. Indonesia's implementation in this regard remains unchanged and therefore continues to meet the minimum standard.

588. Indonesia has the necessary legal basis for spontaneous exchange of information, a process for completing the templates in a timely way and has completed all exchanges. Indonesia has met all of the ToR for the exchange of information process and no recommendations are made.

C. Statistics (ToR IV)

589. The statistics for the year in review are as follows:

Category of ruling	Number of exchanges	Jurisdictions exchanged with
Cross-border unilateral APAs and any other cross-border unilateral tax rulings (such as an advance tax ruling) covering transfer pricing or the application of transfer pricing principles	*De minimis* rule applies	N/A
De minimis rule	1	N/A
Total	1	

D. Matters related to intellectual property regimes (ToR I.A.1.3)

590. Indonesia does not offer an intellectual property regime for which transparency requirements under the Action 5 Report (OECD, 2015[1]) were imposed.

Summary of recommendations on implementation of the transparency framework

Aspect of implementation of the transparency framework that should be improved	Recommendation for improvement
	No recommendations are made.

References

OECD (2021), *BEPS Action 5 on Harmful Tax Practices - Terms of Reference and Methodology for the Conduct of the Peer Reviews of the Action 5 Transparency Framework*, OECD Publishing, Paris, http://www.oecd.org/tax/beps/beps-action-5-harmful-tax-practices-peer-review-transparency-framework.pdf. [3]

OECD (2015), *Countering Harmful Tax Practices More Effectively, Taking into Account Transparency and Substance, Action 5 - 2015 Final Report*, OECD/G20 Base Erosion and Profit Shifting Project, OECD Publishing, Paris, https://dx.doi.org/10.1787/9789264241190-en. [1]

OECD (ed.) (2017b), *Harmful Tax Practices - 2017 Progress Report on Preferential Regimes*, OECD Publishing, Paris, http://dx.doi.org/10.1787/9789264283954-en. [2]

OECD/Council of Europe (2011), *The Multilateral Convention on Mutual Administrative Assistance in Tax Matters: Amended by the 2010 Protocol*, OECD Publishing, Paris, https://dx.doi.org/10.1787/9789264115606-en. [4]

Notes

[1] Participating jurisdictions to the Convention are available here: www.oecd.org/tax/exchange-of-tax-information/convention-on-mutual-administrative-assistance-in-tax-matters.htm. Indonesia also has bilateral agreements with Algeria, Armenia, Australia, Austria, Bangladesh, Belarus, Belgium, Brunei Darussalam, Bulgaria, Cambodia, Canada, China (People's Republic of), Croatia, Czech Republic, Democratic People's Republic of Korea, Denmark, Egypt, Finland, France, Germany, Hong Kong (China), Hungary, India, Iran, Italy, Japan, Jordan, Korea, Kuwait, Lao People's Democratic Republic, Luxembourg, Malaysia, Mexico, Mongolia, Morocco, Netherlands, New Zealand, Norway, Pakistan, Papua New Guinea, Philippines, Poland, Portugal, Qatar, Romania, Russia, Serbia, Seychelles, Singapore, Slovak Republic, South Africa, Spain, Sri Lanka, Sudan, Suriname, Sweden, Syrian Arab Republic, Chinese Taipei, Tajikistan, Thailand, Tunisia, Turkey, Ukraine, United Arab Emirates, United Kingdom, United States, Uzbekistan, Venezuela, Viet Nam.

Ireland

Ireland has met all aspects of the terms of reference (OECD, 2021[3]) (ToR) for the calendar year 2020 (year in review), and no recommendations are made.

Ireland can legally issue three types of rulings within the scope of the transparency framework.

In practice, Ireland issued rulings within the scope of the transparency framework as follows:

Type of ruling	Number of rulings
Past rulings	29
Future rulings in the period 1 April 2016 – 31 December 2016	0
Future rulings in the calendar year 2017	2
Future rulings in the calendar year 2018	39
Future rulings in the calendar year 2019	5
Future rulings in the year in review	4

No peer input was received in respect of the exchanges of information on rulings received from Ireland.

A. The information gathering process (ToR I.A)

591. Ireland can legally issue three types of rulings within the scope of the transparency framework: (i) preferential regimes;[1] (ii) cross-border unilateral APAs and any other cross-border unilateral tax rulings (such as an advance tax ruling) covering transfer pricing or the application of transfer pricing principles; and (iii) permanent establishment rulings.

592. For Ireland, past rulings are any tax rulings within scope that are issued either: (i) on or after 1 January 2014 but before 1 April 2016; or (ii) on or after 1 January 2010 but before 1 January 2014, provided they were still in effect as at 1 January 2014. Future rulings are any tax rulings within scope that are issued on or after 1 April 2016.

593. In the prior years' peer review reports, it was determined that Ireland's undertakings to identify past and future rulings and all potential exchange jurisdictions were sufficient to meet the minimum standard. In addition, it was determined that Ireland's review and supervision mechanism was sufficient to meet the minimum standard. Ireland's implementation remains unchanged, and therefore continues to meet the minimum standard.

594. Ireland has met all of the ToR for the information gathering process and no recommendations are made.

B. The exchange of information (ToR II.B)

595. Ireland has international agreements permitting spontaneous exchange of information, including being a party to (i) the *Multilateral Convention on Mutual Administrative Assistance in Tax Matters: Amended by the 2010 Protocol* (OECD/Council of Europe, 2011[4]) ("the Convention"), (ii) the Directive 2011/16/EU with all other European Union Member States and (iii) bilateral agreements in force with 73 jurisdictions.[2]

596. For the year in review, the timeliness of exchanges is as follows:

Future rulings within the scope of the transparency framework	Number of exchanges transmitted within three months of the information becoming available to the competent authority or immediately after legal impediments have been lifted	Delayed exchanges		
		Number of exchanges transmitted later than three months of the information on rulings becoming available to the competent authority	Reasons for the delays	Any other comments
	4	0	N/A	N/A

Follow up requests received for exchange of the ruling	Number	Average time to provide response	Number of requests not answered
	0	N/A	N/A

597. In the prior years' peer review reports, it was determined that Ireland's process for the completion and exchange of templates were sufficient to meet the minimum standard. With respect to past rulings, no further action was required. Ireland's implementation in this regard remains unchanged and therefore continues to meet the minimum standard.

598. Ireland has the necessary legal basis for spontaneous exchange of information, a process for completing the templates in a timely way and has completed all exchanges. Ireland has met all of the ToR for the exchange of information process and no recommendations are made.

C. Statistics (ToR IV)

599. The statistics for the year in review are as follows:

Category of ruling	Number of exchanges	Jurisdictions exchanged with
Ruling related to a preferential regime	*De minimis* rule applies	N/A
Cross-border unilateral APAs and any other cross-border unilateral tax rulings (such as an advance tax ruling) covering transfer pricing or the application of transfer pricing principles	*De minimis* rule applies	N/A
Permanent establishment rulings	*De minimis* rule applies	N/A
De minimis rule	4	N/A
Total	4	

D. Matters related to intellectual property regimes (ToR I.A.1.3)

600. Ireland offers an intellectual property regime (IP regime)[3] that is subject to the transparency requirements under the Action 5 Report (OECD, 2015[1]). It states that the identification of the benefitting taxpayers will occur as follows:

- ***New entrants benefitting from the grandfathered IP regime***: as this is a new IP regime rather than a grandfathered IP regime, transparency on new entrants is not relevant.
- ***Third category of IP assets***: the relevant part of the annual corporation tax return has been designed to capture the data that Ireland will require for its reporting and exchange of information obligations under the framework. So far, there have been no taxpayers benefitting from the third category of IP assets.
- ***Taxpayers making use of the option to treat the nexus ratio as a rebuttable presumption***: not applicable as the regime does not allow the nexus ratio to be treated as a rebuttable presumption.

Summary of recommendations on implementation of the transparency framework

Aspect of implementation of the transparency framework that should be improved	Recommendation for improvement
	No recommendations are made.

References

OECD (2021), *BEPS Action 5 on Harmful Tax Practices - Terms of Reference and Methodology for the Conduct of the Peer Reviews of the Action 5 Transparency Framework*, OECD Publishing, Paris, http://www.oecd.org/tax/beps/beps-action-5-harmful-tax-practices-peer-review-transparency-framework.pdf. [3]

OECD (2015), *Countering Harmful Tax Practices More Effectively, Taking into Account Transparency and Substance, Action 5 - 2015 Final Report*, OECD/G20 Base Erosion and Profit Shifting Project, OECD Publishing, Paris, https://dx.doi.org/10.1787/9789264241190-en. [1]

OECD (ed.) (2017b), *Harmful Tax Practices - 2017 Progress Report on Preferential Regimes*, OECD Publishing, Paris, http://dx.doi.org/10.1787/9789264283954-en. [2]

OECD/Council of Europe (2011), *The Multilateral Convention on Mutual Administrative Assistance in Tax Matters: Amended by the 2010 Protocol*, OECD Publishing, Paris, https://dx.doi.org/10.1787/9789264115606-en. [4]

Notes

[1] With respect to the following preferential regimes: 1) Shipping regime and 2) Knowledge development box.

[2] Participating jurisdictions to the Convention are available here: www.oecd.org/tax/exchange-of-tax-information/convention-on-mutual-administrative-assistance-in-tax-matters.htm. Ireland also has bilateral agreements with Albania, Armenia, Australia, Austria, Bahrain, Belarus, Belgium, Bosnia and Herzegovina, Botswana, Bulgaria, Canada, Chile, China (People's Republic of), Croatia, Cyprus, Czech Republic, Denmark, Egypt, Estonia, Ethiopia, Finland, France, Georgia, Germany, Greece, Hong Kong (China), Hungary, Iceland, India, Israel, Italy, Japan, Kazakhstan, Korea, Kuwait, Latvia, Lithuania, Luxembourg, Malaysia, Malta, Mexico, Moldova, Montenegro, Morocco, Netherlands, New Zealand, North Macedonia, Norway, Pakistan, Panama, Poland, Portugal, Qatar, Romania, Russia, Saudi Arabia, Serbia, Singapore, Slovak Republic, Slovenia, South Africa, Spain, Sweden, Switzerland, Thailand, Turkey, United Arab Emirates, Ukraine, United Kingdom, United States, Uzbekistan, Viet Nam, and Zambia.

[3] Knowledge development box.

Isle of Man

The Isle of Man has met all aspects of the terms of reference (OECD, 2021[3]) (ToR) for the calendar year 2020 (year in review), and no recommendations are made.

The Isle of Man can legally issue two types of rulings within the scope of the transparency framework.

In practice, the Isle of Man issued rulings within the scope of the transparency framework as follows:

Type of ruling	Number of rulings
Past rulings	2
Future rulings in the period 1 April 2017 – 31 December 2017	0
Future rulings in the calendar year 2018	0
Future rulings in the calendar year 2019	0
Future rulings in the year in review	0

As no exchanges took place, no peer input was received in respect of the exchanges of information on rulings received from the Isle of Man.

A. The information gathering process (ToR I.A)

601. The Isle of Man can legally issue two types of rulings within the scope of the transparency framework: (i) rulings providing for unilateral downward adjustments and (ii) permanent establishment rulings.

602. For the Isle of Man, past rulings are any tax rulings within scope that are issued either: (i) on or after 1 January 2015 but before 1 April 2017; or (ii) on or after 1 January 2012 but before 1 January 2015, provided they were still in effect as at 1 January 2015. Future rulings are any tax rulings within scope that are issued on or after 1 April 2017.

603. In the prior years' peer review reports, it was determined that the Isle of Man's undertakings to identify past and future rulings and all potential exchange jurisdictions were sufficient to meet the minimum standard. In addition, it was determined that the Isle of Man's review and supervision mechanism was sufficient to meet the minimum standard. The Isle of Man's implementation remains unchanged, and therefore continues to meet the minimum standard.

604. The Isle of Man has met all of the ToR for the information gathering process and no recommendations are made.

B. The exchange of information (ToR II.B)

605. The Isle of Man has international agreements permitting spontaneous exchange of information, including being a jurisdiction participating in (i) the *Multilateral Convention on Mutual Administrative Assistance in Tax Matters: Amended by the 2010 Protocol* (OECD/Council of Europe, 2011[4]) ("the Convention") and (ii) bilateral agreements in force with 16 jurisdictions.[1]

606. During the year in review, no exchanges were required to take place and no data on the timeliness of exchanges is reported.

607. In the prior years' peer review reports, it was determined that the Isle of Man's process for the completion and exchange of templates were sufficient to meet the minimum standard. With respect to past rulings, no further action was required. The Isle of Man's implementation in this regard remains unchanged and therefore continues to meet the minimum standard.

608. The Isle of Man has the necessary legal basis for spontaneous exchange of information, a process for completing the templates in a timely way and has completed all exchanges. The Isle of Man has met all of the ToR for the exchange of information process and no recommendations are made.

C. Statistics (ToR IV)

609. As no rulings were issued, no statistics can be reported.

D. Matters related to intellectual property regimes (ToR I.A.1.3)

610. The Isle of Man does not offer an intellectual property regime for which transparency requirements under the Action 5 Report (OECD, 2015[1]) were imposed.

Summary of recommendations on implementation of the transparency framework

Aspect of implementation of the transparency framework that should be improved	Recommendation for improvement
	No recommendations are made.

References

OECD (2021), *BEPS Action 5 on Harmful Tax Practices - Terms of Reference and Methodology for the Conduct of the Peer Reviews of the Action 5 Transparency Framework*, OECD Publishing, Paris, http://www.oecd.org/tax/beps/beps-action-5-harmful-tax-practices-peer-review-transparency-framework.pdf. [3]

OECD (2015), *Countering Harmful Tax Practices More Effectively, Taking into Account Transparency and Substance, Action 5 - 2015 Final Report*, OECD/G20 Base Erosion and Profit Shifting Project, OECD Publishing, Paris, https://dx.doi.org/10.1787/9789264241190-en. [1]

OECD (ed.) (2017b), *Harmful Tax Practices - 2017 Progress Report on Preferential Regimes*, OECD Publishing, Paris, http://dx.doi.org/10.1787/9789264283954-en. [2]

OECD/Council of Europe (2011), *The Multilateral Convention on Mutual Administrative Assistance in Tax Matters: Amended by the 2010 Protocol*, OECD Publishing, Paris, https://dx.doi.org/10.1787/9789264115606-en. [4]

Notes

[1] Participating jurisdictions to the Convention are available here: www.oecd.org/tax/exchange-of-tax-information/convention-on-mutual-administrative-assistance-in-tax-matters.htm. The Isle of Man also has bilateral agreements with Anguilla. Bahrain, British Virgin Islands, Cayman Islands, Estonia, Gibraltar, Guernsey, Jersey, Luxembourg, Malta, Qatar, Seychelles, Singapore, Turks and Caicos Islands, United Kingdom and United States.

Israel

Israel has met all aspects of the terms of reference (OECD, 2021[3]) (ToR) for the calendar year 2020 (year in review), except for identifying future rulings within the scope of the transparency framework (ToR I.A.1.2) and for ensuring that each of the mandatory fields of information required in the template contained in Annex C of the 2015 Action 5 Report (OECD, 2015[1]), especially with regard to the summary section, are present in the information exchanged (ToR II.B.3). Israel receives two recommendations on these points for the year in review.

In the prior year report, as well as in the 2016, 2017 and 2018 peer reviews, Israel had received a recommendation regarding the timely provision of information on rulings to the Competent Authority for exchange of information (ToR II.B.5). Israel resolved this issue and therefore the recommendation is now removed. In the prior year report, Israel had received a recommendation regarding the mandatory fields of information required in the template contained in Annex C of the 2015 Action 5 Report (OECD, 2015[1]), especially with regard to the summary section (ToR II.B.3). As this issue has not been fully addressed, the recommendation remains in place. In addition, as there were new circumstances, one additional recommendation has been made as relevant.

Israel can legally issue five types of rulings within the scope of the transparency framework.

In practice, Israel issued rulings within the scope of the transparency framework as follows:[1]

Type of ruling	Number of rulings
Past rulings	79
Future rulings in the period 1 April 2016 – 31 December 2016	5
Future rulings in the calendar year 2017	3
Future rulings in the calendar year 2018	15
Future rulings in the calendar year 2019	30
Future rulings in the year in review	15

Peer input was received from five jurisdictions in respect of the exchanges of information on rulings received from Israel. The input was generally positive, noting that overall information was complete, in a correct format and almost all received in a timely manner. However, peer input indicated that exchanges on rulings were not timely.

A. The information gathering process (ToR I.A)

611. Israel can legally issue the following five types of rulings within the scope of the transparency framework: (i) preferential regimes;[2] (ii) cross-border unilateral APAs and any other cross-border unilateral tax rulings (such as an advance tax ruling) covering transfer pricing or the application of transfer pricing principles; (iii) rulings providing for unilateral downward adjustments; (iv) permanent establishment rulings; and (v) related party conduit rulings.

Past rulings (ToR I.A.1.1, I.A.1.2, I.A.2.1, I.A.2.2)

612. For Israel, past rulings are any tax rulings within scope that are issued either: (i) on or after 1 January 2014 but before 1 April 2016; or (ii) on or after 1 January 2010 but before 1 January 2014, provided they were still in effect as at 1 January 2014.

613. In the prior years' peer review reports, it was determined that Israel's undertakings to identify past rulings and all potential exchange jurisdictions were sufficient to meet the minimum standard. Israel's undertakings in this regard remain unchanged, and therefore continue to meet the minimum standard.

Future rulings (ToR I.A.1.1, I.A.1.2, I.A.2.1)

614. Future rulings are any tax rulings within scope that are issued on or after 1 April 2016.

615. In the prior years' peer review reports, it was determined that Israel's undertakings to identify future rulings and all potential exchange jurisdictions were sufficient to meet the minimum standard. However, during the year in review, Israel identified an additional eleven future rulings issued in 2019 that were not otherwise identified in the prior year. Although Israel confirms that all rulings issued in 2019 have now been identified, in order to ensure that similar issues are not encountered in future, Israel is recommended to strengthen its information gathering process identifying all future rulings within the scope of the transparency framework.

Review and supervision (ToR I.A.3)

616. In the prior years' peer review reports, it was determined that Israel's review and supervision mechanism was sufficient to meet the minimum standard. As noted above, during the year in review, Israel identified an additional eleven future rulings. As part of the efforts to strengthen the information gathering process, Israel is therefore recommended to strengthen its review and supervision mechanism to ensure that the information gathering process is working effectively.

Conclusion on section A

617. Israel has met all of the ToR for the information gathering process and no recommendations are made, except for identifying all future rulings within the scope of the transparency framework (ToR I.A.1.2). Israel is recommended to strengthen its information gathering process identifying all future rulings within the scope of the transparency framework and its review and supervision mechanism to ensure that the information gathering process is working effectively.

B. The exchange of information (ToR II.B)

Legal basis for spontaneous exchange of information (ToR II.B.1, II.B.2)

618. Israel has the necessary domestic legal basis to exchange information spontaneously. Israel notes that there are no legal or practical impediments that prevent the spontaneous exchange of information on rulings as contemplated in the Action 5 minimum standard.

619. Israel has international agreements permitting spontaneous exchange of information, including being a party to (i) the *Multilateral Convention on Mutual Administrative Assistance in Tax Matters: Amended by the 2010 Protocol* (OECD/Council of Europe, 2011[4]) ("the Convention") and (ii) bilateral agreements in force with 55 jurisdictions.[3]

Completion and exchange of templates (ToR II.B.3, II.B.4, II.B.5, II.B.6, II.B.7)

620. In the prior years' peer review reports, it was determined that Israel's process for the completion and exchange of templates met all the ToR, except for the timely provision of information on rulings to the Competent Authority (ToR II.B.5) and for ensuring that each of the mandatory fields of information required in the template contained in Annex C of the 2015 Action 5 Report (OECD, 2015[1]), especially with regard to the summary section, are present in the information exchanged (ToR II.B.3). With respect to past rulings, no further action was required. Therefore, Israel was recommended to reduce the timeliness for providing the information on future rulings to the Competent Authority and to ensure that it duly completes each of the mandatory fields of information required in the Annex C template. With respect to past rulings, no further action was required.

621. During the prior year, regarding the exchanges of information on rulings received from Israel, peer input indicated that the summary section of the template was not always sufficiently informative and detailed. Israel took note of these remarks and indicates that the EOI department manager instructs the departments issuing the rulings about the necessity to complete the summary section of the Annex C template in line with the internal FHTP suggested guidance. In addition, data is presented to the EOI department manager during weekly department meetings. However, during the year in review, peer input still noted that the information provided in the summary section was too brief and therefore, the recommendation on this point remains.

622. Regarding the recommendation for submitting information to the Competent Authority, peer input still indicated delays. However, these delays do not necessarily relate to the timely provision of information on rulings to the Competent Authority. Furthermore, as mentioned below, Israel still had to perform exchanges for rulings issued in 2018 and 2019 but Israel confirms that exchanges for all rulings have now been performed and that all exchanges for rulings issued during the year in review were transmitted in a timely manner. Israel has also confirmed it has a procedure in place for minimizing delays and the EOI department recruited an additional employee in order to assist data transfers between departments. Therefore, it is not expected that Israel will experience delays on rulings issued in the future, and the recommendation is now removed.

623. For the year in review, the timeliness of exchanges is as follows:

Future rulings within the scope of the transparency framework	Number of exchanges transmitted within three months of the information becoming available to the competent authority or immediately after legal impediments have been lifted	Delayed exchanges		
		Number of exchanges transmitted later than three months of the information on rulings becoming available to the competent authority	Reasons for the delays	Any other comments
	36	99	N/A	N/A

Follow up requests received for exchange of the ruling	Number	Average time to provide response	Number of requests not answered
	0	N/A	N/A

624. The 135 exchanges performed in 2020 refer to: i) 6 future rulings issued in 2018 accounting for 15 exchanges; ii) 30 future rulings issued in 2019 accounting for 84 exchanges; and iii) 15 future rulings issued in 2020 accounting for 36 exchanges.

Conclusion on section B

625. Israel has the necessary legal basis for spontaneous exchange of information. Israel has met all of the ToR for the exchange of information except for ensuring that each of the mandatory fields of information required in the template contained in Annex C of the 2015 Action 5 Report, especially with regard to the summary section, are present in the information exchanged (ToR II.B.3).

626. Israel is recommended to develop a process to complete the templates on future rulings, and in particular the summary section, in accordance with the form agreed under the transparency framework (Tor II.B.3). Although Israel continued to experience delays during the year of review, the prior years' recommendation to ensure that information is made available to the Competent Authority without undue delay (ToR II.B.5) is removed.

C. Statistics (ToR IV)

627. The statistics for the year in review are as follows:

Category of ruling	Number of exchanges	Jurisdictions exchanged with
Ruling related to a preferential regime	135	Argentina, Australia, Belarus, Belgium, Brazil, Bulgaria, Canada, China (People's Republic of), Cyprus, Czech Republic, Denmark, Estonia, France, Germany, Hong Kong (China), Hungary, India, Italy, Ireland, Japan, Korea, Malta, Netherlands, New Zealand, Poland, Romania, Singapore, South Africa, Spain, Switzerland, United Kingdom, United States
Cross-border unilateral APAs and any other cross-border unilateral tax rulings (such as an advance tax ruling) covering transfer pricing or the application of transfer pricing principles	0	N/A
Cross-border rulings providing for a unilateral downward adjustment to the taxpayer's taxable profits that is not directly reflected in the taxpayer's	0	N/A

financial / commercial accounts		
Permanent establishment rulings	0	N/A
Related party conduit rulings	0	N/A
IP regimes: total exchanges on taxpayers benefitting from the third category of IP assets, new entrants benefitting from grandfathered IP regimes; and taxpayers making use of the option to treat the nexus ratio as a rebuttable presumption	0	N/A
Total	135	

D. Matters related to intellectual property regimes (ToR I.A.1.3)

628. Israel offers two intellectual property regimes (IP regime)[4] that are subject to the transparency requirements under the Action 5 Report (OECD, 2015[1]). It states that the identification of the benefitting taxpayers will occur as follows:

- ***New entrants benefitting from the grandfathered IP regime***: the process on the collection of information regarding new entrants in the grandfathered IP regime is described in the previous years' peer review reports, and no recommendations were made. With respect to new entrants in the grandfathered IP regime, exchanges were completed in prior years and no further action was required.
- ***Third category of IP assets***: the regimes provide benefits to the third category of IP assets. The process on the collection of information is described in the previous years' peer review reports and meets the ToR. During the year in review, the Authority for Technological Innovation (i.e. the certifying agency) approved five applications regarding IP assets included in the third category. Information in respect of the five certificates issued in 2020 will be collected in the companies' tax returns for 2020, due at the end of 2021 and exchanged within the timelines required for the Action 5 transparency framework. Israel's implementation on this aspect remains unchanged and continues to meet the ToR.
- ***Taxpayers making use of the option to treat the nexus ratio as a rebuttable presumption***: not applicable as the regime does not allow the nexus ratio to be treated as a rebuttable presumption.

Summary of recommendations on implementation of the transparency framework

Aspect of implementation of the transparency framework that should be improved	Recommendation for improvement
Israel identified additional future rulings that were not previously captured.	Israel is recommended to strengthen its information gathering process identifying all future rulings within the scope of the transparency framework and its review and supervision mechanism to ensure that the information gathering process is working effectively.
During the year in review, as well as in the 2019 peer review reports, concerns were raised regarding the completion of templates in accordance with the form agreed under the transparency framework.	Israel is recommended to develop a process to complete the templates on future rulings, and in particular, the summary section, in accordance with the form agreed under the transparency framework. This recommendation remains unchanged since the 2019 peer review report.

References

OECD (2021), *BEPS Action 5 on Harmful Tax Practices - Terms of Reference and Methodology for the Conduct of the Peer Reviews of the Action 5 Transparency Framework*, OECD Publishing, Paris, http://www.oecd.org/tax/beps/beps-action-5-harmful-tax-practices-peer-review-transparency-framework.pdf. [3]

OECD (2015), *Countering Harmful Tax Practices More Effectively, Taking into Account Transparency and Substance, Action 5 - 2015 Final Report*, OECD/G20 Base Erosion and Profit Shifting Project, OECD Publishing, Paris, https://dx.doi.org/10.1787/9789264241190-en. [1]

OECD (ed.) (2017b), *Harmful Tax Practices - 2017 Progress Report on Preferential Regimes*, OECD Publishing, Paris, http://dx.doi.org/10.1787/9789264283954-en. [2]

OECD/Council of Europe (2011), *The Multilateral Convention on Mutual Administrative Assistance in Tax Matters: Amended by the 2010 Protocol*, OECD Publishing, Paris, https://dx.doi.org/10.1787/9789264115606-en. [4]

Notes

[1] Note: The statistical data for Israel are supplied by and under the responsibility of the relevant Israeli authorities. The use of such data by the OECD is without prejudice to the status of the Golan Heights, East Jerusalem and Israeli settlements in the West Bank under the terms of international law.

[2] With respect to the following preferential regimes: Preferred company regime and Preferred technological enterprise regime.

[3] Participating jurisdictions to the Convention are available here: www.oecd.org/tax/exchange-of-tax-information/convention-on-mutual-administrative-assistance-in-tax-matters.htm. Israel also has bilateral agreements with Australia, Austria, Belarus, Belgium, Brazil, Bulgaria, Canada, China (People's Republic of), Croatia, Czech Republic, Denmark, Estonia, Ethiopia, Finland, France, Georgia, Germany, Greece, Hungary, India, Ireland, Italy, Jamaica, Japan, Korea, Latvia, Lithuania, Luxembourg, Malta, Mexico, Moldova, Netherlands, Norway, Panama, Philippines, Poland, Portugal, Romania, Russia, Serbia, Singapore, Slovak Republic, Slovenia, South Africa, Spain, Sweden, Switzerland, Chinese Taipei, Thailand, Turkey, Ukraine, United Kingdom, United States, Uzbekistan and Viet Nam.

[4] The Preferred company regime which is the grandfathered regime, and the Preferred technological enterprise regime which is the amended regime.

Italy

Italy has met all aspects of the terms of reference (OECD, 2021[3]) (ToR) for the calendar year 2020 (year in review), and no recommendations are made.

Italy can legally issue three types of rulings within the scope of the transparency framework.

In practice, Italy issued rulings within the scope of the transparency framework as follows:

Type of ruling	Number of rulings
Past rulings	58
Future rulings in the period 1 April 2016 – 31 December 2016	39
Future rulings in the calendar year 2017	123
Future rulings in the calendar year 2018	308
Future rulings in the calendar year 2019	206
Future rulings in the year of review	224

Peer input was received from eleven jurisdictions in respect of the exchanges of information on rulings received from Italy. The input was generally positive, noting that information, was complete, in a correct format and received in a timely manner. In general, the information provided in the summary section was considered complete and sufficient for risk assessment purposes and there was no need to request further information. One peer noted that the information was too general to perform risk assessment analysis, and Italy will consider this feedback.

A. The information gathering process (ToR I.A)

629. Italy can legally issue the following three types of rulings within the scope of the transparency framework: (i) preferential regimes;[1] (ii) cross-border unilateral APAs and any other cross-border unilateral tax rulings (such as an advance tax ruling) covering transfer pricing or the application of transfer pricing principles; and (iii) permanent establishment rulings.

630. For Italy, past rulings are any tax rulings within scope that are issued either: (i) on or after 1 January 2014 but before 1 April 2016; or (ii) on or after 1 January 2010 but before 1 January 2014, provided they were still in effect as at 1 January 2014. Future rulings are any tax rulings within scope that are issued on or after 1 April 2016.

631. In the prior years' peer review reports, it was determined that Italy's undertakings to identify past and future rulings and all potential exchange jurisdictions were sufficient to meet the minimum standard. In addition, it was determined that Italy's review and supervision mechanism was sufficient to meet the minimum standard. Italy's implementation remains unchanged, and therefore continues to meet the minimum standard.

632. Italy has met all of the ToR for the information gathering process and no recommendations are made.

B. The exchange of information (ToR II.B)

633. Italy has international agreements permitting spontaneous exchange of information, including being a party to (i) the Multilateral Convention on Mutual Administrative Assistance in Tax Matters: Amended by the 2010 Protocol (OECD/Council of Europe, 2011[4]) ("the Convention"), (ii) the Directive 2011/16/EU with all other European Union Member States and (iii) bilateral agreements in force with 100 jurisdictions.[2]

634. For the year in review, the timeliness of exchanges is as follows:

Future rulings in the scope of the transparency framework	Number of exchanges transmitted within three months of the information becoming available to the competent authority or immediately after legal impediments have been lifted	Delayed exchanges		
		Number of exchanges transmitted later than three months of the information on rulings becoming available to the competent authority	Reasons for the delays	Any other comments
	1073	0	N/A	N/A

Follow up requests received for exchange of the ruling	Number	Average time to provide response	Number of requests not answered
	2	105 days	0

635. The average response time to follow up requests has suffered delays due to the effects of the lockdown imposed by the Italian Government to deal with the COVID-19 pandemic emergency during the first quarter of 2020. The teleworking situation was stabilised towards the end of 2020 and indeed the reply to the second follow up request was provided within 40 days. As this delay was a direct result of the COVID-19 pandemic it is not expected to be a recurring problem once normal conditions resume, and therefore no recommendation is given in this regard. This issue will be reviewed again in the subsequent year's peer review to monitor whether there is a persistent issue.

636. In the prior years' peer review reports, it was determined that Italy's process for the completion and exchange of templates were sufficient to meet the minimum standard. With respect to past rulings, no further action was required. In addition, the Revenue Agency has developed an IT application which will permit automatic downloads of information on rulings from relevant databases and its subsequent transmission to the Competent Authority. This application is currently in an experimental phase and allows for a partial automation of the process. Italy's implementation in this regard remains unchanged and therefore continues to meet the minimum standard. Italy has the necessary legal basis for spontaneous exchange of information, a process for completing the templates in a timely way and has completed all exchanges. Italy has met all of the ToR for the exchange of information process and no recommendations are made.

C. Statistics (ToR IV)

637. The statistics for the year in review are as follows:

Category of ruling	Number of exchanges	Jurisdictions exchanged with
Ruling related to a preferential regime	955	Albania, Argentina, Armenia, Australia, Austria, Azerbaijan, Belgium, Bosnia and Herzegovina, Brazil, Bulgaria, Cameroon, Canada, Chile, China (People's Republic of), Colombia, Côte d'Ivoire, Croatia, Czech Republic, Denmark, Egypt, Estonia, Philippines, Finland, France, Georgia, Germany, Hungary, Japan, Jordan, Greece, Guernsey, Hong Kong (China), India, Indonesia, Ireland, Israel, Kazakhstan, Kenya, Korea, Latvia, Lithuania, Luxembourg, Malaysia, Malta, Morocco, Mauritius, Mexico, Moldova, Montenegro, Nigeria, Norway, New Zealand, Netherlands, Pakistan, Panama, Peru, Poland, Portugal, , Romania, Russia, San Marino, Saudi Arabia, Senegal, Serbia, Singapore, Slovak Republic, Slovenia, South Africa, Spain, Sweden, Switzerland, Thailand, Tunisia, Turkey, Ukraine, United Kingdom, United States, Viet Nam
Cross-border unilateral APAs and any other cross-border unilateral tax rulings (such as an advance tax ruling) covering transfer pricing or the application of transfer pricing principles	111	Argentina, Austria, Belgium, Brazil, China (People's Republic of), Croatia, Czech Republic, Finland, France, Germany, Greece, Hong Kong (China), Hungary, India, Ireland, Japan, Korea, Luxembourg, Morocco, Netherlands, Poland, Portugal, Romania, Russia, Serbia, Singapore, Slovenia, Spain, Sweden, Switzerland, Turkey, Ukraine, United Kingdom, United States
Permanent establishment rulings	7	Belgium, Ireland, Luxembourg, Netherlands, United States
Total	1073	

D. Matters related to intellectual property regimes (ToR I.A.1.3)

638. Italy offered an intellectual property regime (IP regime)[3] that was amended with effect as of 1 January 2017 to the extent it was not nexus compliant (i.e. for benefits for trademarks) and is subject to transparency requirements under the Action 5 Report (OECD, 2015[1]). It states that the identification of the benefitting taxpayers will occur as follows:

- ***New entrants benefitting from the grandfathered IP regime***: not applicable as Italy has completed the exchange of information on new entrants to the grandfathered IP regime that obtained benefits with respect to trademarks.
- ***Third category of IP assets***: not applicable as the regime does not allow the third category of IP assets to qualify for the benefits.
- ***Taxpayers making use of the option to treat the nexus ratio as a rebuttable presumption***: not applicable as the regime does not allow the nexus ratio to be treated as a rebuttable presumption.

Summary of recommendations on implementation of the transparency framework

Aspect of implementation of the transparency framework that should be improved	Recommendation for improvement
	No recommendations are made.

References

OECD (2021), *BEPS Action 5 on Harmful Tax Practices - Terms of Reference and Methodology for the Conduct of the Peer Reviews of the Action 5 Transparency Framework*, OECD Publishing, Paris, http://www.oecd.org/tax/beps/beps-action-5-harmful-tax-practices-peer-review-transparency-framework.pdf. [3]

OECD (2015), *Countering Harmful Tax Practices More Effectively, Taking into Account Transparency and Substance, Action 5 - 2015 Final Report*, OECD/G20 Base Erosion and Profit Shifting Project, OECD Publishing, Paris, https://dx.doi.org/10.1787/9789264241190-en. [1]

OECD (ed.) (2017b), *Harmful Tax Practices - 2017 Progress Report on Preferential Regimes*, OECD Publishing, Paris, http://dx.doi.org/10.1787/9789264283954-en. [2]

OECD/Council of Europe (2011), *The Multilateral Convention on Mutual Administrative Assistance in Tax Matters: Amended by the 2010 Protocol*, OECD Publishing, Paris, https://dx.doi.org/10.1787/9789264115606-en. [4]

Notes

[1] With respect to the following preferential regimes: 1) International shipping and 2) Patent Box.

[2] Participating jurisdictions to the Convention are available here: www.oecd.org/tax/exchange-of-tax-information/convention-on-mutual-administrative-assistance-in-tax-matters.htm. Italy also has bilateral agreements with Albania, Algeria, Argentina, Armenia, Australia, Austria, Azerbaijan, Bangladesh, Barbados, Belarus, Belgium, Bosnia and Herzegovina, Brazil, Bulgaria, Canada, Chile, China (People's Republic of), Congo, Côte d'Ivoire, Croatia, Cyprus, Czech Republic, Denmark, Ecuador, Egypt, Estonia, Ethiopia, Finland, North Macedonia, France, Georgia, Germany, Ghana, Greece, Hong Kong (China), Hungary, Iceland, India, Indonesia, Ireland, Israel, Japan, Jordan, Kazakhstan, Korea, Kuwait, Kyrgyzstan, Latvia, Lebanon, Lithuania, Luxembourg, Malaysia, Malta, Mauritius, Mexico, Moldova, Montenegro, Morocco, Mozambique, Netherlands, New Zealand, Norway, Oman, Pakistan, Philippines, Poland, Portugal, Qatar, Romania, Russia, San Marino, Saudi Arabia, Senegal, Serbia, Singapore, Slovak Republic, Slovenia, South Africa, Spain, Sri Lanka, Sweden, Switzerland, Syrian Arab Republic, Chinese Taipei, Tajikistan, Tanzania, Thailand, Trinidad and Tobago, Tunisia, Turkey, Uganda, Ukraine, United Arab Emirates, United Kingdom, United States, Uruguay, Uzbekistan, Venezuela, Viet Nam and Zambia.

[3] Partial exemption for income/gains derived from certain IP rights.

Jamaica

Jamaica has met all aspects of the terms of reference (OECD, 2021[3]) (ToR) for the calendar year 2020 (year in review) that can be met in the absence of rulings being issued in practice, and no recommendations are made.

Jamaica can legally issue five types of rulings within the scope of the transparency framework.

In practice, Jamaica issued no rulings within the scope of the transparency framework.

As no exchanges were required to take place, no peer input was received in respect of the exchanges of information on rulings received from Jamaica.

A. The information gathering process (ToR I.A)

639. Jamaica can legally issue the following five types of rulings within the scope of the transparency framework: (i) preferential regimes;[1] (ii) cross-border unilateral APAs and any other cross-border unilateral tax rulings (such as an advance tax ruling) covering transfer pricing or the application of transfer pricing principles; (iii) rulings providing for unilateral downward adjustments; (iv) permanent establishment rulings; and (v) related party conduit rulings.

640. For Jamaica, past rulings are any tax rulings within scope that are issued either (i) on or after 1 January 2015 but before 1 April 2017; and (ii) on or after 1 January 2012 but before 1 January 2015, provided they were still in effect as at 1 January 2015. Future rulings are any tax rulings within scope that are issued on or after 1 April 2017.

641. In the prior years' peer review reports, it was determined that Jamaica's undertakings to identify past and future rulings and all potential exchange jurisdictions were sufficient to meet the minimum standard. In the prior year peer review report, it was also noted that Jamaica was preparing a more formal procedure to issue and review rulings for the purposes of the transparency framework, including guidelines to specify which information must be included in rulings applications. During the year in review, there have been no further developments. In addition, it was determined that Jamaica's review and supervision mechanism was sufficient to meet the minimum standard. Jamaica's implementation in this regard remains unchanged, and therefore continues to meet the minimum standard.

642. Jamaica has met all of the ToR for the information gathering process that can be met in the absence of rulings being issued in practice and no recommendations are made.

B. The exchange of information (ToR II.B)

643. Jamaica has international agreements permitting spontaneous exchange of information, including being a party to (i) the *Multilateral Convention on Mutual Administrative Assistance in Tax Matters: Amended by the 2010 Protocol* (OECD/Council of Europe, 2011[4]) ("the Convention") and (ii) bilateral agreements in force with 27 jurisdictions.[2]

644. As Jamaica did not issue any rulings within the scope of the transparency framework in the relevant period, Jamaica was not required to exchange any information on rulings in the year in review and no data on the timeliness of exchanges can be reported.

645. In the prior years' peer review reports, it was determined that Jamaica's process for the completion and exchange of templates were sufficient to meet the minimum standard in the absence of rulings being issued and exchanged in practice. Jamaica's implementation in this regard remains unchanged and therefore continues to meet the minimum standard.

646. Jamaica has the necessary legal basis for spontaneous exchange of information and a process for completing the templates in a timely way. Jamaica has met all of the ToR for the exchange of information process that can be met in the absence of rulings being issued and exchanged in practice and no recommendations are made.

C. Statistics (ToR IV)

647. As no rulings were issued, no statistics can be reported.

D. Matters related to intellectual property regimes (ToR I.A.1.3)

648. Jamaica does not offer an intellectual property regime for which transparency requirements under the Action 5 Report (OECD, 2015[1]) were imposed.

Summary of recommendations on implementation of the transparency framework

Aspect of implementation of the transparency framework that should be improved	Recommendation for improvement
	No recommendations are made.

References

OECD (2021), *BEPS Action 5 on Harmful Tax Practices - Terms of Reference and Methodology for the Conduct of the Peer Reviews of the Action 5 Transparency Framework*, OECD Publishing, Paris, http://www.oecd.org/tax/beps/beps-action-5-harmful-tax-practices-peer-review-transparency-framework.pdf. [3]

OECD (2015), *Countering Harmful Tax Practices More Effectively, Taking into Account Transparency and Substance, Action 5 - 2015 Final Report*, OECD/G20 Base Erosion and Profit Shifting Project, OECD Publishing, Paris, https://dx.doi.org/10.1787/9789264241190-en. [1]

OECD (ed.) (2017b), *Harmful Tax Practices - 2017 Progress Report on Preferential Regimes*, OECD Publishing, Paris, http://dx.doi.org/10.1787/9789264283954-en. [2]

OECD/Council of Europe (2011), *The Multilateral Convention on Mutual Administrative Assistance in Tax Matters: Amended by the 2010 Protocol*, OECD Publishing, Paris, https://dx.doi.org/10.1787/9789264115606-en. [4]

Notes

[1] With respect to the following preferential regimes: Special economic zones.

[2] Participating jurisdictions to the Convention are available here: www.oecd.org/tax/exchange-of-tax-information/convention-on-mutual-administrative-assistance-in-tax-matters.htm. Jamaica also has bilateral agreements with Antigua and Barbuda, Barbados, Belize, Brazil, Canada, China (People's Republic of), Denmark, Dominica, Faroe Islands, Finland, France, Germany, Greenland, Grenada, Guyana, Iceland, Israel, Japan, Mexico, Norway, Saint Kitts and Nevis, Saint Lucia, Saint Vincent and the Grenadines, Spain, Sweden, Trinidad and Tobago, United Kingdom and United States.

Japan

Japan has met all aspects of the terms of reference (OECD, 2021[3]) (ToR) for the calendar year 2020 (year in review), and no recommendations are made.

Japan can legally issue three types of rulings within the scope of the transparency framework.

In practice, Japan issued rulings within the scope of the transparency framework as follows:

Type of ruling	Number of rulings
Past rulings	51
Future rulings in the period 1 April 2016 – 31 December 2016	12
Future rulings in the calendar year 2017	14
Future rulings in the calendar year 2018	16
Future rulings in the calendar year 2019	4
Future rulings in the year of review	29

No peer input was received in respect of the exchanges of information on rulings received from Japan.

A. The information gathering process (ToR I.A)

649. Japan can legally issue the following three types of rulings within the scope of the transparency framework: (i) cross-border unilateral APAs and any other cross-border unilateral tax rulings (such as an advance tax ruling) covering transfer pricing or the application of transfer pricing principles; (ii) permanent establishment rulings; and (iii) related party conduit rulings.

650. For Japan, past rulings are any tax rulings within scope that are issued either: (i) on or after 1 January 2014 but before 1 April 2016; or (ii) on or after 1 January 2010 but before 1 January 2014, provided they were still in effect as at 1 January 2014. Future rulings are any tax rulings within scope that are issued on or after 1 April 2016.

651. In the prior years' peer review reports, it was determined that Japan's undertakings to identify past and future rulings and all potential exchange jurisdictions were sufficient to meet the minimum standard. In addition, it was determined that Japan's review and supervision mechanism was sufficient to meet the minimum standard. Japan's implementation remains unchanged, and therefore continues to meet the minimum standard.

652. Japan has met all of the ToR for the information gathering process and no recommendations are made.

B. The exchange of information (ToR II.B)

653. Japan has international agreements permitting spontaneous exchange of information, including being a party to the (i) *Multilateral Convention on Mutual Administrative Assistance in Tax Matters: Amended by the 2010 Protocol* (OECD/Council of Europe, 2011[4]) ("the Convention") and (ii) bilateral agreements in force with 74 jurisdictions.[1]

654. For the year in review, the timeliness of exchanges is as follows:

Future rulings in the scope of the transparency framework	Number of exchanges transmitted within three months of the information becoming available to the competent authority or immediately after legal impediments have been lifted	Delayed exchanges		
		Number of exchanges transmitted later than three months of the information on rulings becoming available to the competent authority	Reasons for the delays	Any other comments
	14	9	Covid-19 pandemic (see below)	N/A

Follow up requests received for exchange of the ruling	Number	Average time to provide response	Number of requests not answered
	0	N/A	N/A

655. Japan notes that some exchanges were delayed due to the COVID-19 pandemic. In particular, Japan notes that the Express Mail Service from Japan to some jurisdictions has been suspended, and therefore some exchanges were delayed. Japan is currently in the process of resolving this issue, and seeking alternate solutions for exchanges in the meantime. Six exchanges of rulings issued during the year in review were transmitted in 2021 and will be included in next year's peer review.

656. As this is a temporary issue that is a direct result of the COVID-19 pandemic it is not expected to be a recurring problem once normal conditions resume, and therefore no recommendation is given at this

stage for the delayed exchanges. This issue will be reviewed again in the subsequent year's peer review to monitor whether there is a persistent issue.

657. In the prior years' peer review reports, it was determined that Japan's process for the completion and exchange of templates were sufficient to meet the minimum standard. With respect to past rulings, no further action was required. Japan's implementation in this regard remains unchanged and therefore continues to meet the minimum standard.

658. Japan has the necessary legal basis for spontaneous exchange of information, a process for completing the templates in a timely way and has completed all exchanges. Japan has met all of the ToR for the exchange of information process and no recommendations are made.

C. Statistics (ToR IV)

659. The statistics for the year in review are as follows:

Category of ruling	Number of exchanges	Jurisdictions exchanged with
Cross-border unilateral advance pricing agreements (APAs) and any other cross-border unilateral tax rulings (such as an advance tax ruling) covering transfer pricing or the application of transfer pricing principles	23	Belgium, China (People's Republic of), Hong Kong (China), Malaysia, Netherlands, Philippines, Singapore, Sweden, Thailand, United Kingdom, United States
Permanent establishment rulings	0	N/A
Related party conduit rulings	0	N/A
Total	23	

D. Matters related to intellectual property regimes (ToR I.A.1.3)

660. Japan does not offer an intellectual property regime for which transparency requirements under the Action 5 Report (OECD, 2015[1]) were imposed.

Summary of recommendations on implementation of the transparency framework

Aspect of implementation of the transparency framework that should be improved	Recommendation for improvement
	No recommendations are made.

References

OECD (2021), *BEPS Action 5 on Harmful Tax Practices - Terms of Reference and Methodology for the Conduct of the Peer Reviews of the Action 5 Transparency Framework*, OECD Publishing, Paris, http://www.oecd.org/tax/beps/beps-action-5-harmful-tax-practices-peer-review-transparency-framework.pdf. [3]

OECD (2015), *Countering Harmful Tax Practices More Effectively, Taking into Account Transparency and Substance, Action 5 - 2015 Final Report*, OECD/G20 Base Erosion and Profit Shifting Project, OECD Publishing, Paris, https://dx.doi.org/10.1787/9789264241190-en. [1]

OECD (ed.) (2017b), *Harmful Tax Practices - 2017 Progress Report on Preferential Regimes*, OECD Publishing, Paris, http://dx.doi.org/10.1787/9789264283954-en. [2]

OECD/Council of Europe (2011), *The Multilateral Convention on Mutual Administrative Assistance in Tax Matters: Amended by the 2010 Protocol*, OECD Publishing, Paris, https://dx.doi.org/10.1787/9789264115606-en. [4]

Notes

[1] Parties to the Convention are available here: www.oecd.org/tax/exchange-of-tax-information/convention-on-mutual-administrative-assistance-in-tax-matters.htm. Japan also has bilateral agreements in force with Armenia, Australia, Austria, Azerbaijan, Bangladesh, Belarus, Belgium, Brazil, Brunei Darussalam, Bulgaria, Canada, Chile, China (People's Republic of), Croatia, Czech Republic, Denmark, Ecuador, Egypt, Estonia, Fiji, Finland, France, Georgia, Germany, Hong Kong (China), Hungary, Iceland, India, Indonesia, Ireland, Israel, Italy, Jamaica, Kazakhstan, Korea, Kuwait, Kyrgyzstan, Latvia, Lithuania, Luxembourg, Malaysia, Mexico, Moldova, Netherlands, New Zealand, Norway, Oman, Pakistan, Philippines, Poland, Portugal, Qatar, Romania, Russia, Saudi Arabia, Singapore, Slovak Republic, Slovenia, South Africa, Spain, Sri Lanka, Sweden, Switzerland, Tajikistan, Thailand, Turkey, Turkmenistan, Ukraine, United Arab Emirates, United Kingdom, United States, Uzbekistan, Viet Nam, Zambia.

Jersey

Jersey has met all aspects of the terms of reference (OECD, 2021[3]) (ToR) for the calendar year 2020 (year in review), and no recommendations are made.

Jersey can legally issue four types of rulings within the scope of the transparency framework.

In practice, Jersey issued rulings within the scope of the transparency framework as follows:

Type of ruling	Number of rulings
Past rulings	16
Future rulings in the period 1 April 2017 – 31 December 2017	1
Future rulings in the calendar year 2018	0
Future rulings in the calendar year 2019	1
Future rulings in the year in review	0

As no exchanges took place, no peer input was received in respect of the exchanges of information on rulings received from Jersey.

A. The information gathering process (ToR I.A)

661. Jersey can legally issue four types of rulings within the scope of the transparency framework: (i) cross-border unilateral APAs and any other cross-border unilateral tax rulings (such as an advance tax ruling) covering transfer pricing or the application of transfer pricing principles; (ii) rulings providing for unilateral downward adjustments; (iii) permanent establishment rulings; and (iv) related party conduit rulings.

662. For Jersey, past rulings are any tax rulings within scope that are issued either: (i) on or after 1 January 2015 but before 1 April 2017; or (ii) on or after 1 January 2012 but before 1 January 2015, provided they were still in effect as at 1 January 2015. Future rulings are any tax rulings within scope that are issued on or after 1 April 2017.

663. In the prior years' peer review reports, it was determined that Jersey's undertakings to identify past and future rulings and all potential exchange jurisdictions were sufficient to meet the minimum standard. In addition, it was determined that Jersey's review and supervision mechanism was sufficient to meet the minimum standard. Jersey's implementation remains unchanged, and therefore continues to meet the minimum standard.

664. Jersey has met all of the ToR for the information gathering process and no recommendations are made.

B. The exchange of information (ToR II.B)

665. Jersey has international agreements permitting spontaneous exchange of information, including being a jurisdiction participating in (i) the *Multilateral Convention on Mutual Administrative Assistance in Tax Matters: Amended by the 2010 Protocol* (OECD/Council of Europe, 2011[4]) ("the Convention") and (ii) bilateral agreements in force with 16 jurisdictions.[1]

666. During the year in review, no exchanges were required to take place and no data on the timeliness of exchanges is reported.

667. In the prior years' peer review reports, it was determined that Jersey's process for the completion and exchange of templates were sufficient to meet the minimum standard. With respect to past rulings, no further action was required. Jersey's implementation in this regard remains unchanged and therefore continues to meet the minimum standard.

668. Jersey has the necessary legal basis for spontaneous exchange of information, a process for completing the templates in a timely way and has completed all exchanges. Jersey has met all of the ToR for the exchange of information process and no recommendations are made.

C. Statistics (ToR IV)

669. As no rulings were issued, no statistics can be reported.

D. Matters related to intellectual property regimes (ToR I.A.1.3)

670. Jersey does not offer an intellectual property regime for which transparency requirements under the Action 5 Report (OECD, 2015[1]) were imposed.

Summary of recommendations on implementation of the transparency framework

Aspect of implementation of the transparency framework that should be improved	Recommendation for improvement
	No recommendations are made.

References

OECD (2021), *BEPS Action 5 on Harmful Tax Practices - Terms of Reference and Methodology for the Conduct of the Peer Reviews of the Action 5 Transparency Framework*, OECD Publishing, Paris, http://www.oecd.org/tax/beps/beps-action-5-harmful-tax-practices-peer-review-transparency-framework.pdf. [3]

OECD (2015), *Countering Harmful Tax Practices More Effectively, Taking into Account Transparency and Substance, Action 5 - 2015 Final Report*, OECD/G20 Base Erosion and Profit Shifting Project, OECD Publishing, Paris, https://dx.doi.org/10.1787/9789264241190-en. [1]

OECD (ed.) (2017b), *Harmful Tax Practices - 2017 Progress Report on Preferential Regimes*, OECD Publishing, Paris, http://dx.doi.org/10.1787/9789264283954-en. [2]

OECD/Council of Europe (2011), *The Multilateral Convention on Mutual Administrative Assistance in Tax Matters: Amended by the 2010 Protocol*, OECD Publishing, Paris, https://dx.doi.org/10.1787/9789264115606-en. [4]

Notes

[1] Participating jurisdictions to the Convention are available here: www.oecd.org/tax/exchange-of-tax-information/convention-on-mutual-administrative-assistance-in-tax-matters.htm. Jersey also has bilateral agreements with Cyprus, Estonia, Guernsey, Hong Kong (China), Isle of Man, Liechtenstein, Luxembourg, Malta, Mauritius, Qatar, Rwanda, Seychelles, Singapore, United Arab Emirates, United Kingdom and United States.

Jordan

Jordan has met all aspects of the terms of reference (OECD, 2021[3]) (ToR) for the calendar year 2020 (year in review), except for identifying all past and future rulings and all potential exchange jurisdictions with a review and supervision mechanism (ToR I.A), having a domestic legal basis for spontaneous exchange of information and exchanging information on the tax rulings in accordance with the form and timelines under the transparency framework (ToR II.B) and for identifying and exchanging information on all new entrants to the IP regime (ToR I.A.1.3). Jordan receives three recommendations on these points for the year in review.

In the prior year report, as well as partly in the 2017 and 2018 peer review, Jordan had received the same recommendations. As they have not been addressed, the recommendations remain in place.

Jordan can legally issue one type of rulings within the scope of the transparency framework. In practice, Jordan issued no rulings within the scope of the transparency framework.

As no exchanges took place, no peer input was received in respect of the exchanges of information on rulings received from Jordan.

A. The information gathering process (ToR I.A)

671. Jordan can legally issue the following one type of rulings within the scope of the transparency framework: (i) preferential regimes.[1]

Past rulings (ToR I.A.1.1, I.A.1.2, I.A.2.1, I.A.2.2)

672. For Jordan, past rulings are any tax rulings within scope that are issued either (i) on or after 1 January 2015 but before 1 September 2017; and (ii) and on or after 1 January 2012 but before 1 January 2015, provided still in effect as at 1 January 2015. However, as Jordan put in place an administrative process to issue rulings in 2019, there are no past rulings that have been issued by Jordan in the relevant period.

Future rulings (ToR I.A.1.1, I.A.1.2, I.A.2.1)

673. For Jordan, future rulings are any tax rulings within scope that are issued on or after 1 September 2017. No rulings were issued by Jordan during the period in review.

674. During the year in review, Jordan did not have specific mechanisms in place for identifying future rulings and potential exchange jurisdictions within the scope of the transparency framework and relied on a case-by-case approach.The Income and Sales Tax Department (ISTD) within the Ministry of Finance is currently working on introducing a mechanism to identify future rulings that are in the scope of the transparency framework and all jurisdictions for which the tax ruling would be relevant. Jordan indicated that detailed procedures and guidance will be developed between the end of 2021 and early 2022.

Review and supervision (ToR I.A.3)

675. Jordan did not have a review and supervision mechanism under the transparency framework for the year in review. Jordan is currently considering the implementation of review and supervision mechanisms within ISTD to ensure that all relevant information related to future rulings is captured adequately.

Conclusion on section A

676. Jordan does not have specific mechanisms in place for identifying future rulings and potential exchange jurisdictions within the scope of the transparency framework as well as for reviewing and supervising that all relevant information is captured adequately.

677. Jordan is recommended to ensure that it has put in place an effective information gathering process to identify all future rulings and potential exchange jurisdictions, with a review and supervision mechanism, as soon as possible (ToR I.A).

B. The exchange of information (ToR II.B)

Legal basis for spontaneous exchange of information (ToR II.B.1, II.B.2)

678. Jordan does not have the necessary domestic legal basis to exchange information spontaneously. ISTD is currently in the process of putting in place the necessary domestic legal basis to exchange information spontaneously. Jordan can only exchange information on request.

679. Jordan does not have currently in effect an agreement that would allow for spontaneous exchange of information under the transparency framework. Jordan signed the *Multilateral Convention on Mutual*

Administrative Assistance in Tax Matters: Amended by the 2010 Protocol (OECD/Council of Europe, 2011[4]) ("the Convention") on 29 September 2020 and ratified on 11 August 2021. The Convention will enter into force on 1 December 2021. No exchanges could occur under the Convention for the year in review.[2]

680. During the year in review, Jordan indicated that a legal framework allowing for spontaneous exchange of information on relevant tax rulings in order to exchange tax rulings in a timely manner is in the process of being developed and it is expected between the end of 2021 and early 2022.

681. Jordan is encouraged to continue its efforts to expand its international exchange of information instruments to be able to exchange rulings. It is however noted that jurisdictions are assessed on their compliance with the transparency framework in respect of the exchange of information network in effect for the year of the particular annual review.

Completion and exchange of templates (ToR II.B.3, II.B.4, II.B.5, II.B.6, II.B.7)

682. During the year in review, Jordan did not put in place a process to exchange information on rulings in accordance with the form and timelines required by the transparency framework. Jordan is recommended to ensure the timely exchange of information on rulings in the form required by the transparency framework. Jordan is currently considering the implementation of a process within ISTD to ensure the timely exchange of information on future rulings.

Conclusion on section B

683. Jordan does not yet have the necessary domestic legal basis to exchange information spontaneously and a process to exchange information on rulings in the required format and timelines. Jordan is recommended to put in place a domestic legal framework allowing spontaneous exchange of information on the relevant tax rulings and to ensure the timely exchange of information on rulings in the form required by the transparency framework (ToR II.B).

C. Statistics (ToR IV)

684. As no rulings were issued, no statistics can be reported.

D. Matters related to intellectual property regimes (ToR I.A.1.3)

685. Jordan offers one intellectual property regime (IP regime).[3] The assessment of transparency requirements under the Action 5 Report (OECD, 2015[1]), is as follows:

- ***New entrants benefitting from the grandfathered IP regime***: the Development zone regime was reported in the year 2019 as actually harmful. In January 2021, Jordan issued a regulation as well as a legally binding opinion and an administrative act, both annexed to the regulation, amending the regime as of 1 January 2021 with no grandfathering provided to existing taxpayers. The Forum on Harmful Tax Practices (FHTP) approved these documents and concluded that the regime was compliant with the FHTP standard and therefore updated the conclusion to "not harmful (amended)". Throughout the period in which the regime is considered "harmful", Jordan is expected to have information available and to have exchanged information on new entrants as of the relevant date from which the enhanced transparency obligations apply (i.e. 16 October 2017) until the date the regime is amended (i.e. 1 January 2021). During the year in review, Jordan has not identified information on new entrants to the Development zone regime for the relevant period indicated above, and as such has not exchanged information on these taxpayers. Jordan has indicated that a process to identify new entrants to the Development zone regime for the relevant period will be developed between the end of 2021 and early 2022. Therefore, Jordan is recommended to identify information and to put in place a domestic legal framework allowing spontaneous exchange of information on all new entrants to the IP regime (ToR I.A.1.3).

- ***Third category of IP assets***: not applicable to these regimes.
- ***Taxpayers making the use of the option to treat the nexus ratio as a rebuttable presumption:*** not applicable to these regimes.

Summary of recommendations on implementation of the transparency framework

Aspect of implementation of the transparency framework that should be improved	Recommendation for improvement
Jordan does not have specific mechanisms in place for identifying future rulings and potential exchange jurisdictions within the scope of the transparency framework as well as for reviewing and supervising that all relevant information is captured adequately.	Jordan is recommended to ensure that it has put in place an effective information gathering process to identify all future rulings and potential exchange jurisdictions, with a review and supervision mechanism, as soon as possible. This recommendation remains unchanged since the prior year peer review report.
Jordan has not the necessary domestic legal basis to exchange information spontaneously and Jordan does not yet have a process to exchange information on rulings in the required format and timelines.	Jordan is recommended to put in place a domestic legal framework allowing spontaneous exchange of information on the relevant tax rulings and to ensure the timely exchange of information on rulings in the form required by the transparency framework. This recommendation remains unchanged since the prior year peer review report.
Jordan has not identified information on new entrants to the Development zone IP regime during the relevant period, and has not exchanged information on these taxpayers.	Jordan is recommended to identify information and to put in place a domestic legal framework allowing spontaneous exchange of information on all new entrants to the IP regime. This recommendation remains unchanged since the prior year peer review report.

Jurisdiction's response and recent developments

686. With the support of international donors, Jordan is planning to develop a set of procedures and guidelines that will allow ISTD to meet the information gathering process requirements, to implement a legal framework allowing for spontaneous exchange of information and to identify new entrants to the Development zone regime for the relevant period. Jordan expects to complete these processes between the end of 2021 and early 2022.

References

OECD (2021), *BEPS Action 5 on Harmful Tax Practices - Terms of Reference and Methodology for the Conduct of the Peer Reviews of the Action 5 Transparency Framework*, OECD Publishing, Paris, http://www.oecd.org/tax/beps/beps-action-5-harmful-tax-practices-peer-review-transparency-framework.pdf. [3]

OECD (2015), *Countering Harmful Tax Practices More Effectively, Taking into Account Transparency and Substance, Action 5 - 2015 Final Report*, OECD/G20 Base Erosion and Profit Shifting Project, OECD Publishing, Paris, https://dx.doi.org/10.1787/9789264241190-en. [1]

OECD (ed.) (2017b), *Harmful Tax Practices - 2017 Progress Report on Preferential Regimes*, OECD Publishing, Paris, http://dx.doi.org/10.1787/9789264283954-en. [2]

OECD/Council of Europe (2011), *The Multilateral Convention on Mutual Administrative Assistance in Tax Matters: Amended by the 2010 Protocol*, OECD Publishing, Paris, https://dx.doi.org/10.1787/9789264115606-en. [4]

Notes

[1] With respect to the following preferential regimes: 1) Development zone regime; 2) Aqaba special economic zone; and 3) the tax preference (i.e. 5% income tax rate on information technology services performed inside or outside the development zones) granted to the information technology sector by the Investment law and included in the Cabinet Decision no. 14883 of 2016.

[2] Participating jurisdictions to the Convention are available here: www.oecd.org/tax/exchange-of-tax-information/convention-on-mutual-administrative-assistance-in-tax-matters.htm.

[3] Development zone regime.

Kazakhstan

Kazakhstan is taking steps to implement the legal basis for the transparency framework and to commence administrative preparations in line with the terms of reference (OECD, 2021[3]) (ToR) to ensure that it finalises information gathering process (ToR I.A) and that information on rulings will be identified and exchanged in a timely manner (ToR II.B). Kazakhstan receives two recommendations on these points for the year in review.

In the prior year report, as well as in the 2018 peer review, Kazakhstan received the same recommendations. As they have not been addressed, the recommendations remain in place.

Kazakhstan can legally issue one type of rulings within the scope of the transparency framework.

In practice, Kazakhstan issued one past ruling and no future rulings within the scope of the transparency framework.

As no exchanges took place, no peer input was received in respect of the exchanges of information on rulings received from Kazakhstan.

A. The information gathering process (ToR I.A)

687. Kazakhstan can legally issue the following type of rulings within the scope of the transparency framework: cross-border unilateral APAs and any other cross-border unilateral tax rulings (such as an advance tax ruling) covering transfer pricing or the application of transfer pricing principles.

Past rulings (ToR I.A.1.1, I.A.1.2, I.A.2.1, I.A.2.2)

688. For Kazakhstan, past rulings are any tax rulings issued either (i) on or after 1 January 2016 but before 1 April 2018; and (ii) on or after 1 January 2014 but before 1 January 2016, provided still in effect as at 1 January 2016.

689. In the prior year peer review report, it was noted that Kazakhstan issued one past ruling and that the responsible team is continuing to put in place guidelines and practices to collect and record the relevant information for the purposes of the transparency framework. As Kazakhstan has not finalised this process for the year in review, the recommendation remains in place.

Future rulings (ToR I.A.1.1, I.A.1.2, I.A.2.1)

690. For Kazakhstan, future rulings are any tax rulings within scope that are issued on or after 1 April 2018.

691. In the prior year peer review report, Kazakhstan noted that when requesting an APA, the taxpayer must identify all transactions that will be covered by the agreement and provide all necessary information about these related parties. However, for the year in review, it is still not clear whether information on the immediate parent and ultimate parent is being collected. It is noted that guidelines and practices are being implemented to make sure that the relevant information is adequately processed for the purposes of the transparency framework. As such, the recommendation remains in place.

Review and supervision (ToR I.A.3)

692. In the prior year peer review report, it was determined that Kazakhstan was in the process of implementing a review and supervision mechanism. Once issued by the transfer pricing division, rulings should be reviewed by the non-residents taxation division, which will be responsible to collect the relevant information and to make sure that all relevant information is captured adequately and submitted to all relevant jurisdictions without delay. As it is not known whether Kazakhstan has finalised this process for the year in review, the recommendation remains in place.

Conclusion on section A

693. Kazakhstan is recommended to finalise its information gathering process, with a review and supervision mechanism, as soon as possible (ToR I.A).

B. The exchange of information (ToR II.B)

Legal basis for spontaneous exchange of information (ToR II.B.1, II.B.2)

694. In the prior year peer review report, it was noted that Kazakhstan intended to draft regulations that will allow for the spontaneous exchange of information on tax rulings in future. However, for the year in review, Kazakhstan has not yet put in place the necessary domestic legal basis to exchange information spontaneously.

695. Kazakhstan has international agreements permitting spontaneous exchange of information, including being a party to the (i) *Multilateral Convention on Mutual Administrative Assistance in Tax Matters: Amended by the 2010 Protocol* (OECD/Council of Europe, 2011[4]) ("the Convention") and (ii) bilateral agreements in force with 59 jurisdictions.[1]

Completion and exchange of templates (ToR II.B.3, II.B.4, II.B.5, II.B.6, II.B.7)

696. In the prior year peer review report, it was determined that Kazakhstan was still developing a process to complete the templates on relevant rulings, to make them available to the Competent Authority for exchange of information, and to exchange them with relevant jurisdictions. Kazakhstan has not yet put in place such a process for the year in review.

697. As it is not known whether exchanges took place in the year of review, no data on the timeliness of exchanges can be reported.

Conclusion on section B

698. Kazakhstan is recommended to put in place a domestic legal framework allowing spontaneous exchange of information on rulings and to continue its efforts to complete the templates for all relevant rulings and to ensure that the exchanges of information on rulings occur as soon as possible (ToR II.B).

C. Statistics (ToR IV)

699. As there was no information on rulings exchanged by Kazakhstan for the year in review, no statistics can be reported.

D. Matters related to intellectual property regimes (ToR I.A.1.3)

700. Kazakhstan does not offer an intellectual property regime for which transparency requirements under the Action 5 Report (OECD, 2015[1]) were imposed.

Summary of recommendations on implementation of the transparency framework

Aspect of implementation of the transparency framework that should be improved	Recommendation for improvement
Kazakhstan has not yet finalised the steps to have in place its necessary information and gathering process.	Kazakhstan is recommended to finalise its information gathering process, with a review and supervision mechanism, as soon as possible. This recommendation remains unchanged since the 2018 and 2019 peer review reports.
Kazakhstan has not yet finalised the steps to have effective compulsory spontaneous exchange of information on the tax rulings within the scope of the transparency framework.	Kazakhstan is recommended to continue to put in place a domestic legal framework allowing spontaneous exchange of information on rulings and to continue its efforts to complete the templates for all relevant rulings and to ensure that the exchanges of information on rulings occur as soon as possible. This recommendation remains unchanged since the 2018 and 2019 peer review reports.

References

OECD (2021), *BEPS Action 5 on Harmful Tax Practices - Terms of Reference and Methodology for the Conduct of the Peer Reviews of the Action 5 Transparency Framework*, OECD Publishing, Paris, http://www.oecd.org/tax/beps/beps-action-5-harmful-tax-practices-peer-review-transparency-framework.pdf. [3]

OECD (2015), *Countering Harmful Tax Practices More Effectively, Taking into Account Transparency and Substance, Action 5 - 2015 Final Report*, OECD/G20 Base Erosion and Profit Shifting Project, OECD Publishing, Paris, https://dx.doi.org/10.1787/9789264241190-en. [1]

OECD (ed.) (2017b), *Harmful Tax Practices - 2017 Progress Report on Preferential Regimes*, OECD Publishing, Paris, http://dx.doi.org/10.1787/9789264283954-en. [2]

OECD/Council of Europe (2011), *The Multilateral Convention on Mutual Administrative Assistance in Tax Matters: Amended by the 2010 Protocol*, OECD Publishing, Paris, https://dx.doi.org/10.1787/9789264115606-en. [4]

Notes

[1] Participating jurisdictions to the Convention are available here: www.oecd.org/tax/exchange-of-tax-information/convention-on-mutual-administrative-assistance-in-tax-matters.htm. Kazakhstan also has bilateral agreements with Albania, Armenia, Austria, Azerbaijan, Belarus, Belgium, Bulgaria, Canada, China (People's Republic of), Croatia, Czech Republic, Denmark, Estonia, Finland, France, Georgia, Germany, Hungary, Iceland, India, Iran, Ireland, Italy, Japan, Korea, Kyrgyzstan, Latvia, Lithuania, Luxembourg, Malaysia, Moldova, Mongolia, Montenegro, Morocco, Netherlands, North Macedonia, Norway, Pakistan, Poland, Portugal, Qatar, Romania, Russian Federation, Saudi Arabia, Serbia, Singapore, Slovak Republic, Slovenia, Spain, Sweden, Switzerland, Tajikistan, Turkey, Turkmenistan, Ukraine, United Arab Emirates, United Kingdom, United States and Uzbekistan.

Kenya

Kenya has met all aspects of the terms of reference (OECD, 2021[3]) (ToR) for the calendar year 2020 (year in review) that can be met in the absence of rulings being issued in practice, and no recommendations are made.

Kenya can legally issue four types of rulings within the scope of the transparency framework.

In practice, Kenya issue no rulings within the scope of the transparency framework.

As no exchanges were required to take place, no peer input was received in respect of the exchanges of information on rulings received from Kenya.

A. The information gathering process (ToR I.A)

701. Kenya can legally issue the following four types of rulings within the scope of the transparency framework: (i) preferential regimes;[1] (ii) rulings providing for unilateral downward adjustments; (iii) permanent establishment rulings; and (iv) related party conduit rulings.

702. For Kenya, past rulings are any tax rulings within scope that are issued either: (i) on or after 1 January 2016 but before 1 April 2018; or (ii) on or after 1 January 2014 but before 1 January 2016, provided they were still in effect as at 1 January 2016. Future rulings are any tax rulings within scope that are issued on or after 1 April 2018.

703. In the prior years' peer review reports, it was determined that Kenya's undertakings to identify past and future rulings and all potential exchange jurisdictions were sufficient to meet the minimum standard in the absence of rulings being issued. In addition, it was determined that Kenya's review and supervision mechanism was sufficient to meet the minimum standard. Kenya's implementation remains unchanged, and therefore continues to meet the minimum standard.

704. Kenya has met all of the ToR for the information gathering process and no recommendations are made.

B. The exchange of information (ToR II.B)

705. Kenya has international agreements permitting spontaneous exchange of information, including being a party to (i) the *Multilateral Convention on Mutual Administrative Assistance in Tax Matters: Amended by the 2010 Protocol* (OECD/Council of Europe, 2011[4]) ("the Convention") and (ii) bilateral agreements in force with 15 jurisdictions.[2] Kenya is encouraged to continue its efforts to expand its international exchange of information instruments to be able to exchange rulings. It is noted, however, that jurisdictions are assessed on their compliance with the transparency framework in respect of the exchange of information network in effect for the year of the particular annual review.

706. As no rulings are issued in practice, no data on the timeliness of exchanges can be reported.

707. In the prior year peer review report, it was determined that Kenya's process for the completion and exchange of templates were sufficient to meet the minimum standard in the absence of rulings being issued. With respect to past rulings, no further action was required. Kenya's implementation in this regard remains unchanged and therefore continues to meet the minimum standard.

708. Kenya has the necessary legal basis for spontaneous exchange of information and a process for completing the templates in a timely way. Kenya has met all of the ToR for the exchange of information process in the absence of rulings being issued and no recommendations are made.

C. Statistics (ToR IV)

709. As no rulings were issued, no statistics can be reported.

D. Matters related to intellectual property regimes (ToR I.A.1.3)

710. Kenya does not offer an intellectual property regime for which transparency requirements under the Action 5 Report (OECD, 2015[1]) were imposed.

Summary of recommendations on implementation of the transparency framework

Aspect of implementation of the transparency framework that should be improved	Recommendation for improvement
	No recommendations are made.

References

OECD (2021), *BEPS Action 5 on Harmful Tax Practices - Terms of Reference and Methodology for the Conduct of the Peer Reviews of the Action 5 Transparency Framework*, OECD Publishing, Paris, http://www.oecd.org/tax/beps/beps-action-5-harmful-tax-practices-peer-review-transparency-framework.pdf. [3]

OECD (2015), *Countering Harmful Tax Practices More Effectively, Taking into Account Transparency and Substance, Action 5 - 2015 Final Report*, OECD/G20 Base Erosion and Profit Shifting Project, OECD Publishing, Paris, https://dx.doi.org/10.1787/9789264241190-en. [1]

OECD (ed.) (2017b), *Harmful Tax Practices - 2017 Progress Report on Preferential Regimes*, OECD Publishing, Paris, http://dx.doi.org/10.1787/9789264283954-en. [2]

OECD/Council of Europe (2011), *The Multilateral Convention on Mutual Administrative Assistance in Tax Matters: Amended by the 2010 Protocol*, OECD Publishing, Paris, https://dx.doi.org/10.1787/9789264115606-en. [4]

Notes

[1] With respect to the following preferential regimes: 1) Export processing zone and 2) Special economic zone.

[2] Participating jurisdictions to the Convention are available here: www.oecd.org/tax/exchange-of-tax-information/convention-on-mutual-administrative-assistance-in-tax-matters.htm. Kenya also has bilateral agreements with Canada, Denmark, France, Germany, India, Iran, Korea, Norway, Qatar, Seychelles, South Africa, Sweden, United Arab Emirates, United Kingdom and Zambia.

Korea

Korea has met all aspects of the terms of reference (OECD, 2021[3]) (ToR) for the calendar year 2020 (year in review), and no recommendations are made.

Korea can legally issue one type of rulings within the scope of the transparency framework.

In practice, Korea issued rulings within the scope of the transparency framework as follows:

Type of ruling	Number of rulings
Past rulings	45
Future rulings in the period 1 April 2016 – 31 December 2016	1
Future rulings in the calendar year 2017	4
Future rulings in the calendar year 2018	5
Future rulings in the calendar year 2019	5
Future rulings in the year in review	12

Peer input was received from three jurisdictions in respect of the exchanges of information on rulings received from Korea. One peer was positive, noting that information was complete, in a correct format and received in a timely manner. Two peers noted that the information was not received in a timely matter, and one of them additionally noted that more information could be provided in the summary box of the template.

A. The information gathering process (ToR I.A)

711. Korea can legally issue the following type of ruling within the scope of the transparency framework: cross-border unilateral APAs and any other cross-border unilateral tax rulings (such as an advance tax ruling) covering transfer pricing or the application of transfer pricing principles.

712. For Korea, past rulings are any tax rulings within scope that are issued either: (i) on or after 1 January 2014 but before 1 April 2016; or (ii) on or after 1 January 2010 but before 1 January 2014, provided they were still in effect as at 1 January 2014. Future rulings are any tax rulings within scope that are issued on or after 1 April 2016.

713. In the prior years' peer review reports, it was determined that Korea's undertakings to identify past and future rulings and all potential exchange jurisdictions were sufficient to meet the minimum standard. In addition, it was determined that Korea's review and supervision mechanism was sufficient to meet the minimum standard. Korea's implementation remains unchanged, and therefore continues to meet the minimum standard.

714. Korea has met all of the ToR for the information gathering process and no recommendations are made.

B. The exchange of information (ToR II.B)

715. Korea has international agreements permitting spontaneous exchange of information, including being a party to (i) the *Multilateral Convention on Mutual Administrative Assistance in Tax Matters: Amended by the 2010 Protocol* (OECD/Council of Europe, 2011[4]) ("the Convention") and (ii) bilateral agreements in force with 93 jurisdictions.[1]

716. For the year in review, the timeliness of exchanges is as follows:

Future rulings within the scope of the transparency framework	Number of exchanges transmitted within three months of the information becoming available to the competent authority or immediately after legal impediments have been lifted	Delayed exchanges		
		Number of exchanges transmitted later than three months of the information on rulings becoming available to the competent authority	Reasons for the delays	Any other comments
	34	16	See below.	N/A

Follow up requests received for exchange of the ruling	Number	Average time to provide response	Number of requests not answered
	0	N/A	N/A

717. Korea noted that the 16 delayed exchanges, all related to one ruling, were caused by a human error. As soon as the EoI division was notified for the exchanges, the exchanges were made with a limited delay. In order to avoid this issue from happening again in the future, Korea will designate an additional person in the MAP division who is responsible for unilateral APAs. In addition, it has strengthened the communication between the MAP division and the EoI division. Therefore, no recommendation is made. In addition, based on peer input, Korea indicated that it changed its internal policy to provide more information in the summary section of the template.

718. In the prior years' peer review reports, it was determined that Korea's process for the completion and exchange of templates were sufficient to meet the minimum standard. With respect to past rulings, no

further action was required. Korea's implementation in this regard remains unchanged and therefore continues to meet the minimum standard.

719. Korea has the necessary legal basis for spontaneous exchange of information, a process for completing the templates in a timely way and has completed all exchanges. Korea has met all of the ToR for the exchange of information process and no recommendations are made.

C. Statistics (ToR IV)

720. The statistics for the year in review are as follows:

Category of ruling	Number of exchanges	Jurisdictions exchanged with
Cross-border unilateral APAs and any other cross-border unilateral tax rulings (such as an advance tax ruling) covering transfer pricing or the application of transfer pricing principles	50	Argentina, Australia, Canada, Chile, China (People's Republic of), Germany, Hong Kong (China), India, Indonesia, Ireland, Japan, Malaysia, Mexico, Netherlands, Norway, Papua New Guinea, Philippines, Poland, Russia, Singapore, South Africa, Thailand, Turkey, United States
IP regimes: total exchanges on taxpayers benefitting from the third category of IP assets, new entrants benefitting from grandfathered IP regimes; and taxpayers making use of the option to treat the nexus ratio as a rebuttable presumption	0	N/A
Total	50	

D. Matters related to intellectual property regimes (ToR I.A.1.3)

721. Korea offers an intellectual property regime (IP regime)[2] that is subject to the transparency requirements under the Action 5 Report (OECD, 2015[1]). It states that the identification of the benefitting taxpayers will occur as follows:

- ***New entrants benefitting from the grandfathered IP regime***: as this is a new IP regime rather than a grandfathered IP regime, transparency on new entrants is not relevant.
- ***Third category of IP assets***: the regime provides benefits to the third category of IP assets. The process on the collection of information is described in the prior year peer review report and meets the ToR. Korea notes that for the year in review, there was one taxpayer that applied for the third category of IP assets, but as this was a purely domestic taxpayer, no exchanges needed to take place.
- ***Taxpayers making use of the option to treat the nexus ratio as a rebuttable presumption***: not applicable as the regime does not allow the nexus ratio to be treated as a rebuttable presumption.

Summary of recommendations on implementation of the transparency framework

Aspect of implementation of the transparency framework that should be improved	Recommendation for improvement
	No recommendations are made.

References

OECD (2021), *BEPS Action 5 on Harmful Tax Practices - Terms of Reference and Methodology for the Conduct of the Peer Reviews of the Action 5 Transparency Framework*, OECD Publishing, Paris, http://www.oecd.org/tax/beps/beps-action-5-harmful-tax-practices-peer-review-transparency-framework.pdf. [3]

OECD (2015), *Countering Harmful Tax Practices More Effectively, Taking into Account Transparency and Substance, Action 5 - 2015 Final Report*, OECD/G20 Base Erosion and Profit Shifting Project, OECD Publishing, Paris, https://dx.doi.org/10.1787/9789264241190-en. [1]

OECD (ed.) (2017b), *Harmful Tax Practices - 2017 Progress Report on Preferential Regimes*, OECD Publishing, Paris, http://dx.doi.org/10.1787/9789264283954-en. [2]

OECD/Council of Europe (2011), *The Multilateral Convention on Mutual Administrative Assistance in Tax Matters: Amended by the 2010 Protocol*, OECD Publishing, Paris, https://dx.doi.org/10.1787/9789264115606-en. [4]

Notes

1 Participating jurisdictions to the Convention are available here: www.oecd.org/tax/exchange-of-tax-information/convention-on-mutual-administrative-assistance-in-tax-matters.htm. Korea also has bilateral agreements with Albania, Algeria, Australia, Austria, Azerbaijan, Bahrain, Bangladesh, Belarus, Belgium, Brazil, Brunei Darussalam, Bulgaria, Canada, Chile, China (People's Republic of), Colombia, Croatia, Czech Republic, Denmark, Ecuador, Egypt, Estonia, Ethiopia, Fiji, Finland, France, Gabon, Georgia, Germany, Greece, Hong Kong (China), Hungary, Iceland, India, Indonesia, Iran, Ireland, Israel, Italy, Japan, Jordan, Kazakhstan, Kenya, Kuwait, Kyrgyzstan, Lao People's Democratic Republic, Latvia, Lithuania, Luxembourg, Malaysia, Malta, Mexico, Mongolia, Morocco, Myanmar, Nepal, Netherlands, New Zealand, Norway, Oman, Pakistan, Panama, Papua New Guinea, Peru, Philippines, Poland, Portugal, Qatar, Romania, Russia, Saudi Arabia, Serbia, Singapore, Slovak Republic, Slovenia, South Africa, Spain, Sri Lanka, Sweden, Switzerland, Tajikistan, Thailand, Tunisia, Turkey, Turkmenistan, Ukraine, United Arab Emirates, United Kingdom, United States, Uruguay, Uzbekistan, Venezuela and Viet Nam.

2 Special taxation for transfer, acquisition, etc. of technology.

Latvia

Latvia has met all aspects of the terms of reference (OECD, 2021[3]) (ToR) for the calendar year 2020 (year in review), and no recommendations are made.

Latvia can legally issue three types of rulings within the scope of the transparency framework.

In practice, Latvia issued rulings within the scope of the transparency framework as follows:

Type of ruling	Number of rulings
Past rulings	1
Future rulings in the period 1 April 2016 – 31 December 2016	1
Future rulings in the calendar year 2017	2
Future rulings in the calendar year 2018	3
Future rulings in the calendar year 2019	4
Future rulings in the year in review	4

Peer input was received from one jurisdiction in respect of the exchanges of information on rulings received from Latvia. The input was positive, noting that information was complete, in a correct format and received in a timely manner.

A. The information gathering process (ToR I.A)

722. Latvia can legally issue the following three types of rulings within the scope of the transparency framework: (i) preferential regimes;[1] (ii) cross-border unilateral APAs and any other cross-border unilateral tax rulings (such as an advance tax ruling) covering transfer pricing or the application of transfer pricing principles; and (iii) permanent establishment rulings.

723. For Latvia, past rulings are any tax rulings within scope that are issued either: (i) on or after 1 January 2014 but before 1 April 2016; or (ii) on or after 1 January 2010 but before 1 January 2014, provided they were still in effect as at 1 January 2014. Future rulings are any tax rulings within scope that are issued on or after 1 April 2016.

724. In the prior years' peer review reports, it was determined that Latvia's undertakings to identify past and future rulings and all potential exchange jurisdictions were sufficient to meet the minimum standard. In addition, it was determined that Latvia's review and supervision mechanism was sufficient to meet the minimum standard. Latvia's implementation remains unchanged, and therefore continues to meet the minimum standard.

725. Latvia has met all of the ToR for the information gathering process and no recommendations are made.

B. The exchange of information (ToR II.B)

726. Latvia has international agreements permitting spontaneous exchange of information, including being a party to (i) the *Multilateral Convention on Mutual Administrative Assistance in Tax Matters: Amended by the 2010 Protocol* (OECD/Council of Europe, 2011[4]) ("the Convention"), (ii) the Directive 2011/16/EU with all other European Union Member States and (iii) bilateral agreements in force with 62 jurisdictions.[2]

727. For the year in review, the timeliness of exchanges is as follows:

Future rulings within the scope of the transparency framework	Number of exchanges transmitted within three months of the information becoming available to the competent authority or immediately after legal impediments have been lifted	Delayed exchanges		
		Number of exchanges transmitted later than three months of the information on rulings becoming available to the competent authority	Reasons for the delays	Any other comments
	5	0	N/A	N/A

Follow up requests received for exchange of the ruling	Number	Average time to provide response	Number of requests not answered
	0	N/A	N/A

728. In the prior years' peer review reports, it was determined that Latvia's process for the completion and exchange of templates were sufficient to meet the minimum standard. With respect to past rulings, no further action was required. Latvia's implementation in this regard remains unchanged and therefore continues to meet the minimum standard.

729. Latvia has the necessary legal basis for spontaneous exchange of information, a process for completing the templates in a timely way and has completed all exchanges. Latvia has met all of the ToR for the exchange of information process and no recommendations are made.

C. Statistics (ToR IV)

730. The statistics for the year in review are as follows:

Category of ruling	Number of exchanges	Jurisdictions exchanged with
Ruling related to a preferential regime	0	N/A
Cross-border unilateral APAs and any other cross-border unilateral tax rulings (such as an advance tax ruling) covering transfer pricing or the application of transfer pricing principles	*De minimis* rule applies	N/A
Permanent establishment rulings	0	N/A
De minimis rule	5	N/A
Total	5	

D. Matters related to intellectual property regimes (ToR I.A.1.3)

731. Latvia does not offer an intellectual property regime for which transparency requirements under the Action 5 Report (OECD, 2015[1]) were imposed.

Summary of recommendations on implementation of the transparency framework

Aspect of implementation of the transparency framework that should be improved	Recommendation for improvement
	No recommendations are made.

References

OECD (2021), *BEPS Action 5 on Harmful Tax Practices - Terms of Reference and Methodology for the Conduct of the Peer Reviews of the Action 5 Transparency Framework*, OECD Publishing, Paris, http://www.oecd.org/tax/beps/beps-action-5-harmful-tax-practices-peer-review-transparency-framework.pdf. [3]

OECD (2015), *Countering Harmful Tax Practices More Effectively, Taking into Account Transparency and Substance, Action 5 - 2015 Final Report*, OECD/G20 Base Erosion and Profit Shifting Project, OECD Publishing, Paris, https://dx.doi.org/10.1787/9789264241190-en. [1]

OECD (ed.) (2017b), *Harmful Tax Practices - 2017 Progress Report on Preferential Regimes*, OECD Publishing, Paris, http://dx.doi.org/10.1787/9789264283954-en. [2]

OECD/Council of Europe (2011), *The Multilateral Convention on Mutual Administrative Assistance in Tax Matters: Amended by the 2010 Protocol*, OECD Publishing, Paris, https://dx.doi.org/10.1787/9789264115606-en. [4]

Notes

[1] With respect to the following preferential regimes: 1) Shipping tax regime and 2) Special economic zones.

[2] Participating jurisdictions to the Convention are available here: www.oecd.org/tax/exchange-of-tax-information/convention-on-mutual-administrative-assistance-in-tax-matters.htm. Latvia also has bilateral agreements with Albania, Armenia, Austria, Azerbaijan, Belarus, Belgium, Bulgaria, Canada, China (People's Republic of), Croatia, Cyprus, Czech Republic, Denmark, Estonia, Finland, France, Georgia, Germany, Greece, Hong Kong (China), Hungary, Iceland, India, Ireland, Israel, Italy, Japan, Kazakhstan, Korea, Kuwait, Kyrgyzstan, Lithuania, Luxembourg, Malta, Mexico, Moldova, Morocco, Netherlands, North Macedonia, Norway, Poland, Portugal, Qatar, Romania, Russia, Montenegro, Serbia, Singapore, Slovenia, Slovak Republic, Spain, Sweden, Switzerland, Tajikistan, Turkey, Turkmenistan, Ukraine, United Arab Emirates, United Kingdom, United States, Uzbekistan and Viet Nam.

Liechtenstein

Liechtenstein has met all aspects of the terms of reference (OECD, 2021[3]) (ToR) for the calendar year 2020 (year in review), and no recommendations are made.

Liechtenstein can legally issue four types of rulings within the scope of the transparency framework.

In practice, Liechtenstein issued rulings within the scope of the transparency framework as follows:

Type of ruling	Number of rulings
Past rulings	18
Future rulings in the period 1 April 2017 – 31 December 2017	6
Future rulings in the calendar year 2018	5
Future rulings in the calendar year 2019	3
Future rulings in the year in review	14

No peer input was received in respect of the exchanges of information on rulings received from Liechtenstein.

A. The information gathering process (ToR I.A)

732. Liechtenstein can legally issue the following four types of rulings within the scope of the transparency framework: (i) cross-border unilateral APAs and any other cross-border unilateral tax rulings (such as an advance tax ruling) covering transfer pricing or the application of transfer pricing principles; (ii) rulings providing for unilateral downward adjustments; (iii) permanent establishment rulings; and (iv) related party conduit rulings.

733. For Liechtenstein, past rulings are any tax rulings within scope that are issued either: (i) on or after January 2015 but before 1 April 2017; or (ii) on or after 1 January 2012 but before 1 January 2015, provided they were still in effect as at 1 January 2017. Future rulings are any tax rulings within scope that are issued on or after 1 April 2017.

734. In the prior years' peer review reports, it was determined that Liechtenstein's undertakings to identify past and future rulings and all potential exchange jurisdictions were sufficient to meet the minimum standard. In addition, it was determined that Liechtenstein's review and supervision mechanism was sufficient to meet the minimum standard. Liechtenstein's implementation remains unchanged, and therefore continues to meet the minimum standard.

735. Liechtenstein has met all of the ToR for the information gathering process and no recommendations are made.

B. The exchange of information (ToR II.B)

736. Liechtenstein has international agreements permitting spontaneous exchange of information, including being a party to (i) the *Multilateral Convention on Mutual Administrative Assistance in Tax Matters: Amended by the 2010 Protocol* (OECD/Council of Europe, 2011[4]) ("the Convention") and (ii) bilateral agreements in force with 14 jurisdictions.[1]

737. For the year in review, the timeliness of exchanges is as follows:

Future rulings within the scope of the transparency framework	Number of exchanges transmitted within three months of the information becoming available to the competent authority or immediately after legal impediments have been lifted	Delayed exchanges		
		Number of exchanges transmitted later than three months of the information on rulings becoming available to the competent authority	Reasons for the delays	Any other comments
	15	0	N/A	N/A

Follow up requests received for exchange of the ruling	Number	Average time to provide response	Number of requests not answered
	0	N/A	N/A

738. In the prior years' peer review reports, it was determined that Liechtenstein's process for the completion and exchange of templates were sufficient to meet the minimum standard. With respect to past rulings, no further action was required from Liechtenstein. Liechtenstein's implementation in this regard remains unchanged and therefore continues to meet the minimum standard.

739. Liechtenstein has the necessary legal basis for spontaneous exchange of information, a process for completing the templates in a timely way and has completed all exchanges. Liechtenstein has met all of the ToR for the exchange of information process and no recommendations are made.

C. Statistics (ToR IV)

740. The statistics for the year in review are as follows:

Category of ruling	Number of exchanges	Jurisdictions exchanged with
Cross-border unilateral APAs and any other cross-border unilateral tax rulings (such as an advance tax ruling) covering transfer pricing or the application of transfer pricing principles	8	Austria, Germany, Switzerland
Cross-border rulings providing for a unilateral downward adjustment to the taxpayer's taxable profits that is not directly reflected in the taxpayer's financial / commercial accounts	1	*De minimis* rule applies
Permanent establishment rulings	9	Austria, Germany, Switzerland
Related party conduit rulings	0	N/A
Total	18[2]	

D. Matters related to intellectual property regimes (ToR I.A.1.3)

741. Liechtenstein does not offer an intellectual property regime for which transparency requirements under the Action 5 Report (OECD, 2015[1]) were imposed.

Summary of recommendations on implementation of the transparency framework

Aspect of implementation of the transparency framework that should be improved	Recommendation for improvement
	No recommendations are made.

References

OECD (2021), *BEPS Action 5 on Harmful Tax Practices - Terms of Reference and Methodology for the Conduct of the Peer Reviews of the Action 5 Transparency Framework*, OECD Publishing, Paris, http://www.oecd.org/tax/beps/beps-action-5-harmful-tax-practices-peer-review-transparency-framework.pdf. [3]

OECD (2015), *Countering Harmful Tax Practices More Effectively, Taking into Account Transparency and Substance, Action 5 - 2015 Final Report*, OECD/G20 Base Erosion and Profit Shifting Project, OECD Publishing, Paris, https://dx.doi.org/10.1787/9789264241190-en. [1]

OECD (ed.) (2017b), *Harmful Tax Practices - 2017 Progress Report on Preferential Regimes*, OECD Publishing, Paris, http://dx.doi.org/10.1787/9789264283954-en. [2]

OECD/Council of Europe (2011), *The Multilateral Convention on Mutual Administrative Assistance in Tax Matters: Amended by the 2010 Protocol*, OECD Publishing, Paris, https://dx.doi.org/10.1787/9789264115606-en. [4]

Notes

[1] Participating jurisdictions to the Convention are available here: www.oecd.org/tax/exchange-of-tax-information/convention-on-mutual-administrative-assistance-in-tax-matters.htm. Liechtenstein also has bilateral agreements with Andorra, Austria, Czech Republic, Germany, Hungary, Iceland, Jersey, Lithuania, Luxembourg, Monaco, San Marino, Singapore, United Arab Emirates, and United Kingdom.

[2] There were 15 unique exchanges, as three rulings fell into more than one category and were exchanged with more than one jurisdiction under the BEPS Action 5 report.

Lithuania

Lithuania has met all aspects of the terms of reference (OECD, 2021[3]) (ToR) for the calendar year 2020 (year in review), and no recommendations are made.

Lithuania can legally issue five types of rulings within the scope of the transparency framework.

In practice, Lithuania issued rulings within the scope of the transparency framework as follows:

Type of ruling	Number of rulings
Past rulings	5
Future rulings in the calendar year 2017	6
Future rulings in the calendar year 2018	5
Future rulings in the calendar year 2019	9
Future rulings in the year in review	4

No peer input was received in respect of the exchanges of information on rulings received from Lithuania.

A. The information gathering process (ToR I.A)

742. Lithuania can legally issue the following five types of rulings within the scope of the transparency framework: (i) preferential regimes;[1] (ii) cross-border unilateral APAs and any other cross-border unilateral tax rulings (such as an advance tax ruling) covering transfer pricing or the application of transfer pricing principles; (iii) rulings providing for unilateral downward adjustments; (iv) permanent establishment rulings; and (v) related party conduit rulings.

743. For Lithuania, past rulings are any tax rulings within scope that are issued either: (i) on or after 1 January 2015 but before 1 April 2017; or (ii) on or after 1 January 2012 but before 1 January 2015, provided they were still in effect as at 1 January 2015. Future rulings are any tax rulings within scope that are issued on or after 1 April 2017.

744. In the prior years' peer review reports, it was determined that Lithuania's undertakings to identify past and future rulings and all potential exchange jurisdictions were sufficient to meet the minimum standard. In addition, it was determined that Lithuania's review and supervision mechanism was sufficient to meet the minimum standard. For past rulings, Lithuania's implementation remains unchanged, and therefore continues to meet the minimum standard.

745. Lithuania has met all of the ToR for the information gathering process and no recommendations are made.

B. The exchange of information (ToR II.B)

746. Lithuania has international agreements permitting spontaneous exchange of information, including being a party to (i) the *Multilateral Convention on Mutual Administrative Assistance in Tax Matters: Amended by the 2010 Protocol* (OECD/Council of Europe, 2011[4]) ("the Convention"), (ii) the Directive 2011/16/EU with all other European Union Member States and (iii) bilateral agreements in force with 55 jurisdictions.[2]

747. For the year in review, the timeliness of exchanges is as follows:

Future rulings within the scope of the transparency framework	Number of exchanges transmitted within three months of the information becoming available to the competent authority or immediately after legal impediments have been lifted	Delayed exchanges		
		Number of exchanges transmitted later than three months of the information on rulings becoming available to the competent authority	Reasons for the delays	Any other comments
	5	0	N/A	N/A

Follow up requests received for exchange of the ruling	Number	Average time to provide response	Number of requests not answered
	0	N/A	N/A

748. In the prior years' peer review reports, it was determined that Lithuania's process for the completion and exchange of templates were sufficient to meet the minimum standard. With respect to past rulings, no further action was required. Lithuania's implementation in this regard remains unchanged and therefore continues to meet the minimum standard.

749. Lithuania has the necessary legal basis for spontaneous exchange of information, a process for completing the templates in a timely way and has completed all exchanges. Lithuania has met all of the ToR for the exchange of information process and no recommendations are made.

C. Statistics (ToR IV)

750. The statistics for the year in review are as follows:

Category of ruling	Number of exchanges	Jurisdictions exchanged with
Ruling related to a preferential regime	*De minimis* rule applies	N/A
Cross-border unilateral APAs and any other cross-border unilateral tax rulings (such as an advance tax ruling) covering transfer pricing or the application of transfer pricing principles	0	N/A
Cross-border rulings providing for a unilateral downward adjustment to the taxpayer's taxable profits that is not directly reflected in the taxpayer's financial / commercial accounts	0	N/A
Permanent establishment rulings	*De minimis* rule applies	N/A
Related party conduit rulings	0	N/A
De minimis rule	5	N/A
Total	5	

D. Matters related to intellectual property regimes (ToR I.A.1.3)

751. Lithuania offers an intellectual property regime (IP regime) which came into effect from 1 January 2018. It is noted that this regime is not subject to transparency requirements under the Action 5 report (OECD, 2015[1]), because:

- ***New entrants benefitting from the grandfathered IP regime***: as this is a new IP regime rather than a grandfathered IP regime, transparency on new entrants was not relevant.
- ***Third category of IP assets***: not applicable as the regime does not allow the third category of IP assets to qualify for the benefits.
- ***Taxpayers making use of the option to treat the nexus ratio as a rebuttable presumption***: not applicable as the regime does not allow the nexus ratio to be treated as a rebuttable presumption.

Summary of recommendations on implementation of the transparency framework

Aspect of implementation of the transparency framework that should be improved	Recommendation for improvement
	No recommendations are made.

References

OECD (2021), *BEPS Action 5 on Harmful Tax Practices - Terms of Reference and Methodology for the Conduct of the Peer Reviews of the Action 5 Transparency Framework*, OECD Publishing, Paris, http://www.oecd.org/tax/beps/beps-action-5-harmful-tax-practices-peer-review-transparency-framework.pdf. [3]

OECD (2015), *Countering Harmful Tax Practices More Effectively, Taking into Account Transparency and Substance, Action 5 - 2015 Final Report*, OECD/G20 Base Erosion and Profit Shifting Project, OECD Publishing, Paris, https://dx.doi.org/10.1787/9789264241190-en. [1]

OECD (ed.) (2017b), *Harmful Tax Practices - 2017 Progress Report on Preferential Regimes*, OECD Publishing, Paris, http://dx.doi.org/10.1787/9789264283954-en. [2]

OECD/Council of Europe (2011), *The Multilateral Convention on Mutual Administrative Assistance in Tax Matters: Amended by the 2010 Protocol*, OECD Publishing, Paris, https://dx.doi.org/10.1787/9789264115606-en. [4]

Notes

[1] With respect to the following preferential regimes: 1) Free economic zone taxation regime, 2) Tonnage tax regime and 3) IP regime.

[2] Participating jurisdictions to the Convention are available here: www.oecd.org/tax/exchange-of-tax-information/convention-on-mutual-administrative-assistance-in-tax-matters.htm. Lithuania also has bilateral agreements with Armenia, Austria, Azerbaijan, Belarus, Belgium, Bulgaria, Canada, China (People's Republic of), Croatia, Czech Republic, Cyprus, Denmark, Estonia, Finland, France, Georgia, Germany, Greece, Hungary, Iceland, India, Ireland, Israel, Italy, Japan, Kazakhstan, Korea, Kuwait, Kyrgyzstan, Latvia, Luxembourg, Malta, Mexico, Moldova, Netherlands, North Macedonia, Norway, Poland, Portugal, Romania, Russia, Serbia, Singapore, Slovak Republic, Slovenia, Spain, Sweden, Switzerland, Turkey, Turkmenistan, Ukraine, United Arab Emirates, United Kingdom, United States and Uzbekistan.

Luxembourg

Luxembourg has met all aspects of the terms of reference (OECD, 2021[3]) (ToR) for the calendar year 2020 (year in review), and no recommendations are made.

Luxembourg can legally issue four types of rulings within the scope of the transparency framework.

In practice, Luxembourg issued rulings within the scope of the transparency framework as follows:

Type of ruling	Number of rulings
Past rulings	1922
Future rulings in the period 1 April 2016 – 31 December 2016	73
Future rulings in the calendar year 2017	18
Future rulings in the calendar year 2018	9
Future rulings in the calendar year 2019	3
Future rulings in the year in review	0

Peer input was received from one jurisdiction in respect of the exchanges of information on rulings received from Luxembourg. The input was positive, noting that information was complete, in a correct format and received in a timely manner.

A. The information gathering process (ToR I.A)

752. Luxembourg can legally issue the following four types of rulings within the scope of the transparency framework: (i) preferential regimes;[1] (ii) cross-border unilateral APAs and any other cross-border unilateral tax rulings (such as an advance tax ruling) covering transfer pricing or the application of transfer pricing principles; (iii) rulings providing for unilateral downward adjustments; and (iv) permanent establishment rulings.

753. For Luxembourg, past rulings are any tax rulings within scope that are issued either: (i) on or after 1 January 2014 but before 1 April 2016; or (ii) on or after 1 January 2010 but before 1 January 2014, provided they were still in effect as at 1 January 2014. Future rulings are any tax rulings within scope that are issued on or after 1 April 2016.

754. In the prior years' peer review reports, it was determined that Luxembourg's undertakings to identify past and future rulings and all potential exchange jurisdictions were sufficient to meet the minimum standard. In addition, it was determined that Luxembourg's review and supervision mechanism was sufficient to meet the minimum standard. Luxembourg's implementation remains unchanged, and therefore continues to meet the minimum standard.

755. Luxembourg has met all of the ToR for the information gathering process and no recommendations are made.

B. The exchange of information (ToR II.B)

756. Luxembourg has international agreements permitting spontaneous exchange of information, including being a party to (i) the *Multilateral Convention on Mutual Administrative Assistance in Tax Matters: Amended by the 2010 Protocol* (OECD/Council of Europe, 2011[4]) ("the Convention"), (ii) the Directive 2011/16/EU with all other European Union Member States and (iii) bilateral agreements in force with 82 jurisdictions.[2]

757. For the year in review, the timeliness of exchanges is as follows:

Future rulings within the scope of the transparency framework	Number of exchanges transmitted within three months of the information becoming available to the competent authority or immediately after legal impediments have been lifted	Delayed exchanges		
		Number of exchanges transmitted later than three months of the information on rulings becoming available to the competent authority	Reasons for the delays	Any other comments
	0[3]	3	See below	N/A

Follow up requests received for exchange of the ruling	Number	Average time to provide response	Number of requests not answered
	6	1.5 months	0

758. Luxembourg concluded during its verification process of the exchange statistics that the exchanges for one ruling issued in 2019 were omitted in 2019 due to human error, which subsequently resulted in three exchanges in 2020. Luxembourg notes this was a specific and isolated case which will be prevented by a closer collaboration between the authorities involved.

759. In the prior years' peer review reports, it was determined that Luxembourg's process for the completion and exchange of templates were sufficient to meet the minimum standard. With respect to past

rulings, no further action was required. Luxembourg's implementation in this regard remains unchanged and therefore continues to meet the minimum standard.

760. Luxembourg has the necessary legal basis for spontaneous exchange of information, a process for completing the templates in a timely way and has completed all exchanges. Luxembourg has met all of the ToR for the exchange of information process and no recommendations are made.

C. Statistics (ToR IV)

761. The statistics for the year in review are as follows:

Category of ruling	Number of exchanges	Jurisdictions exchanged with
Ruling related to a preferential regime	0	N/A
Cross-border unilateral APAs and any other cross-border unilateral tax rulings (such as an advance tax ruling) covering transfer pricing or the application of transfer pricing principles	*De minimis* rule applies[4]	N/A
Cross-border rulings providing for a unilateral downward adjustment to the taxpayer's taxable profits that is not directly reflected in the taxpayer's financial / commercial accounts	0	N/A
Permanent establishment rulings	0	N/A
De minimis rule	3	N/A
IP regimes: total exchanges on taxpayers benefitting from the third category of IP assets, new entrants benefitting from grandfathered IP regimes; and taxpayers making use of the option to treat the nexus ratio as a rebuttable presumption	7	Belgium, France, Germany, Netherlands, Turkey, United States
Total	10[5]	

D. Matters related to intellectual property regimes (ToR I.A.1.3)

762. Luxembourg offered an intellectual property regime (IP regime)[6] that was abolished as of 1 July 2016 and is subject to transparency requirements under the Action 5 Report (OECD, 2015[1]). It states that the identification of the benefitting taxpayers will occur as follows:

- ***New entrants benefitting from the grandfathered IP regime:*** during the prior year, an IT research application was launched with the aim of identifying the taxpayers who requested the application of the IP regime in their tax return. Some taxpayers only filed their tax return for the fiscal years 2015 and 2016 by late 2017 or in 2018. Information on these remaining new entrants and new IP assets from existing taxpayers was exchanged in 2018, with a small number of additional exchanges taking place early in the year in review. Exchanges took place generally within one month of receipt of the information. This issue is now completed.
- ***Third category of IP assets***: not applicable as the IP regime has been abolished.
- ***Taxpayers making use of the option to treat the nexus ratio as a rebuttable presumption***: not applicable as the IP regime has been abolished.

763. In addition, Luxembourg offers an IP regime that not is subject to the transparency requirements under the Action 5 Report (OECD, 2015[1]), because:

- ***New entrants benefitting from the grandfathered IP regime***: as this is a new IP regime rather than a grandfathered IP regime, transparency on new entrants is not relevant.
- ***Third category of IP assets***: not applicable as the regime does not allow the third category of IP assets to qualify for the benefits.
- ***Taxpayers making use of the option to treat the nexus ratio as a rebuttable presumption***: not applicable as the regime does not allow the nexus ratio to be treated as a rebuttable presumption.

Summary of recommendations on implementation of the transparency framework

Aspect of implementation of the transparency framework that should be improved	Recommendation for improvement
	No recommendations are made.

References

OECD (2021), *BEPS Action 5 on Harmful Tax Practices - Terms of Reference and Methodology for the Conduct of the Peer Reviews of the Action 5 Transparency Framework*, OECD Publishing, Paris, http://www.oecd.org/tax/beps/beps-action-5-harmful-tax-practices-peer-review-transparency-framework.pdf. [3]

OECD (2015), *Countering Harmful Tax Practices More Effectively, Taking into Account Transparency and Substance, Action 5 - 2015 Final Report*, OECD/G20 Base Erosion and Profit Shifting Project, OECD Publishing, Paris, https://dx.doi.org/10.1787/9789264241190-en. [1]

OECD (ed.) (2017b), *Harmful Tax Practices - 2017 Progress Report on Preferential Regimes*, OECD Publishing, Paris, http://dx.doi.org/10.1787/9789264283954-en. [2]

OECD/Council of Europe (2011), *The Multilateral Convention on Mutual Administrative Assistance in Tax Matters: Amended by the 2010 Protocol*, OECD Publishing, Paris, https://dx.doi.org/10.1787/9789264115606-en. [4]

Notes

[1] With respect to the following preferential regimes: 1) Private asset management company, 2) Investment company in risk capital, 3) Provision for fluctuations in reinsurance companies, and 4) Informal capital and partial exemption for income/gains derived from certain IP rights.

[2] Participating jurisdictions to the Convention are available here: www.oecd.org/tax/exchange-of-tax-information/convention-on-mutual-administrative-assistance-in-tax-matters.htm. Luxembourg also has bilateral agreements with Andorra, Armenia, Austria, Azerbaijan, Bahrain, Guernsey, Barbados, Belgium, Brazil, Brunei Darussalam, Bulgaria, Canada, China (People's Republic of), Croatia, Cyprus, Czech Republic, Denmark, Estonia, Finland, France, Georgia, Germany, Greece, Hungary, Iceland, India, Indonesia, Ireland, Isle of Man, Israel, Italy, Japan, Jersey, Kazakhstan, Korea, Kosovo, Lao People's Democratic Republic, Latvia, Liechtenstein, Lithuania, Malaysia, Malta, Mauritius, Mexico, Moldova, Monaco, Morocco, Netherlands, North Macedonia, Norway, Panama, Poland, Portugal, Qatar, Romania, Russia, San Marino, Saudi Arabia, Senegal, Serbia, Seychelles, Singapore, Slovak Republic, Slovenia, South Africa, Spain, Sri Lanka, Sweden, Switzerland, Chinese Taipei, Tajikistan, Thailand, Trinidad and Tobago, Tunisia, Turkey, Ukraine, United Arab Emirates, United Kingdom, United States, Uruguay, Uzbekistan and Viet Nam.

[3] During the year in review, Luxembourg also transmitted an additional 10 exchanges of "other types of rulings" that fall outside of the scope of the transparency framework.

[4] Exchanges related to one ruling issued in 2019, as explained under paragraph 6.

[5] See note 3.

[6] Partial exemption for income/gains derived from certain IP rights.

Malaysia

Malaysia has met all aspects of the terms of reference (OECD, 2021[3]) (ToR) for the calendar year 2020 (year in review), except for identifying all potential exchange jurisdictions for future rulings (ToR I.A.2.1) and for providing information on rulings to the Competent Authority without undue delay and undertaking spontaneous exchange of information on all future tax rulings within the scope of the transparency framework (ToR II.B). Malaysia receives two recommendations on these points for the year in review.

In the prior year report, Malaysia received the same recommendation to identify all potential exchange jurisdictions for future rulings. In the prior year report, as well as in the 2017 and 2018 peer reviews, Malaysia had received the same recommendation to provide information on rulings to the Competent Authority without undue delay and to undertake spontaneous exchange of information on all future tax rulings within the scope of the transparency framework, but also with regard to past rulings. Malaysia resolved the issue with regard to past rulings and therefore the recommendation no longer relates to past rulings. In the prior year report, as well as in the 2017 and 2018 peer reviews, Malaysia had received a recommendation to identify and exchange information on new entrants to the grandfathered regime. Malaysia resolved this issue and therefore this recommendation is now removed.

Malaysia can legally issue five types of rulings within the scope of the transparency framework.

In practice, Malaysia issued rulings within the scope of the transparency framework as follows:[1]

Type of ruling	Number of rulings
Past rulings	249
Future rulings in the period 1 September 2017 – 31 December 2017	7
Future rulings in the calendar year 2018	12
Future rulings in the calendar year 2019	17
Future rulings in the year in review	40

Peer input was received from two jurisdictions in respect of the exchanges of information on rulings received from Malaysia. The input was generally positive, noting that overall information was complete and in a correct format. However, one peer indicated that exchanges on rulings were not timely.

A. The information gathering process (ToR I.A)

764. Malaysia can legally issue the following five types of rulings within the scope of the transparency framework: (i) preferential regimes;[2] (ii) cross-border unilateral APAs and any other cross-border unilateral tax rulings (such as an advance tax ruling) covering transfer pricing or the application of transfer pricing principles; (iii) rulings providing for unilateral downward adjustments; (iv) permanent establishment rulings; and (v) related party conduit rulings.

Past rulings (ToR I.A.1.1, I.A.1.2, I.A.2.1, I.A.2.2)

765. For Malaysia, past rulings are any tax rulings within scope that are issued either (i) on or after 1 January 2015 but before 1 September 2017; and (ii) on or after 1 January 2012 but before 1 January 2015, provided they were still in effect as at 1 January 2015.

766. In the prior years' peer review reports, it was determined that Malaysia's undertakings to identify past rulings and all potential exchange jurisdictions were sufficient to meet the minimum standard. Malaysia's implementation in this regard remains unchanged, and therefore continues to meet the minimum standard.

Future rulings (ToR I.A.1.1, I.A.1.2, I.A.2.1)

767. For Malaysia, future rulings are any tax rulings within scope that are issued on or after 1 September 2017.

768. In the prior year's peer review report, it was determined that Malaysia's undertakings to identify past and future rulings and all potential exchange jurisdictions have met all the ToR, except for identifying all potential exchange jurisdictions for future rulings (ToR I.A.2.1). Therefore, Malaysia was recommended to ensure that all potential exchange jurisdictions are identified swiftly for all future rulings.

769. During the year in review, Malaysia was still in the process of putting in place new requirements for taxpayers to provide the information required for completing the Annex C template upfront, including information on potential exchange jurisdictions. Malaysia is therefore recommended to continue its efforts to ensure that all potential exchange jurisdictions are identified swiftly for all future rulings.

Review and supervision (ToR I.A.3)

770. In the prior years' peer review reports, it was determined that Malaysia's review and supervision mechanism was sufficient to meet the minimum standard. Malaysia's implementation in this regard remains unchanged, and therefore continues to meet the minimum standard.

Conclusion on section A

771. Malaysia has met all of the ToR for the information gathering process except for identifying all potential exchange jurisdictions for future rulings (ToR I.A.2.1). Malaysia is recommended to ensure that all potential exchange jurisdictions are identified swiftly for all future rulings.

B. The exchange of information (ToR II.B)

Legal basis for spontaneous exchange of information (ToR II.B.1, II.B.2)

772. Malaysia has the necessary domestic legal basis to exchange information spontaneously. Malaysia notes that there are no legal or practical impediments that prevent the spontaneous exchange of information on rulings as contemplated in the Action 5 minimum standard.

773. Malaysia has international agreements permitting spontaneous exchange of information, including being a party to (i) the *Multilateral Convention on Mutual Administrative Assistance in Tax Matters: Amended by the 2010 Protocol* (OECD/Council of Europe, 2011[4]) ("the Convention") and (ii) bilateral agreements in force with 73 jurisdictions.[3]

Completion and exchange of templates (ToR II.B.3, II.B.4, II.B.5, II.B.6, II.B.7)

774. In the prior year peer review report, it was determined that Malaysia's internal policies, processes and procedures for the completion and exchange of templates were sufficient to meet the minimum standard, except for the provision of information on rulings to the Competent Authority without undue delay, and the timely spontaneous exchange of information on past and future rulings (ToR II.B). It should be noted that for the peer input, one peer indicated that the summary box of the template was not sufficient.

775. Malaysia's internal procedures and timelines to provide information on rulings to the Competent Authority remain unchanged, and therefore the recommendation to reduce the timelines for providing information on rulings to the Competent Authority without undue delay remains.

776. During the year in review, Malaysia prioritised resources for the exchange of information on past rulings and completed the exchanges on all 160 past rulings. However, Malaysia was not able to complete the exchanges of information on future rulings during the year in review. Therefore, the recommendation to complete the templates for all relevant future rulings and to ensure that the exchanges of information on rulings occur as soon as possible remains. The same recommendation for past rulings has now been removed.

777. For the year in review, the timeliness of exchanges is as follows:

Past rulings within the scope of the transparency framework	Number of exchanges transmitted by 31 December 2020	Delayed exchanges		
		Number of exchanges not transmitted by 31 December 2020	Reasons for the delays	Any other comments
	360	0	N/A	N/A
Future rulings within the scope of the transparency framework	Number of exchanges transmitted within three months of the information becoming available to the competent authority or immediately after legal impediments have been lifted	Delayed exchanges		
		Number of exchanges transmitted later than three months of the information on rulings becoming available to the competent authority	Reasons for the delays	Any other comments
	0	31	N/A	N/A
Total	360	31		

Follow up requests received for exchange of the ruling	Number	Average time to provide response	Number of requests not answered
	0	N/A	N/A

Conclusion on section B

778. Malaysia has the necessary legal basis to undertake spontaneous exchange of information. Malaysia is recommended to continue its efforts to reduce the timeliness for providing the information on rulings to the Competent Authority and to complete the templates for all relevant future rulings and to ensure that the exchanges of information on future rulings occur as soon as possible (ToR II.B).

C. Statistics (ToR IV)

779. The statistics for the year in review are as follows:

Category of ruling	Number of exchanges	Jurisdictions exchanged with
Ruling related to a preferential regime	391	Australia, Belgium, Brazil, Brunei Darussalam, Canada, China (People's Republic of), Czech Republic, Denmark, Egypt, Finland, France, Germany, Hong Kong (China), Hungary, India, Indonesia, Ireland, Italy, Japan, Korea, Liechtenstein, Luxembourg, Myanmar, Macau (China), Mexico, Mauritius, Netherlands, New Zealand, Norway, Pakistan, Panama, Poland, Portugal, Qatar, Romania, Russia, Singapore, South Africa, Spain, Sri Lanka, Sweden, Switzerland, Chinese Taipei, Thailand, Tunisia, Turkey, United Kingdom, Viet Nam
Cross-border unilateral APAs and any other cross-border unilateral tax rulings (such as an advance tax ruling) covering transfer pricing or the application of transfer pricing principles	0	N/A
Cross-border rulings providing for a unilateral downward adjustment to the taxpayer's taxable profits that is not directly reflected in the taxpayer's financial / commercial accounts	0	N/A
Permanent establishment rulings	0	N/A
Related party conduit rulings	0	N/A
IP regimes: total exchanges on taxpayers benefitting from the third category of IP assets, new entrants benefitting from grandfathered IP regimes; and taxpayers making use of the option to treat the nexus ratio as a rebuttable presumption	0	N/A
Total	391	

D. Matters related to intellectual property regimes (ToR I.A.1.3)

780. Malaysia offered three intellectual property regimes (IP regime)[4] that were abolished as of 1 July 2018 and are subject to transparency requirements under the Action 5 Report (OECD, 2015[1]) It states that the identification of the benefitting taxpayers will occur as follows:

- ***New entrants benefitting from the grandfathered IP regime***: Transparency obligations apply for the three regimes, because grandfathering is provided to entrants that entered the regime after the relevant date from which enhanced transparency obligations apply. Malaysia confirms that it has not granted any new approvals into the regime (both new taxpayers and new IP assets from existing taxpayers) after the cut-off date of 16 October 2017. Therefore, the recommendation to identify and exchange information on all new entrants to the grandfathered IP regime as soon as possible (ToR I.A.1.3) can be removed.

- ***Third category of IP assets***: not applicable as the IP regimes have been abolished.
- ***Taxpayers making use of the option to treat the nexus ratio as a rebuttable presumption***: not applicable as the IP regimes have been abolished.

Summary of recommendations on implementation of the transparency framework

Aspect of implementation of the transparency framework that should be improved	Recommendation for improvement
Malaysia experienced difficulties in identifying all potential exchange jurisdictions for future rulings.	Malaysia is recommended to continue its efforts to ensure that all potential exchange jurisdictions are identified swiftly for all future rulings. This recommendation remains unchanged since the prior year peer review report.
Malaysia experienced delays in the provision of rulings to the Competent Authority and did not undertake spontaneous exchange of information on all future tax rulings within the scope of the transparency framework during the year in review.	Malaysia is recommended to continue its efforts to reduce the timeliness for providing the information on rulings to the Competent Authority and to complete the templates for all relevant future rulings and to ensure that the exchanges of information on future rulings occur as soon as possible. This recommendation remains unchanged since the 2017, 2018 and 2019 peer review reports.

References

OECD (2021), *BEPS Action 5 on Harmful Tax Practices - Terms of Reference and Methodology for the Conduct of the Peer Reviews of the Action 5 Transparency Framework*, OECD Publishing, Paris, http://www.oecd.org/tax/beps/beps-action-5-harmful-tax-practices-peer-review-transparency-framework.pdf. [3]

OECD (2015), *Countering Harmful Tax Practices More Effectively, Taking into Account Transparency and Substance, Action 5 - 2015 Final Report*, OECD/G20 Base Erosion and Profit Shifting Project, OECD Publishing, Paris, https://dx.doi.org/10.1787/9789264241190-en. [1]

OECD (ed.) (2017b), *Harmful Tax Practices - 2017 Progress Report on Preferential Regimes*, OECD Publishing, Paris, http://dx.doi.org/10.1787/9789264283954-en. [2]

OECD/Council of Europe (2011), *The Multilateral Convention on Mutual Administrative Assistance in Tax Matters: Amended by the 2010 Protocol*, OECD Publishing, Paris, https://dx.doi.org/10.1787/9789264115606-en. [4]

Notes

[1] During the year in review, it was concluded that Malaysia had included rulings that are not cross-border in the prior years' peer review reports. As these rulings do not fall within the scope of the BEPS Action 5 transparency framework, these rulings are no longer counted for the purpose of the annual peer review.

[2] 1) Pioneer status – contract R&D, 2) Biotechnology industry, 3) Principal hub, 4) MSC Malaysia, 5) Green technology services and 6) Special economic regions, 7) High technology regime and 8) Treasury management centre.

[3] Participating jurisdictions to the Convention are available here: www.oecd.org/tax/exchange-of-tax-information/convention-on-mutual-administrative-assistance-in-tax-matters.htm. Malaysia also has bilateral agreements with Albania, Argentina, Australia, Austria, Bahrain, Bangladesh, Belgium, Bosnia and Herzegovina, Brunei Darussalam, Canada, Chile, China (People's Republic of), Croatia, Czech Republic, Denmark, Egypt, Fiji, Finland, France, Germany, Hong Kong (China), Hungary, India, Indonesia, Iran, Ireland, Italy, Japan, Jordan, Kazakhstan, Korea, Kuwait, Kyrgyzstan, Laos, Lebanon, Luxembourg, Malta, Mauritius, Mongolia, Morocco, Myanmar, Namibia, Netherlands, New Zealand, Norway, Pakistan, Papua New Guinea, Philippines, Poland, Qatar, Romania, Russia, San Marino, Saudi Arabia, Seychelles, Singapore, South Africa, Spain, Slovak Republic, Sri Lanka, Sudan, Sweden, Switzerland, Syrian Arab Republic, Thailand, Turkey, Turkmenistan, United Arab Emirates, United Kingdom, Uzbekistan, Venezuela, Viet Nam, Zimbabwe.

[4] These regimes are: 1) Biotechnology industry, 2) MSC Malaysia and 3) Principal hub.

Malta

Malta has met all aspects of the terms of reference (OECD, 2021[3]) (ToR) for the calendar year 2020 (year in review), and no recommendations are made.

Malta can legally issue four types of rulings within the scope of the transparency framework.

In practice, Malta issued rulings within the scope of the transparency framework as follows:

Type of ruling	Number of rulings
Past rulings	7
Future rulings in the period 1 April 2017 – 31 December 2017	4
Future rulings in the calendar year 2018	7
Future rulings in the calendar year 2019	15
Future rulings in the year in review	17

Peer input was received from one jurisdiction in respect of the exchanges of information on rulings received from Malta. The input was positive, noting that information was complete, in a correct format and received in a timely manner.

A. The information gathering process (ToR I.A)

781. Malta can legally issue the following four types of rulings within the scope of the transparency framework: (i) cross-border unilateral APAs and any other cross-border unilateral tax rulings (such as an advance tax ruling) covering transfer pricing or the application of transfer pricing principles; (ii) rulings providing for unilateral downward adjustments; (iii) permanent establishment rulings; and (iv) related party conduit rulings.

782. For Malta, past rulings are any tax rulings within scope that are issued either: (i) on or after 1 January 2015 but before 1 April 2017; and (ii) on or after 1 January 2012 but before 1 January 2015, provided they were still in effect as at 1 January 2015. Future rulings are any tax rulings within scope that are issued on or after 1 April 2017.

783. In the prior years' peer review reports, it was determined that Malta's undertakings to identify past and future rulings and all potential exchange jurisdictions were sufficient to meet the minimum standard. In addition, it was determined that Malta's review and supervision mechanism was sufficient to meet the minimum standard. Malta's implementation remains unchanged, and therefore continues to meet the minimum standard.

784. Malta has met all of the ToR for the information gathering process and no recommendations are made.

B. The exchange of information (ToR II.B)

785. Malta has international agreements permitting spontaneous exchange of information, including being a party to (i) the *Multilateral Convention on Mutual Administrative Assistance in Tax Matters: Amended by the 2010 Protocol* (OECD/Council of Europe, 2011[4]) ("the Convention"), (ii) Directive 2011/16/EU with all other EU Member States, and (iii) bilateral agreements in force with 77 jurisdictions.[1]

786. For the year in review, the timeliness of exchanges is as follows:

Future rulings within the scope of the transparency framework	Number of exchanges transmitted within three months of the information becoming available to the competent authority or immediately after legal impediments have been lifted	Delayed exchanges		
		Number of exchanges transmitted later than three months of the information on rulings becoming available to the competent authority	Reasons for the delays	Any other comments
	23	3	Application of the EU DAC3 timelines.	N/A

Follow up requests received for exchange of the ruling	Number	Average time to provide response	Number of requests not answered
	0	N/A	N/A

787. Malta notes that two rulings that were issued in 2019 were not timely exchanged, because these were exchanges with EU Member States under the EU DAC3 timelines. Malta notes however that from March 2020, it has changed its procedures and all rulings within the scope of the Action 5 transparency framework will be exchanged within three months after the ruling becomes available to the competent authority.

788. In the prior years' peer review reports, it was determined that Malta's process for the completion and exchange of templates were sufficient to meet the minimum standard. With respect to past rulings, no further action was required. Malta's implementation in this regard remains unchanged and therefore continues to meet the minimum standard.

789. Malta has the necessary legal basis for spontaneous exchange of information, a process for completing the templates in a timely way and has completed all exchanges. Malta has met all of the ToR for the exchange of information process and no recommendations are made.

C. Statistics (ToR IV)

790. The statistics for the year in review are as follows:

Category of ruling	Number of exchanges	Jurisdictions exchanged with
Cross-border unilateral APAs and any other cross-border unilateral tax rulings (such as an advance tax ruling) covering transfer pricing or the application of transfer pricing principles	2	*De minimis* rule applies
Cross-border rulings providing for a unilateral downward adjustment to the taxpayer's taxable profits that is not directly reflected in the taxpayer's financial / commercial accounts	0	N/A
Permanent establishment rulings	0	N/A
Related party conduit rulings	24	Australia, Chile, Curaçao, Cyprus, Czech Republic, Germany, Guernsey, Ireland, Israel, Netherlands, Panama, Poland, Portugal, Qatar, Slovak Republic, Sweden, Thailand, United Kingdom
IP regimes: total exchanges on taxpayers benefitting from the third category of IP assets, new entrants benefitting from grandfathered IP regimes; and taxpayers making use of the option to treat the nexus ratio as a rebuttable presumption	0	N/A
Total	26	

D. Matters related to intellectual property regimes (ToR I.A.1.3)

791. Malta offers an intellectual property regime (IP regime)[2] that is subject to the transparency requirements under the Action 5 Report (OECD, 2015[1]). It states that the identification of the benefitting taxpayers will occur as follows:

- ***New entrants benefitting from the grandfathered IP regime***: as this is a new IP regime rather than a grandfathered IP regime, transparency on new entrants is not relevant.
- ***Third category of IP assets***: the regime provides benefits to the third category of IP assets. The process on the collection of information was described in the prior year peer review report. Malta confirms that for the year in review, there were no taxpayers benefitting from the third category of IP assets. As such, no exchanges needed to take place.
- ***Taxpayers making use of the option to treat the nexus ratio as a rebuttable presumption***: not applicable as the regime does not allow the nexus ratio to be treated as a rebuttable presumption.

Summary of recommendations on implementation of the transparency framework

Aspect of implementation of the transparency framework that should be improved	Recommendation for improvement
	No recommendations are made.

References

OECD (2021), *BEPS Action 5 on Harmful Tax Practices - Terms of Reference and Methodology for the Conduct of the Peer Reviews of the Action 5 Transparency Framework*, OECD Publishing, Paris, http://www.oecd.org/tax/beps/beps-action-5-harmful-tax-practices-peer-review-transparency-framework.pdf. [3]

OECD (2015), *Countering Harmful Tax Practices More Effectively, Taking into Account Transparency and Substance, Action 5 - 2015 Final Report*, OECD/G20 Base Erosion and Profit Shifting Project, OECD Publishing, Paris, https://dx.doi.org/10.1787/9789264241190-en. [1]

OECD (ed.) (2017b), *Harmful Tax Practices - 2017 Progress Report on Preferential Regimes*, OECD Publishing, Paris, http://dx.doi.org/10.1787/9789264283954-en. [2]

OECD/Council of Europe (2011), *The Multilateral Convention on Mutual Administrative Assistance in Tax Matters: Amended by the 2010 Protocol*, OECD Publishing, Paris, https://dx.doi.org/10.1787/9789264115606-en. [4]

Notes

[1] Participating jurisdictions to the Convention are available here: www.oecd.org/tax/exchange-of-tax-information/convention-on-mutual-administrative-assistance-in-tax-matters.htm. Malta also has bilateral agreements with Albania, Andorra, Australia, Austria, Azerbaijan, Bahrain, Barbados, Belgium, Botswana, Bulgaria, Canada, China (People's Republic of), Croatia, Cyprus, Czech Republic, Denmark, Egypt, Estonia, Finland, France, Georgia, Germany, Greece, Guernsey, Hong Kong (China), Hungary, Iceland, India, Ireland, Isle of Man, Israel, Italy, Jersey, Jordan, Korea, Kosovo, Kuwait, Latvia, Lebanon, Libya, Liechtenstein, Lithuania, Luxembourg, Malaysia, Mauritius, Mexico, Moldova, Monaco, Montenegro, Morocco, Netherlands, Norway, Pakistan, Poland, Portugal, Qatar, Romania, Russia, San Marino, Saudi Arabia, Serbia, Singapore, Slovak Republic, Slovenia, South Africa, Spain, Sweden, Switzerland, Syrian Arab Republic, Tunisia, Turkey, Ukraine, United Arab Emirates, United Kingdom, United States, Uruguay and Viet Nam.

[2] Patent box deduction rules.

Mauritius

Mauritius has met all aspects of the terms of reference (OECD, 2021[3]) (ToR) for the calendar year 2020 (year in review), and no recommendations are made.

Mauritius can legally issue three types of rulings within the scope of the transparency framework.

In practice, Mauritius issued rulings within the scope of the transparency framework as follows:

Type of ruling	Number of rulings
Past rulings	20
Future rulings in the period 1 September 2017 – 31 December 2017	0
Future rulings in the calendar year 2018	1
Future rulings in the calendar year 2019	1
Future rulings in the year in review	10

No peer input was received in respect of the exchanges of information on rulings received from Mauritius.

A. The information gathering process (ToR I.A)

792. Mauritius can legally issue the following three types of rulings within the scope of the transparency framework: (i) preferential regimes;[1] (ii) cross-border unilateral APAs and any other cross-border unilateral tax rulings (such as an advance tax ruling) covering transfer pricing or the application of transfer pricing principles; and (iii) permanent establishment rulings.

793. For Mauritius, past rulings are any tax rulings within scope that are issued either: (i) on or after 1 January 2015 but before 1 September 2017; and (ii) on or after 1 January 2012 but before 1 January 2015, provided they were still in effect as at 1 January 2015. Future rulings are any tax rulings within scope that are issued on or after 1 September 2017.

794. In the prior years' peer review reports, it was determined that Mauritius' undertakings to identify past and future rulings and all potential exchange jurisdictions were sufficient to meet the minimum standard. In addition, it was determined that Mauritius' review and supervision mechanism was sufficient to meet the minimum standard. Mauritius' implementation remains unchanged, and therefore continues to meet the minimum standard.

795. Mauritius has met all of the ToR for the information gathering process and no recommendations are made.

B. The exchange of information (ToR II.B)

796. Mauritius has international agreements permitting spontaneous exchange of information, including being a party to (i) the *Multilateral Convention on Mutual Administrative Assistance in Tax Matters: Amended by the 2010 Protocol* (OECD/Council of Europe, 2011[4]) ("the Convention") and (ii) bilateral agreements in force with 46 jurisdictions.[2]

797. For the year in review, the timeliness of exchanges is as follows:

Future rulings within the scope of the transparency framework	Number of exchanges transmitted within three months of the information becoming available to the competent authority or immediately after legal impediments have been lifted	Delayed exchanges		
		Number of exchanges transmitted later than three months of the information on rulings becoming available to the competent authority	Reasons for the delays	Any other comments
	11	1	Due to Covid-19 pandemic	N/A

Follow up requests received for exchange of the ruling	Number	Average time to provide response	Number of requests not answered
	0	N/A	N/A

798. In the prior years' peer review reports, it was determined that Mauritius' process for the completion and exchange of templates were sufficient to meet the minimum standard. With respect to past rulings, no further action was required. Mauritius' implementation in this regard remains unchanged and therefore continues to meet the minimum standard.

799. Mauritius has the necessary legal basis for spontaneous exchange of information, a process for completing the templates in a timely way and has completed all exchanges. Mauritius has met all of the ToR for the exchange of information process and no recommendations are made.

C. Statistics (ToR IV)

800. The statistics for the year in review are as follows:

Category of ruling	Number of exchanges	Jurisdictions exchanged with
Ruling related to a preferential regime	10	India, Guernsey, United Kingdom, United States
Cross-border unilateral APAs and any other cross-border unilateral tax rulings (such as an advance tax ruling) covering transfer pricing or the application of transfer pricing principles	0	N/A
Permanent establishment rulings	2	*De minimis* rule applies
IP regimes: total exchanges on taxpayers benefitting from the third category of IP assets, new entrants benefitting from grandfathered IP regimes; and taxpayers making use of the option to treat the nexus ratio as a rebuttable presumption	0	N/A
Total	12	

D. Matters related to intellectual property regimes (ToR I.A.1.3)

801. Mauritius offered two intellectual property regimes (IP regime)[3] that are abolished as of 1 July 2018 and are subject to transparency requirements under the Action 5 Report (OECD, 2015[1]). It states that the identification of the benefitting taxpayers will occur as follows:

- ***New entrants benefitting from the grandfathered IP regime***: In the prior years' peer review reports, it was determined that Mauritius' process for identifying and exchanging information on new entrants to the grandfathered IP regime were sufficient to meet the minimum standard. Mauritius' implementation in this regard remains unchanged and therefore continues to meet the minimum standard.
- ***Third category of IP assets***: not applicable as the IP regimes have been abolished.
- ***Taxpayers making use of the option to treat the nexus ratio as a rebuttable presumption***: not applicable as the IP regimes have been abolished.

802. In addition, Mauritius offers an IP regime[4] that is subject to the transparency requirements under the Action 5 Report (OECD, 2015[1]). It states that the identification of the benefitting taxpayers will occur as follows:

- ***New entrants benefitting from the grandfathered IP regime***: as this is a new IP regime rather than a grandfathered IP regime, transparency on new entrants is not relevant.
- ***Third category of IP assets***: the regime provides benefits to the third category of IP assets. All taxpayers benefitting from the IP regime should self-identify this in the tax return, which includes a separate box for the third category of IP assets. Only taxpayers with a certificate for the third category of IP assets issued by the Mauritius Research and Innovation Council are eligible. The Research and Innovation Council is still in the process of finalising its certification application process. Once the certification application process is finalised, there will be a co-operation mechanism put in place with the Mauritius Revenue Authority to ensure that any taxpayer's claims to benefit from the third category of assets are verified. Mauritius indicated that there is also the option of directing companies wishing to obtain certification to internationally recognized and accredited firms, where consideration and approval by the relevant local authorities would be

required. Mauritius confirms that during the year in review, no certificates have been issued by the Mauritius Research and Innovation Council.

- ***Taxpayers making use of the option to treat the nexus ratio as a rebuttable presumption***: not applicable as the regime does not allow the nexus ratio to be treated as a rebuttable presumption.

Summary of recommendations on implementation of the transparency framework

Aspect of implementation of the transparency framework that should be improved	Recommendation for improvement
	No recommendations are made.

References

OECD (2021), *BEPS Action 5 on Harmful Tax Practices - Terms of Reference and Methodology for the Conduct of the Peer Reviews of the Action 5 Transparency Framework*, OECD Publishing, Paris, http://www.oecd.org/tax/beps/beps-action-5-harmful-tax-practices-peer-review-transparency-framework.pdf. [3]

OECD (2015), *Countering Harmful Tax Practices More Effectively, Taking into Account Transparency and Substance, Action 5 - 2015 Final Report*, OECD/G20 Base Erosion and Profit Shifting Project, OECD Publishing, Paris, https://dx.doi.org/10.1787/9789264241190-en. [1]

OECD (ed.) (2017b), *Harmful Tax Practices - 2017 Progress Report on Preferential Regimes*, OECD Publishing, Paris, http://dx.doi.org/10.1787/9789264283954-en. [2]

OECD/Council of Europe (2011), *The Multilateral Convention on Mutual Administrative Assistance in Tax Matters: Amended by the 2010 Protocol*, OECD Publishing, Paris, https://dx.doi.org/10.1787/9789264115606-en. [4]

Notes

[1] With respect to the following preferential regimes: 1) Global business license 1, 2) Global business license 2, 3) Global headquarters administration regime, 4) Global treasury activities, 5) Captive insurances, 6) Segment B banking, 7) Investment banking, 8) Freeport zone, 9) Shipping regime, 10) Innovation box and 11) Partial exemption system.

[2] Parties to the Convention are available here: www.oecd.org/tax/exchange-of-tax-information/convention-on-mutual-administrative-assistance-in-tax-matters.htm. Mauritius also has bilateral agreements in force with Australia, Bangladesh, Barbados, Belgium, Botswana, Cabo Verde, China (People's Republic of), Congo, Croatia, Cyprus, Egypt, Eswatini, France, Germany, Ghana, Guernsey, India, Italy, Jersey, Kuwait, Lesotho, Luxembourg, Madagascar, Malaysia, Malta, Monaco, Mozambique, Namibia, Nepal, Oman, Pakistan, Qatar, Rwanda, Senegal, Seychelles, Singapore, South Africa, Sri Lanka, Sweden, Thailand, Tunisia, Uganda, United Arab Emirates, United Kingdom, Zambia and Zimbabwe. In addition, Mauritius' TIEA with the United States permits for the spontaneous exchange of information.

[3] These regimes are: 1) Global business licence 1 and 2) Global business licence 2.

[4] Innovation box.

Mexico

Mexico has met all aspects of the terms of reference (OECD, 2021[3]) (ToR) for the calendar year 2020 (year in review), and no recommendations are made.

Mexico can legally issue two types of rulings within the scope of the transparency framework.

In practice, Mexico issued rulings within the scope of the transparency framework as follows:

Type of ruling	Number of rulings
Past rulings	13
Future rulings in the period 1 April 2016 – 31 December 2016	1
Future rulings in the calendar year 2017	328
Future rulings in the calendar year 2018	294
Future rulings in the calendar year 2019	48
Future rulings in the year in review	44

No peer input was received in respect of the exchanges of information on rulings received from Mexico.

A. The information gathering process (ToR I.A)

803. Mexico can legally issue the following two types of rulings within the scope of the transparency framework: (i) cross-border unilateral APAs and any other cross-border unilateral tax rulings (such as an advance tax ruling) covering transfer pricing or the application of transfer pricing principles and (ii) permanent establishment rulings.

804. For Mexico, past rulings are any tax rulings within scope that are issued either: (i) on or after 1 January 2014 but before 1 April 2016; or (ii) on or after 1 January 2010 but before 1 January 2014, provided they were still in effect as at 1 January 2014. Future rulings are any tax rulings within scope that are issued on or after 1 April 2016.

805. In the prior years' peer review reports, it was determined that Mexico's undertakings to identify past and future rulings and all potential exchange jurisdictions were sufficient to meet the minimum standard. In addition, it was determined that Mexico's review and supervision mechanism was sufficient to meet the minimum standard. Mexico's implementation remains unchanged, and therefore continues to meet the minimum standard.

806. Mexico has met all of the ToR for the information gathering process and no recommendations are made.

B. The exchange of information (ToR II.B)

807. Mexico has international agreements permitting spontaneous exchange of information, including being a party to (i) the *Multilateral Convention on Mutual Administrative Assistance in Tax Matters: Amended by the 2010 Protocol* (OECD/Council of Europe, 2011[4]) ("the Convention"), (ii) bilateral agreements in force with seven jurisdictions and (iii) tax information exchange agreements in force with three jurisdictions.[1]

808. For the year in review, the timeliness of exchanges is as follows:

Future rulings within the scope of the transparency framework	Number of exchanges transmitted within three months of the information becoming available to the competent authority or immediately after legal impediments have been lifted	Delayed exchanges		
		Number of exchanges transmitted later than three months of the information on rulings becoming available to the competent authority	Reasons for the delays	Any other comments
	43	0	N/A	N/A

Follow up requests received for exchange of the ruling	Number	Average time to provide response	Number of requests not answered
	0	N/A	N/A

809. In the prior years' peer review reports, it was determined that Mexico's process for the completion and exchange of templates were sufficient to meet the minimum standard. With respect to past rulings, no further action was required. Mexico's implementation in this regard remains unchanged and therefore continues to meet the minimum standard.

810. Mexico has the necessary legal basis for spontaneous exchange of information, a process for completing the templates in a timely way and has completed all exchanges. Mexico has met all of the ToR for the exchange of information process and no recommendations are made.

C. Statistics (ToR IV)

811. The statistics for the year in review are as follows:

Category of ruling	Number of exchanges	Jurisdictions exchanged with
Cross-border unilateral APAs and any other cross-border unilateral tax rulings (such as an advance tax ruling) covering transfer pricing or the application of transfer pricing principles	43	Canada, France, Luxembourg, Netherlands, Switzerland, United States
Permanent establishment rulings	0	N/A
Total	43	

D. Matters related to intellectual property regimes (ToR I.A.1.3)

812. Mexico does not offer an intellectual property regime for which transparency requirements under the Action 5 Report (OECD, 2015[1]) were imposed.

Summary of recommendations on implementation of the transparency framework

Aspect of implementation of the transparency framework that should be improved	Recommendation for improvement
	No recommendations are made.

References

OECD (2021), *BEPS Action 5 on Harmful Tax Practices - Terms of Reference and Methodology for the Conduct of the Peer Reviews of the Action 5 Transparency Framework*, OECD Publishing, Paris, http://www.oecd.org/tax/beps/beps-action-5-harmful-tax-practices-peer-review-transparency-framework.pdf. [3]

OECD (2015), *Countering Harmful Tax Practices More Effectively, Taking into Account Transparency and Substance, Action 5 - 2015 Final Report*, OECD/G20 Base Erosion and Profit Shifting Project, OECD Publishing, Paris, https://dx.doi.org/10.1787/9789264241190-en. [1]

OECD (ed.) (2017b), *Harmful Tax Practices - 2017 Progress Report on Preferential Regimes*, OECD Publishing, Paris, http://dx.doi.org/10.1787/9789264283954-en. [2]

OECD/Council of Europe (2011), *The Multilateral Convention on Mutual Administrative Assistance in Tax Matters: Amended by the 2010 Protocol*, OECD Publishing, Paris, https://dx.doi.org/10.1787/9789264115606-en. [4]

Notes

[1] Participating jurisdictions to the Convention are available here: www.oecd.org/tax/exchange-of-tax-information/convention-on-mutual-administrative-assistance-in-tax-matters.htm. Mexico also has bilateral agreements with Austria, Canada, Hong Kong (China), Russia, South Africa, Ukraine and the United States. In addition, Mexico has tax information exchange agreements permitting spontaneous exchange of information with Aruba, Canada and the United States.

Morocco

Morocco has met all aspects of the terms of reference (OECD, 2021[3]) (ToR) for the calendar year 2020 (year in review), and no recommendations are made.

In the prior year report, Morocco had received one recommendation. As this recommendation regarding the development of a process to ensure that the exchanges of information on rulings occur in accordance with the form and timelines under the transparency framework has been addressed, it has been removed.

Morocco can legally issue one type of rulings within the scope of the transparency framework.

In practice, Morocco issued rulings within the scope of the transparency framework as follows:

Type of ruling	Number of rulings
Future rulings in the calendar year 2019	0
Future rulings in the year of review	4

No peer input was received in respect of the exchanges of information on rulings received from Morocco.

A. The information gathering process (ToR I.A)

813. Morocco can legally issue the following type of ruling within the scope of the transparency framework: cross-border unilateral APAs and any other cross-border unilateral tax rulings (such as an advance tax ruling) covering transfer pricing or the application of transfer pricing principles.

814. For Morocco, past rulings are any tax rulings issued prior to 1 September 2019. However, there is no obligation for Morocco to conduct spontaneous exchange information on past rulings. Future rulings are any tax rulings within scope that are issued on or after 1 September 2019.

815. In the prior year's peer review report, it was determined that Morocco's undertakings to identify past and future rulings and all potential exchange jurisdictions were sufficient to meet the minimum standard. In addition, it was determined that Morocco's review and supervision mechanism was sufficient to meet the minimum standard. For the year 2019, the ToR for the information gathering process was met in the absence of rulings being issued.

816. As rulings were issued during the year in review, Morocco's implementation of its information gathering process was due to be formalised. Morocco notes that it put in place a centralised administrative process for APAs, as well as other requirements of the transparency framework. As such, the unit in charge of issuing APAs identifies and lists all relevant APAs, and summarises these APAs in accordance with the template contained in Annex C of the Action 5 Report (OECD, 2015[1]). This information is shared with the "Service des échanges de renseignements à l'international" that is responsible for exchanging this information with the relevant jurisdictions.

817. Therefore, Morocco has met all of the ToR for the information gathering process and no recommendations are made.

B. The exchange of information (ToR II.B)

Legal basis for spontaneous exchange of information (ToR II.B.1, II.B.2)

818. Morocco has the necessary domestic legal basis to exchange information spontaneously. Morocco notes that there are no legal or practical impediments that prevent the spontaneous exchange of information on rulings as contemplated in the Action 5 minimum standard.

819. Morocco has international agreements permitting spontaneous exchange of information, including being a party to the (i) *Multilateral Convention on Mutual Administrative Assistance in Tax Matters: Amended by the 2010 Protocol* (OECD/Council of Europe, 2011[4]) ("the Convention") and (ii) bilateral agreements in force with 56 jurisdictions.[1]

Completion and exchange of templates (ToR II.B.3, II.B.4, II.B.5, II.B.6, II.B.7)

820. In the prior year's peer review report, it was determined that Morocco did not have a process to complete the templates on relevant rulings, to make them available to the Competent Authority for exchange of information, and to exchange them with relevant jurisdictions (ToR II.B). Therefore, Morocco was recommended to develop a process to complete the templates on relevant rulings and to ensure that the exchanges of information on rulings occur in accordance with the form and timelines under the transparency framework.

821. During the year in review, Morocco noted that a process has been developed to ensure that information on APAs is transmitted to the Competent Authority responsible for exchange of information by means of the template contained in Annex C of the Action 5 Report (OECD, 2015[1]). Morocco confirms that summaries are drafted in accordance with the internal FHTP guidelines and include all required

information. Furthermore, all the activities by the unit responsible for issuing APAs and by the International Exchange of Information Department to exchange information are centralised at the level of the Legislation, Studies and International Cooperation directorate. This should ensure that all rulings in scope of the transparency framework will be correctly and immediately identified and all information needed for the exchanges is adequately captured. Therefore, the recommendation from the prior year is now removed.

822. Regarding the rulings issued during the year in review, Morocco notes that these were issued in October 2020 and all exchanges related to these rulings have been transmitted by the competent authority to relevant exchange jurisdictions by March 2021. Data on the timeliness of these exchanges will be assessed in next year's peer review.

823. As no exchanges took place during the year in review, no data on the timeliness of exchanges is reported.

Conclusion on section B

824. Morocco has the necessary legal basis for spontaneous exchange of information. Morocco has met all of the ToR for the exchange of information process.

C. Statistics (ToR IV)

825. As there was no information on rulings exchanged by Morocco for the year in review, no statistics can be reported.

D. Matters related to intellectual property regimes (ToR I.A.1.3)

826. Morocco does not offer an intellectual property regime for which transparency requirements under the Action 5 Report (OECD, 2015[1]) were imposed.

Summary of recommendations on implementation of the transparency framework

Aspect of implementation of the transparency framework that should be improved	Recommendation for improvement
	No recommendations are made.

References

OECD (2021), *BEPS Action 5 on Harmful Tax Practices - Terms of Reference and Methodology for the Conduct of the Peer Reviews of the Action 5 Transparency Framework*, OECD Publishing, Paris, http://www.oecd.org/tax/beps/beps-action-5-harmful-tax-practices-peer-review-transparency-framework.pdf. [3]

OECD (2015), *Countering Harmful Tax Practices More Effectively, Taking into Account Transparency and Substance, Action 5 - 2015 Final Report*, OECD/G20 Base Erosion and Profit Shifting Project, OECD Publishing, Paris, https://dx.doi.org/10.1787/9789264241190-en. [1]

OECD (ed.) (2017b), *Harmful Tax Practices - 2017 Progress Report on Preferential Regimes*, OECD Publishing, Paris, http://dx.doi.org/10.1787/9789264283954-en. [2]

OECD/Council of Europe (2011), *The Multilateral Convention on Mutual Administrative Assistance in Tax Matters: Amended by the 2010 Protocol*, OECD Publishing, Paris, https://dx.doi.org/10.1787/9789264115606-en. [4]

Notes

[1] Parties to the Convention are available here: www.oecd.org/tax/exchange-of-tax-information/convention-on-mutual-administrative-assistance-in-tax-matters.htm. Morocco also has bilateral agreements with Arab Maghreb Union jurisdictions and Austria, Bahrain, Belgium, Bulgaria, Canada, China (People's Republic of), Côte d'Ivoire, Croatia, Czech Republic, Denmark, Egypt, Ethiopia, Finland, France, Gabon, Germany, Greece, Guinea, Hungary, India, Indonesia, Ireland, Italy, Jordan, Korea, Kuwait, Latvia, Lebanon, Luxembourg, Malaysia, Mali, Malta, Netherlands, North Macedonia, Norway, Oman, Pakistan, Poland, Portugal, Qatar, Romania, Russia, Senegal, Singapore, Spain, Syrian Arab Republic, Turkey, Ukraine, United Arab Emirates, United Kingdom, United States, Viet Nam.

Namibia

Namibia is taking steps to implement the legal basis for the transparency framework and to commence administrative preparations to ensure that information on rulings will be exchanged in a timely manner, in line with the terms of reference (OECD, 2021[3]) (ToR). Namibia receives two recommendations covering the information gathering process (ToR I.A) and exchange of information (ToR II.B) for the calendar year 2020 (year in review).

This is Namibia's first review of implementation of the transparency framework.

Namibia can legally issue four types of rulings within the scope of the transparency framework.

In practice, Namibia issued no rulings within the scope of the transparency framework.

As no exchanges were required to take place, no peer input was received in respect of the exchanges of information on rulings received from Namibia.

A. The information gathering process (ToR I.A)

827. Namibia can legally issue the following four types of rulings within the scope of the transparency framework: (i) cross-border unilateral APAs and any other cross-border unilateral tax rulings (such as an advance tax ruling) covering transfer pricing or the application of transfer pricing principles; (ii) rulings providing for unilateral downward adjustments; (iii) permanent establishment rulings; and (iv) related party conduit rulings. Namibia's domestic tax laws do not contain a specific provision on issuing rulings.

Past rulings (ToR I.A.1.1, I.A.1.2, I.A.2.1, I.A.2.2)

828. For Namibia, past rulings are any tax rulings issued prior to 1 March 2020. However, there is no obligation for Namibia to conduct spontaneous exchange information on past rulings.

Future rulings (ToR I.A.1.1, I.A.1.2, I.A.2.1)

829. For Namibia, future rulings are any tax rulings within scope that are issued on or after 1 March 2020.

830. No rulings were issued by Namibia during the future rulings period in the year in review. However, Namibia indicates that there are not yet processes in place to ensure the implementation of the obligations relating to the transparency framework.

Review and supervision (ToR I.A.3)

831. Namibia did not yet have a review and supervision mechanism under the transparency framework for the year in review.

Conclusion on section A

832. Namibia is recommended to ensure that it has put in place an effective information gathering process to identify all relevant future rulings and all potential exchange jurisdictions and to implement a review and supervision mechanism, as soon as possible (ToR I.A).

B. The exchange of information (ToR II.B)

Legal basis for spontaneous exchange of information (ToR II.B.1, II.B.2)

833. Namibia notes that although it does not have an explicit domestic legal basis to exchange information spontaneously, international agreements can override secrecy provisions prohibiting the exchange of information. Therefore, Namibia will be able to exchange information on rulings with jurisdictions that are treaty partners. Furthermore, there are no legal or practical impediments that prevent the spontaneous exchange of information on rulings as contemplated in the Action 5 minimum standard.

834. Namibia has international agreements permitting spontaneous exchange of information, including bilateral agreements in force with 11 jurisdictions.[1] Namibia signed the *Multilateral Convention on Mutual Administrative Assistance in Tax Matters: Amended by the 2010 Protocol* (OECD/Council of Europe, 2011[4]) ("the Convention") on 29 September 2020 and ratified on 9 December 2020. The Convention entered into force on 1 April 2021. No exchanges could occur under the Convention for the year in review.[2]

Completion and exchange of templates (ToR II.B.3, II.B.4, II.B.5, II.B.6, II.B.7)

835. Namibia does not yet have a process to complete the templates on all relevant rulings, to make them available to the Competent Authority for exchange of information, and to exchange them with relevant jurisdictions.

836. During the year in review, no exchanges were required to take place and no data on the timeliness of exchanges is reported.

Conclusion on section B

837. Namibia is recommended to develop a process to complete the templates for all relevant rulings and to ensure that the exchanges of information on rulings occur in accordance with the form and timelines under the transparency framework going forward (ToR II.B).

C. Statistics (ToR IV)

838. As there was no information on rulings exchanged by Namibia for the year in review, no statistics can be reported.

D. Matters related to intellectual property regimes (ToR I.A.1.3)

839. Namibia does not offer an intellectual property regime for which transparency requirements under the Action 5 Report (OECD, 2015[1]) were imposed.

Summary of recommendations on implementation of the transparency framework

Aspect of implementation of the transparency framework that should be improved	Recommendation for improvement
Namibia does not yet have the necessary information gathering process in place.	Namibia is recommended to ensure that it has put in place an effective information gathering process to identify all relevant past and future rulings and all potential exchange jurisdictions and to implement a review and supervision mechanism, as soon as possible.
Namibia does not yet have a process to complete the templates on relevant rulings, to make them available to the Competent Authority for exchange of information, and to exchange them with relevant jurisdictions.	Namibia is recommended to develop a process to complete the templates for all relevant rulings and to ensure that the exchanges of information on rulings occur in accordance with the form and timelines under the transparency framework going forward.

References

OECD (2021), *BEPS Action 5 on Harmful Tax Practices - Terms of Reference and Methodology for the Conduct of the Peer Reviews of the Action 5 Transparency Framework*, OECD Publishing, Paris, http://www.oecd.org/tax/beps/beps-action-5-harmful-tax-practices-peer-review-transparency-framework.pdf. [3]

OECD (2015), *Countering Harmful Tax Practices More Effectively, Taking into Account Transparency and Substance, Action 5 - 2015 Final Report*, OECD/G20 Base Erosion and Profit Shifting Project, OECD Publishing, Paris, https://dx.doi.org/10.1787/9789264241190-en. [1]

OECD (ed.) (2017b), *Harmful Tax Practices - 2017 Progress Report on Preferential Regimes*, OECD Publishing, Paris, http://dx.doi.org/10.1787/9789264283954-en. [2]

OECD/Council of Europe (2011), *The Multilateral Convention on Mutual Administrative Assistance in Tax Matters: Amended by the 2010 Protocol*, OECD Publishing, Paris, https://dx.doi.org/10.1787/9789264115606-en. [4]

Notes

[1] Namibia has bilateral agreements with Botswana, France, Germany, India, Malaysia, Mauritius, Romania, Russia, South Africa, Sweden, United Kingdom.

[2] Participating jurisdictions to the Convention are available here: www.oecd.org/tax/exchange-of-tax-information/convention-on-mutual-administrative-assistance-in-tax-matters.htm.

Netherlands

The Netherlands has met all aspects of the terms of reference (OECD, 2021[3]) (ToR) for the calendar year 2020 (year in review), except for the timely provision of information on rulings to the Competent Authority for exchange of information (ToR II.B.5). The Netherlands receives one recommendation on this point for the year in review.

In the prior year report, the Netherlands received no recommendations. However, as there were new circumstances, a recommendation has been made as relevant.

The Netherlands can legally issue four types of rulings within the scope of the transparency framework.

In practice, the Netherlands issued rulings within the scope of the transparency framework as follows:

Type of ruling	Number of rulings
Past rulings	2 206
Future rulings in the period 1 April 2016 – 31 December 2016	297
Future rulings in the calendar year 2017	214
Future rulings in the calendar year 2018	272
Future rulings in the calendar year 2019	403
Future rulings in the year in review	263

Peer input was received from fourteen jurisdictions in respect of the exchanges of information on rulings received from the Netherlands. The input was generally positive, noting that overall information was complete and in a correct format. However, three peers indicated that exchanges on rulings were not timely.

A. The information gathering process (ToR I.A)

840. The Netherlands can legally issue the following four types of rulings within the scope of the transparency framework: (i) preferential regimes;[1] (ii) cross-border unilateral APAs and any other cross-border unilateral tax rulings (such as an advance tax ruling) covering transfer pricing or the application of transfer pricing principles; (iii) rulings providing for unilateral downward adjustments;[2] and (iv) permanent establishment rulings.

841. For the Netherlands, past rulings are any tax rulings within scope that are issued either: (i) on or after 1 January 2014 but before 1 April 2016; or (ii) on or after 1 January 2010 but before 1 January 2014, provided they were still in effect as at 1 January 2014. Future rulings are any tax rulings within scope that are issued on or after 1 April 2016.

842. In the prior years' peer review reports, it was determined that the Netherlands' undertakings to identify past and future rulings and all potential exchange jurisdictions were sufficient to meet the minimum standard. In addition, it was determined that the Netherlands' review and supervision mechanism was sufficient to meet the minimum standard. The Netherlands' implementation remains unchanged, and therefore continues to meet the minimum standard.

843. The Netherlands has met all of the ToR for the information gathering process and no recommendations are made.

B. The exchange of information (ToR II.B)

Legal basis for spontaneous exchange of information (ToR II.B.1, II.B.2)

844. The Netherlands has the necessary domestic legal basis to exchange information spontaneously. The Netherlands notes that there are no legal or practical impediments that prevent the spontaneous exchange of information on rulings as contemplated in the Action 5 minimum standard.

845. The Netherlands has international agreements permitting spontaneous exchange of information, including being a party to (i) the *Multilateral Convention on Mutual Administrative Assistance in Tax Matters:* Amended *by the 2010 Protocol* (OECD/Council of Europe, 2011[4]) ("the Convention"), (ii) the Directive 2011/16/EU with all other European Union Member States and (iii) bilateral agreements in force with 142 jurisdictions.[3]

Completion and exchange of templates (ToR II.B.3, II.B.4, II.B.5, II.B.6, II.B.7)

846. In the prior years' peer review reports, it was determined that the Netherlands' process for the completion and exchange of templates were sufficient to meet the minimum standard. However, it should be noted that for the peer input, three peers indicated that information in the summary box of the template could provide more detail.

847. Furthermore, peer input indicated that during the year in review, some information on rulings were exchanged with a delay. The Netherlands confirms that in all cases, information on rulings was exchanged within three months after the information became available to the Competent Authority. However, the Netherlands indicates that in some cases, a delay has taken place in the period between the issuance of the ruling and the transmission to the Competent Authority as the Tax Administration needed additional time to complete the Annex C template. The Netherlands is currently investigating this issue and therefore, the Netherlands is recommended to ensure that information is made available to the Competent Authority without undue delay (ToR II.B.5).

848. For the year in review, the timeliness of exchanges is as follows:

Future rulings within the scope of the transparency framework	Number of exchanges transmitted within three months of the information becoming available to the competent authority or immediately after legal impediments have been lifted	Delayed exchanges		
		Number of exchanges transmitted later than three months of the information on rulings becoming available to the competent authority	Reasons for the delays	Any other comments
	772	0	N/A	N/A

Follow up requests received for exchange of the ruling	Number	Average time to provide response	Number of requests not answered
	6	50 days	4

849. It was noted by the Netherlands that four follow up requests have not yet been answered due to ongoing inquiries.

Conclusion on section B

850. The Netherlands has the necessary legal basis for spontaneous exchange of information. The Netherlands has met all of the ToR for the exchange of information process except for the timely provision of information on rulings to the Competent Authority for exchange of information (ToR II.B.5). The Netherlands is recommended to ensure that information is made available to the Competent Authority without undue delay.

C. Statistics (ToR IV)

851. The statistics for the year in review are as follows:

Category of ruling	Number of exchanges	Jurisdictions exchanged with
Ruling related to a preferential regime	580	Argentina, Australia, Austria, Belarus, Belgium, Brazil, Canada, Chile, China (People's Republic of), Colombia, Costa Rica, Cyprus, Czech Republic, Denmark, Dominican Republic, Ecuador, Egypt, Finland, France, Germany, Greece, Guatemala, Hong Kong (China), Hungary, Iceland, India, Indonesia, Ireland, Israel, Italy, Japan, Jersey, Kazakhstan, Korea, Latvia, Lithuania, Luxembourg, Malaysia, Malta, Mexico, Monaco, Morocco, New Zealand, Norway, Oman, Panama, Peru, Philippines, Poland, Portugal, Qatar, Romania, Russia, Saudi Arabia, Senegal, Serbia, Singapore, Slovak Republic, South Africa, Spain, Sweden, Switzerland, Chinese Taipei, Thailand, Tunisia, Turkey, Uganda, Ukraine, United Kingdom, United States, Uruguay, Viet Nam
Cross-border unilateral APAs and any other cross-border unilateral tax rulings (such as an advance tax ruling) covering transfer pricing or the application of transfer pricing principles	125	Argentina, Australia, Belarus, Bosnia and Herzegovina, Brazil, Canada, Chile, China (People's Republic of), Colombia, Guernsey, Hong Kong (China), Iceland, India, Indonesia,

		Israel, Japan, Kazakhstan, Korea, Malaysia, Mauritius, Mexico, New Zealand, Norway, Russia, Saudi Arabia, Singapore, Slovenia, South Africa, Switzerland, Chinese Taipei, Thailand, Turkey, Ukraine, United States
Cross-border rulings providing for a unilateral downward adjustment to the taxpayer's taxable profits that is not directly reflected in the taxpayer's financial / commercial accounts	0	N/A
Permanent establishment rulings	67	Australia, Bonaire, Brazil, Canada, China (People's Republic of), Curaçao, Hong Kong (China), India, Indonesia, Israel, Japan, Korea, Malaysia, Mexico, New Zealand, Norway, Philippines, Russia, Saint Lucia, Singapore, South Africa, Switzerland, Chinese Taipei, Thailand, Turkey, United States
De minimis rule	N/A	N/A
IP regimes: total exchanges on taxpayers benefitting from the third category of IP assets, new entrants benefitting from grandfathered IP regimes; and taxpayers making use of the option to treat the nexus ratio as a rebuttable presumption	Included in "rulings related to a preferential regime".	N/A
Total	772	

D. Matters related to intellectual property regimes (ToR I.A.1.3)

852. The Netherlands offers an intellectual property regime (IP regime)[4] that is subject to the transparency requirements under the Action 5 Report (OECD, 2015[1]). It states that the identification of the benefitting taxpayers will occur as follows:

- ***New entrants benefitting from the grandfathered IP regime***: the application of the IP regime[5] is usually offered by way of ruling. In those cases, the Netherlands identified taxpayers entering new into the regime or bringing new assets into the regime through the rulings process. For those cases in which no ruling was granted but the benefit was claimed directly in the tax return, the Netherlands' process was described in the previous' year peer review report. The Netherlands confirms that all exchanges have now taken place.
- ***Third category of IP assets***: the regime allows the third category of IP assets to benefit from the preferential tax treatment. Most taxpayers apply for a ruling in order to obtain this benefit with regard to the IP regime,[6] and information would be exchanged using the process for future rulings. For those taxpayers that use the third category of IP assets without having applied for a ruling, the Netherlands' process was described in the previous' year peer review report. The Netherlands continues to meet the standard.
- ***Taxpayers making use of the option to treat the nexus ratio as a rebuttable presumption***: not applicable as the regime does not allow the nexus ratio to be treated as a rebuttable presumption.

Summary of recommendations on implementation of the transparency framework

Aspect of implementation of the transparency framework that should be improved	Recommendation for improvement
The Netherlands experienced delays in the provision of rulings to the Competent Authority.	The Netherlands is recommended to ensure that information is made available to the Competent Authority without undue delay.

Jurisdiction's response and recent developments

853. With respect to the input by three peers that the information included in the summary section of the template could provide more detail, the Netherlands notes that the templates exchanged meet the minimum standard and therefore all required elements have been included. In most of the cases, more than the required information was provided. The Netherlands also notes that in some instances, it was not possible to exchange certain details (such as the amount of the transaction or annual turnover and profits), as such information was not yet available at the time of issuance of the ruling.

References

OECD (2021), *BEPS Action 5 on Harmful Tax Practices - Terms of Reference and Methodology for the Conduct of the Peer Reviews of the Action 5 Transparency Framework*, OECD Publishing, Paris, http://www.oecd.org/tax/beps/beps-action-5-harmful-tax-practices-peer-review-transparency-framework.pdf. [3]

OECD (2015), *Countering Harmful Tax Practices More Effectively, Taking into Account Transparency and Substance, Action 5 - 2015 Final Report*, OECD/G20 Base Erosion and Profit Shifting Project, OECD Publishing, Paris, https://dx.doi.org/10.1787/9789264241190-en. [1]

OECD (ed.) (2017b), *Harmful Tax Practices - 2017 Progress Report on Preferential Regimes*, OECD Publishing, Paris, http://dx.doi.org/10.1787/9789264283954-en. [2]

OECD/Council of Europe (2011), *The Multilateral Convention on Mutual Administrative Assistance in Tax Matters: Amended by the 2010 Protocol*, OECD Publishing, Paris, https://dx.doi.org/10.1787/9789264115606-en. [4]

Notes

[1] With respect to the following preferential regimes: 1) Innovation box and 2) International shipping.

[2] From 1 July 2019, a new ruling policy is in place which no longer allows rulings with regard to unilateral downward adjustments to be concluded.

[3] Participating jurisdictions to the Convention are available here: www.oecd.org/tax/exchange-of-tax-information/convention-on-mutual-administrative-assistance-in-tax-matters.htm. The Netherlands also has bilateral agreements with Albania, Algeria, Argentina, Armenia, Australia, Austria, Azerbaijan, Bahrain, Bangladesh, Barbados, Belarus, Belgium, Bermuda, Bosnia and Herzegovina, Brazil, Bulgaria, Canada, China (People's Republic of), Croatia, Curaçao, Czech Republic, Denmark, Egypt, Estonia, Ethiopia, Finland, France, Georgia, Germany, Ghana, Greece, Hong Kong (China), Hungary, Iceland, India, Indonesia, Ireland, Israel, Italy, Japan, Jordan, Kazakhstan, Kenya, Korea, Kuwait, Latvia, Lithuania, Luxembourg, Malaysia, Malta, Mexico, Moldova, Montenegro, Morocco, New Zealand, Nigeria, North Macedonia, Norway, Oman, Pakistan, Panama, Philippines, Poland, Portugal, Qatar, Romania, Russia, Sint Maarten, Saudi Arabia, Serbia, Singapore, Slovak Republic, Slovenia, South Africa, Spain, Sri Lanka, Suriname, Sweden, Switzerland, Chinese Taipei, Tajikistan, Thailand, Tunisia, Turkey, Uganda, Ukraine, United Arab Emirates, United Kingdom, United States, Uzbekistan, Venezuela, Viet Nam, Zambia and Zimbabwe.

[4] Innovation box.

[5] The non-lump-sum IP regime.

In the lump-sum-regime, 25% of the profit of a taxpayer with a maximum of € 25,000 can be taxed in the IP regime. This means that the maximum IP regime deduction is € 20,000 per taxpayer in 2017.

[6] The non-lump-sum IP regime.

New Zealand

New Zealand has met all aspects of the terms of reference (OECD, 2021[3]) (ToR) for the calendar year 2020 (year in review), and no recommendations are made.

New Zealand can legally issue five types of rulings within the scope of the transparency framework, but in practice only issues three types of rulings within the scope of the transparency framework.

In practice, New Zealand issued rulings within the scope of the transparency framework as follows:

Type of ruling	Number of rulings
Past rulings	69
Future rulings in the period 1 April 2016 – 31 December 2016	14
Future rulings in the calendar year 2017	15
Future rulings in the calendar year 2018	8
Future rulings in the calendar year 2019	21
Future rulings in the year in review	18

Peer input was received from one jurisdiction in respect of the exchanges of information on rulings received from New Zealand. The input was positive, noting that information was complete, in a correct format and received in a timely manner.

A. The information gathering process (ToR I.A)

854. New Zealand can legally issue five types of rulings within the scope of the transparency framework, but in practice issues the three following types of rulings within the scope of the transparency framework: (i) cross-border unilateral APAs and any other cross-border unilateral tax rulings (such as an advance tax ruling) covering transfer pricing or the application of transfer pricing principles; (ii) permanent establishment rulings; and (iii) related party conduit rulings.

855. For New Zealand, past rulings are any tax rulings within scope that are issued either: (i) on or after 1 January 2014 but before 1 April 2016; or (ii) on or after 1 January 2010 but before 1 January 2014, provided they were still in effect as at 1 January 2014. Future rulings are any tax rulings within scope that are issued on or after 1 April 2016.

856. In the prior years' peer review reports, it was determined that New Zealand's undertakings to identify past and future rulings and all potential exchange jurisdictions were sufficient to meet the minimum standard. In addition, it was determined that New Zealand's review and supervision mechanism was sufficient to meet the minimum standard. New Zealand's implementation remains unchanged, and therefore continues to meet the minimum standard.

857. New Zealand has met all of the ToR for the information gathering process and no recommendations are made.

B. The exchange of information (ToR II.B)

858. New Zealand has international agreements permitting spontaneous exchange of information, including being a party to (i) the *Multilateral Convention on Mutual Administrative Assistance in Tax Matters: Amended by the 2010 Protocol* (OECD/Council of Europe, 2011[4]) ("the Convention") and (ii) bilateral agreements in force with 40 jurisdictions.[1]

859. For the year in review, the timeliness of exchanges is as follows:

Future rulings within the scope of the transparency framework	Number of exchanges transmitted within three months of the information becoming available to the competent authority or immediately after legal impediments have been lifted	Delayed exchanges		
		Number of exchanges transmitted later than three months of the information on rulings becoming available to the competent authority	Reasons for the delays	Any other comments
	32	0	N/A	N/A

Follow up requests received for exchange of the ruling	Number	Average time to provide response	Number of requests not answered
	0	N/A	N/A

860. In the prior years' peer review reports, it was determined that New Zealand's process for the completion and exchange of templates were sufficient to meet the minimum standard. With respect to past rulings, no further action was required. New Zealand's implementation in this regard remains unchanged and therefore continues to meet the minimum standard.

861. New Zealand has the necessary legal basis for spontaneous exchange of information, a process for completing the templates in a timely way and has completed all exchanges. New Zealand has met all of the ToR for the exchange of information process and no recommendations are made.

C. Statistics (ToR IV)

862. The statistics for the year in review are as follows:

Category of ruling	Number of exchanges	Jurisdictions exchanged with
Cross-border unilateral APAs and any other cross-border unilateral tax rulings (such as an advance tax ruling) covering transfer pricing or the application of transfer pricing principles	30	Australia, China (People's Republic of), France, Hong Kong (China), Japan, Korea, Netherlands, Singapore, Switzerland, United Kingdom, United States
Permanent establishment rulings	*De minimis* rule applies	N/A
Related party conduit rulings	0	N/A
De minimis rule	2	N/A
Total	32	

D. Matters related to intellectual property regimes (ToR I.A.1.3)

863. New Zealand does not offer an intellectual property regime for which transparency requirements under the Action 5 Report (OECD, 2015[1]) were imposed.

Summary of recommendations on implementation of the transparency framework

Aspect of implementation of the transparency framework that should be improved	Recommendation for improvement
	No recommendations are made.

References

OECD (2021), *BEPS Action 5 on Harmful Tax Practices - Terms of Reference and Methodology for the Conduct of the Peer Reviews of the Action 5 Transparency Framework*, OECD Publishing, Paris, http://www.oecd.org/tax/beps/beps-action-5-harmful-tax-practices-peer-review-transparency-framework.pdf. [3]

OECD (2015), *Countering Harmful Tax Practices More Effectively, Taking into Account Transparency and Substance, Action 5 - 2015 Final Report*, OECD/G20 Base Erosion and Profit Shifting Project, OECD Publishing, Paris, https://dx.doi.org/10.1787/9789264241190-en. [1]

OECD (ed.) (2017b), *Harmful Tax Practices - 2017 Progress Report on Preferential Regimes*, OECD Publishing, Paris, http://dx.doi.org/10.1787/9789264283954-en. [2]

OECD/Council of Europe (2011), *The Multilateral Convention on Mutual Administrative Assistance in Tax Matters: Amended by the 2010 Protocol*, OECD Publishing, Paris, https://dx.doi.org/10.1787/9789264115606-en. [4]

Notes

[1] Participating jurisdictions to the Convention are available here: www.oecd.org/tax/exchange-of-tax-information/convention-on-mutual-administrative-assistance-in-tax-matters.htm. New Zealand also has bilateral agreements with Australia, Austria, Belgium, Canada, Chile, China (People's Republic of), Czech Republic, Denmark, Fiji, Finland, France, Germany, Hong Kong (China), India, Indonesia, Ireland, Italy, Japan, Korea, Malaysia, Mexico, Netherlands, Norway, Papua New Guinea, Philippines, Poland, Russia, Samoa, Singapore, South Africa, Spain, Sweden, Switzerland, Chinese Taipei, Thailand, Turkey, United Arab Emirates, United Kingdom, United States, Viet Nam.

Norway

Norway has met all aspects of the terms of reference (OECD, 2021[3]) (ToR) for the calendar year 2020 (year in review), and no recommendations are made.

Norway can legally issue three types of rulings within the scope of the transparency framework.

In practice, Norway issued rulings within the scope of the transparency framework as follows:

Type of ruling	Number of rulings
Past rulings	1
Future rulings in the period 1 April 2016 – 31 December 2016	0
Future rulings in the calendar year 2017	1
Future rulings in the calendar year 2018	0
Future rulings in the calendar year 2019	0
Future rulings in the year in review	0

No peer input was received in respect of the exchanges of information on rulings received from Norway.

A. The information gathering process (ToR I.A)

864. Norway can legally issue the following three types of rulings within the scope of the transparency framework: (i) preferential regimes;[1] (ii) cross-border unilateral APAs covering transfer pricing or the application of transfer pricing principles in relation to realisation of natural gas for companies liable to tax under the Petroleum Tax Act; and (iii) related party conduit rulings.

865. For Norway, past rulings are any tax rulings within scope that are issued either: (i) on or after 1 January 2014 but before 1 April 2016; or (ii) on or after 1 January 2010 but before 1 January 2014, provided they were still in effect as at 1 January 2014. Future rulings are any tax rulings within scope that are issued on or after 1 April 2016.

866. In the prior years' peer review reports, it was determined that Norway's undertakings to identify past and future rulings and all potential exchange jurisdictions were sufficient to meet the minimum standard. In addition, it was determined that Norway's review and supervision mechanism was sufficient to meet the minimum standard. Norway's implementation remains unchanged, and therefore continues to meet the minimum standard.

867. Norway has met all of the ToR for the information gathering process and no recommendations are made.

B. The exchange of information (ToR II.B)

868. Norway has international agreements permitting spontaneous exchange of information, including being a party to (i) the *Multilateral Convention on Mutual Administrative Assistance in Tax Matters: Amended by the 2010 Protocol* (OECD/Council of Europe, 2011[4]) ("the Convention"), (ii) the Nordic Convention on Assistance in Tax Matters and (iii) bilateral agreements in force with 84 jurisdictions.[2]

869. As Norway did not issue any rulings within the scope of the transparency framework in the relevant period, Norway was not required to exchange any information on rulings in the year in review and no data on the timeliness of exchanges can be reported.

870. In the prior years' peer review reports, it was determined that Norway's process for the completion and exchange of templates were sufficient to meet the minimum standard. With respect to past rulings, no further action was required. Norway's implementation in this regard remains unchanged and therefore continues to meet the minimum standard.

871. Norway has the necessary legal basis for spontaneous exchange of information, a process for completing the templates in a timely way and has completed all exchanges. Norway has met all of the ToR for the exchange of information process and no recommendations are made.

C. Statistics (ToR IV)

872. As no rulings were issued, no statistics can be reported.

D. Matters related to intellectual property regimes (ToR I.A.1.3)

873. Norway does not offer an intellectual property regime for which transparency requirements under the Action 5 Report (OECD, 2015[1]) were imposed.

Summary of recommendations on implementation of the transparency framework

Aspect of implementation of the transparency framework that should be improved	Recommendation for improvement
	No recommendations are made.

References

OECD (2021), *BEPS Action 5 on Harmful Tax Practices - Terms of Reference and Methodology for the Conduct of the Peer Reviews of the Action 5 Transparency Framework*, OECD Publishing, Paris, http://www.oecd.org/tax/beps/beps-action-5-harmful-tax-practices-peer-review-transparency-framework.pdf. [3]

OECD (2015), *Countering Harmful Tax Practices More Effectively, Taking into Account Transparency and Substance, Action 5 - 2015 Final Report*, OECD/G20 Base Erosion and Profit Shifting Project, OECD Publishing, Paris, https://dx.doi.org/10.1787/9789264241190-en. [1]

OECD (ed.) (2017b), *Harmful Tax Practices - 2017 Progress Report on Preferential Regimes*, OECD Publishing, Paris, http://dx.doi.org/10.1787/9789264283954-en. [2]

OECD/Council of Europe (2011), *The Multilateral Convention on Mutual Administrative Assistance in Tax Matters: Amended by the 2010 Protocol*, OECD Publishing, Paris, https://dx.doi.org/10.1787/9789264115606-en. [4]

Notes

[1] With respect to the following regime: International shipping.

[2] Participating jurisdictions to the Convention are available here: www.oecd.org/tax/exchange-of-tax-information/convention-on-mutual-administrative-assistance-in-tax-matters.htm. Parties to the Nordic Convention on Assistance in Tax Matters are Denmark, Faroe Islands, Finland, Iceland and Sweden. Norway also has bilateral agreements with Albania, Argentina, Australia, Austria, Azerbaijan, Bangladesh, Barbados, Belgium, Benin, Bonaire, Bosnia and Herzegovina, Brazil, Bulgaria, Canada, Chile, China (People's Republic of), Croatia, Curaçao, Cyprus, Czech Republic, Egypt, Estonia, France, Gambia, Georgia, Germany, Greece, Hungary, India, Indonesia, Ireland, Israel, Italy, Ivory Coast, Jamaica, Japan, Kazakhstan, Kenya, Korea, Latvia, Lithuania, Luxembourg, Malawi, Malaysia, Malta, Mexico, Montenegro, Morocco, Nepal, Netherlands, New Zealand, North Macedonia, Pakistan, Philippines, Poland, Portugal, Qatar, Romania, Russia, Saba, Senegal, Serbia, Sierra Leone, Singapore, Saint Eustatius, Sint Maarten, Slovak Republic, Slovenia, South Africa, Spain, Sri Lanka, Switzerland, Tanzania, Thailand, Tunisia, Turkey, Uganda, Ukraine, United Kingdom, United States, Venezuela, Viet Nam, Zambia and Zimbabwe.

Peru

Peru has met all aspects of the terms of reference (OECD, 2021[3]) (ToR) for the calendar year 2020 (year in review), and no recommendations are made.

Peru can legally issue one type of ruling within the scope of the transparency framework.

In practice, Peru issued no rulings within the scope of the transparency framework.

As no exchanges were required to take place, no peer input was received in respect of the exchanges of information on rulings received from Peru.

A. The information gathering process (ToR I.A)

874. Peru can legally issue the following type of ruling within the scope of the transparency framework: cross-border unilateral APAs and any other cross-border unilateral tax rulings (such as an advance tax ruling) covering transfer pricing or the application of transfer pricing principles.[1]

875. For Peru, past rulings are any tax rulings within scope that are issued either: (i) on or after 1 January 2015 but before 1 September 2017; or (ii) on or after 1 January 2012 but before 1 January 2015, provided they were still in effect as at 1 January 2015. Future rulings are any tax rulings within scope that are issued on or after 1 September 2017.

876. In the prior years' peer review reports, it was determined that Peru's undertakings to identify past and future rulings and all potential exchange jurisdictions were sufficient to meet the minimum standard. In addition, it was determined that Peru's review and supervision mechanism was sufficient to meet the minimum standard. In the year in review, Peru clarified that officials from the Large National Taxpayer Unit manually verify all tax rulings issued to identify those that fall within the scope of the transparency framework and report this information to the relevant departments. For the purpose of formalising the process, Peru notes that a structured procedure will be established by the end of 2022 to capture and verify relevant information appropriately. The new procedure will formalise the process to identify APAs and particular consultations issued on transfer pricing or the application of transfer pricing principles matters as well as the relevant exchange jurisdictions at the time of the taxpayer's request. It will also detail the steps of the review and supervision mechanism. Peru's implementation remains unchanged, and therefore continues to meet the minimum standard.

877. Peru has met all of the ToR for the information gathering process and no recommendations are made.

B. The exchange of information (ToR II.B)

878. Peru has international agreements permitting spontaneous exchange of information, including being a party to (i) the *Multilateral Convention on Mutual Administrative Assistance in Tax Matters: Amended by the 2010 Protocol* (OECD/Council of Europe, 2011[4]) ("the Convention"), (ii) bilateral agreements in force with seven jurisdictions, and (iii) tax information exchange agreements in force with two jurisdictions.[2]

879. As Peru did not issue any past or future rulings within the scope of the transparency framework in the relevant periods, Peru was not required to exchange any information on rulings in the year in review and no data on the timeliness of exchanges can be reported.

880. In the prior years' peer review reports, it was determined that Peru's process for the completion and exchange of templates were sufficient to meet the minimum standard. With respect to past rulings, no further action was required. Peru's implementation in this regard remains unchanged and therefore continues to meet the minimum standard.

881. Peru has the necessary legal basis for spontaneous exchange of information, a process for completing the templates in a timely way and has completed all exchanges. For the purpose of formalising the process, Peru notes that a structured procedure for the completion and exchange of templates will be established by the end of 2022. Peru has met all of the ToR for the exchange of information process and no recommendations are made.

C. Statistics (ToR IV)

882. As no rulings were issued, no statistics can be reported.

D. Matters related to intellectual property regimes (ToR I.A.1.3)

883. Peru does not offer an intellectual property regime for which transparency requirements under the Action 5 Report (OECD, 2015[1]) were imposed.

Summary of recommendations on implementation of the transparency framework

Aspect of implementation of the transparency framework that should be improved	Recommendation for improvement
	No recommendations are made.

References

OECD (2021), *BEPS Action 5 on Harmful Tax Practices - Terms of Reference and Methodology for the Conduct of the Peer Reviews of the Action 5 Transparency Framework*, OECD Publishing, Paris, http://www.oecd.org/tax/beps/beps-action-5-harmful-tax-practices-peer-review-transparency-framework.pdf. [3]

OECD (2015), *Countering Harmful Tax Practices More Effectively, Taking into Account Transparency and Substance, Action 5 - 2015 Final Report*, OECD/G20 Base Erosion and Profit Shifting Project, OECD Publishing, Paris, https://dx.doi.org/10.1787/9789264241190-en. [1]

OECD (ed.) (2017b), *Harmful Tax Practices - 2017 Progress Report on Preferential Regimes*, OECD Publishing, Paris, http://dx.doi.org/10.1787/9789264283954-en. [2]

OECD/Council of Europe (2011), *The Multilateral Convention on Mutual Administrative Assistance in Tax Matters: Amended by the 2010 Protocol*, OECD Publishing, Paris, https://dx.doi.org/10.1787/9789264115606-en. [4]

Notes

[1] Rulings other than APAs are known in Peru as "particular consultations". Particular consultations are issued in accordance with article 95-A of the Tax Code and relate to the tax regime applicable to specific facts or situations addressed by a taxpayer with a legitimate interest. Particular consultations are specific rulings on which the particular taxpayer is entitled to rely. However, Peru clarified that particular consultations cannot be issued on any of the categories of rulings within the scope of the transparency framework except for issues covering transfer pricing or the application of transfer pricing principles that fall outside the scope of an APA. Therefore, particular consultations fall in the "any other cross-border unilateral tax rulings (such as an advance tax ruling) covering transfer pricing or the application of transfer pricing principles".

[2] Participating jurisdictions to the Convention are available here: www.oecd.org/tax/exchange-of-tax-information/convention-on-mutual-administrative-assistance-in-tax-matters.htm. Peru also has bilateral agreements with Brazil, Canada, Chile, Korea, Mexico, Portugal and Switzerland; and tax information exchange agreements in force with Ecuador and the United States.

Philippines

The Philippines is taking steps to implement the legal basis for exchange under the transparency framework, and by commencing administrative preparations to ensure that information on rulings will be exchanged once the new legal basis is in place. The Philippines has met all aspects of the terms of reference (OECD, 2021[3]) (ToR) for the calendar year 2020 (year in review), except for identifying all potential exchange jurisdictions for both past and future rulings (ToR I.A.2.1 and ToR I.A.2.2) and having in place a domestic legal framework allowing spontaneous exchange of information on rulings by ensuring the timely exchange of information on rulings in the form required by the transparency framework (ToR II.B). The Philippines receives three recommendations on this point for the year in review.

In the prior year report, as well as in the 2017 and 2018 peer reviews, the Philippines had received four recommendations. The Philippines has resolved the issue regarding the review and supervision mechanism, and therefore this recommendation is now removed. As the other issues have not been addressed, the recommendations remain in place.

Philippines can legally issue one type of rulings within the scope of the transparency framework.

In practice, the Philippines issued rulings within the scope of the transparency framework as follows:

Type of ruling	Number of rulings
Past rulings	78
Future rulings in the period 1 September 2017 – 31 December 2017	4
Future rulings in the calendar year 2018	30
Future rulings in the calendar year 2019	10
Future rulings in the year in review	15

As no exchanges took place, no peer input was received in respect of the exchanges of information on rulings received from the Philippines.

A. The information gathering process (ToR I.A)

884. The Philippines can legally issue the following type of rulings within the scope of the transparency framework: permanent establishment rulings.

Past rulings (ToR I.A.1.1, I.A.1.2, I.A.2.1, I.A.2.2)

885. For the Philippines, past rulings are any tax rulings within scope that are issued either: (i) on or after 1 January 2015 but before 1 September 2017; or (ii) on or after 1 January 2012 but before 1 January 2015, provided they were still in effect as at 1 January 2015.

886. In the prior years' peer review reports, it was determined that the Philippines' undertakings to identify past rulings met the ToR. However, the Philippines was recommended to apply the "best efforts approach" to identify potential exchange jurisdictions, in particular for the ultimate parent company, as this was the only type of information on potential exchange jurisdictions that was not provided by the taxpayer upon application.

887. During the year in review, the Philippines experienced similar problems and therefore the prior years' recommendation remains. The Philippines notes that it is currently addressing these issues, including capacity building and working in co-operation with the Department of Finance.

Future rulings (ToR I.A.1.1, I.A.1.2, I.A.2.1)

888. For the Philippines, future rulings are any tax rulings within scope that are issued on or after 1 September 2017.

889. In the prior years' peer review reports, it was determined that the Philippines' undertakings in respect of future rulings met the ToR, except for identifying all potential exchange jurisdictions (ToR I.A.2.1). As for past rulings, the only required information on potential exchange jurisdictions that was not provided by the taxpayer upon application was related to the ultimate parent company. Therefore, the Philippines was recommended to ensure that all potential exchange jurisdictions are identified swiftly for future rulings.

890. During the year in review, the Philippines experienced similar problems and therefore the prior years' recommendation remains. The Philippines notes that it is currently addressing these issues, including capacity building and working in co-operation with the Department of Finance.

Review and supervision (ToR I.A.3)

891. In the prior years' peer review reports, it was not clear whether the Philippines had a review and supervision process in place (ToR I.A.3). Therefore, the Philippines was recommended to have in place a review and supervision mechanism to ensure that all relevant information is captured adequately.

892. During the year in review, the Philippines clarified that the process for ensuring all relevant information is captured accurately is guided by the Revenue Memorandum Order No. (RMO) 72-2010, and involves the Office of the Commissioner reviewing the data collected by the International Tax Affairs Division and the Legal Service. Therefore, the prior years' recommendation is now removed.

Conclusion on section A

893. The Philippines has met all of the ToR for the information gathering process, except for applying the "best efforts approach" for past rulings (ToR I.A.2.2), identifying all potential exchange jurisdictions for future rulings (ToR I.A.2.1). The Philippines is recommended to apply the best efforts approach for past

rulings with respect to identifying the ultimate parent company, and to ensure that all potential exchange jurisdictions are identified swiftly for future rulings.

B. The exchange of information (ToR II.B)

Legal basis for spontaneous exchange of information (ToR II.B.1, II.B.2)

894. The Philippines does not have the necessary domestic legal basis to exchange information on rulings spontaneously. This is because the Philippines is legally prohibited from sharing information on, or copies of, rulings other than to the applicant taxpayer. The Philippines is currently in the process of issuing regulations to allow the Philippines to spontaneously exchange information on rulings.

895. The Philippines has international agreements permitting spontaneous exchange of information, including double tax agreements with 43 jurisdictions.[1] The Philippines signed the *Multilateral Convention on Mutual Administrative Assistance in Tax Matters: Amended by the 2010 Protocol* (OECD/Council of Europe, 2011[4]) ("the Convention"), which is currently with the Philippine Senate for concurrence. Once the Convention enters into force, the spontaneous exchange of information could also be undertaken with jurisdictions that are covered by the Convention.

Completion and exchange of templates (ToR II.B.3, II.B.4, II.B.5, II.B.6, II.B.7)

896. As the Philippines does not yet have the legal basis for exchanges, the process for the completion and exchange of templates has not been put in place. The Philippines is recommended to put in place a process for the completion and exchange of templates to ensure the exchanges can take place as soon as the legal basis is in force.

897. For the year in review, as there is no domestic legal basis for exchange, no data on the timeliness of exchanges can be reported.

Conclusion on section B

898. The Philippines is recommended to continue its efforts to put in place a domestic legal framework allowing spontaneous exchange of information on rulings and to ensure the timely exchange of information on rulings in the form required by the transparency framework (ToR II.B).

C. Statistics (ToR IV)

899. As there was no information on rulings exchanged by the Philippines for the year in review, no statistics can be reported.

D. Matters related to intellectual property regimes (ToR I.A.1.3)

900. The Philippines does not offer an intellectual property regime for which transparency requirements under the Action 5 Report (OECD, 2015[1]) were imposed.

Summary of recommendations on implementation of the transparency framework

Aspect of implementation of the transparency framework that should be improved	Recommendation for improvement

The Philippines does not currently collect information on all potential exchange jurisdictions, particularly the ultimate parent company for past rulings.	The Philippines is recommended to apply the "best efforts approach" to identify potential exchange jurisdictions for all past rulings. This recommendation remains unchanged since the 2017, 2018 and 2019 peer review reports.
The Philippines does not currently collect information on all potential exchange jurisdictions, particularly the ultimate parent company for future rulings.	The Philippines is recommended to ensure that all potential exchange jurisdictions are identified swiftly for future rulings. This recommendation remains unchanged since the 2017, 2018 and 2019 peer review reports.
The Philippines does not yet have the necessary domestic legal framework in place for exchanging information on rulings or a process in place to ensure the timely exchange of information on rulings in the form required by the transparency framework.	The Philippines is recommended to continue to put in place a domestic legal framework allowing spontaneous exchange of information on rulings and to ensure the timely exchange of information on rulings in the form required by the transparency framework. This recommendation remains unchanged since the 2017, 2018 and 2019 peer review reports.

References

OECD (2021), *BEPS Action 5 on Harmful Tax Practices - Terms of Reference and Methodology for the Conduct of the Peer Reviews of the Action 5 Transparency Framework*, OECD Publishing, Paris, http://www.oecd.org/tax/beps/beps-action-5-harmful-tax-practices-peer-review-transparency-framework.pdf. [3]

OECD (2015), *Countering Harmful Tax Practices More Effectively, Taking into Account Transparency and Substance, Action 5 - 2015 Final Report*, OECD/G20 Base Erosion and Profit Shifting Project, OECD Publishing, Paris, https://dx.doi.org/10.1787/9789264241190-en. [1]

OECD (ed.) (2017b), *Harmful Tax Practices - 2017 Progress Report on Preferential Regimes*, OECD Publishing, Paris, http://dx.doi.org/10.1787/9789264283954-en. [2]

OECD/Council of Europe (2011), *The Multilateral Convention on Mutual Administrative Assistance in Tax Matters: Amended by the 2010 Protocol*, OECD Publishing, Paris, https://dx.doi.org/10.1787/9789264115606-en. [4]

Notes

[1] The Philippines has bilateral agreements in force with Australia, Austria, Bahrain, Bangladesh, Belgium, Brazil, Canada, China (People's Republic of), Czech Republic, Denmark, Finland, France, Germany, Hungary, India, Indonesia, Israel, Italy, Japan, Korea, Kuwait, Malaysia, Mexico, Netherlands, New Zealand, Nigeria, Norway, Pakistan, Poland, Qatar, Romania, Russia, Singapore, Spain, Sri Lanka, Sweden, Switzerland, Thailand, Turkey, United Arab Emirates, United Kingdom, United States and Viet Nam.

Poland

Poland has met all aspects of the terms of reference (OECD, 2021[3]) (ToR) for the calendar year 2020 (year in review), and no recommendations are made.

Poland can legally issue five types of rulings within the scope of the transparency framework.

In practice, Poland issued rulings within the scope of the transparency framework as follows:

Type of ruling	Number of rulings
Past rulings	84
Future rulings in the period 1 April 2016 – 31 December 2016	6
Future rulings in the calendar year 2017	20
Future rulings in the calendar year 2018	16
Future rulings in the calendar year 2019	100
Future rulings in the year in review	108

Peer input was received from four jurisdictions in respect of the exchanges of information on rulings received from Poland. The input was generally positive, noting that overall information was complete, in a correct format and received in a timely manner. One peer recommended to provide information on the duration of rulings.

A. The information gathering process (ToR I.A)

901. Poland can legally issue the following five types of rulings within the scope of the transparency framework: (i) preferential regimes; (ii) cross-border unilateral APAs and any other cross-border unilateral tax rulings (such as an advance tax ruling) covering transfer pricing or the application of transfer pricing principles; (iii) rulings providing for unilateral downward adjustments; (iv) permanent establishment rulings; and (v) related party conduit rulings.

For Poland, past rulings are any tax rulings within scope that are issued either: (i) on or after 1 January 2014 but before 1 April 2016; or (ii) on or after 1 January 2010 but before 1 January 2014, provided they were still in effect as at 1 January 2014.

902. In the prior years' peer review reports, it was determined that Poland's undertakings to identify past and future rulings and all potential exchange jurisdictions were sufficient to meet the minimum standard. In addition, it was determined that Poland's review and supervision mechanism was sufficient to meet the minimum standard. Poland's implementation remains unchanged, and therefore continues to meet the minimum standard.

903. Poland has met all of the ToR for the information gathering process and no recommendations are made.

B. The exchange of information (ToR II.B)

904. Poland has international agreements permitting spontaneous exchange of information, including being a party to (i) the *Multilateral Convention on Mutual Administrative Assistance in Tax Matters: Amended by the 2010 Protocol* (OECD/Council of Europe, 2011[4]) ("the Convention"), (ii) the Directive 2011/16/EU with all other European Union Member States and (iii) bilateral agreements in force with 89 jurisdictions.[1]

905. For the year in review, the timeliness of exchanges is as follows:

Future rulings within the scope of the transparency framework	Number of exchanges transmitted within three months of the information becoming available to the competent authority or immediately after legal impediments have been lifted	Delayed exchanges		
		Number of exchanges transmitted later than three months of the information on rulings becoming available to the competent authority	Reasons for the delays	Any other comments
	245	3	COVID-19 pandemic	Suspended shipment to some jurisdictions

Follow up requests received for exchange of the ruling	Number	Average time to provide response	Number of requests not answered
	0	N/A	N/A

906. In the prior years' peer review reports, it was determined that Poland's process for the completion and exchange of templates were sufficient to meet the minimum standard. With respect to past rulings, no further action was required. Poland's implementation in this regard remains unchanged and therefore continues to meet the minimum standard.

907. Poland has the necessary legal basis for spontaneous exchange of information, a process for completing the templates in a timely way and has completed all exchanges. Only small proportion of

exchanges were delayed as a direct impact of the COVID-19 pandemic, and as it is not expected to be a recurring problem once normal conditions resume, no recommendation is given for the delayed exchanges. Poland has met all of the ToR for the exchange of information process and no recommendations are made.

C. Statistics (ToR IV)

908. The statistics for the year in review are as follows:

Category of ruling	Number of exchanges	Jurisdictions exchanged with
Rulings related to a preferential regime	4	*De minimis* rule applies
Cross-border unilateral APAs and any other cross-border unilateral tax rulings (such as an advance tax ruling) covering transfer pricing or the application of transfer pricing principles	1	*De minimis* rule applies
Cross-border rulings providing for a unilateral downward adjustment to the taxpayer's taxable profits that is not directly reflected in the taxpayer's financial / commercial accounts	112	Australia, Canada, China (People's Republic of), Georgia, Iceland, India, Indonesia, Israel, Japan, Korea, Kuwait, Mexico, Morocco, New Zealand, North Macedonia, Norway, Russia, Serbia, Singapore, South Africa, Switzerland, Chinese Taipei, Thailand, Turkey, Ukraine, United States, Viet Nam
Permanent establishment rulings	7	Korea, Switzerland, United States
Related party conduit rulings	124	Australia, Canada, Chile, China (People's Republic of), Egypt, Greenland, India, Indonesia, Israel, Japan, Kazakhstan, Korea, Liechtenstein, Malaysia, Mexico, Morocco, New Zealand, Norway, Pakistan, Philippines, Qatar, Russia, Serbia, Singapore, South Africa, Switzerland, Turkey, United States
Total	248	

D. Matters related to intellectual property regimes (ToR I.A.1.3)

909. Poland offers an intellectual property regime (IP regime)[2] that is not subject to the transparency requirements under the Action 5 Report (OECD, 2015[1]), because:

- ***New entrants benefitting from the grandfathered IP regime***: as this is a new IP regime rather than a grandfathered IP regime, transparency on new entrants is not relevant.
- ***Third category of IP assets***: not applicable as the regime does not allow the third category of IP assets to qualify for the benefits.
- ***Taxpayers making the use of the option to treat the nexus ratio as a rebuttable presumption***: not applicable the regime does not allow the nexus ratio to be treated as a rebuttable presumption.

Summary of recommendations on implementation of the transparency framework

Aspect of implementation of the transparency framework that should be improved	Recommendation for improvement
	No recommendations are made.

References

OECD (2021), *BEPS Action 5 on Harmful Tax Practices - Terms of Reference and Methodology for the Conduct of the Peer Reviews of the Action 5 Transparency Framework*, OECD Publishing, Paris, http://www.oecd.org/tax/beps/beps-action-5-harmful-tax-practices-peer-review-transparency-framework.pdf. [3]

OECD (2015), *Countering Harmful Tax Practices More Effectively, Taking into Account Transparency and Substance, Action 5 - 2015 Final Report*, OECD/G20 Base Erosion and Profit Shifting Project, OECD Publishing, Paris, https://dx.doi.org/10.1787/9789264241190-en. [1]

OECD (ed.) (2017b), *Harmful Tax Practices - 2017 Progress Report on Preferential Regimes*, OECD Publishing, Paris, http://dx.doi.org/10.1787/9789264283954-en. [2]

OECD/Council of Europe (2011), *The Multilateral Convention on Mutual Administrative Assistance in Tax Matters: Amended by the 2010 Protocol*, OECD Publishing, Paris, https://dx.doi.org/10.1787/9789264115606-en. [4]

Notes

[1] Parties to the Convention are available here: www.oecd.org/tax/exchange-of-tax-information/convention-on-mutual-administrative-assistance-in-tax-matters.htm. Poland also has bilateral agreements with Albania, Armenia, Australia, Austria, Azerbaijan, Bangladesh, Belarus, Belgium, Bosnia and Herzegovina, Bulgaria, Canada, Chile, China (People's Republic of), Croatia, Cyprus, Czech Republic, Denmark, Egypt, Estonia, Ethiopia, Finland, France, Georgia, Germany, Greece, Guernsey, Hungary, Iceland, India, Indonesia, Iran, Ireland, Isle of Man, Israel, Italy, Jamaica, Japan, Jersey, Jordan, Kazakhstan, Korea, Kuwait, Kyrgyzstan, Latvia, Lebanon, Lithuania, Luxembourg, Malaysia, Malta, Mexico, Moldova, Mongolia, Montenegro, Morocco, Netherlands, New Zealand, North Macedonia, Norway, Pakistan, Peru, Philippines, Portugal, Qatar, Romania, Russia, Saudi Arabia, Serbia, Singapore, Slovak Republic, Slovenia, South Africa, Spain, Sri Lanka, Sweden, Switzerland, Syrian Arab Republic, Chinese Taipei, Tajikistan, Thailand, Tunisia, Turkey, Ukraine, United Arab Emirates, United Kingdom, United States, Uzbekistan, Vanuatu, Viet Nam and Zimbabwe.

[2] IP box.

Portugal

Portugal has met all aspects of the terms of reference (OECD, 2021[3]) (ToR) for the calendar year 2020 (year in review), and no recommendations are made.

Portugal can legally issue two types of rulings within the scope of the transparency framework.

In practice, Portugal issued rulings within the scope of the transparency framework as follows:

Type of ruling	Number of rulings
Past rulings	24
Future rulings in the period 1 April 2016 – 31 December 2016	2
Future rulings in the calendar year 2017	11
Future rulings in the calendar year 2018	11
Future rulings in the calendar year 2019	6
Future rulings in the year in review	6

No peer input was received in respect of the exchanges of information on rulings received from Portugal.

A. The information gathering process (ToR I.A)

910. Portugal can legally issue the following two types of rulings within the scope of the transparency framework: (i) cross-border unilateral APAs and any other cross-border unilateral tax rulings (such as an advance tax ruling) covering transfer pricing or the application of transfer pricing principles; and (ii) permanent establishment rulings.

911. For Portugal, past rulings are any tax rulings within scope that are issued either: (i) on or after 1 January 2014 but before 1 April 2016; or (ii) on or after 1 January 2010 but before 1 January 2014, provided they were still in effect as at 1 January 2014. Future rulings are any tax rulings within scope that are issued on or after 1 April 2016.

912. In the prior years' peer review reports, it was determined that Portugal's undertakings to identify past and future rulings and all potential exchange jurisdictions were sufficient to meet the minimum standard. In addition, it was determined that Portugal's review and supervision mechanism was sufficient to meet the minimum standard. Portugal's implementation remains unchanged, and therefore continues to meet the minimum standard.

913. Portugal has met all of the ToR for the information gathering process and no recommendations are made.

B. The exchange of information (ToR II.B)

914. Portugal has international agreements permitting spontaneous exchange of information, including being a party to (i) the *Multilateral Convention on Mutual Administrative Assistance in Tax Matters: Amended by the 2010 Protocol* (OECD/Council of Europe, 2011[4]) ("the Convention"), (ii) the Directive 2011/16/EU with all other European Union Member States and (iii) bilateral agreements in force with 78 jurisdictions.[1]

915. For the year in review, the timeliness of exchanges is as follows:

Future rulings within the scope of the transparency framework	Number of exchanges transmitted within three months of the information becoming available to the competent authority or immediately after legal impediments have been lifted	Delayed exchanges		
		Number of exchanges transmitted later than three months of the information on rulings becoming available to the competent authority	Reasons for the delays	Any other comments
	20	0	N/A	N/A

Follow up requests received for exchange of the ruling	Number	Average time to provide response	Number of requests not answered
	0	N/A	N/A

916. In the prior years' peer review reports, it was determined that Portugal's process for the completion and exchange of templates were sufficient to meet the minimum standard. With respect to past rulings, no further action was required. Portugal's implementation in this regard remains unchanged and therefore continues to meet the minimum standard.

917. Portugal has the necessary legal basis for spontaneous exchange of information, a process for completing the templates in a timely way and has completed all exchanges. Portugal has met all of the ToR for the exchange of information process and no recommendations are made.

C. Statistics (ToR IV)

918. The statistics for the year in review are as follows:

Category of ruling	Number of exchanges	Jurisdictions exchanged with
Cross-border unilateral APAs and any other cross-border unilateral tax rulings (such as an advance tax ruling) covering transfer pricing or the application of transfer pricing principles	18	Belgium, China (People's Republic of), Italy, France, Germany, Korea, Netherlands, Spain, Switzerland, United Kingdom, United States
Permanent establishment rulings	2	*De minimis* rule applies
IP regimes: total exchanges on taxpayers benefitting from the third category of IP assets, new entrants benefitting from grandfathered IP regimes; and taxpayers making use of the option to treat the nexus ratio as a rebuttable presumption	0	N/A
Total	20	

D. Matters related to intellectual property regimes (ToR I.A.1.3)

919. Portugal offers an intellectual property regime (IP regime)[2] that is subject to the transparency requirements under the Action 5 Report (OECD, 2015[1]). It states that the identification of the benefitting taxpayers will occur as follows:

- ***New entrants benefitting from the grandfathered IP regime***: Portugal did not identify any new entrants benefitting from the grandfathered IP regime that should be subject to spontaneous exchange of information with other jurisdictions.
- ***Third category of IP assets***: not applicable as the regime does not allow the third category of IP assets to qualify for the benefits.
- ***Taxpayers making use of the option to treat the nexus ratio as a rebuttable presumption***: not applicable as the regime does not allow the nexus ratio to be treated as a rebuttable presumption.

Summary of recommendations on implementation of the transparency framework

Aspect of implementation of the transparency framework that should be improved	Recommendation for improvement
	No recommendations are made.

References

OECD (2021), *BEPS Action 5 on Harmful Tax Practices - Terms of Reference and Methodology for the Conduct of the Peer Reviews of the Action 5 Transparency Framework*, OECD Publishing, Paris, http://www.oecd.org/tax/beps/beps-action-5-harmful-tax-practices-peer-review-transparency-framework.pdf. [3]

OECD (2015), *Countering Harmful Tax Practices More Effectively, Taking into Account Transparency and Substance, Action 5 - 2015 Final Report*, OECD/G20 Base Erosion and Profit Shifting Project, OECD Publishing, Paris, https://dx.doi.org/10.1787/9789264241190-en. [1]

OECD (ed.) (2017b), *Harmful Tax Practices - 2017 Progress Report on Preferential Regimes*, OECD Publishing, Paris, http://dx.doi.org/10.1787/9789264283954-en. [2]

OECD/Council of Europe (2011), *The Multilateral Convention on Mutual Administrative Assistance in Tax Matters: Amended by the 2010 Protocol*, OECD Publishing, Paris, https://dx.doi.org/10.1787/9789264115606-en. [4]

Notes

[1] Participating jurisdictions to the Convention are available here: www.oecd.org/tax/exchange-of-tax-information/convention-on-mutual-administrative-assistance-in-tax-matters.htm. Portugal also has bilateral agreements with Algeria, Andorra, Angola, Austria, Bahrain, Barbados, Belgium, Brazil, Bulgaria, Cabo Verde, Canada, Chile, China (People's Republic of), Colombia, Côte d'Ivoire, Croatia, Cuba, Cyprus, Czech Republic, Denmark, Estonia, Ethiopia, France, Georgia, Germany, Greece, Guinea-Bissau, Hong Kong (China), Hungary, Iceland, India, Indonesia, Ireland, Israel, Italy, Japan, Korea, Kuwait, Latvia, Lithuania, Luxembourg, Macau (China), Malta, Mexico, Moldova, Montenegro, Morocco, Mozambique, Netherlands, Norway, Oman, Pakistan, Panama, Peru, Poland, Qatar, Romania, Russia, San Marino, Sao Tome and Principe, Saudi Arabia, Senegal, Singapore, Slovak Republic, Slovenia, South Africa, Spain, Sweden, Switzerland, Tunisia, Turkey, Ukraine, United Arab Emirates, United Kingdom, United States, Uruguay, Venezuela and Viet Nam.

[2] Partial exemption for income from patents and other industrial property rights.

Qatar

Qatar has met all aspects of the terms of reference (OECD, 2021[3]) (ToR) for the calendar year 2020 (year in review), and no recommendations are made.

Qatar can legally issue five types of rulings within the scope of the transparency framework.

In practice, Qatar issued rulings within the scope of the transparency framework as follows:

Type of ruling	Number of rulings
Past rulings	0
Future rulings in the period 1 September 2018 – 31 December 2018	0
Future rulings in the calendar year 2019	1
Future rulings in the year in review	1

No peer input was received in respect of the exchanges of information on rulings received from Qatar.

A. The information gathering process (ToR I.A)

920. Qatar can legally issue the following five types of rulings within the scope of the transparency framework: (i) preferential regimes;[1] (ii) cross-border unilateral APAs and any other cross-border unilateral tax rulings (such as an advance tax ruling) covering transfer pricing or the application of transfer pricing principles; (iii) rulings providing for unilateral downward adjustments; (iv) permanent establishment rulings; and (v) related party conduit rulings.

921. For Qatar, past rulings are any tax rulings issued prior to 1 September 2018. Future rulings are any tax rulings within scope that are issued on or after 1 September 2018.

922. In the prior year peer review report, it was determined that Qatar's undertakings to identify future rulings and all potential exchange jurisdictions were sufficient to meet the minimum standard. In addition, it was determined that Qatar's review and supervision mechanism was sufficient to meet the minimum standard. Qatar's implementation in this regard remains unchanged, and therefore continues to meet the minimum standard.

923. Qatar has met all of the ToR for the information gathering process and no recommendations are made.

B. The exchange of information (ToR II.B)

924. Qatar has international agreements permitting spontaneous exchange of information, including being a party to (i) the *Multilateral Convention on Mutual Administrative Assistance in Tax Matters: Amended by the 2010 Protocol* (OECD/Council of Europe, 2011[4]) ("the Convention") and (ii) bilateral agreements in force with 75 jurisdictions.[2]

925. For the year in review, the timeliness of exchanges is as follows:

Future rulings within the scope of the transparency framework	Number of exchanges transmitted within three months of the information becoming available to the competent authority or immediately after legal impediments have been lifted	Delayed exchanges		
		Number of exchanges transmitted later than three months of the information on rulings becoming available to the competent authority	Reasons for the delays	Any other comments
	2	0	N/A	N/A

Follow up requests received for exchange of the ruling	Number	Average time to provide response	Number of requests not answered
	0	N/A	N/A

926. In the prior years' peer review reports, it was determined that Qatar's process for the completion and exchange of templates were sufficient to meet the minimum standard. With respect to past rulings, no action was required. Qatar's implementation in this regard remains unchanged and therefore continues to meet the minimum standard.

927. Qatar has the necessary legal basis for spontaneous exchange of information, a process for completing the templates in a timely way and has completed all exchanges. Qatar has met all of the ToR for the exchange of information process and no recommendations are made.

C. Statistics (ToR IV)

928. The statistics for the year in review are as follows:

Category of ruling	Number of exchanges	Jurisdictions exchanged with
Ruling related to a preferential regime	*De minimis* rule applies	N/A
Cross-border unilateral APAs and any other cross-border unilateral tax rulings (such as an advance tax ruling) covering transfer pricing or the application of transfer pricing principles	*De minimis* rule applies	N/A
Cross-border rulings providing for a unilateral downward adjustment to the taxpayer's taxable profits that is not directly reflected in the taxpayer's financial / commercial accounts	0	N/A
Permanent establishment rulings	0	N/A
Related party conduit rulings	0	N/A
De minimis rule	2	N/A
IP regimes: total exchanges on taxpayers benefitting from the third category of IP assets, new entrants benefitting from grandfathered IP regimes; and taxpayers making use of the option to treat the nexus ratio as a rebuttable presumption	0	N/A
Total	2	

D. Matters related to intellectual property regimes (ToR I.A.1.3)

929. Qatar offers two intellectual property regimes (IP regimes)[3] that are not currently subject to the transparency requirements under the Action 5 Report (OECD, 2015[1]), because:

- ***New entrants benefitting from the grandfathered IP regime***: not applicable for the year in review, as Qatar was in the process of amending the regime and had not taken a decision on whether it will provide grandfathering to existing taxpayers.
- ***Third category of IP assets***: not applicable for the year in review, as Qatar was in the process of amending the regime.
- ***Taxpayers making use of the option to treat the nexus ratio as a rebuttable presumption***: not applicable for the year in review, as Qatar was in the process of amending the regime.

Summary of recommendations on implementation of the transparency framework

Aspect of implementation of the transparency framework that should be improved	Recommendation for improvement
	No recommendations are made.

References

OECD (2021), *BEPS Action 5 on Harmful Tax Practices - Terms of Reference and Methodology for the Conduct of the Peer Reviews of the Action 5 Transparency Framework*, OECD Publishing, Paris, http://www.oecd.org/tax/beps/beps-action-5-harmful-tax-practices-peer-review-transparency-framework.pdf. [3]

OECD (2015), *Countering Harmful Tax Practices More Effectively, Taking into Account Transparency and Substance, Action 5 - 2015 Final Report*, OECD/G20 Base Erosion and Profit Shifting Project, OECD Publishing, Paris, https://dx.doi.org/10.1787/9789264241190-en. [1]

OECD (ed.) (2017b), *Harmful Tax Practices - 2017 Progress Report on Preferential Regimes*, OECD Publishing, Paris, http://dx.doi.org/10.1787/9789264283954-en. [2]

OECD/Council of Europe (2011), *The Multilateral Convention on Mutual Administrative Assistance in Tax Matters: Amended by the 2010 Protocol*, OECD Publishing, Paris, https://dx.doi.org/10.1787/9789264115606-en. [4]

Notes

[1] Rulings issued in relation to certain exemptions and concessionary rate under the Qatar Financial Centre (QFC) Tax Regulations.

[2] Participating jurisdictions to the Convention are available here: www.oecd.org/tax/exchange-of-tax-information/convention-on-mutual-administrative-assistance-in-tax-matters.htm. Qatar also has bilateral agreements with Albania, Algeria, Armenia, Austria, Azerbaijan, Barbados, Belarus, Belgium, Bermuda, Bosnia and Herzegovina, Brunei Darussalam, Bulgaria, Chad, China (People's Republic of), Croatia, Cuba, Cyprus, Ecuador, Eritrea, Ethiopia, Fiji, France, Gambia, Georgia, Greece, Guernsey, Hong Kong (China), Hungary, India, Indonesia, Iran, Ireland, Isle of Man, Italy, Japan, Jersey, Jordan, Kazakhstan, Kenya, Korea, Kyrgyzstan, Latvia, Lebanon, Luxembourg, Malaysia, Malta, Mauritania, Mauritius, Mexico, Monaco, Morocco, Nepal, Netherlands, Nigeria, North Macedonia, Norway, Pakistan, Panama, Paraguay, Philippines, Poland, Portugal, Romania, Russia, San Marino, Senegal, Serbia, Seychelles, Singapore, Slovenia, Somalia, South Africa, Spain, Sri Lanka, Sudan.

[3] These regimes are: 1) Free zone at science & technology park and 2) Free zone areas.

Romania

Romania has met all aspects of the terms of reference (OECD, 2021[3]) (ToR) for the calendar year 2020 (year in review), and no recommendations are made.

In the prior year report, as well as in the 2017 and 2018 peer reviews, Romania had received one recommendation. Romania has resolved this issue, and the recommendation has been removed.

Romania can legally issue two types of rulings within the scope of the transparency framework.

In practice, Romania issued rulings within the scope of the transparency framework as follows:

Type of ruling	Number of rulings
Past rulings	16
Future rulings in the period 1 April 2017 – 31 December 2017	5
Future rulings in the calendar year 2018	1
Future rulings in the calendar year 2019	4
Future rulings in the year in review	5

No peer input was received in respect of the exchanges of information on rulings received from Romania.

A. The information gathering process (ToR I.A)

930. Romania can legally issue the following two types of rulings within the scope of the transparency framework: (i) cross-border unilateral APAs and any other cross-border unilateral tax rulings (such as an advance tax ruling) covering transfer pricing or the application of transfer pricing principles and (ii) permanent establishment rulings.

931. For Romania, past rulings are any tax rulings within scope that are issued either: (i) on or after 1 January 2015 but before 1 April 2017; or (ii) on or after 1 January 2012 but before 1 January 2015, provided they were still in effect as at 1 January 2015. Future rulings are any tax rulings within scope that are issued on or after 1 April 2017.

932. In the prior years' peer review reports, it was determined that Romania's undertakings to identify past and future rulings and all potential exchange jurisdictions were sufficient to meet the minimum standard. In addition, it was determined that Romania's review and supervision mechanism was sufficient to meet the minimum standard. Romania's implementation remains unchanged, and therefore continues to meet the minimum standard.

933. Romania has met all of the ToR for the information gathering process and no recommendations are made.

B. The exchange of information (ToR II.B)

Legal basis for spontaneous exchange of information (ToR II.B.1, II.B.2)

934. Romania has the necessary domestic legal basis to exchange information spontaneously. Romania notes that there are no legal or practical impediments that prevent the spontaneous exchange of information on rulings as contemplated in the Action 5 minimum standard.

935. Romania has international agreements permitting spontaneous exchange of information, including being a party to (i) the *Multilateral Convention on Mutual Administrative Assistance in Tax Matters: Amended by the 2010 Protocol* (OECD/Council of Europe, 2011[4]) ("the Convention"), (ii) the Directive 2011/16/EU with all other European Union Member States and (iii) bilateral agreements in force with 88 jurisdictions.[1]

Completion and exchange of templates (ToR II.B.3, II.B.4, II.B.5, II.B.6, II.B.7)

936. In the prior year peer review report, it was determined that Romania' process for the completion and exchange of templates was sufficient to meet the minimum standard except for the timely exchange of information on future rulings (ToR II.B.6).

937. During the year in review, Romania addressed this issue by creating a new unit within the National Agency for Fiscal Administration (NAFA) as the result of an internal reorganisation. This unit is specifically dedicated to the exchange of information on cross-border tax rulings. Romania confirms that information on these rulings will be exchanged on a quarterly basis. In addition, Romania confirms that all rulings within the scope of the transparency framework that were issued until the end of 2020 have now been exchanged. Therefore, the prior year recommendation is now removed.

938. For the year in review, the timeliness of exchanges is as follows:

Future rulings within the scope of the transparency framework	Number of exchanges transmitted within three months of the information becoming available to the competent authority or immediately after legal impediments have been lifted	Delayed exchanges		
		Number of exchanges transmitted later than three months of the information on rulings becoming available to the competent authority	Reasons for the delays	Any other comments
	5[2]	0	N/A	N/A

Follow up requests received for exchange of the ruling	Number	Average time to provide response	Number of requests not answered
	0	N/A	N/A

939. It is noted that Romania issued two rulings in the second semester of 2020, which were exchanged in February 2021 with a delay, because Romania used the EU DAC3 timelines. From 1 January 2021, Romania changed its procedure and now applies the Action 5 timelines for rulings issued within the scope of the transparency framework. As the information on the two rulings is exchanged with a relatively short delay, and this is not a recurring issue, no recommendation is made. This will be also reflected in next year's peer review report.

Conclusion on Section B

940. Romania has the necessary legal basis for spontaneous exchange of information, a process for completing the templates in a timely way and has completed all exchanges. Romania has met all of the ToR for the exchange of information process and no recommendations are made.

C. Statistics (ToR IV)

941. The statistics for the year in review are as follows:

Category of ruling	Number of exchanges	Jurisdictions exchanged with
Cross-border unilateral APAs and any other cross-border unilateral tax rulings (such as an advance tax ruling) covering transfer pricing or the application of transfer pricing principles	5	Austria, Korea, Luxembourg, Netherlands
Permanent establishment rulings	0	N/A
Total	5	

D. Matters related to intellectual property regimes (ToR I.A.1.3)

942. Romania does not offer an intellectual property regime for which transparency requirements under the Action 5 Report (OECD, 2015[1]) were imposed.

Summary of recommendations on implementation of the transparency framework

Aspect of implementation of the transparency framework that should be improved	Recommendation for improvement
	No recommendations are made.

References

OECD (2021), *BEPS Action 5 on Harmful Tax Practices - Terms of Reference and Methodology for the Conduct of the Peer Reviews of the Action 5 Transparency Framework*, OECD Publishing, Paris, http://www.oecd.org/tax/beps/beps-action-5-harmful-tax-practices-peer-review-transparency-framework.pdf. [3]

OECD (2015), *Countering Harmful Tax Practices More Effectively, Taking into Account Transparency and Substance, Action 5 - 2015 Final Report*, OECD/G20 Base Erosion and Profit Shifting Project, OECD Publishing, Paris, https://dx.doi.org/10.1787/9789264241190-en. [1]

OECD (ed.) (2017b), *Harmful Tax Practices - 2017 Progress Report on Preferential Regimes*, OECD Publishing, Paris, http://dx.doi.org/10.1787/9789264283954-en. [2]

OECD/Council of Europe (2011), *The Multilateral Convention on Mutual Administrative Assistance in Tax Matters: Amended by the 2010 Protocol*, OECD Publishing, Paris, https://dx.doi.org/10.1787/9789264115606-en. [4]

Notes

[1] Participating jurisdictions to the Convention are available here: www.oecd.org/tax/exchange-of-tax-information/convention-on-mutual-administrative-assistance-in-tax-matters.htm. Romania also has bilateral agreements with Albania, Algeria, Armenia, Australia, Austria, Azerbaijan, Bangladesh, Belarus, Belgium, Bosnia and Herzegovina, Bulgaria, Canada, China (People's Republic of), Croatia, Cyprus, Czech Republic, Democratic People's Republic of Korea, Denmark, Ecuador, Egypt, Estonia, Ethiopia, Finland, France, Georgia, Germany, Greece, Hong Kong (China), Hungary, Iceland, India, Indonesia, Iran, Ireland, Israel, Italy, Japan, Jordan, Kazakhstan, Korea, Kuwait, Latvia, Lebanon, Lithuania, Luxembourg, Malaysia, Malta, Mexico, Moldova, Montenegro, Morocco, Namibia, Netherlands, Nigeria, North Macedonia, Norway, Pakistan, Philippines, Poland, Portugal, Qatar, Russia, San Marino, Saudi Arabia, Serbia, Montenegro, Singapore, Slovenia, Slovak Republic, South Africa, Spain, Sri Lanka, Sudan, Sweden, Switzerland, Syrian Arab Republic, Tajikistan, Thailand, Tunisia, Turkey, Turkmenistan, Ukraine, United Arab Emirates, United Kingdom, United States, Uruguay, Uzbekistan, Viet Nam and Zambia.

[2] Out of these five exchanges, two exchanges relate to rulings issued in 2019 and three exchanges relate to rulings issued in 2020. In 2021, two additional exchanges of rulings issued in 2020 took place as described in the report.

Russia

The Russian Federation ("Russia") has met all aspects of the terms of reference (OECD, 2021[3]) (ToR) for the calendar year 2020 (year in review), and no recommendations are made.

Russia can legally issue five types of rulings within the scope of the transparency framework.

In practice, Russia issued rulings within the scope of the transparency framework as follows:

Type of ruling	Number of rulings
Past rulings	1
Future rulings in the period 1 April 2016 – 31 December 2016	0
Future rulings in the calendar year 2017	0
Future rulings in the calendar year 2018	0
Future rulings in the calendar year 2019	0
Future rulings in the year in review	0

As no exchanges were required to take place during the year in review, no peer input was received in respect of the exchanges of information on rulings received from Russia.

A. The information gathering process (ToR I.A)

943. Russia can legally issue five types of rulings within the scope of the transparency framework: (i) preferential regimes;[1] (ii) cross-border unilateral APAs and any other cross-border unilateral tax rulings (such as an advance tax ruling) covering transfer pricing or the application of transfer pricing principles; (iii) rulings providing for unilateral downward adjustments; (iv) permanent establishment rulings; and (iv) related party conduit rulings.

944. For Russia, past rulings are any tax rulings within scope that are issued either: (i) on or after 1 January 2014 but before 1 April 2016; or (ii) on or after 1 January 2010 but before 1 January 2014, provided they were still in effect as at 1 January 2014. Future rulings are any tax rulings within scope that are issued on or after 1 April 2016.

945. In the prior years' peer review reports, it was determined that Russia's undertakings to identify past and future rulings and all potential exchange jurisdictions were sufficient to meet the minimum standard. In addition, it was determined that Russia's review and supervision mechanism was sufficient to meet the minimum standard. Russia's implementation remains unchanged, and therefore continues to meet the minimum standard.

946. Russia has met all of the ToR for the information gathering process and no recommendations are made.

B. The exchange of information (ToR II.B)

947. Russia has international agreements permitting spontaneous exchange of information, including being a party to (i) the *Multilateral Convention on Mutual Administrative Assistance in Tax Matters: Amended by the 2010 Protocol* (OECD/Council of Europe, 2011[4]) ("the Convention") and (ii) bilateral agreements in force with 84 jurisdictions.[2]

948. As Russia was not required to exchange any information on rulings for the year in review, no data on the timeliness of exchanges can be reported.

949. In the prior years' peer review reports, it was determined that Russia's process for the completion and exchange of templates were sufficient to meet the minimum standard. With respect to past rulings, no further action was required. Russia's implementation in this regard remains unchanged and therefore continues to meet the minimum standard.

950. Russia has the necessary legal basis for spontaneous exchange of information, a process for completing the templates in a timely way and has completed all exchanges. Russia has met all of the ToR for the exchange of information process and no recommendations are made.

C. Statistics (ToR IV)

951. As no exchanges were required to take place during the year in review, no statistics can be reported.

D. Matters related to intellectual property regimes (ToR I.A.1.3)

952. Russia does not offer an intellectual property regime for which transparency requirements under the Action 5 Report (OECD, 2015[1]) were imposed.

Summary of recommendations on implementation of the transparency framework

Aspect of implementation of the transparency framework that should be improved	Recommendation for improvement
	No recommendations are made.

References

OECD (2021), *BEPS Action 5 on Harmful Tax Practices - Terms of Reference and Methodology for the Conduct of the Peer Reviews of the Action 5 Transparency Framework*, OECD Publishing, Paris, http://www.oecd.org/tax/beps/beps-action-5-harmful-tax-practices-peer-review-transparency-framework.pdf. [3]

OECD (2015), *Countering Harmful Tax Practices More Effectively, Taking into Account Transparency and Substance, Action 5 - 2015 Final Report*, OECD/G20 Base Erosion and Profit Shifting Project, OECD Publishing, Paris, https://dx.doi.org/10.1787/9789264241190-en. [1]

OECD (ed.) (2017b), *Harmful Tax Practices - 2017 Progress Report on Preferential Regimes*, OECD Publishing, Paris, http://dx.doi.org/10.1787/9789264283954-en. [2]

OECD/Council of Europe (2011), *The Multilateral Convention on Mutual Administrative Assistance in Tax Matters: Amended by the 2010 Protocol*, OECD Publishing, Paris, https://dx.doi.org/10.1787/9789264115606-en. [4]

Notes

1 With respect to the following preferential regimes: 1) Special economic/industry zones.

2 Participating jurisdictions to the Convention are available here: www.oecd.org/tax/exchange-of-tax-information/convention-on-mutual-administrative-assistance-in-tax-matters.htm. Russia also has bilateral agreements with Albania, Algeria, Argentina, Armenia, Australia, Austria, Azerbaijan, Belarus, Belgium, Botswana, Bulgaria, Canada, Chile, China (People's Republic of), Croatia, Cuba, Cyprus, Czech Republic, Democratic People's Republic of Korea, Denmark, Ecuador, Egypt, Finland, France, Georgia, Germany, Greece, Hungary, Iceland, India, Indonesia, Iran, Ireland, Israel, Italy, Japan, Kazakhstan, Korea, Kuwait, Kyrgyzstan, Latvia, Lebanon, Lithuania, Luxembourg, Malaysia, Mali, Malta, Morocco, Mexico, Moldova, Mongolia, Montenegro, Namibia, Netherlands, New Zealand, Nigeria, North Macedonia, Norway, Philippines, Poland, Portugal, Qatar, Romania, Saudi Arabia, Serbia, Singapore, Slovak Republic, Slovenia, South Africa, Spain, Sri Lanka, Sweden, Syrian Arab Republic, Tajikistan, Thailand, Turkey, Turkmenia, Ukraine, United Arab Emirates, United Kingdom, United States, Uzbekistan, Venezuela and Viet Nam.

Saint Kitts and Nevis

Saint Kitts and Nevis has met all aspects of the terms of reference (OECD, 2021[3]) (ToR) for the calendar year 2020 (year in review), and no recommendations are made.

Saint Kitts and Nevis can legally issue five types of rulings within the scope of the transparency framework.

In practice, Saint Kitts and Nevis issued no rulings within the scope of the transparency framework.

As no exchanges were required to take place, no peer input was received in respect of the exchanges of information on rulings received from Saint Kitts and Nevis.

A. The information gathering process (ToR I.A)

953. Saint Kitts and Nevis can legally issue the following five types of rulings within the scope of the transparency framework: (i) preferential regimes;[1] (ii) cross-border unilateral APAs and any other cross-border unilateral tax rulings (such as an advance tax ruling) covering transfer pricing or the application of transfer pricing principles; (iii) rulings providing for unilateral downward adjustments; (iv) permanent establishment rulings; and (v) related party conduit rulings.

954. For Saint Kitts and Nevis, past rulings are any tax rulings within scope that are issued prior to 1 September 2018. However, there is no obligation for Saint Kitts and Nevis to conduct spontaneous exchange information on past rulings. Future rulings are any tax rulings within scope that are issued on or after 1 September 2018.

955. In the prior years' peer review reports, it was determined that Saint Kitts and Nevis's undertakings to identify rulings and all potential exchange jurisdictions were sufficient to meet the minimum standard. In addition, it was determined that Saint Kitts and Nevis's review and supervision mechanism was sufficient to meet the minimum standard. Saint Kitts and Nevis's implementation remains unchanged, and therefore continues to meet the minimum standard.

956. Saint Kitts and Nevis has met all of the ToR for the information gathering process and no recommendations are made.

B. The exchange of information (ToR II.B)

957. Saint Kitts and Nevis has international agreements permitting spontaneous exchange of information, including being a party to the *Multilateral Convention on Mutual Administrative Assistance in Tax Matters: Amended by the 2010 Protocol* (OECD/Council of Europe, 2011[4]) ("the Convention").

958. As Saint Kitts and Nevis did not issue any future rulings within the scope of the transparency framework in the relevant period, Saint Kitts and Nevis was not required to exchange any information on rulings in the year in review and no data on the timeliness of exchanges can be reported.

959. In the prior years' peer review reports, it was determined that Saint Kitts and Nevis' process for the completion and exchange of templates were sufficient to meet the minimum standard. Saint Kitts and Nevis' implementation in this regard remains unchanged and therefore continues to meet the minimum standard.

960. Saint Kitts and Nevis has the necessary legal basis for spontaneous exchange of information and a process for completing the templates in a timely way. Saint Kitts and Nevis has met all of the ToR for the exchange of information process and no recommendations are made.

C. Statistics (ToR IV)

961. As no rulings were issued, no statistics can be reported.

D. Matters related to intellectual property regimes (ToR I.A.1.3)

962. Saint Kitts and Nevis offered three preferential regimes, which also provided benefits to income from intellectual property,[2] that are not subject to the transparency requirements under the Action 5 Report (OECD, 2015[1]), because:

- ***New entrants benefitting from the grandfathered IP regime***: no exchanges were needed to take place as described in the prior year peer review report.
- ***Third category of IP assets***: not applicable as the IP regimes have been abolished.
- ***Taxpayers making use of the option to treat the nexus ratio as a rebuttable presumption***: not applicable as the IP regimes have been abolished.

Summary of recommendations on implementation of the transparency framework

Aspect of implementation of the transparency framework that should be improved	Recommendation for improvement
	No recommendations are made.

References

OECD (2021), *BEPS Action 5 on Harmful Tax Practices - Terms of Reference and Methodology for the Conduct of the Peer Reviews of the Action 5 Transparency Framework*, OECD Publishing, Paris, http://www.oecd.org/tax/beps/beps-action-5-harmful-tax-practices-peer-review-transparency-framework.pdf. [3]

OECD (2015), *Countering Harmful Tax Practices More Effectively, Taking into Account Transparency and Substance, Action 5 - 2015 Final Report*, OECD/G20 Base Erosion and Profit Shifting Project, OECD Publishing, Paris, https://dx.doi.org/10.1787/9789264241190-en. [1]

OECD (ed.) (2017b), *Harmful Tax Practices - 2017 Progress Report on Preferential Regimes*, OECD Publishing, Paris, http://dx.doi.org/10.1787/9789264283954-en. [2]

OECD/Council of Europe (2011), *The Multilateral Convention on Mutual Administrative Assistance in Tax Matters: Amended by the 2010 Protocol*, OECD Publishing, Paris, https://dx.doi.org/10.1787/9789264115606-en. [4]

Notes

[1] 1) Nevis LLC, 2) Nevis business corporation and 3) Companies act – exempt companies.

[2] See note 1.

Saint Lucia

Saint Lucia has met all aspects of the terms of reference (OECD, 2021[3]) (ToR) for the calendar year 2020 (year in review) that can be met in the absence of rulings being issued in practice, except for identifying all potential exchange jurisdictions for future rulings (ToR I.A.2.1). Saint Lucia receives one recommendation on this point for the year in review.

In the prior year report, as well as in the 2018 peer review, Saint Lucia had received two recommendations regarding its information gathering process (ToR I.A), and regarding the timely exchange of information (ToR II.B). Saint Lucia has resolved these issues, except for identifying all potential exchange jurisdictions for future rulings, and therefore one recommendation on this point remains.

Saint Lucia can legally issue two types of rulings within the scope of the transparency framework.

In practice, Saint Lucia issued no rulings within the scope of the transparency framework.

As no exchanges were required to take place, no peer input was received in respect of the exchanges of information on rulings received from Saint Lucia.

A. The information gathering process (ToR I.A)

963. Saint Lucia can legally issue the following two types of rulings within the scope of the transparency framework: (i) preferential regimes[1] and (ii) permanent establishment rulings.

Past rulings (ToR I.A.1.1, I.A.1.2, I.A.2.1, I.A.2.2)

964. For Saint Lucia, past rulings are any tax rulings issued prior to 1 September 2018. However, there is no obligation for Saint Lucia to conduct spontaneous exchange information on past rulings.

Future rulings (ToR I.A.1.1, I.A.1.2, I.A.2.1)

965. For Saint Lucia, future rulings are any tax rulings within scope that are issued on or after 1 September 2018.

966. In the prior years' peer review reports, it was determined that Saint Lucia had not put in place the appropriate processes for future rulings for the purposes of the transparency framework. Therefore, Saint Lucia was recommended to continue its work to make sure the necessary information gathering processes to meet the requirements of the transparency framework is put in place.

967. During the year in review, Saint Lucia approved a new rulings framework. The new rulings framework sets out a process to identify future rulings within scope and all information on potential exchange jurisdictions. Saint Lucia's Inland Revenue Department (IRD) is responsible for the review and authorisation of rulings issued in Saint Lucia. Within the IRD, an Exchange of Information (EOI) Unit and a Rulings Committee were established, which is overseen by the Legal Officer of the IRD. The EOI Unit is responsible for determining whether rulings fall into the scope of the transparency framework, and for the exchange of information of rulings in scope. The Rulings Committee is responsible for the review of all applications and information sources, and sends information to the EOI Unit. The EOI Unit cooperates with the Rulings Committee to ensure all relevant information is obtained. The Legal Officer also provides legal advice to the Comptroller of the IRD, who is the Competent Authority.

968. When a taxpayer requests a ruling, it also needs to provide information on potential exchange jurisdictions. However, Saint Lucia confirmed that taxpayers are not required to provide information on permanent establishments and ultimate parent companies, which means that not all information on potential exchange jurisdictions is collected. As such, the recommendation remains but it is now targeted to one specific aspect that still needs to be addressed.

Review and supervision (ToR I.A.3)

969. In accordance with the rulings framework, a dedicated team within the Rulings Committee will be trained on the identification of rulings within the scope of the transparency framework. This team is also responsible for the review of the accuracy of the information obtained. Furthermore, the Rulings Committee includes a member of the EOI Unit to facilitate the screening and sharing of information received. This review and supervision mechanism is already in place and therefore the recommendation on this point is now removed.

Conclusion on section A

970. Saint Lucia has met all of the ToR for the information gathering process that can be met in the absence of rulings being issued in practice, except for identifying all potential exchange jurisdictions for future rulings (ToR I.A.2.1). Saint Lucia is recommended to ensure that all potential exchange jurisdictions are identified swiftly for all future rulings.

B. The exchange of information (ToR II.B)

Legal basis for spontaneous exchange of information (ToR II.B.1, II.B.2)

971. Saint Lucia has the necessary domestic legal basis to exchange information spontaneously. Saint Lucia notes that there are no legal or practical impediments that prevent the spontaneous exchange of information on rulings as contemplated in the Action 5 minimum standard.

972. Saint Lucia has international agreements permitting spontaneous exchange of information, including being a party to (i) the *Multilateral Convention on Mutual Administrative Assistance in Tax Matters: Amended by the 2010 Protocol* (OECD/Council of Europe, 2011[4]) ("the Convention") and (ii) bilateral agreements in force with 16 jurisdictions.[2]

Completion and exchange of templates (ToR II.B.3, II.B.4, II.B.5, II.B.6, II.B.7)

973. In the prior years' peer review reports, it was determined that Saint Lucia had not put in place the appropriate processes for the completion and exchange of templates. Therefore, Saint Lucia was recommended to continue its work to complete its processes for the completion and exchange of templates as soon as possible.

974. During the year in review, Saint Lucia approved a new rulings framework, whereby the Rulings Committee, assisted by the EOI Unit, is responsible for completing the template contained in Annex C of the Action 5 Report (OECD, 2015[1]), which includes providing a summary of the ruling in line with the internal FHTP suggested guidance and the instructions in the Annex C template. The template would then be quality-checked by a supervisor in the IRD, and then provided to the Comptroller of the IRD for final approval and exchange. As the Comptroller of the IRD oversees the issuance of rulings by the IRD, and is also the Competent Authority for Saint Lucia, all tax rulings would therefore be readily available to the Competent Authority. As such, the recommendation is now removed.

975. As Saint Lucia did not issue any future rulings within the scope of the transparency framework in the relevant period, Saint Lucia was not required to exchange any information on rulings in the year in review and no data on the timeliness of exchanges can be reported.

Conclusion on section B

976. Saint Lucia has the necessary legal basis for spontaneous exchange of information and has a process for completing the templates in a timely way. Saint Lucia has met all of the ToR for the exchange of information process that can be met in the absence of rulings being issued in practice and no recommendations are made.

C. Statistics (ToR IV)

977. As no rulings were issued, no statistics can be reported.

D. Matters related to intellectual property regimes (ToR I.A.1.3)

978. Saint Lucia does not offer an intellectual property regime for which transparency requirements under the Action 5 Report (OECD, 2015[1]) were imposed.

Summary of recommendations on implementation of the transparency framework

Aspect of implementation of the transparency framework that should be improved	Recommendation for improvement
Saint Lucia does not require taxpayers to provide all necessary information to identify all potential exchange jurisdictions for future rulings.	Saint Lucia is recommended to ensure that all potential exchange jurisdictions are identified swiftly for all future rulings. This recommendation remains unchanged since the 2018 and 2019 peer review reports but it is now targeted to only this specific aspect that still needs to be put in place.

References

OECD (2021), *BEPS Action 5 on Harmful Tax Practices - Terms of Reference and Methodology for the Conduct of the Peer Reviews of the Action 5 Transparency Framework*, OECD Publishing, Paris, http://www.oecd.org/tax/beps/beps-action-5-harmful-tax-practices-peer-review-transparency-framework.pdf. [3]

OECD (2015), *Countering Harmful Tax Practices More Effectively, Taking into Account Transparency and Substance, Action 5 - 2015 Final Report*, OECD/G20 Base Erosion and Profit Shifting Project, OECD Publishing, Paris, https://dx.doi.org/10.1787/9789264241190-en. [1]

OECD (ed.) (2017b), *Harmful Tax Practices - 2017 Progress Report on Preferential Regimes*, OECD Publishing, Paris, http://dx.doi.org/10.1787/9789264283954-en. [2]

OECD/Council of Europe (2011), *The Multilateral Convention on Mutual Administrative Assistance in Tax Matters: Amended by the 2010 Protocol*, OECD Publishing, Paris, https://dx.doi.org/10.1787/9789264115606-en. [4]

Notes

[1] 1) International business company, 2) International trust and 3) International partnership regimes.

[2] Participating jurisdictions to the Convention are available here: www.oecd.org/tax/exchange-of-tax-information/convention-on-mutual-administrative-assistance-in-tax-matters.htm. Saint Lucia also has bilateral agreements with CARICOM jurisdictions and the United States.

San Marino

San Marino has met all aspects of the terms of reference (OECD, 2021[3]) (ToR) for the calendar year 2020 (year in review), and no recommendations are made.

San Marino can legally issue two types of rulings within the scope of the transparency framework.

In practice, San Marino issued rulings within the scope of the transparency framework as follows:

Type of ruling	Number of rulings
Past rulings	1
Future rulings in the period 1 April 2017 – 31 December 2017	0
Future rulings in the calendar year 2018	0
Future rulings in the calendar year 2019	0
Future rulings in the year in review	0

No peer input was received in respect of the exchanges of information on rulings received from San Marino.

A. The information gathering process (ToR I.A)

979. San Marino can legally issue the following two types of rulings within the scope of the transparency framework: (i) preferential regimes[1] and (ii) permanent establishment rulings.

980. For San Marino, past rulings are any tax rulings within scope that are issued either (i) on or after 1 January 2015 but before 1 April 2017; and (ii) on or after 1 January 2012 but before 1 January 2015, provided they were still in effect as at 1 January 2015. Future rulings are any tax rulings within scope that are issued on or after 1 April 2017.

981. In the prior year peer review report, it was determined that San Marino's undertakings to identify past and future rulings and all potential exchange jurisdictions were sufficient to meet the minimum standard. In addition, it was determined that San Marino's review and supervision mechanism was sufficient to meet the minimum standard. San Marino's implementation remains unchanged, and therefore continues to meet the minimum standard.

982. San Marino has met all of the ToR for the information gathering process and no recommendations are made.

B. The exchange of information (ToR II.B)

983. San Marino has international agreements permitting spontaneous exchange of information, including being a party to (i) the *Multilateral Convention on Mutual Administrative Assistance in Tax Matters: Amended by the 2010 Protocol* (OECD/Council of Europe, 2011[4]) ("the Convention") and (ii) bilateral agreements in force with 23 jurisdictions.[2]

984. For the year in review, the timeliness of exchanges is as follows:

Past rulings within the scope of the transparency framework	Number of exchanges transmitted by 31 December 2020	Delayed exchanges		
		Number of exchanges not transmitted by 31 December 2020	Reasons for the delays	Any other comments
	1[3]	0	N/A	See below.

Follow up requests received for exchange of the ruling	Number	Average time to provide response	Number of requests not answered
	0	N/A	N/A

985. The exchange reported in the table above relates to a permanent establishment ruling issued by San Marino in 2016. This past ruling was identified by the Tax Office in November 2019 and exchanged with the relevant exchange jurisdiction in February 2020. This exchange has already been reported in the prior year peer review report.

986. In the prior year peer review report, it was determined that San Marino's process for the completion and exchange of templates were sufficient to meet the minimum standard. It was also determined that San Marino concluded all remaining exchanges for past rulings during the year in review. San Marino's implementation in this regard remains unchanged and therefore continues to meet the minimum standard.

987. San Marino has the necessary legal basis for spontaneous exchange of information, a process for completing the templates in a timely way and has completed all exchanges. San Marino has met all of the ToR for the exchange of information process and no recommendations are made.

C. Statistics (ToR IV)

988. The statistics for the year in review are as follows:

Category of ruling	Number of exchanges	Jurisdictions exchanged with
Ruling related to a preferential regime	0	N/A
Permanent establishment rulings	*De minimis* rule applies	N/A
De minimis rule	1	N/A
IP regimes: total exchanges on taxpayers benefitting from the third category of IP assets, new entrants benefitting from grandfathered IP regimes; and taxpayers making use of the option to treat the nexus ratio as a rebuttable presumption	0	N/A
Total	1	

D. Matters related to intellectual property regimes (ToR I.A.1.3)

989. San Marino offered three intellectual property regimes (IP regime)[4] that are not subject to the transparency requirements under the Action 5 Report (OECD, 2015[1]), because:

- ***New entrants benefitting from the grandfathered IP regime***: not applicable, as described in the prior year peer review report.
- ***Third category of IP assets***: not applicable as the regimes do not allow the third category of IP assets to qualify for the benefits.
- ***Taxpayers making use of the option to treat the nexus ratio as a rebuttable presumption***: not applicable as the regimes do not allow the nexus ratio to be treated as a rebuttable presumption.

990. San Marino offered one IP regime[5] that is subject to the transparency requirements under the Action 5 Report (OECD, 2015[1]). It states that the identification of the benefitting taxpayers will occur as follows:

- ***New entrants benefitting from the grandfathered IP regime:*** not applicable because the identification process informed that there were no new entrants in the relevant period that benefitted from the grandfathered regime and therefore no information needed to be exchanged.
- ***Third category of IP assets:*** not applicable as the regime does not allow the third category of IP assets to qualify for the benefits.
- ***Taxpayers making use of the option to treat the nexus ratio as a rebuttable presumption***: not applicable as the regime does not allow the nexus ratio to be treated as a rebuttable presumption.

Summary of recommendations on implementation of the transparency framework

Aspect of implementation of the transparency framework that should be improved	Recommendation for improvement
	No recommendations are made.

References

OECD (2021), *BEPS Action 5 on Harmful Tax Practices - Terms of Reference and Methodology for the Conduct of the Peer Reviews of the Action 5 Transparency Framework*, OECD Publishing, Paris, http://www.oecd.org/tax/beps/beps-action-5-harmful-tax-practices-peer-review-transparency-framework.pdf. [3]

OECD (2015), *Countering Harmful Tax Practices More Effectively, Taking into Account Transparency and Substance, Action 5 - 2015 Final Report*, OECD/G20 Base Erosion and Profit Shifting Project, OECD Publishing, Paris, https://dx.doi.org/10.1787/9789264241190-en. [1]

OECD (ed.) (2017b), *Harmful Tax Practices - 2017 Progress Report on Preferential Regimes*, OECD Publishing, Paris, http://dx.doi.org/10.1787/9789264283954-en. [2]

OECD/Council of Europe (2011), *The Multilateral Convention on Mutual Administrative Assistance in Tax Matters: Amended by the 2010 Protocol*, OECD Publishing, Paris, https://dx.doi.org/10.1787/9789264115606-en. [4]

Notes

[1] With respect to the following preferential regime: IP regime. In the prior year report, it was noted that San Marino could legally issue rulings with respect to the following preferential regimes: 1) New companies regime (New companies regime provided by art. 73, law no. 166/2013), 2) High tech regime (Regime for high-tech start-up companies under law no. 71/2013 and delegated decree no. 116/2014) and 3) IP regime. San Marino has since clarified that rulings can be issued only with respect to the IP regime.

[2] Participating jurisdictions to the Convention are available here: www.oecd.org/tax/exchange-of-tax-information/convention-on-mutual-administrative-assistance-in-tax-matters.htm. San Marino also has bilateral agreements with Austria, Azerbaijan, Barbados, Belgium, Croatia, Cyprus, Georgia, Greece, Hungary, Italy, Liechtenstein, Luxembourg, Malaysia, Malta, Portugal, Qatar, Romania, Saint Kitts and Nevis, Serbia, Seychelles, Singapore, United Arab Emirates and Viet Nam.

[3] This exchange is the same exchange as the one included in the prior year peer review report as a delayed exchange.

[4] 1) IP regime, 2) High tech regime (Regime for high-tech start-up companies under law no. 71/2013 and delegated decree no. 116/2014), and 3) High innovative enterprise regime (High innovative enterprise regime introduced by delegated decree no. 101/2019 of 13 June 2019).

[5] New companies regime (New companies regime provided by art. 73, law no. 166/2013).

Senegal

Senegal has met all aspects of the terms of reference (OECD, 2021[3]) (ToR) for the calendar year 2020 (year in review) that can be met in the absence of rulings being issued in practice, and no recommendations are made.

Senegal can legally issue one type of ruling within the scope of the transparency framework.

In practice, Senegal issued no rulings within the scope of the transparency framework.

As no rulings were issued, no exchanges were required to take place, and no peer input was received in respect of the exchanges of information on rulings received from Senegal.

A. The information gathering process (ToR I.A)

991. Senegal can legally issue the following type of ruling within the scope of the transparency framework: cross-border unilateral APAs and any other cross-border unilateral tax rulings (such as an advance tax ruling) covering transfer pricing or the application of transfer pricing principles.

992. For Senegal, past rulings are any tax rulings within scope that are issued either (i) on or after 1 January 2016 but before 1 April 2018; and (ii) on or after 1 January 2014 but before 1 January 2016, provided still in effect as at 1 January 2016. Future rulings are any tax rulings within scope that are issued on or after 1 April 2018.

993. In the prior years' peer review reports, it was determined that there was no need to identify potential exchange jurisdictions as no past rulings were issued during the past rulings period. In addition, it was determined that Senegal's undertakings to identify future rulings and all potential exchange jurisdictions were sufficient to meet the minimum standard, and that Senegal's review and supervision mechanism was sufficient to meet the minimum standard. Senegal's implementation remains unchanged, and therefore continues to meet the minimum standard.

994. Senegal has met all of the ToR for the information gathering process that can be met in the absence of rulings being issued and no recommendations are made.

B. The exchange of information (ToR II.B)

995. Senegal has international agreements permitting spontaneous exchange of information, including being a party to (i) the *Multilateral Convention on Mutual Administrative Assistance in Tax Matters: Amended by the 2010 Protocol* (OECD/Council of Europe, 2011[4]) ("the Convention") and (ii) bilateral agreements in force with 21 jurisdictions.[1]

996. As no rulings are issued in practice, no data on the timeliness of exchanges can be reported.

997. In the prior year peer review report, it was determined that Senegal's process for the completion and exchange of templates were sufficient to meet the minimum standard in the absence of rulings being issued. With respect to past rulings, no further action was required. Senegal's implementation in this regard remains unchanged and therefore continues to meet the minimum standard.

998. Senegal has the necessary legal basis for spontaneous exchange of information, a process for completing the templates in a timely way. Senegal has met all of the ToR for the exchange of information process in the absence of rulings being issued and no recommendations are made.

C. Statistics (ToR IV)

999. As no rulings were issued, no statistics can be reported.

D. Matters related to intellectual property regimes (ToR I.A.1.3)

1000. Senegal does not offer an intellectual property regime for which transparency requirements under the Action 5 Report (OECD, 2015[1]) were imposed.

Summary of recommendations on implementation of the transparency framework

Aspect of implementation of the transparency framework that should be improved	Recommendation for improvement
	No recommendations are made.

References

OECD (2021), *BEPS Action 5 on Harmful Tax Practices - Terms of Reference and Methodology for the Conduct of the Peer Reviews of the Action 5 Transparency Framework*, OECD Publishing, Paris, http://www.oecd.org/tax/beps/beps-action-5-harmful-tax-practices-peer-review-transparency-framework.pdf. [3]

OECD (2015), *Countering Harmful Tax Practices More Effectively, Taking into Account Transparency and Substance, Action 5 - 2015 Final Report*, OECD/G20 Base Erosion and Profit Shifting Project, OECD Publishing, Paris, https://dx.doi.org/10.1787/9789264241190-en. [1]

OECD (ed.) (2017b), *Harmful Tax Practices - 2017 Progress Report on Preferential Regimes*, OECD Publishing, Paris, http://dx.doi.org/10.1787/9789264283954-en. [2]

OECD/Council of Europe (2011), *The Multilateral Convention on Mutual Administrative Assistance in Tax Matters: Amended by the 2010 Protocol*, OECD Publishing, Paris, https://dx.doi.org/10.1787/9789264115606-en. [4]

Notes

[1] Participating jurisdictions to the Convention are available here: www.oecd.org/tax/exchange-of-tax-information/convention-on-mutual-administrative-assistance-in-tax-matters.htm. Senegal also has bilateral agreements with West African Economic and Monetary Union jurisdictions, African and Malagasy Common Organisation jurisdictions and Belgium, Canada, Chinese Taipei, France, Italy, Kuwait, Lebanon, Malaysia, Mauritania, Mauritius, Morocco, Norway, Portugal, Spain, United Arab Emirates and United Kingdom.

Seychelles

Seychelles has met all aspects of the terms of reference (OECD, 2021[3]) (ToR) for the calendar year 2020 (year in review), and no recommendations are made.

Seychelles can legally issue five types of rulings within the scope of the transparency framework.

In practice, Seychelles issued no rulings within the scope of the transparency framework.

As no exchanges were required to take place, no peer input was received in respect of the exchanges of information on rulings received from Seychelles.

A. The information gathering process (ToR I.A)

1001. Seychelles can legally issue the following five types of rulings within the scope of the transparency framework: (i) preferential regimes;[1] (ii) cross-border unilateral APAs and any other cross-border unilateral tax rulings (such as an advance tax ruling) covering transfer pricing or the application of transfer pricing principles; (iii) rulings providing for unilateral downward adjustments; (iv) permanent establishment rulings; and (v) related party conduit rulings.

1002. For Seychelles, past rulings are any tax rulings within scope that are issued either: (i) on or after 1 January 2015 but before 1 April 2017; or (ii) on or after 1 January 2012 but before 1 January 2015, provided they were still in effect as at 1 January 2015. Future rulings are any tax rulings within scope that are issued on or after 1 April 2017.

1003. In the prior years' peer review reports, it was determined that Seychelles' undertakings to identify past and future rulings and all potential exchange jurisdictions were sufficient to meet the minimum standard. In addition, it was determined that Seychelles' review and supervision mechanism was sufficient to meet the minimum standard. Seychelles' implementation remains unchanged, and therefore continues to meet the minimum standard. It is noted that the Seychelles Revenue Commission (SRC) is continuing to develop a new form to request a private ruling to capture all the needed information. Until that takes place, Seychelles would continue to use its information gathering powers under the Revenue Administration Act to obtain information on all potential exchange jurisdictions.

1004. Seychelles has met all of the ToR for the information gathering process that can be met in the absence of exchanges being issued and no recommendations are made.

B. The exchange of information (ToR II.B)

1005. Seychelles has international agreements permitting spontaneous exchange of information, including being a party to (i) the *Multilateral Convention on Mutual Administrative Assistance in Tax Matters: Amended by the 2010 Protocol* (OECD/Council of Europe, 2011[4]) ("the Convention") and (ii) bilateral agreements in force with 28 jurisdictions.[2]

1006. As Seychelles did not issue any past or future rulings within the scope of the transparency framework in the relevant periods, Seychelles did not exchange any information on rulings in the year in review and no data on the timeliness of exchanges can be reported.

1007. In the prior years' peer review reports, it was determined that Seychelles' process for the completion and exchange of templates were sufficient to meet the minimum standard. With respect to past rulings, no action was required. Seychelles' implementation in this regard remains unchanged and therefore continues to meet the minimum standard.

1008. Seychelles has the necessary legal basis for spontaneous exchange of information and a process for completing the templates in a timely way. Seychelles has met all of the ToR for the exchange of information process that can be met in the absence of exchanges being issued and no recommendations are made.

C. Statistics (ToR IV)

1009. As no rulings were issued, no statistics can be reported.

D. Matters related to intellectual property regimes (ToR I.A.1.3)

1010. Seychelles offered three intellectual property regimes (IP regime)[3] that were abolished as of 1 January 2019 and not subject to the transparency requirements under the Action 5 Report (OECD, 2015[1]), because:

- ***New entrants benefitting from the grandfathered IP regime***: the IP regimes have been abolished without grandfathering for taxpayers entering after the relevant date from which enhanced transparency obligations apply. As such, no enhanced transparency requirements apply.
- ***Third category of IP assets***: not applicable as the IP regimes have been abolished.
- ***Taxpayers making use of the option to treat the nexus ratio as a rebuttable presumption***: not applicable as the IP regimes have been abolished.

Summary of recommendations on implementation of the transparency framework

Aspect of implementation of the transparency framework that should be improved	Recommendation for improvement
	No recommendations are made.

References

OECD (2021), *BEPS Action 5 on Harmful Tax Practices - Terms of Reference and Methodology for the Conduct of the Peer Reviews of the Action 5 Transparency Framework*, OECD Publishing, Paris, http://www.oecd.org/tax/beps/beps-action-5-harmful-tax-practices-peer-review-transparency-framework.pdf. [3]

OECD (2015), *Countering Harmful Tax Practices More Effectively, Taking into Account Transparency and Substance, Action 5 - 2015 Final Report*, OECD/G20 Base Erosion and Profit Shifting Project, OECD Publishing, Paris, https://dx.doi.org/10.1787/9789264241190-en. [1]

OECD (ed.) (2017b), *Harmful Tax Practices - 2017 Progress Report on Preferential Regimes*, OECD Publishing, Paris, http://dx.doi.org/10.1787/9789264283954-en. [2]

OECD/Council of Europe (2011), *The Multilateral Convention on Mutual Administrative Assistance in Tax Matters: Amended by the 2010 Protocol*, OECD Publishing, Paris, https://dx.doi.org/10.1787/9789264115606-en. [4]

Notes

[1] With respect to the following preferential regimes: 1) International business companies, 2) Companies special license, 3) International trade zone licensees, 4) Offshore banking, 5) Non domestic insurance business, 6) Fund administration business, 7) Securities business under the securities act and 8) Reinsurance business.

[2] Participating jurisdictions to the Convention are available here: www.oecd.org/tax/exchange-of-tax-information/convention-on-mutual-administrative-assistance-in-tax-matters.htm. Seychelles also has bilateral agreements with Bahrain, Barbados, Belgium, Bermuda, Botswana, China (People's Republic of), Cyprus, Eswatini, Ethiopia, Guernsey, Indonesia, Isle of Man, Jersey, Kenya, Luxembourg, Malaysia, Mauritius, Monaco, Oman, Qatar, San Marino, Singapore, South Africa, Sri Lanka, Thailand, United Arab Emirates, Viet Nam and Zambia.

[3] These regimes are: 1) International business companies; 2) Companies special license; and 3) International trade zone.

Singapore

Singapore has met all aspects of the terms of reference (OECD, 2021[3]) (ToR) for the calendar year 2020 (year in review), and no recommendations are made.

Singapore can legally issue five types of rulings within the scope of the transparency framework.

In practice, Singapore issued rulings within the scope of the transparency framework as follows:

Type of ruling	Number of rulings
Past rulings	1 008
Future rulings in the calendar year 2017	85
Future rulings in the calendar year 2018	222
Future rulings in the calendar year 2019	274
Future rulings in the year in review	211

Peer input was received from six jurisdictions in respect of the exchanges of information on rulings received from Singapore. The input was generally positive, noting that overall information was complete, in a correct format and almost all received in a timely manner. Two peers noted that exchanges on rulings were not timely, which is reflected in the report.

A. The information gathering process (ToR I.A)

1011. Singapore can legally issue the following five types of rulings within the scope of the transparency framework: (i) preferential regimes;[1] (ii) cross-border unilateral APAs and any other cross-border unilateral tax rulings (such as an advance tax ruling) covering transfer pricing or the application of transfer pricing principles; (iii) rulings providing for unilateral downward adjustments; (iv) permanent establishment rulings; and (v) related party conduit rulings.

1012. For Singapore, past rulings are any tax rulings within scope that are issued either: (i) on or after 1 January 2015 but before 1 April 2017; or (ii) on or after 1 January 2012 but before 1 January 2015, provided they were still in effect as at 1 January 2015. Future rulings are any tax rulings within scope that are issued on or after 1 April 2017.

1013. In the prior years' peer review reports, it was determined that Singapore's undertakings to identify past and future rulings and all potential exchange jurisdictions were sufficient to meet the minimum standard. In addition, it was determined that Singapore's review and supervision mechanism was sufficient to meet the minimum standard. Singapore's implementation remains unchanged, and therefore continues to meet the minimum standard.

1014. Singapore has met all of the ToR for the information gathering process and no recommendations are made.

B. The exchange of information (ToR II.B)

1015. In the prior years' peer review reports, it was determined that Singapore's process for the completion and exchange of templates were sufficient to meet the minimum standard. With respect to past rulings, no further action was required. Singapore's implementation in this regard remains unchanged and therefore continues to meet the minimum standard.

1016. Singapore has international agreements permitting spontaneous exchange of information, including being a party to (i) the *Multilateral Convention on Mutual Administrative Assistance in Tax Matters: Amended by the 2010 Protocol* (OECD/Council of Europe, 2011[4]) ("the Convention") and (ii) bilateral agreements in force with 84 jurisdictions.[2]

1017. For the year in review, the timeliness of exchanges is as follows:

Future rulings within the scope of the transparency framework	Number of exchanges transmitted within three months of the information becoming available to the competent authority or immediately after legal impediments have been lifted	Delayed exchanges		
		Number of exchanges transmitted later than three months of the information on rulings becoming available to the competent authority	Reasons for the delays	Any other comments
	504	91	See below	N/A

Follow up requests received for exchange of the ruling	Number	Average time to provide response	Number of requests not answered
	1	37 days	0

1018. Singapore explained that most of the delays for the exchanges were due to a system error, as some files were not processed by the system. This error was discovered when the system reports showed that there were delayed exchanges. The delayed exchanges have been completed in the year in review, with an average delay of 49 days. The system issue has also been resolved. In addition, there were two delayed exchanges arising from the need to seek clarification with regard to the legal basis for spontaneous exchange of information under one of the new bilateral agreements that entered into force in the year in review. Once the clarification was obtained, Singapore completed the exchanges and these two exchanges were delayed by seven days. As the majority of Singapore's exchanges were conducted within FHTP timelines, and the delays were due to issues that are not anticipated to be recurring issues and were already solved during the year in review, no recommendation is made.

1019. Singapore has the necessary legal basis for spontaneous exchange of information, a process for completing the templates in a timely way and has completed all exchanges. Singapore has met all of the ToR for the exchange of information process and no recommendations are made.

C. Statistics (ToR IV)

1020. The statistics for the year in review are as follows:

Category of ruling	Number of exchanges	Jurisdictions exchanged with
Ruling/letters of awards related to a preferential regime	585	Argentina, Australia, Austria, Belgium, Brazil, Canada, Chile, China (People's Republic of), Colombia, Denmark, France, Germany, Hong Kong (China), Hungary, India, Indonesia, Ireland, Israel, Italy, Japan, Jersey, Korea, Luxembourg, Malaysia, Malta, Mauritius, Mexico, Netherlands, New Zealand, Norway, Panama, Poland, Russia, Saudi Arabia, Seychelles, South Africa, Spain, Sweden, Switzerland, Turkey, United Kingdom, United States
Cross-border unilateral APAs and any other cross-border unilateral tax rulings (such as an advance tax ruling) covering transfer pricing or the application of transfer pricing principles	10	Australia, France, Hong Kong (China), Japan, Korea, Malaysia, Netherlands
Cross-border rulings providing for a unilateral downward adjustment to the taxpayer's taxable profits that is not directly reflected in the taxpayer's financial / commercial accounts	0	N/A
Permanent establishment rulings	0	N/A
Related party conduit rulings	0	N/A
Total	595	

D. Matters related to intellectual property regimes (ToR I.A.1.3)

1021. Singapore has two preferential regimes, which also offered benefits to income from intellectual property (IP regimes).[3] The IP parts of both regimes were abolished as of 30 June 2018 and are subject to transparency requirements under the Action 5 Report (OECD, 2015[1]). It states that the identification of the benefitting taxpayers occurred as follows:

- ***New entrants benefitting from the grandfathered IP regime***: transparency obligations apply for the two IP regimes, and Singapore has completed the exchanges during the prior years in review.
- ***Third category of IP assets***: not applicable as the IP regimes have been abolished.

- ***Taxpayers making use of the option to treat the nexus ratio as a rebuttable presumption***: not applicable as the IP regimes have been abolished.

1022. Singapore offers an IP regime[4] which came into effect from 1 July 2018. It is noted that this regime is not subject to the transparency requirements under the Action 5 Report (OECD, 2015[1]), because:

- ***New entrants benefitting from the grandfathered IP regime***: the regime is a new nexus-compliant regime and therefore there is no grandfathered IP regime for which enhanced transparency requirements will apply.
- ***Third category of IP assets***: not applicable as the regime does not allow the third category of IP assets to qualify for the benefits.
- ***Taxpayers making the use of the option to treat the nexus ratio as a rebuttable presumption***: not applicable as the regime does not allow the nexus ratio to be treated as a rebuttable presumption.

Summary of recommendations on implementation of the transparency framework

Aspect of implementation of the transparency framework that should be improved	Recommendation for improvement
	No recommendations are made.

References

OECD (2021), *BEPS Action 5 on Harmful Tax Practices - Terms of Reference and Methodology for the Conduct of the Peer Reviews of the Action 5 Transparency Framework*, OECD Publishing, Paris, http://www.oecd.org/tax/beps/beps-action-5-harmful-tax-practices-peer-review-transparency-framework.pdf. [3]

OECD (2015), *Countering Harmful Tax Practices More Effectively, Taking into Account Transparency and Substance, Action 5 - 2015 Final Report*, OECD/G20 Base Erosion and Profit Shifting Project, OECD Publishing, Paris, https://dx.doi.org/10.1787/9789264241190-en. [1]

OECD (ed.) (2017b), *Harmful Tax Practices - 2017 Progress Report on Preferential Regimes*, OECD Publishing, Paris, http://dx.doi.org/10.1787/9789264283954-en. [2]

OECD/Council of Europe (2011), *The Multilateral Convention on Mutual Administrative Assistance in Tax Matters: Amended by the 2010 Protocol*, OECD Publishing, Paris, https://dx.doi.org/10.1787/9789264115606-en. [4]

Notes

[1] 1) Development and expansion incentive - services, 2) Pioneer service company, 3) Aircraft leasing scheme, 4) Finance and treasury centre, 5) Insurance business development, 6) Financial sector incentive, 7) Global trader programme.

[2] Participating jurisdictions to the Convention are available here: www.oecd.org/tax/exchange-of-tax-information/convention-on-mutual-administrative-assistance-in-tax-matters.htm. Singapore also has bilateral agreements with Albania, Australia, Bahrain, Bangladesh, Barbados, Belarus, Belgium, Brunei Darussalam, Bulgaria, Cambodia, Canada, China (People's Republic of), Cyprus, Czech Republic, Denmark, Ecuador, Egypt, Estonia, Ethiopia, Fiji, Finland, France, Georgia, Germany, Ghana, Guernsey, Hungary, India, Indonesia, Ireland, Isle of Man, Israel, Italy, Japan, Jersey, Kazakhstan, Korea, Kuwait, Lao People's Democratic Republic, Latvia, Libya, Lithuania, Luxembourg, Malaysia, Malta, Mauritius, Mexico, Mongolia, Morocco, Myanmar, Netherlands, New Zealand, Nigeria, Norway, Oman, Pakistan, Papua New Guinea, Philippines, Poland, Portugal, Qatar, Romania, Russia, Rwanda, San Marino, Saudi Arabia, Seychelles, Slovak Republic, Slovenia, South Africa, Spain, Sri Lanka, Sweden, Thailand, Tunisia, Turkey, Turkmenistan, Ukraine, United Arab Emirates, United Kingdom, United States, Uruguay, Uzbekistan and Viet Nam.

[3] 1) Pioneer service company and 2) Development and expansion incentive – services.

[4] IP development incentive.

Sint Maarten

Sint Maarten has met all aspects of the terms of reference (OECD, 2021[3]) (ToR) for the calendar year 2020 (year in review) that can be met in the absence of rulings being issued in practice, and no recommendations are made.

Sint Maarten can legally issue five types of rulings within the scope of the transparency framework.

In practice, Sint Maarten issued no rulings within the scope of the transparency framework.

As no exchanges were required to take place, no peer input was received in respect of the exchanges of information on rulings received from Sint Maarten.

A. The information gathering process (ToR I.A)

1023. Sint Maarten can legally issue the following five types of rulings within the scope of the transparency framework: (i) preferential regimes;[1] (ii) cross-border unilateral APAs and any other cross-border unilateral tax rulings (such as an advance tax ruling) covering transfer pricing or the application of transfer pricing principles; (iii) rulings providing for unilateral downward adjustments; (iv) permanent establishment rulings; and (v) related party conduit rulings.

1024. For Sint Maarten, past rulings are any tax rulings within scope that are issued either: (i) on or after 1 January 2015 but before 1 September 2017; or (ii) on or after 1 January 2012 but before 1 January 2015, provided they were still in effect as at 1 January 2015. Future rulings are any tax rulings within scope that are issued on or after 1 September 2017.

1025. In the prior year peer review report, it was determined that Sint Maarten's undertakings to identify past and future rulings and all potential exchange jurisdictions were sufficient to meet the minimum standard. In addition, it was determined that Sint Maarten's review and supervision mechanism was sufficient to meet the minimum standard. Sint Maarten's implementation remains unchanged, and therefore continues to meet the minimum standard.

1026. Sint Maarten has met all of the ToR for the information gathering process and no recommendations are made.

B. The exchange of information (ToR II.B)

1027. Sint Maarten has international agreements permitting spontaneous exchange of information, including being a jurisdiction participating in (i) the *Multilateral Convention on Mutual Administrative Assistance in Tax Matters: Amended by the 2010 Protocol* (OECD/Council of Europe, 2011[4]) ("the Convention") and (ii) bilateral agreements in force with three jurisdictions.[2]

1028. As Sint Maarten did not issue any rulings within the scope of the transparency framework in the relevant period, Sint Maarten was not required to exchange any information on rulings in the year in review and no data on the timeliness of exchanges can be reported.

1029. In the prior year peer review report, it was determined that Sint Maarten's process for the completion and exchange of templates were sufficient to meet the minimum standard. With respect to past rulings, no further action was required. Sint Maarten's implementation in this regard remains unchanged and therefore continues to meet the minimum standard.

1030. Sint Maarten has the necessary legal basis for spontaneous exchange of information, a process for completing the templates in a timely way and has completed all exchanges. [country] has met all of the ToR for the exchange of information process and no recommendations are made.

C. Statistics (ToR IV)

1031. As no rulings were issued, no statistics can be reported.

D. Matters related to intellectual property regimes (ToR I.A.1.3)

1032. Sint Maarten does not offer an intellectual property regime for which transparency requirements under the Action 5 Report (OECD, 2015[1]) were imposed.

Summary of recommendations on implementation of the transparency framework

Aspect of implementation of the transparency framework that should be improved	Recommendation for improvement
	No recommendations are made.

References

OECD (2021), *BEPS Action 5 on Harmful Tax Practices - Terms of Reference and Methodology for the Conduct of the Peer Reviews of the Action 5 Transparency Framework*, OECD Publishing, Paris, http://www.oecd.org/tax/beps/beps-action-5-harmful-tax-practices-peer-review-transparency-framework.pdf. [3]

OECD (2015), *Countering Harmful Tax Practices More Effectively, Taking into Account Transparency and Substance, Action 5 - 2015 Final Report*, OECD/G20 Base Erosion and Profit Shifting Project, OECD Publishing, Paris, https://dx.doi.org/10.1787/9789264241190-en. [1]

OECD (ed.) (2017b), *Harmful Tax Practices - 2017 Progress Report on Preferential Regimes*, OECD Publishing, Paris, http://dx.doi.org/10.1787/9789264283954-en. [2]

OECD/Council of Europe (2011), *The Multilateral Convention on Mutual Administrative Assistance in Tax Matters: Amended by the 2010 Protocol*, OECD Publishing, Paris, https://dx.doi.org/10.1787/9789264115606-en. [4]

Notes

[1] Tax exempt company.

[2] Participating jurisdictions to the Convention are available here: www.oecd.org/tax/exchange-of-tax-information/convention-on-mutual-administrative-assistance-in-tax-matters.htm. Sint Maarten also has bilateral agreements with the Netherlands, Norway and the United States.

Slovak Republic

The Slovak Republic has met all aspects of the terms of reference (OECD, 2021[3]) (ToR) for the calendar year 2020 (year in review), and no recommendations are made.

The Slovak Republic can legally issue two types of rulings within the scope of the transparency framework.

In practice, the Slovak Republic issued rulings within the scope of the transparency framework as follows:

Type of ruling	Number of rulings
Past rulings	1
Future rulings in the period 1 April 2016 – 31 December 2016	2
Future rulings in the calendar year 2017	5
Future rulings in the calendar year 2018	3
Future rulings in the calendar year 2019	3
Future rulings in the year in review	3

No peer input was received in respect of the exchanges of information on rulings received from the Slovak Republic.

A. The information gathering process (ToR I.A)

1033. The Slovak Republic can legally issue the following two types of rulings within the scope of the transparency framework: (i) cross-border unilateral APAs and any other cross-border unilateral tax rulings (such as an advance tax ruling) covering transfer pricing or the application of transfer pricing principles and (ii) permanent establishment rulings.

1034. For the Slovak Republic, past rulings are any tax rulings within scope that are issued either: (i) on or after 1 January 2014 but before 1 April 2016; or (ii) on or after 1 January 2010 but before 1 January 2014, provided they were still in effect as at 1 January 2014. Future rulings are any tax rulings within scope that are issued on or after 1 April 2016.

1035. In the prior years' peer review reports, it was determined that the Slovak Republic's undertakings to identify past and future rulings and all potential exchange jurisdictions were sufficient to meet the minimum standard. In addition, it was determined that the Slovak Republic's review and supervision mechanism was sufficient to meet the minimum standard. The Slovak Republic's implementation remains unchanged, and therefore continues to meet the minimum standard.

1036. The Slovak Republic has met all of the ToR for the information gathering process and no recommendations are made.

B. The exchange of information (ToR II.B)

1037. The Slovak Republic has international agreements permitting spontaneous exchange of information, including being a party to (i) the *Multilateral Convention on Mutual Administrative Assistance in Tax Matters: Amended by the 2010 Protocol* (OECD/Council of Europe, 2011[4]) ("the Convention"), (ii) the Directive 2011/16/EU with all other European Union Member States and (iii) bilateral agreements in force with 70 jurisdictions.[1]

1038. For the year in review, the timeliness of exchanges is as follows:

Future rulings within the scope of the transparency framework	Number of exchanges transmitted within three months of the information becoming available to the competent authority or immediately after legal impediments have been lifted	Delayed exchanges		
		Number of exchanges transmitted later than three months of the information on rulings becoming available to the competent authority	Reasons for the delays	Any other comments
	3	0	N/A	N/A

Follow up requests received for exchange of the ruling	Number	Average time to provide response	Number of requests not answered
	0	N/A	N/A

1039. In the prior years' peer review reports, it was determined that the Slovak Republic's process for the completion and exchange of templates were sufficient to meet the minimum standard. With respect to past rulings, no further action was required. The Slovak Republic's implementation in this regard remains unchanged and therefore continues to meet the minimum standard.

1040. The Slovak Republic has the necessary legal basis for spontaneous exchange of information, a process for completing the templates in a timely way and has completed all exchanges. The Slovak

Republic has met all of the ToR for the exchange of information process and no recommendations are made.

C. Statistics (ToR IV)

1041. The statistics for the year in review are as follows:

Category of ruling	Number of exchanges	Jurisdictions exchanged with
Cross-border unilateral APAs and any other cross-border unilateral tax rulings (such as an advance tax ruling) covering transfer pricing or the application of transfer pricing principles	*De minimis* rule applies	N/A
Permanent establishment rulings	0	N/A
De minimis rule	3	N/A
IP regimes: total exchanges on taxpayers benefitting from the third category of IP assets, new entrants benefitting from grandfathered IP regimes; and taxpayers making use of the option to treat the nexus ratio as a rebuttable presumption	0	N/A
Total	3	0

D. Matters related to intellectual property regimes (ToR I.A.1.3)

1042. The Slovak Republic offers an intellectual property regime (IP regime)[2] that is not subject to the transparency requirements under the Action 5 Report (OECD, 2015[1]), because:

- ***New entrants benefitting from the grandfathered IP regime***: as this is a new IP regime rather than a grandfathered IP regime, transparency on new entrants was not relevant.
- ***Third category of IP assets***: not applicable as the regimes do not allow the third category of IP assets to qualify for the benefits.
- ***Taxpayers making use of the option to treat the nexus ratio as a rebuttable presumption***: not applicable as the regimes do not allow the nexus ratio to be treated as a rebuttable presumption.

Summary of recommendations on implementation of the transparency framework

Aspect of implementation of the transparency framework that should be improved	Recommendation for improvement
	No recommendations are made.

References

OECD (2021), *BEPS Action 5 on Harmful Tax Practices - Terms of Reference and Methodology for the Conduct of the Peer Reviews of the Action 5 Transparency Framework*, OECD Publishing, Paris, http://www.oecd.org/tax/beps/beps-action-5-harmful-tax-practices-peer-review-transparency-framework.pdf. [3]

OECD (2015), *Countering Harmful Tax Practices More Effectively, Taking into Account Transparency and Substance, Action 5 - 2015 Final Report*, OECD/G20 Base Erosion and Profit Shifting Project, OECD Publishing, Paris, https://dx.doi.org/10.1787/9789264241190-en. [1]

OECD (ed.) (2017b), *Harmful Tax Practices - 2017 Progress Report on Preferential Regimes*, OECD Publishing, Paris, http://dx.doi.org/10.1787/9789264283954-en. [2]

OECD/Council of Europe (2011), *The Multilateral Convention on Mutual Administrative Assistance in Tax Matters: Amended by the 2010 Protocol*, OECD Publishing, Paris, https://dx.doi.org/10.1787/9789264115606-en. [4]

Notes

1 Participating jurisdictions to the Convention are available here: www.oecd.org/tax/exchange-of-tax-information/convention-on-mutual-administrative-assistance-in-tax-matters.htm. The Slovak Republic also has bilateral agreements with Armenia, Australia, Austria, Belarus, Belgium, Bosnia and Herzegovina, Brazil, Bulgaria, Canada, China (People's Republic of), Croatia, Cyprus, Czech Republic, Denmark, Estonia, Ethiopia, Finland, France, Georgia, Germany, Greece, Hungary, Iceland, India, Indonesia, Iran, Ireland, Israel, Italy, Japan, Kazakhstan, Korea, Kuwait, Latvia, Libya, Lithuania, Luxembourg, Malaysia, Malta, Mexico, Moldova, Mongolia, Montenegro, Netherlands, Nigeria, North Macedonia, Norway, Poland, Portugal, Romania, Russia, Serbia, Singapore, Slovenia, South Africa, Spain, Sri Lanka, Sweden, Switzerland, Syrian Arab Republic, Chinese Taipei, Tunisia, Turkey, Turkmenistan, Ukraine, United Arab Emirates, United Kingdom, United States, Uzbekistan and Viet Nam.

2 Patent-box.

Slovenia

Slovenia has met all aspects of the terms of reference (OECD, 2021[3]) (ToR) for the calendar year 2020 (year in review), and no recommendations are made.

Slovenia can legally issue three types of rulings within the scope of the transparency framework.

In practice, Slovenia issued rulings within the scope of the transparency framework as follows:

Type of ruling	Number of rulings
Past rulings	8
Future rulings in the period 1 April 2016 – 31 December 2016	0
Future rulings in the calendar year 2017	1
Future rulings in the calendar year 2018	1
Future rulings in the calendar year 2019	2
Future rulings in the year in review	0

No peer input was received in respect of the exchanges of information on rulings received from Slovenia.

A. The information gathering process (ToR I.A)

1043. Slovenia can legally issue the following three types of rulings within the scope of the transparency framework: (i) cross-border unilateral APAs and any other cross-border unilateral tax rulings (such as an advance tax ruling) covering transfer pricing or the application of transfer pricing principles; (ii) permanent establishment rulings; and (iii) related party conduit rulings.

1044. For Slovenia, past rulings are any tax rulings within scope that are issued either: (i) on or after 1 January 2014 but before 1 April 2016; or (ii) on or after 1 January 2010 but before 1 January 2014, provided they were still in effect as at 1 January 2014. Future rulings are any tax rulings within scope that are issued on or after 1 April 2016.

1045. In the prior years' peer review reports, it was determined that Slovenia's undertakings to identify past and future rulings and all potential exchange jurisdictions were sufficient to meet the minimum standard. In addition, it was determined that Slovenia's review and supervision mechanism was sufficient to meet the minimum standard. Slovenia's implementation remains unchanged, and therefore continues to meet the minimum standard.

1046. Slovenia has met all of the ToR for the information gathering process and no recommendations are made.

B. The exchange of information (ToR II.B)

1047. Slovenia has international agreements permitting spontaneous exchange of information, including being a party to (i) the *Multilateral Convention on Mutual Administrative Assistance in Tax Matters: Amended by the 2010 Protocol* (OECD/Council of Europe, 2011[4]) ("the Convention"), (ii) the Directive 2011/16/EU with all other European Union Member States and (iii) bilateral agreements in force with 60 jurisdictions.[1]

1048. As Slovenia did not issue any rulings within the scope of the transparency framework in the relevant period, Slovenia was not required to exchange any information on rulings in the year in review and no data on the timeliness of exchanges can be reported.

1049. In the prior years' peer review reports, it was determined that Slovenia's process for the completion and exchange of templates were sufficient to meet the minimum standard. With respect to past rulings, no further action was required. Slovenia's implementation in this regard remains unchanged and therefore continues to meet the minimum standard.

1050. Slovenia has the necessary legal basis for spontaneous exchange of information, a process for completing the templates in a timely way and has completed all exchanges. Slovenia has met all of the ToR for the exchange of information process and no recommendations are made.

C. Statistics (ToR IV)

1051. As no rulings were issued, no statistics can be reported.

D. Matters related to intellectual property regimes (ToR I.A.1.3)

1052. Slovenia does not offer an intellectual property regime for which transparency requirements under the Action 5 Report (OECD, 2015[1]) were imposed.

Summary of recommendations on implementation of the transparency framework

Aspect of implementation of the transparency framework that should be improved	Recommendation for improvement
	No recommendations are made.

References

OECD (2021), *BEPS Action 5 on Harmful Tax Practices - Terms of Reference and Methodology for the Conduct of the Peer Reviews of the Action 5 Transparency Framework*, OECD Publishing, Paris, http://www.oecd.org/tax/beps/beps-action-5-harmful-tax-practices-peer-review-transparency-framework.pdf. [3]

OECD (2015), *Countering Harmful Tax Practices More Effectively, Taking into Account Transparency and Substance, Action 5 - 2015 Final Report*, OECD/G20 Base Erosion and Profit Shifting Project, OECD Publishing, Paris, https://dx.doi.org/10.1787/9789264241190-en. [1]

OECD (ed.) (2017b), *Harmful Tax Practices - 2017 Progress Report on Preferential Regimes*, OECD Publishing, Paris, http://dx.doi.org/10.1787/9789264283954-en. [2]

OECD/Council of Europe (2011), *The Multilateral Convention on Mutual Administrative Assistance in Tax Matters: Amended by the 2010 Protocol*, OECD Publishing, Paris, https://dx.doi.org/10.1787/9789264115606-en. [4]

Notes

1 Participating jurisdictions to the Convention are available here: www.oecd.org/tax/exchange-of-tax-information/convention-on-mutual-administrative-assistance-in-tax-matters.htm. Slovenia also has bilateral agreements with Albania, Armenia, Austria, Azerbaijan, Belgium, Belarus, Bosnia and Herzegovina, Bulgaria, Canada, China (People's Republic of), Croatia, Cyprus, Czech Republic, Denmark, Estonia, Finland, France, Georgia, Germany, Greece, Hungary, Iceland, India, Iran, Ireland, Isle Of Man, Israel, Italy, Japan, Kazakhstan, Korea, Kosovo, Kuwait, Latvia, Lithuania, Luxembourg, Malta, Moldova, Netherlands, North Macedonia, Norway, Poland, Portugal, Qatar, Romania, Russia, Serbia, Montenegro, Singapore, Slovak Republic, Spain, Sweden, Switzerland, Thailand, Turkey, Ukraine, United Arab Emirates, United Kingdom, United States and Uzbekistan.

South Africa

South Africa has met all aspects of the terms of reference (OECD, 2021[3]) (ToR) for the calendar year 2020 (year in review), and no recommendations are made.

South Africa can legally issue one type of ruling within the scope of the transparency framework.

In practice, South Africa issued rulings within the scope of the transparency framework as follows:

Type of ruling	Number of rulings
Past rulings	1
Future rulings in the period 1 April 2016 – 31 December 2016	0
Future rulings in the calendar year 2017	0
Future rulings in the calendar year 2018	0
Future rulings in the calendar year 2019	0
Future rulings in the year in review	0

As no exchanges were required to take place, no peer input was received in respect of the exchanges of information on rulings received from South Africa.

A. The information gathering process (ToR I.A)

1053. South Africa can legally issue the following type of ruling within the scope of the transparency framework: preferential regimes.[1]

1054. For South Africa, past rulings are any tax rulings within scope that are issued either: (i) on or after 1 January 2014 but before 1 April 2016; or (ii) on or after 1 January 2010 but before 1 January 2014, provided they were still in effect as at 1 January 2014. Future rulings are any tax rulings within scope that are issued on or after 1 April 2016.

1055. In the prior years' peer review reports, it was determined that South Africa's undertakings to identify past and future rulings and all potential exchange jurisdictions were sufficient to meet the minimum standard. In addition, it was determined that South Africa's review and supervision mechanism was sufficient to meet the minimum standard. South Africa's implementation remains unchanged, and therefore continues to meet the minimum standard.

1056. South Africa's has met all of the ToR for the information gathering process and no recommendations are made.

B. The exchange of information (ToR II.B)

1057. South Africa has international agreements permitting spontaneous exchange of information, including being a party to (i) the *Multilateral Convention on Mutual Administrative Assistance in Tax Matters: Amended by the 2010 Protocol* (OECD/Council of Europe, 2011[4]) ("the Convention") and (ii) bilateral agreements in force with 69 jurisdictions.[2]

1058. As South Africa was not required to exchange any information on rulings for the year in review and no data on the timeliness of exchanges can be reported.

1059. In the prior years' peer review reports, it was determined that South Africa's process for the completion and exchange of templates were sufficient to meet the minimum standard. With respect to past rulings, no further action was required. South Africa's implementation in this regard remains unchanged and therefore continues to meet the minimum standard.

1060. South Africa has the necessary legal basis for spontaneous exchange of information, a process for completing the templates in a timely way and has completed all exchanges. South Africa has met all of the ToR for the exchange of information process and no recommendations are made.

C. Statistics (ToR IV)

1061. As no rulings were issued, no statistics can be reported.

D. Matters related to intellectual property regimes (ToR I.A.1.3)

1062. South Africa does not offer an intellectual property regime for which transparency requirements under the Action 5 Report (OECD, 2015[1]) were imposed.

Summary of recommendations on implementation of the transparency framework

Aspect of implementation of the transparency framework that should be improved	Recommendation for improvement
	No recommendations are made.

References

OECD (2021), *BEPS Action 5 on Harmful Tax Practices - Terms of Reference and Methodology for the Conduct of the Peer Reviews of the Action 5 Transparency Framework*, OECD Publishing, Paris, http://www.oecd.org/tax/beps/beps-action-5-harmful-tax-practices-peer-review-transparency-framework.pdf. [3]

OECD (2015), *Countering Harmful Tax Practices More Effectively, Taking into Account Transparency and Substance, Action 5 - 2015 Final Report*, OECD/G20 Base Erosion and Profit Shifting Project, OECD Publishing, Paris, https://dx.doi.org/10.1787/9789264241190-en. [1]

OECD (ed.) (2017b), *Harmful Tax Practices - 2017 Progress Report on Preferential Regimes*, OECD Publishing, Paris, http://dx.doi.org/10.1787/9789264283954-en. [2]

OECD/Council of Europe (2011), *The Multilateral Convention on Mutual Administrative Assistance in Tax Matters: Amended by the 2010 Protocol*, OECD Publishing, Paris, https://dx.doi.org/10.1787/9789264115606-en. [4]

Notes

[1] With respect to the following preferential regimes: 1) Shipping regime and 2) Headquarters regime.

[2] Participating jurisdictions to the Convention are available here: www.oecd.org/tax/exchange-of-tax-information/convention-on-mutual-administrative-assistance-in-tax-matters.htm. South Africa also has bilateral agreements with Algeria, Australia, Austria, Belarus, Belgium, Botswana, Brazil, Bulgaria, Cameroon, Canada, Chile, China (People's Republic of), Croatia, Cyprus, Czech Republic, Democratic Republic of the Congo, Denmark, Egypt, Eswatini, Ethiopia, Finland, France, Ghana, Greece, Hong Kong (China), Hungary, India, Indonesia, Iran, Ireland, Italy, Japan, Kenya, Korea, Lesotho, Luxembourg, Malaysia, Malta, Mauritius, Mexico, Mozambique, Namibia, Netherlands, New Zealand, Nigeria, Norway, Oman, Pakistan, Poland, Portugal, Qatar, Rwanda, Samoa, Saudi Arabia, Seychelles, Singapore, Slovak Republic, Spain, Sweden, Tanzania, Turkey, Turks and Caicos Islands, Uganda, Ukraine, United Arab Emirates, United Kingdom, United States, Uruguay and Zimbabwe.

Spain

Spain has met all aspects of the terms of reference (OECD, 2021[3]) (ToR) for the calendar year 2020 (year in review), except for collecting and exchanging information on new assets of existing taxpayers benefitting from the grandfathered IP regime (ToR I.A.1.3). Spain receives one recommendation on this point for the year in review.

In the prior year report, as well as in the 2017 and 2018 peer reviews, Spain had received the same recommendation. As it has not been addressed, the recommendation remains in place.

Spain can legally issue three types of rulings within the scope of the transparency framework.

In practice, Spain issued rulings within the scope of the transparency framework as follows:

Type of ruling	Number of rulings
Past rulings	146
Future rulings in the period 1 April 2016 – 31 December 2016	28
Future rulings in the calendar year 2017	46
Future rulings in the calendar year 2018	22
Future rulings in the calendar year 2019	19
Future rulings in the year of review	43

Peer input was received from two jurisdictions in respect of the exchanges of information on rulings received from Spain. The input was positive, noting that information was complete, in a correct format and received in a timely manner.

A. The information gathering process (ToR I.A)

1063. Spain can legally issue the following three types of rulings within the scope of the transparency framework: (i) preferential regimes;[1] (ii) cross-border unilateral APAs and any other cross-border unilateral tax rulings (such as an advance tax ruling) covering transfer pricing or the application of transfer pricing principles; and (iii) permanent establishment rulings.

1064. For Spain, past rulings are any tax rulings within scope that are issued either: (i) on or after 1 January 2014 but before 1 April 2016; or (ii) on or after 1 January 2010 but before 1 January 2014, provided they were still in effect as at 1 January 2014. Future rulings are any tax rulings within scope that are issued on or after 1 April 2016.

1065. In the prior years' peer review reports, it was determined that Spain's undertakings to identify past and future rulings and all potential exchange jurisdictions were sufficient to meet the minimum standard. In addition, it was determined that Spain's review and supervision mechanism was sufficient to meet the minimum standard. Spain's implementation remains unchanged, and therefore continues to meet the minimum standard.

1066. Spain has met all of the ToR for the information gathering process and no recommendations are made.

B. The exchange of information (ToR II.B)

1067. Spain has international agreements permitting spontaneous exchange of information, including being a party to the (i) *Multilateral Convention on Mutual Administrative Assistance in Tax Matters: Amended by the 2010 Protocol* (OECD/Council of Europe, 2011[4]) ("the Convention"), (ii) the Directive 2011/16/EU with all other European Union Member States and (iii) bilateral agreements in force with 93 jurisdictions.[2]

1068. For the year in review, the timeliness of exchanges is as follows:

Future rulings in the scope of the transparency framework	Number of exchanges transmitted within three months of the information becoming available to the competent authority or immediately after legal impediments have been lifted	Delayed exchanges		
		Number of exchanges transmitted later than three months of the information on rulings becoming available to the competent authority	Reasons for the delays	Any other comments
	77	0	N/A	N/A

Follow up requests received for exchange of the ruling	Number	Average time to provide response	Number of requests not answered
	0	N/A	N/A

1069. In the prior years' peer review reports, it was determined that Spain's process for the completion and exchange of templates were sufficient to meet the minimum standard. With respect to past rulings, no further action was required. Spain's implementation in this regard remains unchanged and therefore continues to meet the minimum standard.

1070. Spain has the necessary legal basis for spontaneous exchange of information, a process for completing the templates in a timely way and has completed all exchanges. Spain has met all of the ToR for the exchange of information process and no recommendations are made.

C. Statistics (ToR IV)

1071. The statistics for the year in review are as follows:

Category of ruling	Number of exchanges	Jurisdictions exchanged with
Ruling related to a preferential regime	0	N/A
Cross-border unilateral advance pricing agreements (APAs) and any other cross-border unilateral tax rulings (such as an advance tax ruling) covering transfer pricing or the application of transfer pricing principles	71	Argentina, Barbados, Belgium, Brazil, Canada, China (People's Republic of), Colombia, France, Germany, Indonesia, Ireland, Italy, Malaysia, Mexico, Netherlands, Norway, Poland, Portugal, Romania, Russia, Switzerland, United Kingdom, United States
Permanent establishment rulings	6	Belgium, Germany, Hong Kong (China), Japan, Switzerland
IP regimes: total exchanges on taxpayers benefitting from the third category of IP assets, new entrants benefitting from grandfathered IP regimes; and taxpayers making use of the option to treat the nexus ratio as a rebuttable presumption	0	N/A
Total	77	

D. Matters related to intellectual property regimes (ToR I.A.1.3)

1072. Spain offers three intellectual property regimes (IP regime)[3] that are subject to the transparency requirements under the Action 5 Report (OECD, 2015[1]). It states that the identification of the benefitting taxpayers will occur as follows:

- ***New entrants benefitting from the grandfathered IP regime***: Transparency obligations apply for the regimes, because grandfathering is provided to entrants that entered the regime after the relevant date from which enhanced transparency obligations apply. In the previous years' peer review reports, it was explained that Spain adopted a new tax form in August 2017 so that it could identify the new taxpayers for which the enhanced transparency requirements apply. However, Spain was not able to identify new IP assets entering the regime after the relevant date and benefiting from grandfathering. Spain was therefore recommended to identify and exchange relevant information on new assets of existing taxpayers benefitting from the grandfathered IP regime.

  In order to act on this recommendation, Spain tried to include a new reporting obligation in the tax form that was adopted in August 2017. However, in October 2017 the tax form was appealed before the National Court. The appeal to the National Court was resolved on 25 May 2020, but has now been appealed before the Supreme Court. Therefore, the judicial process is still ongoing and the tax form has not yet been amended. As such, this information has not been able to be collected for exchange. Therefore, the prior years' recommendation remains.
- ***Third category of IP assets***: not applicable as the regimes do not allow the third category of IP assets to qualify for the benefits.
- ***Taxpayers making use of the option to treat the nexus ratio as a rebuttable presumption***: not applicable as the regimes do not allow the nexus ratio to be treated as a rebuttable presumption.

Summary of recommendations on implementation of the transparency framework

Aspect of implementation of the transparency framework that should be improved	Recommendation for improvement
Spain has not exchanged information on new assets of existing taxpayers benefitting from the grandfathered regime, as this information was not available during the year in review.	Spain is recommended to continue its efforts to identify and exchange relevant information on new assets of existing taxpayers benefitting from the grandfathered IP regime. This recommendation remains unchanged since the 2017, 2018 and 2019 peer review reports.

Jurisdiction's response and recent developments

1073. Spain notes the following regarding the recommendation for identifying and exchanging information on new assets of existing taxpayers in the grandfathered IP regime. As the proposal to amend the tax return to obtain the relevant information is still pending on the Court, Spain has taken alternative steps to address the issue. Based on an IT search, Spain has identified all taxpayers able to benefit from grandfathering during the relevant period. Spain will exchange the information on those taxpayers with the relevant jurisdictions before the end of 2021 and this will be taken into account in next year's peer review.

References

OECD (2021), *BEPS Action 5 on Harmful Tax Practices - Terms of Reference and Methodology for the Conduct of the Peer Reviews of the Action 5 Transparency Framework*, OECD Publishing, Paris, http://www.oecd.org/tax/beps/beps-action-5-harmful-tax-practices-peer-review-transparency-framework.pdf. [3]

OECD (2015), *Countering Harmful Tax Practices More Effectively, Taking into Account Transparency and Substance, Action 5 - 2015 Final Report*, OECD/G20 Base Erosion and Profit Shifting Project, OECD Publishing, Paris, https://dx.doi.org/10.1787/9789264241190-en. [1]

OECD (ed.) (2017b), *Harmful Tax Practices - 2017 Progress Report on Preferential Regimes*, OECD Publishing, Paris, http://dx.doi.org/10.1787/9789264283954-en. [2]

OECD/Council of Europe (2011), *The Multilateral Convention on Mutual Administrative Assistance in Tax Matters: Amended by the 2010 Protocol*, OECD Publishing, Paris, https://dx.doi.org/10.1787/9789264115606-en. [4]

Notes

[1] With respect to the following preferential regimes: 1) Partial exemption for income from certain intangible assets and 2) Shipping regime.

[2] Parties to the Convention are available here: www.oecd.org/tax/exchange-of-tax-information/convention-on-mutual-administrative-assistance-in-tax-matters.htm. Spain also has bilateral agreements with: Albania, Algeria, Andorra, Argentina, Armenia, Australia, Austria, Barbados, Belarus, Belgium, Bolivia, Bosnia and Herzegovina, Brazil, Bulgaria, Canada, Chile, China (People's Republic of), Colombia, Costa Rica, Croatia, Cuba, Cyprus, Czech Republic, Dominican Republic, Ecuador, Egypt, El Salvador, Estonia, Finland, France, Georgia, Germany, Greece, Hong Kong (China), Hungary, Iceland, India, Indonesia, Iran, Ireland, Israel, Italy, Jamaica, Japan, Kazakhstan, Korea, Kuwait, Kyrgyzstan, Latvia, Lithuania, Luxembourg, Malaysia, Malta, Mexico, Moldova, Morocco, Netherlands, New Zealand, Nigeria, North Macedonia, Norway, Oman, Pakistan, Panama, Philippines, Poland, Portugal, Qatar, Romania, Russia, Saudi Arabia, Senegal, Serbia, Singapore, Slovak Republic, Slovenia, South Africa, Sweden, Switzerland, Tajikistan, Thailand, Trinidad and Tobago, Tunisia, Turkey, Turkmenistan, Ukraine, United Arab Emirates, United Kingdom, United States, Uruguay, Uzbekistan, Venezuela and Viet Nam.

[3] These regimes are the partial exemptions for income from certain intangible assets for: 1) Federal regime, 2) Basque country and 3) Navarra.

Sri Lanka

Sri Lanka did not provide a completed peer review questionnaire to the Secretariat. It is not known whether Sri Lanka has implemented the transparency framework in line with the terms of reference (OECD, 2021[3]) (ToR) for the calendar year 2020 (year in review). Sri Lanka receives two recommendations covering the information gathering process (ToR I.A) and exchange of information (ToR II.B) for the year in review.

In the prior year report, as well as in the 2017 and 2018 peer reviews, Sri Lanka received the same recommendations. As they have not been addressed, the recommendations remain in place.

It is not known whether Sri Lanka can legally issue any types of ruling within the scope of the transparency framework, or whether in practice Sri Lanka issued any such rulings.

No peer input was received in respect of the exchanges of information on rulings received from Sri Lanka.

A. The information gathering process (ToR I.A)

1074. Sri Lanka was not yet able to complete the peer review questionnaire. It is not known whether Sri Lanka has implemented the transparency framework during the year in review.

Conclusion on section A

1075. Sri Lanka is recommended to ensure that it has put in place an effective information gathering process to identify all relevant past and future rulings and all potential exchange jurisdictions and to implement a review and supervision mechanism, as soon as possible (ToR I.A).

B. The exchange of information (ToR II.B)

Legal basis for spontaneous exchange of information (ToR II.B.1, II.B.2)

1076. It is not known whether Sri Lanka has the necessary domestic legal basis to exchange information spontaneously. Sri Lanka is recommended to put in place a domestic legal framework allowing spontaneous exchange of information on rulings if needed.

1077. Sri Lanka has international agreements permitting spontaneous exchange of information, including being a party to (i) the *Multilateral Convention on Mutual Administrative Assistance in Tax Matters: Amended by the 2010 Protocol* (OECD/Council of Europe, 2011[4]) ("the Convention"), (ii) bilateral agreements in force with 44 jurisdictions.[1]

Completion and exchange of templates (ToR II.B.3, II.B.4, II.B.5, II.B.6, II.B.7)

1078. It is not known whether Sri Lanka has put in place a process to exchange information on rulings in accordance with the form and timelines required by the transparency framework. Sri Lanka is recommended to ensure the timely exchange of information on rulings in the form required by the transparency framework.

Conclusion on section B

1079. Sri Lanka is recommended to put in place a domestic legal framework allowing spontaneous exchange of information on rulings and develop a process to complete the templates on relevant rulings and to ensure that the exchanges of information on rulings occur in accordance with the form and timelines under the transparency framework (ToR II.B).

C. Statistics (ToR IV)

1080. As the Secretariat is not aware whether information on rulings was exchanged by Sri Lanka for the year in review, no statistics can be reported.

D. Matters related to intellectual property regimes (ToR I.A.1.3)

1081. Sri Lanka does not offer an intellectual property regime for which transparency requirements under the Action 5 Report (OECD, 2015[1]) were imposed.

Summary of recommendations on implementation of the transparency framework

Aspect of implementation of the transparency framework that should be improved	Recommendation for improvement
It is not known whether Sri Lanka has put in place the necessary information gathering process.	Sri Lanka is recommended to finalise its information gathering process for identifying all future rulings and potential exchange jurisdictions, with a review and supervision mechanism, as soon as possible. This recommendation remains unchanged since the 2017, 2018 and 2019 peer review reports.
It is not known whether Sri Lanka has a process to complete the templates on relevant rulings, to make them available to the Competent Authority for exchange of information, and to exchange them with relevant jurisdictions.	Sri Lanka is recommended to put in place a domestic legal framework allowing spontaneous exchange of information on rulings and to develop a process to complete the templates on relevant rulings and to ensure that the exchanges of information on rulings occur in accordance with the form and timelines under the transparency framework. This recommendation remains unchanged since the 2017, 2018 and 2019 peer review reports.

References

OECD (2021), *BEPS Action 5 on Harmful Tax Practices - Terms of Reference and Methodology for the Conduct of the Peer Reviews of the Action 5 Transparency Framework*, OECD Publishing, Paris, http://www.oecd.org/tax/beps/beps-action-5-harmful-tax-practices-peer-review-transparency-framework.pdf. [3]

OECD (2015), *Countering Harmful Tax Practices More Effectively, Taking into Account Transparency and Substance, Action 5 - 2015 Final Report*, OECD/G20 Base Erosion and Profit Shifting Project, OECD Publishing, Paris, https://dx.doi.org/10.1787/9789264241190-en. [1]

OECD (ed.) (2017b), *Harmful Tax Practices - 2017 Progress Report on Preferential Regimes*, OECD Publishing, Paris, http://dx.doi.org/10.1787/9789264283954-en. [2]

OECD/Council of Europe (2011), *The Multilateral Convention on Mutual Administrative Assistance in Tax Matters: Amended by the 2010 Protocol*, OECD Publishing, Paris, https://dx.doi.org/10.1787/9789264115606-en. [4]

Notes

[1] Participating jurisdictions to the Convention are available here: www.oecd.org/tax/exchange-of-tax-information/convention-on-mutual-administrative-assistance-in-tax-matters.htm. Sri Lanka also has bilateral agreements Sri Lanka also has bilateral agreements in force with Australia, Bangladesh, Bahrain, Belarus, Belgium, Canada, China (People's Republic of), Czech Republic, Denmark, Finland, France, Germany, Hong Kong (China), India, Indonesia, Iran, Italy, Japan, Korea, Kuwait, Luxembourg, Malaysia, Mauritius, Nepal, Netherlands, Norway, Oman, Pakistan, Palestinian Authority, Philippines, Poland, Qatar, Romania, Russia, Saudi Arabia, Seychelles, Singapore, Sweden, Switzerland, Thailand, United Arab Emirates, United Kingdom, United States, and Viet Nam.

Sweden

Sweden has met all aspects of the terms of reference (OECD, 2021[3]) (ToR) for the calendar year 2020 (year in review), and no recommendations are made.

In the prior year report, as well as in the 2016, 2017 and 2018 peer reviews, Sweden had received one recommendation for identifying all potential exchange jurisdictions for future rulings (ToR I.A.2.1). During the year in review, Sweden has resolved this issue and therefore the recommendation is now removed.

Sweden can legally issue three types of rulings within the scope of the transparency framework.

In practice, Sweden issued rulings within the scope of the transparency framework as follows:

Type of ruling	Number of rulings
Past rulings	28
Future rulings in the period 1 April 2016 – 31 December 2016	5
Future rulings in the calendar year 2017	3
Future rulings in the calendar year 2018	6
Future rulings in the calendar year 2019	1
Future rulings in the year in review	1

No peer input was received in respect of the exchanges of information on rulings received from Sweden.

A. The information gathering process (ToR I.A)

1082. Sweden can legally issue the following three types of rulings within the scope of the transparency framework: (i) preferential regimes;[1] (ii) permanent establishment rulings; and (iii) related party conduit rulings.

Past rulings (ToR I.A.1.1, I.A.1.2, I.A.2.1, I.A.2.2)

1083. For Sweden, past rulings are any tax rulings within scope that are issued either: (i) on or after 1 January 2014 but before 1 April 2016; or (ii) on or after 1 January 2010 but before 1 January 2014, provided they were still in effect as at 1 January 2014.

1084. In the prior years' peer review reports, it was determined that Sweden's undertakings to identify past rulings and all potential exchange jurisdictions were sufficient to meet the minimum standard. Sweden's implementation in this regard remains unchanged, and therefore continues to meet the minimum standard.

Future rulings (ToR I.A.1.1, I.A.1.2, I.A.2.1)

1085. For Sweden, future rulings are any tax rulings within scope that are issued on or after 1 April 2016.

1086. In the prior years' peer review reports, Sweden was recommended to amend its rulings practice in order to be able to identify all potential exchange jurisdictions for future rulings (ToR I.A.2.1).

1087. During the year in review, the Swedish Parliament approved legislation on 21 October 2020, taking effect from 1 December 2020 that addresses the requirements under the Action 5 transparency framework for all three types of rulings Sweden can legally issue. As it has been determined that answers to external legal questions can also constitute rulings within the scope of the Action 5 transparency framework, the Swedish Tax Agency (STA) has also amended its ruling practice by issuing internal guidance. In accordance with this legislation and internal guidance, taxpayers (other than natural persons) applying for a ruling, or asking an external legal question that may result in a ruling, now have to submit their jurisdiction of residence, as well as those of their immediate parent company, ultimate parent company, head offices, ultimate beneficial owners and other legal persons that are likely to be affected by the ruling. To ensure compliance, the new legislation includes penalties. The STA also organised workshops for employees who work with written legal answers and appointed additional employees to analyse if an answer to an external legal question may result in a ruling and to require the taxpayers to submit the abovementioned information when needed. As such, the STA will be able to identify all potential exchange jurisdictions regarding future rulings, and therefore, the prior year recommendation is removed.

Review and supervision (ToR I.A.3)

1088. In the prior years' peer review reports, it was determined that Sweden's review and supervision mechanism was sufficient to meet the minimum standard. Sweden's implementation in this regard remains unchanged, and therefore continues to meet the minimum standard.

Conclusion on section A

1089. Sweden has met all of the ToR for the information gathering process and no recommendations are made.

B. The exchange of information (ToR II.B)

1090. Sweden has international agreements permitting spontaneous exchange of information, including being a party to (i) the *Multilateral Convention on Mutual Administrative Assistance in Tax Matters: Amended by the 2010 Protocol* (OECD/Council of Europe, 2011[4]) ("the Convention"), (ii) the Directive 2011/16/EU with all other European Union Member States, (iii) the Nordic Convention on Assistance in Tax Matters and (iv) bilateral agreements in force with 67 jurisdictions.[2]

1091. For the year in review, the timeliness of exchanges is as follows:

Future rulings within the scope of the transparency framework	Number of exchanges transmitted within three months of the information becoming available to the competent authority or immediately after legal impediments have been lifted	Delayed exchanges		
		Number of exchanges transmitted later than three months of the information on rulings becoming available to the competent authority	Reasons for the delays	Any other comments
	3	0	N/A	N/A

Follow up requests received for exchange of the ruling	Number	Average time to provide response	Number of requests not answered
	0	N/A	N/A

1092. In the prior years' peer review reports, it was determined that Sweden's process for the completion and exchange of templates were sufficient to meet the minimum standard. With respect to past rulings, no further action was required from Sweden. Sweden's implementation in this regard remains unchanged and therefore continues to meet the minimum standard.

1093. Sweden has the necessary legal basis for spontaneous exchange of information, a process for completing the templates in a timely way and has completed all exchanges. Sweden has met all of the ToR for the exchange of information process and no recommendations are made.

C. Statistics (ToR IV)

1094. The statistics for the year in review are as follows:

Category of ruling	Number of exchanges	Jurisdictions exchanged with
Ruling related to a preferential regime	0	N/A
Permanent establishment rulings	*De minimis* rule applies	N/A
Related party conduit rulings	0	N/A
De minimis rule	3	N/A
Total	3	

D. Matters related to intellectual property regimes (ToR I.A.1.3)

1095. Sweden does not offer an intellectual property regime for which transparency requirements under the Action 5 Report (OECD, 2015[1]) were imposed.

Summary of recommendations on implementation of the transparency framework

Aspect of implementation of the transparency framework that should be improved	Recommendation for improvement
	No recommendations are made.

References

OECD (2021), *BEPS Action 5 on Harmful Tax Practices - Terms of Reference and Methodology for the Conduct of the Peer Reviews of the Action 5 Transparency Framework*, OECD Publishing, Paris, http://www.oecd.org/tax/beps/beps-action-5-harmful-tax-practices-peer-review-transparency-framework.pdf. [3]

OECD (2015), *Countering Harmful Tax Practices More Effectively, Taking into Account Transparency and Substance, Action 5 - 2015 Final Report*, OECD/G20 Base Erosion and Profit Shifting Project, OECD Publishing, Paris, https://dx.doi.org/10.1787/9789264241190-en. [1]

OECD (ed.) (2017b), *Harmful Tax Practices - 2017 Progress Report on Preferential Regimes*, OECD Publishing, Paris, http://dx.doi.org/10.1787/9789264283954-en. [2]

OECD/Council of Europe (2011), *The Multilateral Convention on Mutual Administrative Assistance in Tax Matters: Amended by the 2010 Protocol*, OECD Publishing, Paris, https://dx.doi.org/10.1787/9789264115606-en. [4]

Notes

[1] With respect to the following preferential regime: Tonnage tax regime.

[2] Participating jurisdictions to the Convention are available here: www.oecd.org/tax/exchange-of-tax-information/convention-on-mutual-administrative-assistance-in-tax-matters.htm. Parties to the Nordic Convention on Assistance in Tax Matters are Denmark, Faroe Islands, Finland, Iceland, Norway and Sweden. Sweden also has bilateral agreements with Albania, Argentina, Armenia, Australia, Austria, Barbados, Belarus, Belgium, Bosnia and Herzegovina, Botswana, Brazil, Bulgaria, Canada, Chile, China (People's Republic of), Croatia, Czech Republic, Egypt, Estonia, France, Georgia, Germany, Greece, Hungary, India, Indonesia, Ireland, Israel, Italy, Jamaica, Japan, Kazakhstan, Kenya, Korea, Latvia, Lithuania, Luxembourg, Malaysia, Malta, Mauritius, Mexico, Montenegro, Namibia, Netherlands, New Zealand, Nigeria, North Macedonia, Pakistan, Poland, Portugal, Romania, Russia, Saudi Arabia, Serbia, Singapore, Slovak Republic, Slovenia, South Africa, Spain, Sri Lanka, Switzerland, Thailand, Trinidad and Tobago, Tunisia, Turkey, Ukraine, United Kingdom, United States, Viet Nam and Zambia.

Switzerland

Switzerland has met all aspects of the terms of reference (OECD, 2021[3]) (ToR) for the calendar year 2020 (year in review), except for identifying all past rulings within the scope of the transparency framework (ToR I.A.1.2) and the timely exchange of information on past and future rulings (ToR II.B.6). Switzerland receives two recommendations on this point for the year in review.

In the prior year report, Switzerland had received three recommendations. Switzerland resolved the recommendation regarding the timely provision of information on rulings to the Competent Authority and therefore this recommendation is now removed. Efforts have been made during the year in review to address the other two recommendations, although the issues have not been fully addressed for the year in review. As such, these recommendations remain in place.

Switzerland can legally issue four types of rulings within the scope of the transparency framework.

In practice, Switzerland issued rulings within the scope of the transparency framework as follows:

Type of ruling	Number of rulings
Past rulings	882[1]
Future rulings in the calendar year 2017	300
Future rulings in the calendar year 2018	228
Future rulings in the calendar year 2019	293
Future rulings in the year in review	214

Peer input was received from eight jurisdictions in respect of the exchanges of information on rulings received from Switzerland. The input was generally positive, noting that overall information was complete, in a correct format and almost all received in a timely manner. However, some peer input indicated that not all exchanges on rulings were conducted in a timely manner.

A. The information gathering process (ToR I.A)

1096. Switzerland can legally issue the following four types of rulings within the scope of the transparency framework: (i) preferential regimes;[2] (ii) cross-border unilateral APAs and any other cross-border unilateral tax rulings (such as an advance tax ruling) covering transfer pricing or the application of transfer pricing principles; (iii) permanent establishment rulings; and (iv) related party conduit rulings.

Past rulings (ToR I.A.1.1, I.A.1.2, I.A.2.1, I.A.2.2)

1097. For Switzerland, past rulings are any tax rulings within scope that are issued on or after 1 January 2010 until 31 December 2016, provided they were still in effect as at 1 January 2018.

1098. In the prior year peer review report, it was determined that Switzerland's undertakings to identify past rulings and all potential exchange jurisdictions have met all the ToR, except for identifying all past rulings within the scope of the transparency framework (ToR I.A.1.2). Therefore, Switzerland was recommended to strengthen its information gathering process identifying all past rulings within the scope of the transparency framework.

1099. During the year in review, Switzerland identified eleven additional past rulings. Switzerland also notes that no further past rulings have been identified since, and only one past ruling still has to be exchanged. Although this indicates that Switzerland is strengthening its information gathering process to identify all past rulings, the prior year recommendation remains in place in order to ensure that similar issues are not encountered in future.

Future rulings (ToR I.A.1.1, I.A.1.2, I.A.2.1)

1100. For Switzerland, future rulings are any tax rulings within scope that are issued on or after 1 January 2017, provided they are still in effect on or after 1 January 2018.

1101. In the prior years' peer review reports, it was determined that Switzerland's undertakings to identify future rulings and all potential exchange jurisdictions were sufficient to meet the minimum standard. Switzerland's undertakings in this regard remain unchanged, and therefore continue to meet the minimum standard.

Review and supervision (ToR I.A.3)

1102. In the prior year peer review reports, Switzerland was recommended, as part of the efforts to enhance the information gathering process, to strengthen its review and supervision mechanism to ensure that the information gathering process is working effectively. During the year in review, Switzerland identified additional past rulings compared to those reported in the prior year report. Although this indicates that Switzerland is strengthening its review and supervision mechanism to ensure that the information gathering process is working effectively, the prior year recommendation remains in place in order to ensure that similar issues are not encountered in future.

Conclusion on section A

1103. Switzerland has met all of the ToR for the information gathering process except for identifying all past rulings within the scope of the transparency framework (ToR I.A.1.2). Switzerland is recommended to strengthen its information gathering process by identifying all past rulings within the scope of the transparency framework and its review and supervision mechanism to ensure that the information gathering process is working effectively.

B. The exchange of information (ToR II.B)

Legal basis for spontaneous exchange of information (ToR II.B.1, II.B.2)

1104. Switzerland has the necessary domestic legal basis to exchange information spontaneously. Switzerland notes that there are no legal or practical impediments that prevent the spontaneous exchange of information on rulings as contemplated in the Action 5 minimum standard.

1105. Switzerland's international agreement permitting spontaneous exchange of information is the *Multilateral Convention on Mutual Administrative Assistance in Tax Matters: Amended by the 2010 Protocol* (OECD/Council of Europe, 2011[4]) ("the Convention"). The necessary domestic and international legal framework for spontaneous exchange of information entered into force on 1 January 2017, allowing for exchanges from 1 January 2018.

Completion and exchange of templates (ToR II.B.3, II.B.4, II.B.5, II.B.6, II.B.7)

1106. In the prior year peer review report, it was determined that Switzerland's process for the completion and exchange of templates met all the ToR, except for the timely provision of information on rulings to the Competent Authority (ToR II.B.5) and the timely exchange of information on past and future rulings (ToR II.B.6).

1107. During the year in review, Switzerland continued to experience recurring delayed exchanges for both past rulings and future rulings. However, additional steps have been taken to receive information on rulings from the cantonal authorities without undue delay and to ensure quality and accuracy of the information received. Accordingly, Switzerland confirmed these delays relate to the identification of past rulings, as described above, and to the timely exchange of information on past and future rulings, as described below. Therefore, the recommendation to continue its efforts to strengthen its process and allocation of resources and to ensure the accurate and timely completion of the template summaries, in order to reduce the timeliness for providing the information on past and future rulings to the Competent Authority (ToR II.B.5) is now removed.

1108. For the year in review, the timeliness of exchanges is as follows:

Past rulings within the scope of the transparency framework	Number of exchanges transmitted by 31 December 2020	Delayed exchanges		
		Number of exchanges not transmitted by 31 December 2020	Reasons for the delays	Any other comments
	184	30	See below	N/A
Future rulings within the scope of the transparency framework	Number of exchanges transmitted within three months of the information becoming available to the competent authority or immediately after legal impediments have been lifted	Delayed exchanges		
		Number of exchanges transmitted later than three months of the information on rulings becoming available to the competent authority	Reasons for the delays	Any other comments
	174	395	See below	N/A
Total	358	425		

Follow up requests received for exchange of the ruling	Number	Average time to provide response	Number of requests not answered
	0	N/A	N/A

1109. Switzerland encountered delays with the exchange of information on both past rulings and future rulings due to legal impediments, consultation with the cantonal tax authorities and the COVID-19 pandemic. Regarding legal impediments, Switzerland indicates that there were pending proceedings as a result of objections raised by taxpayers. With respect to the consultation with the cantonal tax authorities, Switzerland notes that the process was delayed because the Competent Authority had to revert to the cantonal tax authorities, which, in turn, needed to revert to taxpayers in some cases. In relation to the COVID-19 pandemic, Switzerland notes that both the Competent Authorities and the cantonal tax authorities experienced delays due to restricted working conditions.

1110. In the prior year peer review report, it was determined that the Competent Authority had internally reorganised to respond to the increased workload. New staff had been recruited and new teams had been set up, with less diversified and more clearly defined tasks. Furthermore, the IT System had been enhanced so that the steps of the transmission can be monitored more accurately. During the year in review, the efforts of the Competent Authority to enhance the process were impacted by the COVID-19 pandemic. Switzerland notes that in 2021 the situation normalised and the Competent Authority has been able to resume a more timely schedule. Switzerland also indicates that the implementation of the Common Transmission System and the set-up of a ticketing service to efficiently address technical problems related to the IT platform should allow the Competent Authority to enhance the process henceforth.

1111. Therefore, the recommendation to continue to ensure that all information on past and future rulings is exchanged as soon as possible (ToR II.B.6) remains in place.

Conclusion on section B

1112. Switzerland has met all of the ToR for the exchange of information process except for the timely exchange of information on past and future rulings (ToR II.B.6). Switzerland is recommended to continue to ensure that all information on past and future rulings is exchanged as soon as possible.

C. Statistics (ToR IV)

1113. The statistics for the year in review are as follows:

Category of ruling	Number of exchanges	Jurisdictions exchanged with
Ruling related to a preferential regime	373	Argentina, Australia, Austria, Azerbaijan, Barbados, Belgium, Brazil, Canada, Chile, China (People's Republic of), Colombia, Croatia, Cyprus, Czech Republic, Denmark, Estonia, Finland, Faroe Islands, France, Germany, Guernsey, Greece, Greenland, Hong Kong (China), Hungary, Iceland, India, Indonesia, Ireland, Israel, Italy, Japan, Korea, Latvia, Liechtenstein, Lithuania, Luxembourg, Malaysia, Mauritius, Mexico, Netherlands, New Zealand, Nigeria, Norway, Panama, Poland, Portugal, Russia, Saudi Arabia, Singapore, Slovak Republic, South Africa, Spain, Sweden, Turkey, United Kingdom, Uruguay
Cross-border unilateral APAs and any other cross-border unilateral tax rulings (such as an advance tax ruling) covering transfer pricing or the application of transfer pricing principles	366	Austria, Australia, Belgium, Brazil, Canada, Cameroon, China (People's Republic of), Cyprus, Czech Republic, Denmark, Finland, France, Germany, Guernsey, Hong Kong (China), Hungary, India, Ireland, Italy, Japan,

		Jersey, Korea, Latvia, Liechtenstein, Lithuania, Luxembourg, Malta, Marshall Islands, Mauritius, Malaysia, Mexico, Netherlands, New Zealand, Nigeria, Norway, Panama, Poland, Portugal, Russia, Saudi Arabia, Seychelles, Singapore, Slovak Republic, Slovenia, South Africa, Spain, Sweden, Turkey, United Kingdom, Uruguay
Permanent establishment rulings	151	Argentina, Australia, Austria, Barbados, Belgium, Brazil, Canada, Chile, China (People's Republic of), Colombia, Cyprus, Czech Republic, Denmark, Estonia, Finland, France, Germany, Greece, Guernsey, Hong Kong (China), Hungary, India, Indonesia, Ireland, Israel, Italy, Japan, Jersey, Korea, Latvia, Liechtenstein, Lithuania, Luxembourg, Mauritius, Mexico, Netherlands, New Zealand, Norway, Poland, Portugal, Russia, Saudi Arabia, Singapore, South Africa, Spain, Sweden, United Kingdom
Related party conduit rulings	20	Australia, Denmark, France, Germany, Ireland, Italy, Japan, Luxembourg, Malta, Netherlands, Norway, Poland, Portugal, Russia, Singapore, Spain, Sweden, United Kingdom
Total	910[3]	

D. Matters related to intellectual property regimes (ToR I.A.1.3)

1114. Switzerland offers a patent box, an intellectual property regime (IP regime)[4] that was introduced as of 1 January 2020. According to the FHTP, the patent box is designed in compliance with FHTP standards and therefore concluded "not harmful".

- ***New entrants benefitting from the grandfathered IP regime***: not applicable.
- ***Third category of IP assets***: not applicable as the regime does not allow the third category of IP assets to qualify for the benefits.
- ***Taxpayers making the use of the option to treat the nexus ratio as a rebuttable presumption***: not applicable as the regime does not allow the nexus ratio to be treated as a rebuttable presumption.

Summary of recommendations on implementation of the transparency framework

Aspect of implementation of the transparency framework that should be improved	Recommendation for improvement
Switzerland identified additional past rulings that were not previously captured.	Switzerland is recommended to strengthen its information gathering process by identifying all past rulings within the scope of the transparency framework and its review and supervision mechanism to ensure that the information gathering process is working effectively. This recommendation remains unchanged since the prior year peer review report.
Switzerland experienced delays in the exchange of information on past and future rulings.	Switzerland is recommended to continue to ensure that all information on past and future rulings is exchanged as soon

	as possible. This recommendation remains unchanged since the prior year peer review report.

References

OECD (2021), *BEPS Action 5 on Harmful Tax Practices - Terms of Reference and Methodology for the Conduct of the Peer Reviews of the Action 5 Transparency Framework*, OECD Publishing, Paris, http://www.oecd.org/tax/beps/beps-action-5-harmful-tax-practices-peer-review-transparency-framework.pdf. [3]

OECD (2015), *Countering Harmful Tax Practices More Effectively, Taking into Account Transparency and Substance, Action 5 - 2015 Final Report*, OECD/G20 Base Erosion and Profit Shifting Project, OECD Publishing, Paris, https://dx.doi.org/10.1787/9789264241190-en. [1]

OECD (ed.) (2017b), *Harmful Tax Practices - 2017 Progress Report on Preferential Regimes*, OECD Publishing, Paris, http://dx.doi.org/10.1787/9789264283954-en. [2]

OECD/Council of Europe (2011), *The Multilateral Convention on Mutual Administrative Assistance in Tax Matters: Amended by the 2010 Protocol*, OECD Publishing, Paris, https://dx.doi.org/10.1787/9789264115606-en. [4]

Notes

[1] Switzerland identified an additional eleven past rulings during the year in review.

[2] Until 31 December 2019, the following preferential regimes were available: 1) Auxiliary company regime (previously referred to as domiciliary company regime, 2) Mixed company regime, 3) Commissionaire ruling regime, 4) Holding company regime (cantonal level), 5) Licence box (Canton of Nidwalden only). As per 1 January 2020, Switzerland abolished said regimes and simultaneously, introduced an IP regime at cantonal level. This regime, which is mandatory for all of the Swiss cantons, replaced the previous Canton of Nidwalden licence box regime, which the FHTP had reviewed and found to be nexus compliant before (see comments under E.).

[3] Switzerland explained that in some cases the ruling templates identified in the statistics on exchanges above fall in two or more categories (107 in two categories, 1 in three categories, 16 in four categories) which has led to some multiple counting in this table. For the year in review, 753 individual exchanges took place.

[4] See footnote 2 and conclusion of FHTP as per update November 2020.

Thailand

Thailand has met all aspects of the terms of reference (OECD, 2021[3]) (ToR) for the calendar year 2020 (year in review), except for identifying future rulings within the scope of the transparency framework (ToR I.A.1.2), having the domestic legal framework for spontaneous exchange of information on rulings (ToR II.B.1) and the timely exchange of information on past and future rulings (ToR II.B.6). Thailand receives three recommendations on these points for the year in review.

In the prior year report, as well as in the 2018 peer review, Thailand had received two recommendations. However, as there were new circumstances, an additional recommendation has been made as relevant.

Thailand can legally issue one type of ruling within the scope of the transparency framework.

In practice, Thailand issued rulings within the scope of the transparency framework as follows:

Type of ruling	Number of rulings
Past rulings	182
Future rulings in the period 1 April 2018 – 31 December 2018	36
Future rulings in the calendar year 2019	157
Future rulings in the year in review	23

As no exchanges took place, no peer input was received in respect of the exchanges of information on rulings received from Thailand.

A. The information gathering process (ToR I.A)

1115. Thailand can legally issue the following type of rulings within the scope of the transparency framework: preferential regimes.[1]

Past rulings (ToR I.A.1.1, I.A.1.2, I.A.2.1, I.A.2.2)

1116. For Thailand, past rulings are any tax rulings within scope that are issued either: (i) on or after 1 January 2016 but before 1 April 2018; or (ii) on or after 1 January 2014 but before 1 January 2016, provided they were still in effect as at 1 January 2016.

1117. In the prior years' peer review reports, it was determined that Thailand's undertakings to identify past rulings and all potential exchange jurisdictions were sufficient to meet the minimum standard. Thailand's undertakings in this regard remain unchanged, and therefore continue to meet the minimum standard.

Future rulings (ToR I.A.1.1, I.A.1.2, I.A.2.1)

1118. For Thailand, future rulings are any tax rulings within scope that are issued on or after 1 April 2018.

1119. In the prior years' peer review reports, it was determined that Thailand's undertakings to identify past rulings and all potential exchange jurisdictions were sufficient to meet the minimum standard. However, during the year in review, Thailand found that the database for future rulings issued in 2019 and 2020 might be incomplete due to a technical issue when migrating data from paper into the database. As Thailand is still taking action on this issue and in order to ensure that similar issues are not encountered in future, Thailand is recommended to strengthen its information gathering process identifying all future rulings within the scope of the transparency framework.

Review and supervision (ToR I.A.3)

1120. In the prior years' peer review reports, it was determined that Thailand's review and supervision mechanism was sufficient to meet the minimum standard. As noted above, during the year in review, Thailand identified a technical issue with the database for future rulings issued in 2019 and 2020. As part of the efforts to strengthen the information gathering process, Thailand is therefore recommended to strengthen its review and supervision mechanism to ensure that the information gathering process is working effectively.

Conclusion on section A

1121. Thailand has met all of the ToR for the information gathering process except for identifying all future rulings within the scope of the transparency framework (ToR I.A.1.2). Thailand is recommended to strengthen its information gathering process identifying all future rulings within the scope of the transparency framework and its review and supervision mechanism to ensure that the information gathering process is working effectively.

B. The exchange of information (ToR II.B)

Legal basis for spontaneous exchange of information (ToR II.B.1, II.B.2)

1122. In the prior year peer review report, it was determined that Thailand did not have the necessary domestic legal basis to exchange information spontaneously. Thailand notes that there is a legal impediment that prevents the spontaneous exchange of information on rulings as contemplated in the Action 5 minimum standard. In particular, Section 10 of the Revenue Code protects taxpayers' information from disclosure to any other persons unless there is a power to do so under the law. As tax rulings concern the information of taxpayers, Thailand is prohibited to exchange them to treaty partners without requests.

1123. Thailand is in the process of implementing a new legal provision with respect to exchange of information to address this issue. This will involve an amendment to Section 10 of the Revenue Code. This Exchange of Information Bill is currently undergoing the legislative process and is expected to enter into force by 2021. Thailand is recommended to finalise the amendments to put the domestic legal basis in place to commence exchanges as soon as possible.

1124. Thailand has international agreements permitting spontaneous exchange of information, including bilateral agreements in force with 61 jurisdictions.[2] Thailand signed the *Multilateral Convention on Mutual Administrative Assistance in Tax Matters: Amended by the 2010 Protocol* (OECD/Council of Europe, 2011[4]) ("the Convention"). Thailand is encouraged to continue its efforts to ratify the Convention and expand its international exchange of information instruments to be able to exchange information on rulings. It is noted, however, that jurisdictions are assessed on their compliance with the transparency framework in respect of the exchange of information network in effect for the year of the particular annual review.

Completion and exchange of templates (ToR II.B.3, II.B.4, II.B.5, II.B.6, II.B.7)

1125. In the prior year peer review report, it was determined that Thailand's process for the completion and exchange of templates were sufficient to meet the minimum standard. Although Thailand could not legally exchange the information, Thailand is preparing the templates to be in a position to complete the exchanges as soon as the legal basis is in force. However, Thailand notes that although the appropriate process for the completion and exchange of templates has been implemented, in practice, the Revenue Department lacked the appropriate resources to be able to complete all templates in accordance with the timelines under the transparency framework. Therefore, Thailand is recommended to ensure that all information on past and future rulings is exchanged as soon as possible after the legal basis is in force.

1126. For the year in review, the timeliness of exchanges is as follows:

Past rulings within the scope of the transparency framework	Number of exchanges transmitted by 31 December 2020	Delayed exchanges		
		Number of exchanges not transmitted by 31 December 2020	Reasons for the delays	Any other comments
	0	182	See previous paragraph	N/A
Future rulings within the scope of the transparency framework	Number of exchanges transmitted within three months of the information becoming available to the competent authority or immediately after legal impediments have been lifted	Delayed exchanges		
		Number of exchanges transmitted later than three months of the information on rulings becoming available to the competent authority	Reasons for the delays	Any other comments
	0	201	See previous paragraph	N/A
Total	0	383		

Follow up requests received for exchange of the ruling	Number	Average time to provide response	Number of requests not answered
	0	N/A	N/A

Conclusion on section B

1127. Thailand is recommended to finalise the amendments to put the domestic legal basis in place to commence exchanges and to ensure that all information on past and future rulings is exchanged as soon as possible (ToR II.B.1 and II.B.6).

C. Statistics (ToR IV)

1128. As there was no information on rulings exchanged by Thailand for the year in review, no statistics can be reported.

D. Matters related to intellectual property regimes (ToR I.A.1.3)

1129. Thailand offers an intellectual property regime (IP regime)[3] that is not subject to the transparency requirements under the Action 5 Report (OECD, 2015[1]), because:

- ***New entrants benefitting from the grandfathered IP regime***: as this is a new IP regime rather than a grandfathered IP regime, transparency on new entrants is not relevant.
- ***Third category of IP assets***: not applicable as the regime does not allow the third category of IP assets to qualify for the benefits.
- ***Taxpayers making use of the option to treat the nexus ratio as a rebuttable presumption***: not applicable as the regime does not allow the nexus ratio to be treated as a rebuttable presumption.

Summary of recommendations on implementation of the transparency framework

Aspect of implementation of the transparency framework that should be improved	Recommendation for improvement
Thailand found that the database for future rulings issued in 2019 and 2020 may be incomplete due to a technical issue when migrating data from paper into the database.	Thailand is recommended to strengthen its information gathering process identifying all future rulings within the scope of the transparency framework and its review and supervision mechanism to ensure that the information gathering process is working effectively.
Thailand does not yet have the necessary legal framework in place for exchanging information on rulings.	Thailand is recommended to finalise the amendments to put the domestic legal basis in place to commence exchanges as soon as possible. This recommendation remains unchanged since the prior year peer review report.
Thailand did not undertake spontaneous exchange of information on all tax rulings within the scope of the transparency framework during the year in review.	Thailand is recommended to ensure that all information on past and future rulings is exchanged as soon as possible after the domestic legal basis is in force. This recommendation remains unchanged since the 2018 and 2019 peer review reports.

References

OECD (2021), *BEPS Action 5 on Harmful Tax Practices - Terms of Reference and Methodology for the Conduct of the Peer Reviews of the Action 5 Transparency Framework*, OECD Publishing, Paris, http://www.oecd.org/tax/beps/beps-action-5-harmful-tax-practices-peer-review-transparency-framework.pdf. [3]

OECD (2015), *Countering Harmful Tax Practices More Effectively, Taking into Account Transparency and Substance, Action 5 - 2015 Final Report*, OECD/G20 Base Erosion and Profit Shifting Project, OECD Publishing, Paris, https://dx.doi.org/10.1787/9789264241190-en. [1]

OECD (ed.) (2017b), *Harmful Tax Practices - 2017 Progress Report on Preferential Regimes*, OECD Publishing, Paris, http://dx.doi.org/10.1787/9789264283954-en. [2]

OECD/Council of Europe (2011), *The Multilateral Convention on Mutual Administrative Assistance in Tax Matters: Amended by the 2010 Protocol*, OECD Publishing, Paris, https://dx.doi.org/10.1787/9789264115606-en. [4]

Notes

[1] With respect to the following preferential regimes: 1) International headquarters and treasury centre, 2) International trading centre and 3) International business centre.

[2] Participating jurisdictions to the Convention are available here: www.oecd.org/tax/exchange-of-tax-information/convention-on-mutual-administrative-assistance-in-tax-matters.htm. Thailand also has bilateral agreements with Armenia, Australia, Austria, Bahrain, Bangladesh, Belarus, Belgium, Bulgaria, Cambodia, Canada, Chile, China (People's Republic of), Cyprus, Czech Republic, Denmark, Estonia, Finland, France, Germany, Hong Kong (China), Hungary, India, Indonesia, Ireland, Israel, Italy, Japan, Korea, Kuwait, Lao People's Democratic Republic, Luxembourg, Malaysia, Mauritius, Myanmar, Nepal, Netherlands, New Zealand, Norway, Oman, Pakistan, Philippines, Poland, Romania, Russia, Seychelles, Singapore, Slovenia, South Africa, Spain, Sri Lanka, Sweden, Switzerland, Chinese Taipei, Tajikistan, Turkey, Ukraine, United Arab Emirates, United Kingdom, United States, Uzbekistan and Viet Nam.

[3] International business centre.

Turkey

Turkey has met all aspects of the terms of reference (OECD, 2021[3]) (ToR) for the calendar year 2020 (year in review), and no recommendations are made.

In the prior year report, as well as in the 2017 and 2018 peer review reports, Turkey received a recommendation for identifying and exchanging information on new entrants to the grandfathered IP regime and exchanging information on all taxpayers benefitting from the third category of assets in the IP regime (ToR I.A.1.3). Turkey has addressed this issue and therefore the recommendation is now removed.

Turkey can legally issue one type of rulings within the scope of the transparency framework.

In practice, Turkey issued rulings within the scope of the transparency framework as follows:

Type of ruling	Number of rulings
Past rulings	3
Future rulings in the period 1 April 2016 – 31 December 2016	0
Future rulings in the calendar year 2017	8
Future rulings in the calendar year 2018	0
Future rulings in the calendar year 2019	0
Future rulings in the year in review	0

No peer input was received in respect of the exchanges of information on rulings received from Turkey.

A. The information gathering process (ToR I.A)

1130. Turkey can legally issue the following type of ruling within the scope of the transparency framework: cross-border unilateral APAs and any other cross-border unilateral tax rulings (such as an advance tax ruling) covering transfer pricing or the application of transfer pricing principles.

1131. For Turkey, past rulings are any tax rulings within scope that are issued either: (i) on or after 1 January 2014 but before 1 April 2016; or (ii) on or after 1 January 2010 but before 1 January 2014, provided they were still in effect as at 1 January 2014. Future rulings are any tax rulings within scope that are issued on or after 1 April 2016.

1132. In the prior years' peer review reports, it was determined that Turkey's undertakings to identify past and future rulings and all potential exchange jurisdictions were sufficient to meet the minimum standard. In addition, it was determined that Turkey's review and supervision mechanism was sufficient to meet the minimum standard. Turkey's implementation remains unchanged, and therefore continues to meet the minimum standard.

1133. Turkey has met all of the ToR for the information gathering process and no recommendations are made.

B. The exchange of information (ToR II.B)

1134. Turkey has international agreements permitting spontaneous exchange of information, including being a party to (i) the *Multilateral Convention on Mutual Administrative Assistance in Tax Matters: Amended by the 2010 Protocol* (OECD/Council of Europe, 2011[4]) ("the Convention") and (ii) bilateral agreements in force with 86 jurisdictions.[1]

1135. As Turkey did not issue any rulings within the scope of the transparency framework in the relevant period, Turkey was not required to exchange any information on rulings in the year in review and no data on the timeliness of exchanges can be reported.

1136. In the prior years' peer review reports, it was determined that Turkey's process for the completion and exchange of templates were sufficient to meet the minimum standard. With respect to past rulings, no further action was required. Turkey's implementation in this regard remains unchanged and therefore continues to meet the minimum standard.

1137. Turkey has the necessary legal basis for spontaneous exchange of information, a process for completing the templates in a timely way and has completed all exchanges. Turkey has met all of the ToR for the exchange of information process and no recommendations are made.

C. Statistics (ToR IV)

1138. The statistics for the year in review are as follows:

Category of ruling	Number of exchanges	Jurisdictions exchanged with
Cross-border unilateral APAs and any other cross-border unilateral tax rulings (such as an advance tax ruling) covering transfer pricing or the application of transfer pricing principles	0	N/A
IP regimes: total exchanges on taxpayers benefitting from the third category of IP assets, new entrants benefitting from grandfathered IP	23[2]	Canada, Germany, Greece, Italy, Korea, Netherlands, United States, United Kingdom

regimes; and taxpayers making use of the option to treat the nexus ratio as a rebuttable presumption		
Total	23	

D. Matters related to intellectual property regimes (ToR I.A.1.3)

1139. Turkey offers two intellectual property regimes (IP regime) that are subject to transparency requirements under the Action 5 Report (OECD, 2015[1]). It states that the identification of the benefitting taxpayers will occur as follows:

Technology development zone regime:

- ***New entrants benefitting from the grandfathered IP regime***: Transparency obligations apply for the regime, because grandfathering is provided to entrants that entered the regime after the relevant date from which enhanced transparency obligations apply. In addition, the regime has been found to be actually harmful to the extent of extended grandfathering to taxpayers that entered the regime between 1 July 2016 and 19 October 2017. Therefore, the period for enhanced transparency for new entrants on the grandfathered regime is from 6 February 2015 until 19 October 2017. During the year in review, Turkey identified both new taxpayers and new IP assets of existing taxpayers entering the regime and information has been exchanged. Therefore, Turkey's process for identifying and exchanging information on new entrants to the grandfathered IP regime is now sufficient to meet the minimum standard.
- ***Third category of IP assets***: In order for taxpayers to benefit from the third category of IP assets, the Ministry of Industry and Technology issues project completion documents, after the research-development project is completed and the assets have been created. A company requests the completion document electronically and the Ministry of Industry and Technology assesses the application to determine whether the relevant IP assets have been created in the zone and the resulting income is therefore eligible for the tax benefit. After the document is approved and issued electronically by the Ministry, it is provided to the taxpayer. Turkey has also obliged taxpayers to declare their exempted IP income on a quarterly basis for the third category of IP assets in the temporary tax return. During the year in review, Turkey identified these taxpayers and information has been exchanged. Therefore, Turkey's process for identifying and exchanging information on the third category of IP assets is now sufficient to meet the minimum standard.
- ***Taxpayers making use of the option to treat the nexus ratio as a rebuttable presumption***: not applicable as the regime does not allow the nexus ratio to be treated as a rebuttable presumption.

5/B regime:

- ***New entrants benefitting from the grandfathered IP regime***: as this is a new IP regime rather than a grandfathered IP regime, transparency on new entrants was not required.
- ***Third category of IP assets***: not applicable as the regime does not allow the third category of IP assets to qualify for the benefits.
- ***Taxpayers making use of the option to treat the nexus ratio as a rebuttable presumption***: not applicable as the regime does not allow the nexus ratio to be treated as a rebuttable presumption.

Summary of recommendations on implementation of the transparency framework

Aspect of implementation of the transparency framework that should be improved	Recommendation for improvement
	No recommendations are made.

References

OECD (2021), *BEPS Action 5 on Harmful Tax Practices - Terms of Reference and Methodology for the Conduct of the Peer Reviews of the Action 5 Transparency Framework*, OECD Publishing, Paris, http://www.oecd.org/tax/beps/beps-action-5-harmful-tax-practices-peer-review-transparency-framework.pdf. [3]

OECD (2015), *Countering Harmful Tax Practices More Effectively, Taking into Account Transparency and Substance, Action 5 - 2015 Final Report*, OECD/G20 Base Erosion and Profit Shifting Project, OECD Publishing, Paris, https://dx.doi.org/10.1787/9789264241190-en. [1]

OECD (ed.) (2017b), *Harmful Tax Practices - 2017 Progress Report on Preferential Regimes*, OECD Publishing, Paris, http://dx.doi.org/10.1787/9789264283954-en. [2]

OECD/Council of Europe (2011), *The Multilateral Convention on Mutual Administrative Assistance in Tax Matters: Amended by the 2010 Protocol*, OECD Publishing, Paris, https://dx.doi.org/10.1787/9789264115606-en. [4]

Notes

[1] Parties to the Convention are available here: www.oecd.org/tax/exchange-of-tax-information/convention-on-mutual-administrative-assistance-in-tax-matters.htm. Turkey also has bilateral agreements with Albania, Algeria, Australia, Austria, Azerbaijan, Bahrain, Bangladesh, Belarus, Belgium, Bosnia and Herzegovina, Brazil, Bulgaria, Canada, China (People's Republic of), Croatia, Czech Republic, Denmark, Egypt, Estonia, Ethiopia, Finland, France, Gambia, Georgia, Germany, Greece, Hungary, India, Indonesia, Iran, Ireland, Israel, Italy, Japan, Jordan, Kazakhstan, Korea, Kosovo, Kuwait, Kyrgyzstan, Latvia, Lebanon, Lithuania, Luxembourg, Malaysia, Malta, Mexico, Moldova, Mongolia, Montenegro, Morocco, Netherlands, New Zealand, North Macedonia, Norway, Oman, Pakistan, Philippines, Poland, Portugal, Qatar, Romania, Russian Federation, Saudi Arabia, Serbia, Singapore, Slovak Republic, Slovenia, South Africa, Spain, Sudan, Sweden, Switzerland, Syrian Arab Republic, Tajikistan, Thailand, Tunisia, Turkish Republic of Northern Cyprus, Turkmenistan, Ukraine, United Arab Emirates, United Kingdom, United States, Uzbekistan, Viet Nam and Yemen.

[2] Exchanges that are made related to IP regimes are not counted as issued rulings, therefore, there is a difference between the number of exchanges and the number of issued rulings.

Ukraine

Ukraine has met all aspects of the terms of reference (OECD, 2021[3]) (ToR) for the calendar year 2020 (year in review) that can be met in the absence of rulings being issued in practice, and no recommendations are made.

Ukraine can legally issue one type of ruling within the scope of the transparency framework.

In practice, Ukraine issued no rulings within the scope of the transparency framework.

As no exchanges were required to take place, no peer input was received in respect of the exchanges of information on rulings received from Ukraine.

A. The information gathering process (ToR I.A)

1140. Ukraine can legally issue the following type of ruling within the scope of the transparency framework: cross-border unilateral APAs and any other cross-border unilateral tax rulings (such as an advance tax ruling) covering transfer pricing or the application of transfer pricing principles.

1141. For Ukraine, past rulings are any tax rulings within scope that are issued either: (i) on or after 1 January 2016, but before 1 April 2018; and (ii) on or after 1 January 2014, but before 1 January 2016, provided still in effect as at 1 January 2016. Future rulings are any tax rulings within scope that are issued on or after 1 April 2018.

1142. In the prior years' peer review report, it was determined that Ukraine's undertakings to identify past and future rulings and all potential exchange jurisdictions were sufficient to meet the minimum standard. In addition, it was determined that Ukraine's review and supervision mechanism was sufficient to meet the minimum standard. Ukraine's implementation remains unchanged, and therefore continues to meet the minimum standard.

1143. Ukraine has met all of the ToR for the information gathering process that can be met in the absence of rulings being issued and no recommendations are made.

B. The exchange of information (ToR II.B)

1144. Ukraine has international agreements permitting spontaneous exchange of information, including being a party to (i) the *Multilateral Convention on Mutual Administrative Assistance in Tax Matters: Amended by the 2010 Protocol* (OECD/Council of Europe, 2011[4]) ("the Convention") and (ii) bilateral agreements in force with 75 jurisdictions.[1]

1145. As no rulings have been issued, no exchanges were required for the year in review and no data on timeliness is reported.

1146. In the prior year peer review report, it was determined that Ukraine's process for the completion and exchange of templates were sufficient to meet the minimum standard. With respect to past rulings, no action was required. Ukraine's implementation in this regard remains unchanged and therefore continues to meet the minimum standard.

1147. Ukraine has the necessary legal basis for spontaneous exchange of information and a process for completion of templates and exchange of information on rulings. Ukraine has met all of the ToR for the exchange of information process that can be met in the absence of rulings being issued and no recommendations are made.

C. Statistics (ToR IV)

1148. As no rulings were issued, no statistics can be reported.

D. Matters related to intellectual property regimes (ToR I.A.1.3)

1149. Ukraine does not offer an intellectual property regime for which transparency requirements under the Action 5 Report (OECD, 2015[1]) were imposed.

Summary of recommendations on implementation of the transparency framework

Aspect of implementation of the transparency framework that should be improved	Recommendation for improvement
	No recommendations are made.

References

OECD (2021), *BEPS Action 5 on Harmful Tax Practices - Terms of Reference and Methodology for the Conduct of the Peer Reviews of the Action 5 Transparency Framework*, OECD Publishing, Paris, http://www.oecd.org/tax/beps/beps-action-5-harmful-tax-practices-peer-review-transparency-framework.pdf. [3]

OECD (2015), *Countering Harmful Tax Practices More Effectively, Taking into Account Transparency and Substance, Action 5 - 2015 Final Report*, OECD/G20 Base Erosion and Profit Shifting Project, OECD Publishing, Paris, https://dx.doi.org/10.1787/9789264241190-en. [1]

OECD (ed.) (2017b), *Harmful Tax Practices - 2017 Progress Report on Preferential Regimes*, OECD Publishing, Paris, http://dx.doi.org/10.1787/9789264283954-en. [2]

OECD/Council of Europe (2011), *The Multilateral Convention on Mutual Administrative Assistance in Tax Matters: Amended by the 2010 Protocol*, OECD Publishing, Paris, https://dx.doi.org/10.1787/9789264115606-en. [4]

Notes

[1] Participating jurisdictions to the Convention are available here: www.oecd.org/tax/exchange-of-tax-information/convention-on-mutual-administrative-assistance-in-tax-matters.htm. Ukraine also has bilateral agreements with Algeria, Armenia, Austria, Azerbaijan, Belarus, Belgium, Brazil, Bulgaria, Canada, China (People's Republic of), Croatia, Cyprus, Czech Republic, Denmark, Egypt, Estonia, Finland, France, Georgia, Germany, Greece, Hungary, Iceland, India, Indonesia, Iran, Ireland, Israel, Italy, Japan, Jordan, Kazakhstan, Korea, Kuwait, Kyrgyzstan, Latvia, Lebanon, Libya, Lithuania, Luxembourg, Malaysia, Malta, Mexico, Moldova, Mongolia, Montenegro, Morocco, Netherlands, North Macedonia, Norway, Pakistan, Poland, Portugal, Qatar, Romania, Russia, Saudi Arabia, Serbia, Singapore, Slovak Republic, Slovenia, South Africa, Spain, Sweden, Switzerland, Syrian Arab Republic, Tajikistan, Thailand, Turkey, Turkmenistan, United Arab Emirates, United Kingdom, United States, Uzbekistan and Viet Nam.

United Kingdom

The United Kingdom has met all aspects of the terms of reference (OECD, 2021[3]) (ToR) for the calendar year 2020 (year in review), and no recommendations are made.

The United Kingdom can legally issue three types of rulings within the scope of the transparency framework.

In practice, the United Kingdom issued rulings within the scope of the transparency framework as follows:

Type of ruling	Number of rulings
Past rulings	599
Future rulings in the period 1 April 2016 – 31 December 2016	71
Future rulings in the calendar year 2017	16
Future rulings in the calendar year 2018	20
Future rulings in the calendar year 2019	14
Future rulings in the year in review	13

Peer input was received from three jurisdictions in respect of the exchanges of information on rulings received from the United Kingdom. The input was positive, noting that information was complete, in a correct format and received in a timely manner.

A. The information gathering process (ToR I.A)

1150. The United Kingdom can legally issue three types of rulings within the scope of the transparency framework: (i) preferential regimes;[1] (ii) cross-border unilateral APAs and any other cross-border unilateral tax rulings (such as an advance tax ruling) covering transfer pricing or the application of transfer pricing principles; and (iii) permanent establishment rulings.

1151. For the United Kingdom, past rulings are any tax rulings within scope that are issued either: (i) on or after 1 January 2014 but before 1 April 2016; or (ii) on or after 1 January 2010 but before 1 January 2014, provided they were still in effect as at 1 January 2014. Future rulings are any tax rulings within scope that are issued on or after 1 April 2016.

1152. In the prior years' peer review reports, it was determined that the United Kingdom's undertakings to identify past and future rulings and all potential exchange jurisdictions were sufficient to meet the minimum standard. In addition, it was determined that The United Kingdom's review and supervision mechanism was sufficient to meet the minimum standard. The United Kingdom's implementation remains unchanged, and therefore continues to meet the minimum standard.

1153. The United Kingdom has met all of the ToR for the information gathering process and no recommendations are made.

B. The exchange of information (ToR II.B)

1154. The United Kingdom has international agreements permitting spontaneous exchange of information, including being a party to (i) the *Multilateral Convention on Mutual Administrative Assistance in Tax Matters: Amended by the 2010 Protocol* (OECD/Council of Europe, 2011[4]) ("the Convention") and (ii) bilateral agreements in force with 122 jurisdictions.[2]

1155. For the year in review, the timeliness of exchanges is as follows:

Future rulings within the scope of the transparency framework	Number of exchanges transmitted within three months of the information becoming available to the competent authority or immediately after legal impediments have been lifted	Delayed exchanges		
		Number of exchanges transmitted later than three months of the information on rulings becoming available to the competent authority	Reasons for the delays	Any other comments
	15	0	N/A	N/A

Follow up requests received for exchange of the ruling	Number	Average time to provide response	Number of requests not answered
	2	4 months	0

1156. During the year in review, the United Kingdom experienced a short delay in responding to a follow up request. The United Kingdom notes that clarification from the requesting jurisdiction was needed and that the follow up request was responded within 90 days of the receipt of the clarification.

1157. In the prior years' peer review reports, it was determined that the United Kingdom's process for the completion and exchange of templates were sufficient to meet the minimum standard. With respect to past rulings, no further action was required. The United Kingdom's implementation in this regard remains unchanged and therefore continues to meet the minimum standard.

1158. The United Kingdom has the necessary legal basis for spontaneous exchange of information, a process for completing the templates in a timely way and has completed all exchanges. The United Kingdom has met all of the ToR for the exchange of information process and no recommendations are made.

C. Statistics (ToR IV)

1159. The statistics for the year in review are as follows:

Category of ruling	Number of exchanges	Jurisdictions exchanged with
Ruling related to a preferential regime	0	N/A
Cross-border unilateral APAs and any other cross-border unilateral tax rulings (such as an advance tax ruling) covering transfer pricing or the application of transfer pricing principles	11	Australia, China (People's Republic of), Guernsey, Hong Kong (China), Mexico, Norway, Qatar, Saudi Arabia, Switzerland, United States
Permanent establishment rulings	4	Norway, Singapore, United States
IP regimes: total exchanges on taxpayers benefitting from the third category of IP assets, new entrants benefitting from grandfathered IP regimes; and taxpayers making use of the option to treat the nexus ratio as a rebuttable presumption	0	N/A
Total	15	

D. Matters related to intellectual property regimes (ToR I.A.1.3)

1160. The United Kingdom offers an intellectual property regime (IP regime)[3] that is subject to the transparency requirements under the Action 5 Report (OECD, 2015[1]). It states that the identification of the benefitting taxpayers occurs as follows:

- ***New entrants benefitting from the grandfathered IP regime***: in the prior years' peer review reports, it was determined that the United Kingdom's process for identifying and exchanging information on new entrants to the grandfathered IP regime were sufficient to meet the minimum standard. The United Kingdom's implementation in this regard remains unchanged and therefore continues to meet the minimum standard.
- ***Third category of IP assets***: not applicable as the regime does not allow the third category of IP assets to qualify for the benefits.
- ***Taxpayers making use of the option to treat the nexus ratio as a rebuttable presumption***: the United Kingdom did not record any elections to use the rebuttable presumption during the year in review.

Summary of recommendations on implementation of the transparency framework

Aspect of implementation of the transparency framework that should be improved	Recommendation for improvement
	No recommendations are made.

References

OECD (2021), *BEPS Action 5 on Harmful Tax Practices - Terms of Reference and Methodology for the Conduct of the Peer Reviews of the Action 5 Transparency Framework*, OECD Publishing, Paris, http://www.oecd.org/tax/beps/beps-action-5-harmful-tax-practices-peer-review-transparency-framework.pdf. [3]

OECD (2015), *Countering Harmful Tax Practices More Effectively, Taking into Account Transparency and Substance, Action 5 - 2015 Final Report*, OECD/G20 Base Erosion and Profit Shifting Project, OECD Publishing, Paris, https://dx.doi.org/10.1787/9789264241190-en. [1]

OECD (ed.) (2017b), *Harmful Tax Practices - 2017 Progress Report on Preferential Regimes*, OECD Publishing, Paris, http://dx.doi.org/10.1787/9789264283954-en. [2]

OECD/Council of Europe (2011), *The Multilateral Convention on Mutual Administrative Assistance in Tax Matters: Amended by the 2010 Protocol*, OECD Publishing, Paris, https://dx.doi.org/10.1787/9789264115606-en. [4]

Notes

[1] With respect to the following preferential regimes: 1) Patent box and 2) Shipping regime.

[2] Participating jurisdictions to the Convention are available here: www.oecd.org/tax/exchange-of-tax-information/convention-on-mutual-administrative-assistance-in-tax-matters.htm. The United Kingdom also has bilateral agreements with Albania, Algeria, Antigua and Barbuda, Argentina, Armenia, Australia, Azerbaijan, Bahrain, Bangladesh, Barbados, Belarus, Belize, Bolivia, Bosnia and Herzegovina, Botswana, British Virgin Islands, Brunei, Bulgaria, Cayman Islands, Chile, China (People's Republic of), Colombia, Côte d'Ivoire, Croatia, Cyprus, Czech Republic, Denmark, Egypt, Estonia, Eswatini, Ethiopia, Falkland Islands, Faroe Islands, Fiji, Finland, Gambia, Georgia, Ghana, Gibraltar, Greece, Grenada, Guernsey, Guyana, Hong Kong (China), Hungary, Iceland, India, Indonesia, Ireland, Isle of Man, Israel, Jamaica, Japan, Jersey, Jordan, Kazakhstan, Kenya, Kiribati, Korea, Kosovo, Kuwait, Latvia, Lesotho, Libya, Lithuania, Malawi, Malaysia, Malta, Mauritius, Mexico, Moldova, Mongolia, Montenegro, Montserrat, Morocco, Myanmar, Namibia, New Zealand, Nigeria, North Macedonia, Norway, Oman, Pakistan, Panama, Papua New Guinea, Philippines, Poland, Portugal, Qatar, Romania, Russia, Saudi Arabia, Senegal, Serbia, Sierra Leone, Singapore, Slovak Republic, Slovenia, Solomon Islands, South Africa, Spain, Sri Lanka, Saint Kitts and Nevis, Sudan, Chinese Taipei, Tajikistan, Thailand, Trinidad and Tobago, Tunisia, Turkey, Turkmenistan, Tuvalu, Uganda, Ukraine, United Arab Emirates, United States, Uruguay, Uzbekistan, Venezuela, Viet Nam, Zambia and Zimbabwe.

[3] Patent box.

United States

The United States has met all aspects of the terms of reference (OECD, 2021[3]) (ToR) for the calendar year 2020 (year in review), and no recommendations are made.

The United States can legally issue three types of rulings within the scope of the transparency framework.

In practice, The United States issued rulings within the scope of the transparency framework as follows:

Type of ruling	Number of rulings
Past rulings	114
Future rulings in the period 1 April 2016 – 31 December 2016	21
Future rulings in the calendar year 2017	30
Future rulings in the calendar year 2018	27
Future rulings in the calendar year 2019	30
Future rulings in the year in review	18

Peer input was received from five jurisdictions in respect of the exchanges of information on rulings received from the United States. The input was generally positive, noting that information was complete, in a correct format and received in a timely manner.

A. The information gathering process (ToR I.A)

1161. The United States can legally issue three types of rulings within the scope of the transparency framework: (i) cross-border unilateral APAs and any other cross-border unilateral tax rulings (such as an advance tax ruling) covering transfer pricing or the application of transfer pricing principles; (ii) permanent establishment rulings; and (iii) related party conduit rulings.

1162. For the United States, past rulings are any tax rulings within scope that are issued either: (i) on or after 1 January 2014 but before 1 April 2016; or (ii) on or after 1 January 2010 but before 1 January 2014, provided they were still in effect as at 1 January 2014. Future rulings are any tax rulings within scope that are issued on or after 1 April 2016.

1163. In the prior years' peer review reports, it was determined that the United States' undertakings to identify past and future rulings and all potential exchange jurisdictions were sufficient to meet the minimum standard. In addition, it was determined that the United States' review and supervision mechanism was sufficient to meet the minimum standard. The United States' implementation remains unchanged, and therefore continues to meet the minimum standard.

1164. The United States has met all of the ToR for the information gathering process and no recommendations are made.

B. The exchange of information (ToR II.B)

1165. The United States has international agreements permitting spontaneous exchange of information, including being a party to (i) the original *Multilateral Convention on Mutual Administrative Assistance in Tax Matters* (OECD/Council of Europe, 2011[4]) ("the Convention") and (ii) bilateral agreements in force with 49 jurisdictions.[1]

1166. For the year in review, the timeliness of exchanges is as follows:

Future rulings within the scope of the transparency framework	Number of exchanges transmitted within three months of the information becoming available to the competent authority or immediately after legal impediments have been lifted	Delayed exchanges		
		Number of exchanges transmitted later than three months of the information on rulings becoming available to the competent authority	Reasons for the delays	Any other comments
	78	0	N/A	N/A

Follow up requests received for exchange of the ruling	Number	Average time to provide response	Number of requests not answered
	0	N/A	N/A

1167. In the prior years' peer review reports, it was determined that the United States' process for the completion and exchange of templates were sufficient to meet the minimum standard. With respect to past rulings, no further action was required. The United States' implementation in this regard remains unchanged and therefore continues to meet the minimum standard. It should be noted that for the peer input, two peers indicated that information included in the summary section of Annex C of the Action 5 report was not sufficient for risk assessment purposes in all cases, whilst one peer noted that the information provided resulted in the instigation of an investigation with favourable results.

1168. The United States has the necessary legal basis for spontaneous exchange of information, a process for completing the templates in a timely way and has completed all exchanges. The United States has met all of the ToR for the exchange of information process and no recommendations are made.

C. Statistics (ToR IV)

1169. The statistics for the year in review are as follows:

Category of ruling	Number of exchanges	Jurisdictions exchanged with
Ruling related to a preferential regime	0	N/A
Cross-border unilateral APAs and any other cross-border unilateral tax rulings (such as an advance tax ruling) covering transfer pricing or the application of transfer pricing principles	78	Australia, Austria, Belgium, Canada, China, Columbia, Croatia, Czech Republic, Denmark, Dominican Republic, Finland, France, Germany, Honduras, Hungary, Indonesia, Italy, Japan, Luxembourg, Mexico, Netherlands, New Zealand, Norway, Poland, Portugal, Russia, Slovenia, South Africa, Spain, Sweden, Thailand Turkey, Ukraine, United Kingdom
Permanent establishment rulings	0	N/A
Related party conduit rulings	0	N/A
Total	78	

D. Matters related to intellectual property regimes (ToR I.A.1.3)

1170. The United States does not offer an intellectual property regime for which transparency requirements under the Action 5 Report (OECD, 2015[1]) were imposed.

Summary of recommendations on implementation of the transparency framework

Aspect of implementation of the transparency framework that should be improved	Recommendation for improvement
	No recommendations are made.

Jurisdiction's response and recent developments

1171. With respect to peer input indicating insufficiency for risk assessment purposes, the United States reviewed the exchanged templates and confirmed that all required elements of the standard were included. The United States, following its established practices for exchanging templates, consistently monitors the quality and content of outgoing templates.

References

OECD (2021), *BEPS Action 5 on Harmful Tax Practices - Terms of Reference and Methodology for the Conduct of the Peer Reviews of the Action 5 Transparency Framework*, OECD Publishing, Paris, http://www.oecd.org/tax/beps/beps-action-5-harmful-tax-practices-peer-review-transparency-framework.pdf. [3]

OECD (2015), *Countering Harmful Tax Practices More Effectively, Taking into Account Transparency and Substance, Action 5 - 2015 Final Report*, OECD/G20 Base Erosion and Profit Shifting Project, OECD Publishing, Paris, https://dx.doi.org/10.1787/9789264241190-en. [1]

OECD (ed.) (2017b), *Harmful Tax Practices - 2017 Progress Report on Preferential Regimes*, OECD Publishing, Paris, http://dx.doi.org/10.1787/9789264283954-en. [2]

OECD/Council of Europe (2011), *The Multilateral Convention on Mutual Administrative Assistance in Tax Matters: Amended by the 2010 Protocol*, OECD Publishing, Paris, https://dx.doi.org/10.1787/9789264115606-en. [4]

Notes

[1] Participating jurisdictions to the original Convention are available here: www.oecd.org/tax/exchange-of-tax-information/convention-on-mutual-administrative-assistance-in-tax-matters.htm. The United States also has bilateral agreements with Australia, Austria, Barbados, Belgium, Bulgaria, Canada, China (People's Republic of), Czech Republic, Denmark, Egypt, Estonia, Finland, France, Germany, Greece, Hungary, Iceland, India, Indonesia, Ireland, Israel, Italy, Jamaica, Japan, Kazakhstan, Latvia, Lithuania, Luxembourg, Malta, Mexico, Netherlands, New Zealand, Norway, Pakistan, Poland, Portugal, Romania, Russia, Slovak Republic, Slovenia, South Africa, Spain, Sri Lanka, Sweden, Switzerland, Thailand, Turkey, Ukraine and the United Kingdom.

Uruguay

Uruguay has met all aspects of the terms of reference (OECD, 2021[3]) (ToR) for the calendar year 2020 (year in review), and no recommendations are made.

Uruguay can legally issue one type of rulings within the scope of the transparency framework.

In practice, Uruguay issued rulings within the scope of the transparency framework as follows:

Type of ruling	Number of rulings
Past rulings	1
Future rulings in the period 1 April 2018 – 31 December 2018	0
Future rulings in the calendar year 2019	0
Future rulings in the year in review	0

No peer input was received in respect of the exchanges of information on rulings received from Uruguay.

A. The information gathering process (ToR I.A)

1172. Uruguay can legally issue the following type of ruling within the scope of the transparency framework: cross-border unilateral APAs and any other cross-border unilateral tax rulings (such as an advance tax ruling) covering transfer pricing or the application of transfer pricing principles

1173. For Uruguay, past rulings are any tax rulings within scope that are issued either: (i) on or after 1 January 2016 but before 1 April 2018; or (ii) on or after 1 January 20114 but before 1 January 2016, provided they were still in effect as at 1 January 2016. Future rulings are any tax rulings within scope that are issued on or after 1 April 2018.

1174. In the prior year peer review report, it was determined that Uruguay's undertakings to identify past and future rulings and all potential exchange jurisdictions were sufficient to meet the minimum standard. In addition, it was determined that Uruguay's review and supervision mechanism was sufficient to meet the minimum standard. Uruguay's implementation remains unchanged, and therefore continues to meet the minimum standard.

1175. Uruguay has met all of the ToR for the information gathering process and no recommendations are made.

B. The exchange of information (ToR II.B)

1176. Uruguay has international agreements permitting spontaneous exchange of information, including being a party to (i) the *Multilateral Convention on Mutual Administrative Assistance in Tax Matters: Amended by the 2010 Protocol* (OECD/Council of Europe, 2011[4]) ("the Convention") and (ii) bilateral agreements in force with 21 jurisdictions.[1]

1177. As Uruguay did not issue any rulings within the scope of the transparency framework in the relevant period, Uruguay was not required to exchange any information on rulings in the year in review and no data on the timeliness of exchanges can be reported.

1178. In the prior years' peer review reports, it was determined that Uruguay's process for the completion and exchange of templates were sufficient to meet the minimum standard. With respect to past rulings, no further action was required. Uruguay's implementation in this regard remains unchanged and therefore continues to meet the minimum standard.

1179. Uruguay has the necessary legal basis for spontaneous exchange of information, a process for completing the templates in a timely way and has completed all exchanges. Uruguay has met all of the ToR for the exchange of information process and no recommendations are made.

C. Statistics (ToR IV)

1180. As no rulings were issued, no statistics can be reported.

D. Matters related to intellectual property regimes (ToR I.A.1.3)

1181. In the year in review, Uruguay offered three intellectual property regimes (IP regime).[2] However, these are not subject to the transparency requirements under the Action 5 Report, because:

- ***New entrants benefitting from the grandfathered IP regime***: not applicable, as explained in the prior year peer review report.

- ***Third category of IP assets***: not applicable as the regimes do not allow the third category of IP assets to qualify for the benefits.
- ***Taxpayers making use of the option to treat the nexus ratio as a rebuttable presumption***: not applicable as the regimes do not allow the nexus ratio to be treated as a rebuttable presumption.

Summary of recommendations on implementation of the transparency framework

Aspect of implementation of the transparency framework that should be improved	Recommendation for improvement
	No recommendations are made.

References

OECD (2021), *BEPS Action 5 on Harmful Tax Practices - Terms of Reference and Methodology for the Conduct of the Peer Reviews of the Action 5 Transparency Framework*, OECD Publishing, Paris, http://www.oecd.org/tax/beps/beps-action-5-harmful-tax-practices-peer-review-transparency-framework.pdf. [3]

OECD (2015), *Countering Harmful Tax Practices More Effectively, Taking into Account Transparency and Substance, Action 5 - 2015 Final Report*, OECD/G20 Base Erosion and Profit Shifting Project, OECD Publishing, Paris, https://dx.doi.org/10.1787/9789264241190-en. [1]

OECD (ed.) (2017b), *Harmful Tax Practices - 2017 Progress Report on Preferential Regimes*, OECD Publishing, Paris, http://dx.doi.org/10.1787/9789264283954-en. [2]

OECD/Council of Europe (2011), *The Multilateral Convention on Mutual Administrative Assistance in Tax Matters: Amended by the 2010 Protocol*, OECD Publishing, Paris, https://dx.doi.org/10.1787/9789264115606-en. [4]

Notes

[1] Participating jurisdictions to the Convention are available here: www.oecd.org/tax/exchange-of-tax-information/convention-on-mutual-administrative-assistance-in-tax-matters.htm. Uruguay also has bilateral agreements with Belgium, Chile, Ecuador, Finland, Germany, India, Italy, Korea, Liechtenstein, Luxembourg, Malta, Mexico, Paraguay, Portugal, Romania, Singapore, Spain, Switzerland, United Arab Emirates, United Kingdom and Viet Nam.

[2] These are: (i) Benefits under law 16.906 for biotechnology, (ii) Benefits under lit S art. 52 for biotechnology and for software and (iii) Free zones regimes.

Viet Nam

Viet Nam has met all aspects of the terms of reference (OECD, 2021[3]) (ToR) for the calendar year 2020 (year in review), except for having in place a process for completion of templates and exchange of information on rulings (ToR II.B). Viet Nam receives one recommendation on this point for the year in review.

In the prior year report, as well as in the 2017 and 2018 peer reviews, Viet Nam had received the same recommendation. As it has not been addressed, the recommendation remains in place.

Viet Nam can legally issue one type of ruling within the scope of the transparency framework.

In practice, Viet Nam issued no rulings within the scope of the transparency framework.

As no exchanges were required to take place, no peer input was received in respect of the exchanges of information on rulings received from Viet Nam.

A. The information gathering process (ToR I.A)

1182. Viet Nam can legally issue the following type of rulings within the scope of the transparency framework: cross-border unilateral APAs and any other cross-border unilateral tax rulings (such as an advance tax ruling) covering transfer pricing or the application of transfer pricing principles.

1183. For Viet Nam, past rulings are any tax rulings within scope that are issued either: (i) on or after 1 January 2015 but before 1 September 2017; or (ii) on or after 1 January 2012 but before 1 January 2015, provided they were still in effect as at 1 January 2015. Future rulings are any tax rulings within scope that are issued on or after 1 September 2017. In last year's report, Viet Nam indicated it had put the APA program on hold due to the new assessment requirements set out in the revised Tax Administration Law promulgated in 2019 and in effect as of July 2020. As a result, none of the APA requests previously received were approved, no APAs were issued during the year in review and no new APA requests have been accepted.

1184. In the prior years' peer review reports, it was determined that Viet Nam's undertakings to identify past and future rulings and all potential exchange jurisdictions were sufficient to meet the minimum standard. In addition, it was determined that Viet Nam's review and supervision mechanism was sufficient to meet the minimum standard. Viet Nam's implementation remains unchanged, and therefore continues to meet the minimum standard.

1185. Viet Nam has met all of the ToR for the information gathering process and no recommendations are made.

B. The exchange of information (ToR II.B)

Legal basis for spontaneous exchange of information (ToR II.B.1, II.B.2)

1186. Viet Nam has the necessary domestic legal basis to exchange information spontaneously. Viet Nam notes that there are no legal or practical impediments that prevent the spontaneous exchange of information on rulings as contemplated in the Action 5 minimum standard.

1187. Viet Nam has international agreements permitting spontaneous exchange of information, including being a party to bilateral agreements in force with 76 jurisdictions.[1]

Completion and exchange of templates (ToR II.B.3, II.B.4, II.B.5, II.B.6, II.B.7)

1188. In the prior years' peer review reports, it was determined that Viet Nam's process for the completion and exchange of templates met all the ToR, except for the completion and exchange of templates (ToR II.B). Therefore, Viet Nam was recommended to continue to put in place a process to complete the templates for all relevant rulings and to ensure the timely exchange of information on rulings in the form required by the transparency framework.

1189. During the year in review, Viet Nam continued to work on the development of a process to complete the templates on relevant rulings, to make them available to the Competent Authority for exchange of information, and to exchange them with relevant jurisdictions. This process has been further developed in 2021, following the issuance of a revised APA regulation (i.e. Ministry of Finance's circular no. 45/2021/TT-BTC dated 18 June 2021) and the restructuring of the Large Taxpayers Department, including refinement of Large Taxpayers Office's functions. Viet Nam indicated that further detailed instructions on the implementation of this process are going to be developed in 2021. This will be assessed in next year's peer review. Therefore, for the year in review, the prior year recommendation remains.

1190. As no rulings within the scope of the transparency framework have been issued in practice, Viet Nam was not required to complete any exchanges of information and there is no data to report on the timeliness of exchanges.

Conclusion on section B

1191. Viet Nam has the necessary legal basis for spontaneous exchange of information. Viet Nam is currently putting in place a process for completion of templates and exchange of information on rulings (ToR II.B). Viet Nam is recommended to develop a process to complete the templates on relevant rulings and to ensure that the exchanges of information on rulings occur in accordance with the form and timelines under the transparency framework.

C. Statistics (ToR IV)

1192. As there was no information on rulings required to be exchanged by Viet Nam for the year in review, no statistics can be reported.

D. Matters related to intellectual property regimes (ToR I.A.1.3)

1193. Viet Nam does not offer an intellectual property regime for which transparency requirements under the Action 5 Report (OECD, 2015[1]) were imposed.

Summary of recommendations on implementation of the transparency framework

Aspect of implementation of the transparency framework that should be improved	Recommendation for improvement
Viet Nam is currently putting in place a process for completion of templates and exchange of information on rulings.	Viet Nam is recommended to develop a process to complete the templates on relevant rulings and to ensure that the exchanges of information on rulings occur in accordance with the form and timelines under the transparency framework. This recommendation remains unchanged since the 2017, 2018 and 2019cpeer review reports.

References

OECD (2021), *BEPS Action 5 on Harmful Tax Practices - Terms of Reference and Methodology for the Conduct of the Peer Reviews of the Action 5 Transparency Framework*, OECD Publishing, Paris, http://www.oecd.org/tax/beps/beps-action-5-harmful-tax-practices-peer-review-transparency-framework.pdf. [3]

OECD (2015), *Countering Harmful Tax Practices More Effectively, Taking into Account Transparency and Substance, Action 5 - 2015 Final Report*, OECD/G20 Base Erosion and Profit Shifting Project, OECD Publishing, Paris, https://dx.doi.org/10.1787/9789264241190-en. [1]

OECD (ed.) (2017b), *Harmful Tax Practices - 2017 Progress Report on Preferential Regimes*, OECD Publishing, Paris, http://dx.doi.org/10.1787/9789264283954-en. [2]

OECD/Council of Europe (2011), *The Multilateral Convention on Mutual Administrative Assistance in Tax Matters: Amended by the 2010 Protocol*, OECD Publishing, Paris, https://dx.doi.org/10.1787/9789264115606-en. [4]

Notes

[1] Viet Nam has bilateral agreements with Australia, Austria, Azerbaijan, Bangladesh, Belarus, Belgium, Brunei Darussalam, Bulgaria, Cambodia, Canada, China (People's Republic of), Croatia, Cuba, Czech Republic, Democratic People's Republic of Korea, Denmark, Estonia, Finland, France, Germany, Hong Kong (China), Hungary, Iceland, India, Indonesia, Iran, Ireland, Israel, Italy, Japan, Kazakhstan, Korea, Kuwait, Lao People's Democratic Republic, Latvia, Luxembourg, Macau (China), Malaysia, Malta, Mongolia, Morocco, Mozambique, Myanmar, Netherlands, New Zealand, Norway, Oman, Pakistan, Palestinian Authority, Panama, Philippines, Poland, Portugal, Qatar, Romania, Russia, San Marino, Saudi Arabia, Serbia, Seychelles, Singapore, Slovak Republic, Spain, Sri Lanka, Sweden, Switzerland, Chinese Taipei, Thailand, Tunisia, Turkey, Ukraine, United Arab Emirates, United Kingdom, Uruguay, Uzbekistan and Venezuela.

www.ingramcontent.com/pod-product-compliance
Ingram Content Group UK Ltd.
Pitfield, Milton Keynes, MK11 3LW, UK
UKHW051456290926
15471UKWH00008B/1234

9 789264 522534